Informatik aktuell

Herausgeber: W. Brauer
im Auftrag der Gesellschaft für Informatik (GI)

Klaus David
Kurt Geihs (Hrsg.)

Kommunikation in Verteilten Systemen (KiVS)

16. Fachtagung Kommunikation
in Verteilten Systemen (KiVS 2009)
Kassel, 2.–6. März 2009

Eine Veranstaltung der Gesellschaft für Informatik (GI)
unter Beteiligung der Informationstechnischen
Gesellschaft (ITG/VDE)
Ausgerichtet von der Universität Kassel

ITG INFORMATIONSTECHNISCHE GESELLSCHAFT IM VDE

Herausgeber

Klaus David
Kurt Geihs
Universität Kassel, FB 16
Wilhelmshöher Allee 73, 34121 Kassel

Bibliographische Information der Deutschen Bibliothek
Die Deutsche Bibliothek verzeichnet diese Publikation in der Deutschen Nationalbibliografie; detaillierte bibliografische Daten sind im Internet über http://dnb.ddb.de abrufbar.

CR Subject Classification (2001):

ISSN 1431-472-X
ISBN-13 978-3-540-92665-8 Springer Berlin Heidelberg New York

Springer Berlin Heidelberg New York
Springer ist ein Unternehmen von Springer Science+Business Media

springer.de

Printed in Germany

Satz: Reproduktionsfertige Vorlage vom Autor/Herausgeber
Gedruckt auf säurefreiem Papier SPIN: 12581702 33/3142-543210

Vorwort der Tagungsleiter

Herzlich willkommen zur 16. GI/ITG-Fachtagung „Kommunikation in Verteilten Systemen (KiVS) 2009“ in Kassel!

Nach der erfolgreichen Konferenz 2007 in Bern, die hohe Maßstäbe bei Qualität und Organisation setzte, freuen wir uns, Sie in Kassel zur 16. Ausgabe der KiVS-Tagung begrüßen zu können. Der Programmausschuss hat auch dieses Mal ein anspruchsvolles und vielfältiges Programm zusammengestellt. Aus den insgesamt 65 eingereichten Beiträgen wurden 20 Langbeiträge und acht Kurzbeiträge zur Präsentation ausgewählt. Zwei eingeladene Vorträge und zwei Podiumsdiskussionen bereichern das Tagungsprogramm. Zusätzlich finden sieben Workshops und fünf Tutorien zu aktuellen Spezialthemen statt. Abgerundet wird das Programm durch Exkursionen zu Firmen, Vorträge und Vorführungen von Preisträgern sowie einer geselligen Abendveranstaltung.

Die KiVS-Tagungsreihe blickt auf eine relativ lange Geschichte zurück. Die erste Tagung, damals noch als Workshop bezeichnet, wurde 1979 in Berlin veranstaltet. Seither fand sie in zweijährigem Rhythmus statt und hat sich im deutschsprachigen Raum als wichtigstes Forum für Forschung und Entwicklung in den Bereichen Kommunikation und Verteilte Systeme etabliert. Die KiVS-Tagung ist in Fachkreisen bekannt und geschätzt für die Standortbestimmung der Technik und die Diskussion neuer Trends. Anhand der Veränderung der thematischen Schwerpunkte über die Jahre zeigt sich eindrucksvoll (und fast schon ein wenig beängstigend) die Rasanz und Brisanz der Entwicklung: Beispielsweise ging es 1979 um X.25, Bildschirmtext und OSI-Referenzmodell, 1989 um ATM, OSI-Dienste und heterogene Rechnernetze, 1999 um Multimedia, Electronic Commerce und Sicherheit und 2009 spannt die KiVS einen Bogen von Mobilfunk über Selbst-adaptive Systeme bis hin zu Sicherheit und Service-Oriented Computing.

Mit der Universität Kassel wurde eine junge Universität und ein noch junger Informatik-Fachbereich mit der Ausrichtung der Tagung beauftragt. Die Universität wurde 1971 als Gesamthochschule Kassel gegründet. Nach starkem Wachstum und Ausbau des Fächerspektrums benennt sie sich 1993 in Universität Gesamthochschule Kassel um. Seit 2001 bietet sie einen zweigestuften Diplomstudiengang Informatik an. Ein neues Entwicklungskonzept und eine damit einhergehende fachliche Profilierung führen dann im Jahr 2002 zur Umbenennung in Universität Kassel. Das wissenschaftliche Profil der Universität Kassel ist geprägt durch einen in Deutschland ungewöhnlich vielschichtigen Verbund von Kompetenzen, die sich auf Natur und Technik, Kultur und Gesellschaft konzentrieren. Aufgrund dieser Fächervielfalt bietet die Universität Kassel die Themenbreite, um viele Forschungsfragen in interdisziplinärer Kooperation bearbeiten zu können. Die Bildung interdisziplinärer Forschungsschwerpunkte wird daher nachhaltig gefördert.

Unser Dank gilt den Autoren für die Beiträge und dem Programmausschuss für die zeitaufwändige Begutachtung und Auswahl der Präsentationen. Alle Mitglieder des lokalen Organisationskomitees, an vorderster Stelle Iris Rossbach, Alexander Bolz und Michael Wagner verdienen ein dickes Dankeschön für die organisatorische Vorbereitung und Durchführung der Tagung. Nicht zuletzt sei auch den Sponsoren gedankt, ohne deren Beiträge die Konferenz nicht in dieser Weise hätte ausgerichtet werden können.

Wir wünschen allen Teilnehmerinnen und Teilnehmern eine erfolgreiche und unterhaltsame Tagung mit vielen neuen Erkenntnissen und Kontakten!

Kassel, im März 2009

Klaus David und Kurt Geihs
Tagungsleiter
KiVS'09

Organisation

Die 16. Fachtagung „Kommunikation in Verteilten Systemen“(KiVS 2009) wurde von den Fachgebieten „Verteilte Systeme“ (Prof. Dr. Kurt Geihs) und „Kommunikationstechnik“ (Prof. Dr. Klaus David) an der Universität Kassel ausgerichtet und war eine Veranstaltung der Gesellschaft für Informatik (GI) unter Beteiligung der Informationstechnischen Gesellschaft im VDE (ITG/VDE).

Tagungsleitung

Kurt Geihs (Universität Kassel)
Klaus David (Universität Kassel)

Programmkomitee

Sebastian Abeck	Universität Karlsruhe
Heribert Baldus	Philips
Christian Becker	Universität Mannheim
Götz-Philip Brasche	Microsoft
Torsten Braun	Universität Bern
Berthold Butscher	Fraunhofer Fokus
Georg Carle	Universität Tübingen
Daniel Catrein	Ericsson
Joachim Charzinski	Nokia Siemens Networks
Klaus David	Universität Kassel
Hermann de Meer	Universität Passau
Jörg Eberspächer	TU München
Wolfgang Effelsberg	Universität Mannheim
Stefan Fischer	Universität Lübeck
Kurt Geihs	Universität Kassel
Oliver Heckmann	Google
Heinz-Gerd Hegering	Leibniz-Rechenzentrum München
Ralf-Guido Herrtwich	Daimler
Dieter Hogrefe	Universität Göttingen
Holger Karl	Universität Paderborn
Peter Kaufmann	Deutsches Forschungsnetz
Wolfgang Kellerer	DOCOMO Euro-Labs
Hartmut König	TU Cottbus
Arne Koschel	FH Hannover
Udo Krieger	Universität Bamberg
Reinhold Kröger	FH Wiesbaden

Paul J. Kühn	Universität Stuttgart
Winfried Lamersdorf	Universität Hamburg
Rolf Lehnert	TU Dresden
Christof Lindemann	Universität Leipzig
Norbert Luttenberger	Universität Kiel
Martin Mauve	Universität Düsseldorf
Paul Müller	Universität Kaiserslautern
Christian Prehofer	Nokia
Peter Reichl	Forschungszentrum Telekommunikation Wien
Hartmut Ritter	FU Berlin
Kurt Rothermel	Universität Stuttgart
Günter Schäfer	TU Ilmenau
Alexander Schill	TU Dresden
Jochen Schiller	FU Berlin
Jens Schmitt	Universität Kaiserslautern
Otto Spaniol	RWTH Aachen
Ralf Steinmetz	TU Darmstadt
Burkhard Stiller	Universität Zürich
Heiner Stüttgen	NEC
Klaus Wehrle	RWTH Aachen
Torben Weis	Universität Duisburg-Essen
Lars C. Wolf	TU Braunschweig
Bernd Wolfinger	Universität Hamburg
Adam Wolisz	TU Berlin
Michael Zapf	Universität Kassel
Martina Zitterbart	Universität Karlsruhe

Inhaltsverzeichnis

I Funknetze

II Standardization and Research – How Do These Two Fit Together?

III Adaptive Systeme

IV Service-Oriented Computing

V Leistungsbewertung

VI Sicherheit

VII Kurzbeiträge

VIII Preisträger

Teil I

Funknetze

Practical Rate-Based Congestion Control for Wireless Mesh Networks

Sherif M. ElRakabawy and Christoph Lindemann

University of Leipzig, Department of Computer Science,
Johannisgasse 26, 04103 Leipzig, Germany

Abstract. We introduce an adaptive pacing scheme to overcome the drawbacks of TCP in wireless mesh networks with Internet connectivity. The pacing scheme is implemented at the wireless TCP sender as well as at the mesh gateway, and reacts according to the direction of TCP flows running across the wireless network and the Internet. TCP packets are transmitted rate-based within the TCP congestion window according to the current out-of-interference delay and the coefficient of variation of recently measured round-trip times. Opposed to the majority of previous work which builds on simulations, we implement a Linux prototype of our approach and evaluate its feasibility in a real 20-node mesh testbed. In an experimental performance study, we compare the goodput and fairness of our approach against the widely deployed TCP NewReno. Experiments show that our approach, which we denote as Mesh Adaptive Pacing (MAP), can achieve up to 150% more goodput than TCP NewReno and significantly improves fairness between competing flows. MAP is incrementally deployable since it is TCP-compatible, does not require cross-layer information from intermediate nodes along the path, and requires no modifications in the wired domain.

1 Introduction

In recent years, wireless mesh networks (e.g. [2], [9], [13]) have been within the focus of research in the networking community. Wireless mesh networks typically aim to provide cost-efficient Internet access with minimal infrastructure expenditure, which makes it particularly attractive for suburban areas with little or no broadband availability. Mesh nodes, which are typically wireless routers mounted on buildings, form a multihop backbone to forward packets hop-by-hop between the Internet and other mesh nodes. Mesh participants with mesh gateways (MGs), which have direct access to the Internet, can share it with other participants.

Within several research topics in wireless mesh networks, TCP performance has acquired great attention. Wireless mesh networks using IEEE 802.11 namely possess several properties, which are different to the wired Internet for which the widely deployed TCP NewReno implementation has been optimized. Opposed to wired networks, in IEEE 802.11 networks, the wireless channel is a scarce resource shared among nodes within their radio range. Furthermore, channel capture, hidden and exposed terminal effects [8], and the IEEE 802.11 medium access control constitute features of wireless mesh networks not present in a wired IP network. Since the congestion control of TCP NewReno is based on lost data packets, the size of its congestion window is overshooting rather than proactively sensing incipient congestion by monitoring the network traffic. Hence, TCP NewReno possesses quite poor performance in wireless mesh networks, as well as exhibits severe unfairness among competing TCP flows.

Besides TCP improvements for the Internet [16], a few approaches (e.g. [6], [9], and [21]) have been proposed for improving TCP performance in wireless mesh networks with Internet connectivity. Unfortunately, most of these approaches have been only designed and evaluated in network simulators. In this paper, we introduce and evaluate a feasible approach for improving TCP goodput and fairness in a real wireless mesh testbed rather than in simulators. We introduce a rate-based congestion control algorithm for TCP over real IEEE 802.11 mesh networks, implementing rate-based scheduling of transmissions within the TCP congestion window. We propose to distinguish the direction of the TCP flow: For wired-to-wireless TCP flows, we introduce an adaptive pacing scheme at the mesh gateway. For wireless-to-wired flows, we propose an adaptive pacing scheme at the TCP sender. The proposed approach is denoted as *Mesh Adaptive Pacing (MAP)*. In a performance study, we show that, depending on the current network state and traffic patterns, MAP can achieve up to 150% more goodput than the widely deployed TCP NewReno, and significantly improves fairness between competing flows. Opposed to previous proposals for improving TCP over IEEE 802.11 mesh networks, MAP does neither rely on modifications at the routing or the link layer nor requires cross-layer information from intermediate nodes along the path.

The remainder of this paper is organized as follows. Section 2 summarizes related work on TCP for wireless mesh networks, while Section 3 describes the miniaturized wireless mesh testbed which we have built for evaluating our approach. Section 4 introduces the Mesh Adaptive Pacing scheme. An experimental performance study of MAP versus TCP NewReno using our wireless mesh testbed is given in Section 5. Finally, concluding remarks are given.

2 Related Work

ElRakabawy et al. ([5], [6]) and Wei et al. [20] showed that pacing for TCP can improve goodput and fairness both for wired as well as for wireless multihop networks. The authors in [20] found out that pacing yields reduced burstiness of traffic, increased synchronization among flows as well as fragmented SACK blocks in a flow. In [5] and [6], TCP with Adaptive Pacing and Gateway Adaptive Pacing were introduced and evaluated using ns-2 [7]. The results showed that adaptive pacing yields significant performance improvement with respect to standard TCP. Opposed to [20], our approach is tailored for wireless mesh networks and not for the Internet, which possesses fundamentally different characteristics. Beyond [5], MAP supports flows between hosts in the Internet and wireless mesh nodes. Furthermore, opposed to [5] and [6], we evaluate our approach in a real mesh testbed rather than only in simulations.

In [17], Scheuermann et al. proposed a novel hop-by-hop congestion control protocol for multihop wireless networks. In their scheme, backpressure towards the source node is established implicitly by passively observing the medium. Sundaresam et al. [19] introduced ATP, and Anastasi et al. proposed TPA [1], which are both new transport protocols for multihop wireless networks. ATP employs pure rate-based transmission of packets, where the transmission rate is determined using feedback from intermediate nodes along the path. TPA uses a similar congestion control algorithm as TCP, in such that packets are transmitted window-based. Opposed to [1], [17] and [19] we consider mesh networks with Internet connectivity rather than pure multihop wireless networks.

Yang et al. [21] proposed a pacing scheme at the IP layer to improve TCP fairness in hybrid wireless/wired networks. They derived the pacing rate by the minimum transmission delay observed for a node, the most recent transmission delay, and a random delay. In contrast to [21], MAP employs adaptive pacing rather than static pacing. Employing such an adaptive pacing scheme, MAP does not lead to unnecessary goodput degradation if there is no contention between active flows.

Gambiroza et al. [9] studied TCP performance and fairness in wireless mesh networks comprising numerous wireless relay nodes and a connection to the wired Internet. They proposed a distributed link layer algorithm for achieving fairness among active TCP flows. MAP constitutes a modification at the transport layer rather than a modification at the link layer as in [9]. In contrast to [9], MAP does not require any control traffic for achieving fairness among active TCP flows.

Opposed to [5], [6], [9], [19], and [21], our approach is tailored and evaluated in a real mesh testbed rather than simulations. This makes our approach feasible and improves the reliability of the acquired results.

3 The Leipzig Wireless Mesh Testbed

To study the performance of MAP in reality and compare it to the widely deployed TCP NewReno, we built up a miniaturized wireless mesh testbed. The testbed, which is depicted in Figure 1, comprises 20 wireless mesh nodes. Each node consists of a Siemens ESPRIMO P2510 PC with an Intel Celeron 3.2 GHz processor and two IEEE 802.11b Netgear wireless PCI network interface cards (NICs) with Atheros chipsets. Opposed to other testbeds like ORBIT [14], each wireless card is connected to a variable signal attenuator and a 2.1dBi low-gain antenna. Using the variable attenuators, the signal power of the wireless PCI cards can be adaptively shrunk in order to limit the maximum transmission range of each node. Thus, large wireless mesh networks can be scaled down to a few meters, making quick

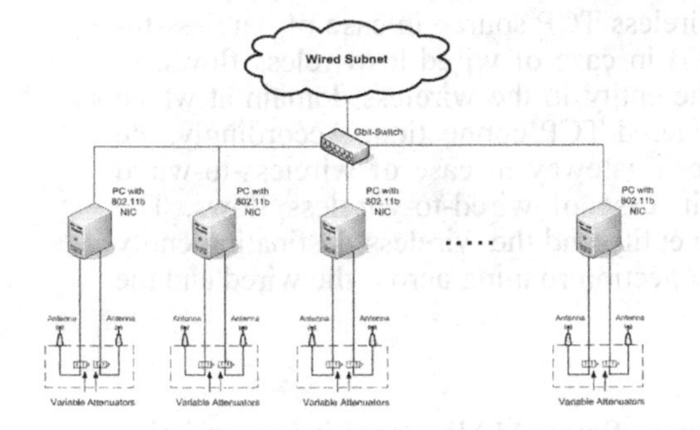

Fig 1: Leipzig wireless mesh testbed

topology and parameter modifications for efficient evaluation of network protocols possible. Besides single-radio communication, the testbed also supports dual-radio communication between mesh nodes by assigning a different channel to each of the two wireless PCI cards of a node. Testbed nodes run a SuSE Linux 10.2 operating system with a custom-compiled kernel version 2.6.18 with the high-resolution timer subsystem patch [10]. As driver for the wireless PCI cards, we employ the Linux Madwifi kernel device driver version 0.9.3.2 for Atheros chipsets. For mesh routing, we employ the Optimized Link State Routing Protocol (OLSR) version 0.5.2 for Linux [3] [12], which incorporates the ETX metric [4] for selecting routes based on the current loss probability of the links. Each wireless node further possesses a Gigabit Ethernet NIC, which is connected to the wired subnet through a Gigabit switch. This allows conducting wired-to-wireless and wireless-to-wired experiments with connections between the wired subnet and the wireless mesh domain. Thereby, any wireless mesh node can act as a mesh gateway.

4 The Mesh Adaptive Pacing Scheme

The main deficiency of TCP's congestion control algorithm over IEEE 802.11 is that it implements reactive rather than proactive congestion control. That is, a packet loss must actually occur before TCP starts throttling its transmission rate. Thus, proactive congestion control, as proposed by MAP, aims to avoid congestion before it actually occurs. Our approach adapts TCP's transmission in order to overcome the spatial reuse constraint as well as the link layer unfairness of IEEE 802.11. Thereby, the transmission rate is adjusted proactively according to the current load in the network rather than reactively after a packet loss actually occurs. Since our approach is only implemented at the wireless TCP sender and above the network layer of the mesh gateway, it is fully TCP-compatible. Specifically, modifications of TCP in the wired domain or changes in IEEE 802.11 are not required.

In general, the network entity at which adaptive pacing is implemented depends on the direction of a TCP flow. We distinguish between two flow directions: wireless-to-wired flows as well as wired-to-wireless flows. While wireless-to-wired flows describe the case where a wireless node constitutes the TCP source and a host in the wired domain is the TCP destination, wired-to-wireless flows correspond to the opposite flow direction. For wireless-to-wired flows, the adaptive pacing scheme is implemented at the wireless TCP source. For wired-to-wireless flows, adaptive pacing is implemented at the mesh gateway, which is responsible for forwarding the packets to the wireless domain according to the computed adaptive pacing rate.

Subsequently, we discuss the components of MAP in detail. Thereby, we use the term *wireless source entity* to refer to the wireless TCP source in case of wireless-to-wired flows, and to the mesh gateway (MG) in case of wired-to-wireless flows. In other words, the wireless source entity is the entity in the wireless domain at which adaptive pacing is implemented for a considered TCP connection. Accordingly, the *wireless destination entity* describes the mesh gateway in case of wireless-to-wired flows, and the wireless TCP destination in case of wired-to-wireless flows. The communication between the wireless source entity and the wireless destination entity corresponds to the wireless part of a TCP connection running across the wired and the wireless domain.

4.1 Network Load Adaptation

In order to achieve fairness between competing flows, MAP adapts its transmission rate according to the current load in the network. Thus, opposed to the aggressive strategy of standard TCP, it throttles its transmission rate to share the available bandwidth with other flows contending for the same channel. MAP identifies the current load in the vicinity by measuring the current degree of contention by means of recently measured wireless RTT samples. The term *wireless RTT* denotes the round-trip time in the wireless part of the network, i.e. the time taken for a TCP packet to be transmitted between a wireless node and MG plus the time taken for the corresponding TCP ACK packet to be transmitted between MG and the wireless node. The RTT delay in the wired part of the network does not need to be considered since the adaptive pacing approach is deployed only within the wireless domain.

MAP uses the coefficient of variation of recently measured wireless round trip times, cov_{RTT}, as a key measure for the degree of the contention on the network path. This measure is given by:

$$cov_{RTT} = \frac{\sqrt{\frac{1}{N-1}\sum_{i=1}^{N}(RTT^{i}_{wireless} - \overline{RTT}_{wireless})^2}}{\overline{RTT}_{wireless}} \qquad (1)$$

Here, N is the number of considered wireless RTT samples, $\overline{RTT}_{wireless}$ is the mean of the samples, and $RTT^{i}_{wireless}$ denotes the value of the i-th wireless RTT sample. The coefficient of variation cov_{RTT} can be obtained purely end-to-end without provoking congestion or packet losses.

4.2 The Spatial Reuse Constraint

Besides the measure of contention on the network path, MAP also accounts for the spatial reuse constraint of IEEE 802.11 mesh networks. That is, due to the hidden terminal problem and the absence of perfect scheduling at link layer, concurrent wireless nodes in a chain cannot transmit simultaneously without causing collisions. A crucial factor that has a significant impact on the spatial reuse constraint of a mesh network is the carrier sensing range of wireless nodes. Physical carrier sensing is a mechanism incorporated in IEEE 802.11 [18], by which a wireless node senses the medium before it transmits a packet. Only if the sensed signal power is below a certain threshold, denoted as carrier sense threshold T_{cs}, does the node initiate a transmission. As the radio signal of a node attenuates with the distance, the range in which the node can sense the transmission of another node is limited. The carrier sensing range defines the range in which the current transmission of a node can be sensed by other nodes. The key role of the carrier sensing range lies in determining which hops on a chain of nodes are prone to be potential hidden terminals. That is, nodes which operate beyond each other's carrier sensing range on a chain comprise mutual hidden terminals. Thus, the transmission of each of the nodes cannot be sensed by the other node, respectively, resulting increased collision at link layer. Figure 2 shows a wireless chain of 6 nodes and a mesh gateway which is connected to the Internet. Assume a TCP connection is running between node 1 as a TCP source and a wired TCP host in the Internet as a TCP destination (i.e. a wireless-to-wired flow). We consider the wireless part of the communication, i.e. the transmission between the nodes of the chain. In this case, nodes 1 and 4 comprise mutual hidden terminals, since both nodes operate beyond each other's carrier sensing ranges. Namely, node 4 cannot sense the transmission from node 1 to node 2 and thus may transmit packets to node 5, resulting collisions with the ongoing transmission between nodes 1 and 2.

From the point of view of the TCP source, i.e. node 1, the first node which is positioned right at the border of its carrier sensing range, node 4 in this case, is the first node that comprises a potential hidden terminal. That means that collisions can be avoided if node 1 defers its transmission until node 4 finishes its transmission to node 5. Note that which node comprises the hidden terminal is mainly determined by the carrier sensing range and does not have to be the 4th node on the chain as given in Figure 2. This means that the hidden terminal varies with varying carrier sensing range. Let node i be the TCP source node and node (i+x), $x \geq 2$, be the hidden terminal to node i. We refer to the time elapsed between transmitting a TCP packet by the TCP source node i and receiving the packet at node (i+x+1) as the *out-of-interference delay (OID)*. Note that the same circumstances apply for wired-to-wireless case, where MG would act as the wireless source entity, node 1 would act as the wireless destination entity, and node 4 would be the hidden terminal.

The challenge is to approximate *OID* by determining the hidden terminal for the wireless source entity node. In order to identify the hidden terminal for the wireless source entity, we have to determine the carrier sensing range in terms of number of hops. The next node right at the border of the carrier sensing range comprises the potential hidden terminal. Subsequently, we introduce the *Adaptive Out-of-Interference Delay* approach, which incorporates an effective way for estimating the carrier sensing range of the wireless source entity and approximating the out-of-interference delay accordingly.

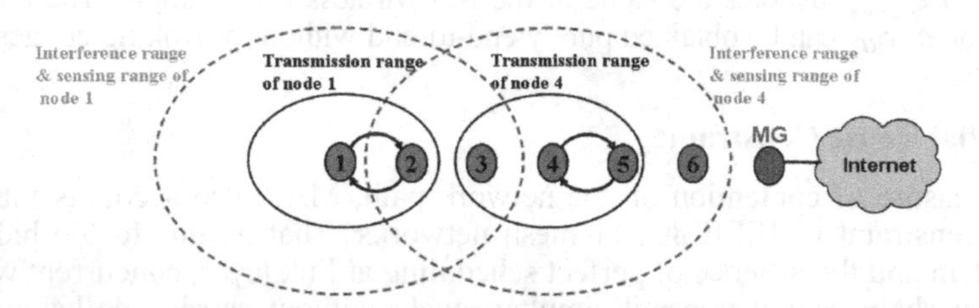

Fig. 2: Spatial reuse constraint: Hidden terminals in a chain are dependent on current carrier sensing range

4.3 Approximating the Out-of-Interference Delay

The main challenge in approximating the carrier sensing range of the wireless source entity, i.e. a wireless TCP source or the mesh gateway, lies in the lack of fundamental information such as transmission range and distance between wireless nodes. Such information can be easily inquired in simulations, but are not available in real life. As we set the preservation of the end-to-end semantics of TCP as a strict design goal, we introduce an approach for approximating the carrier sensing range purely end-to-end without any support from intermediate nodes. All parameters required for approximating the carrier sensing range are available at the wireless source entity and can be inquired from the IEEE 802.11 driver.

We approximate the carrier sensing range in terms of number of hops, not in meters, by estimating how many hops it takes for the transmission signal of the wireless source entity to get attenuated such that it falls below the carrier sensing threshold T_{cs}. That is, the first hop that comes after the threshold T_{cs} is undercut is a potential hidden terminal for the wireless source entity.

The first step towards estimating the carrier sensing range in terms of number of hops is to estimate the signal attenuation for the first hop on the path from wireless source entity to TCP destination. Let P_{out} be the actual outgoing signal power of the wireless source entity. Following the Equivalent Isotropically Radiated Power (EIRP) [15] equation we get:

$$P_{out} = P_{tx} + G_{ant} - A_{cab} - A_v \quad (2)$$

where P_{tx} denotes the transmission power of the wireless NIC at the wireless source entity, G_{ant} denotes the signal gain of the mini antenna, and A_{cab} and A_v describe the signal attenuation caused by the coaxial cable and the variable attenuator, respectively. The parameters A_{cab} and A_v only correspond to the deployed testbed and are set to zero if no cables and/or no hardware attenuators are used in the mesh network. The signal attenuation for the first hop, L_1, is given by the difference between the received power P_{rx} at the second node in the wireless chain and the outgoing signal power from the wireless source entity, i.e. first node in the chain, P_{out}:

$$L_1 = P_{out} - P_{rx} \quad (3)$$

The received power P_{rx} can be easily inquired from the IEEE 802.11 driver at the wireless source entity using the Received Signal Strength Indication mechanism (RSSI) [18] due to the link symmetry between the wireless source entity and the second node in the chain.

The next step is to derive an equation for estimating the signal attenuation for an arbitrary number of hops, *n*. Such an equation shall approximate the signal attenuation of the wireless source entity at nodes which are *n* hops away. The signal attenuation equation as described by the ITU-R indoor propagation model [15] is given by

$$L = 20\log_{10}(f_c) + 10p\log_{10}(d) \qquad (4)$$

where f_c denotes the frequency of the transmitted signal, i.e. a channel in the 2.4 GHz band in our case, p denotes the path loss exponent, and d describes the distance between transmitter and receiver in meters. The path loss exponent p depends on the operating environment of the wireless nodes and ranges from 2 for propagation in free space up to 5 in dense indoor environments. Due to findings from extensive measurements in our testbed and following [15], we set $p = 3$.

Let d_1 be the distance of the first hop in the chain, i.e. between the wireless source entity and the second wireless node, then we get according to Eq. 4

$$L_1 = 20\log_{10}(f_c) + 10p\log_{10}(d_1) \qquad (5)$$

Since the exact distance between the wireless nodes is unknown, we set the distance of the first n hops as $\sum_{i=1}^{n} d_i = d_1 n + \delta$, where δ determines the deviation between the distance $d_1 n$ and the actual distance of the first n hops. For the signal attenuation of the wireless source entity after n hops, L_n, we get:

$$\begin{aligned} L_n &= 20\log_{10}(f_c) + 10p\log_{10}(\textstyle\sum_{i=1}^{n} d_i) \\ &= 20\log_{10}(f_c) + 10p\log_{10}(d_1 n + \delta) \\ &= 20\log_{10}(f_c) + 10p\left(\log_{10}(d_1) + \log_{10}(n) + \log_{10}\left(1 + \frac{\delta}{d_1 n}\right)\right) \qquad (6) \\ &= L_1 + 10p\log_{10}(n) + 10p\log_{10}\left(1 + \frac{\delta}{d_1 n}\right) \\ &= L_1 + 10p\log_{10}(n) + \varepsilon \end{aligned}$$

where ε describes the approximation error, which is determined by δ. Since ε is a logarithmic factor, its ratio to the overall attenuation L_n diminishes with increasing distance.

In a real large-scale mesh network, $\sum_{i=1}^{n} d_i$ may well be determined more accurately, either by deploying localization techniques in IEEE 802.11 [11], or by using GPS localization. In case such localization information are available at the TCP source, an even more accurate approximation of L_n may be achieved.

Finally, we can derive the carrier sensing range H_{cs} in terms of number of hops for an h-hop chain:

$$H_{cs} = \min\{k \mid k \in \{1, 2, ..., h\} \wedge P_{out} - L_k < T_{cs}\} \qquad (7)$$

In other words, H_{cs} is the smallest number of hops k for which the actually sensed power of the wireless source entity (i.e. P_{out} - L_k) is below the carrier sensing threshold T_{cs}. This implies that (H_{cs} + 1) is the first node in the chain which cannot sense the transmission of the wireless source entity, and thus comprises a potential hidden terminal.

By means of the estimated carrier sensing range H_{cs} as well as wireless RTT measurements at the wireless source entity, the out-of-interference delay *OID* of TCP data packets can be derived. The wireless RTT is composed of the sum of the delay experienced by the data packet on the way from the wireless source entity to wireless destination entity and the delay experienced by the ACK packet forwarded from the wireless destination entity to the wireless source entity. Each of these delays comprises the time to forward the packet over h wireless hops, where each forwarding requires a queuing delay t_q and transmission delays t_{data} and t_{ACK}, respectively. Using the measured wireless RTT, we get:

$$RTT_{wireless} = h\left(t_q + t_{data} + t_{LLD}\right) + h\left(t_q + t_{ACK} + t_{LLA}\right) \quad (8)$$

Here, t_{LLD} and t_{LLA} denote the average wireless link layer delay required for transmitting the TCP data packet and the TCP ACK packet, respectively. This delay comprises the transmission time of IEEE 802.11 control packets, link layer backoff, and potential retransmissions at link layer. Since information on link layer backoff and retransmissions are not available at the wireless source entity, we approximate t_{LLD} and t_{LLA} by defining the corresponding upper and lower bounds:

$$\frac{ACK_{LL}}{b_{base}} \le t_{LLD} \le \frac{ACK_{LL}}{b_{base}} + 3\left(\frac{s_{data}}{b} + cw_{cur} \cdot t_{slot}\right) \quad (9)$$

and

$$\frac{ACK_{LL}}{b_{base}} \le t_{LLA} \le \frac{ACK_{LL}}{b_{base}} + 3\left(\frac{s_{ACK}}{b} + cw_{cur} \cdot t_{slot}\right) \quad (10)$$

Here, ACK_{LL} denotes the link layer ACK size (14 bytes), b_{base} is the base bandwidth for transmitting of IEEE 802.11 control packets (1 Mbit/s), b is the bandwidth for data packets, cw_{cur} denotes the current size of the IEEE 802.11 contention window, s_{data} and s_{ACK} denote the packet sizes of TCP data and ACK packets, and t_{slot} corresponds to the IEEE 802.11 slot time. The lower bounds apply when the TCP packet (data or ACK) can be transmitted with no retransmissions. The upper bounds correspond to the case when it takes the maximum number of retransmissions to deliver the TCP packet. According to the IEEE specifications [18], a total of 4 attempts (i.e. 3 retransmissions) are distinguished at link layer before the packet is dropped. We omit the DIFS and SIFS intervals [18] due to their negligible sizes. We consider the case with RTS/CTS deactivated. In case RTS/CTS is activated, the corresponding transmission times of the RTS and CTS packets at a bandwidth of b_{base} are considered in Eqs. 9 and 10. By choosing the median values within the upper and lower bounds for t_{LLD} and t_{LLA} we get an approximation error of at maximum 3%-6%.

Solving for t_q in Eq. 8 while using $t_{data} = s_{data}/b$ and $t_{ACK} = s_{ACK}/b$, we derive the average queuing delay as:

$$t_q = \frac{1}{2}\left(\frac{RTT_{wireless}}{h} - \frac{s_{data} + s_{ACK}}{b} - t_{LLD} - t_{LLA}\right) \quad (11)$$

Subsequently, we can estimate the out-of-interference delay of the TCP data packet:

$$OID = \left(H_{cs} + 1\right)\left(t_q + \frac{s_{data}}{b}\right) \quad (12)$$

The number of hops h on the network path to the wireless destination entity and the bandwidth of the wireless network interface b can be easily inquired without extra overhead from the kernel routing table and the IEEE 802.11 driver, respectively. Note that we use raw $RTT_{wireless}$ measures rather than EWMA-smoothed ones in order to be able to determine short-term RTT variations.

In theory, the maximum spatial reuse with minimum collisions can be achieved with a transmission rate $R_{max}=1/OID$. Thus, an upper bound for the capacity of a path with h hops in an IEEE 802.11 wireless mesh network is given by $h/(H_{cs} + 1)$ packets. Let $T_{one\text{-}way}$ denote the time a packet traverses from the wireless source entity to the wireless destination entity. This quantity can be computed as $T_{one-way} = OID \cdot h/(H_{cs}+1)$. Subsequently, the number of packets in flight on the way from the wireless source entity to the wireless destination entity with a transmission rate of R_{max} is given by:

$$\tilde{P} = R_{max} \cdot T_{one-way} = \frac{1}{(H_{cs}+1)} h \qquad (13)$$

Thus, the number of packets in flight $\tilde{P}$ transmitted with the maximum transmission rate R_{max} reflects the maximum capacity of the network path.

4.4 The MAP Pacing Rate

The adaptive transmission rate of MAP accounts for both the current contention on the network path and the spatial reuse constraint. Thus, the transmission rate formula incorporates both cov_{RTT} and OID:

$$R = \frac{1}{\widehat{OID} \cdot (1 + 2cov_{RTT})} \qquad (14)$$

The coefficient of variation quantifies the percentage of sample deviation from the mean. However, since we want to quantify the size of the spectrum in which the samples fluctuate around the mean, we double the value cov_{RTT} in the rate formula.

We average the measured out-of-interference delay samples and employ a reasonable history size N for the computation of the coefficient of variation using an exponentially weighted moving average (EWMA) with averaging weight α:

$$\widehat{OID} = \alpha \cdot \widehat{OID}_{old} + (1-\alpha) \cdot OID \qquad (15)$$

As validated by our experiments, suitable values for the EWMA weight α and the history size N are 0.7 and 50, respectively.

5 Comparative Performance Study

We evaluate the performance of MAP versus the widely deployed TCP NewReno by means of our Leipzig wireless mesh testbed. The considered performance measures are derived from 10 batches with 95% confidence intervals by the batch means method ([5], [6]). For all experiments, we set the TCP packet size to 1,460 bytes and the TCP receiver's advertised window to 64 packets. Consistent with previous work ([2], [9]), the RTS/CTS handshake is disabled, since it rather degrades TCP goodput due to the increased link layer overhead. We set the IEEE 802.11 data rate to 11 Mbit/s and the attenuation level of the variable attenuators to 16dB, unless otherwise stated. This provides a transmission range of 0.5m.

5.1 Wireless Chain Topology

The first topology we consider is an equally spaced wireless chain comprising 10 mesh nodes, where node 10 acts as mesh router to the wired subnet. Nodes in the chain are positioned such that only direct neighbors can communicate with each other over one hop. An FTP connection runs between the leftmost wireless node (i.e. node 1) and a wired host in the subnet.

In order to evaluate MAP versus TCP NewReno in a variety of different network conditions, we vary network-related parameters to reflect typical real world settings. For one, we consider the goodput of MAP and TCP NewReno in the wireless-to-wired case (i.e. from node 1 to the wired host), as well as in the wired-to-wireless case (i.e. from the wired host to node 1). Furthermore, we set the attenuation level of the variable attenuators such that the signal between nodes is either optimal (at low attenuation level) or very weak (at high attenuation level). Such high attenuation level and/or weak inter-node signal often occurs in real wireless mesh networks, in cases where either links between nodes suffer from high external interference or the distance between nodes is considerably large. Figures 3 to 6 show the results of this experiment, plotted as goodput versus chain length in terms of number of hops.

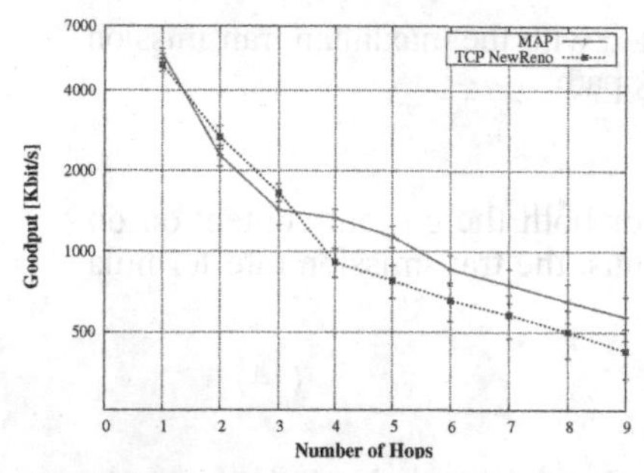

Fig. 3: Wireless chain: Goodput vs. number of hops for wireless-to-wired flow and high link quality

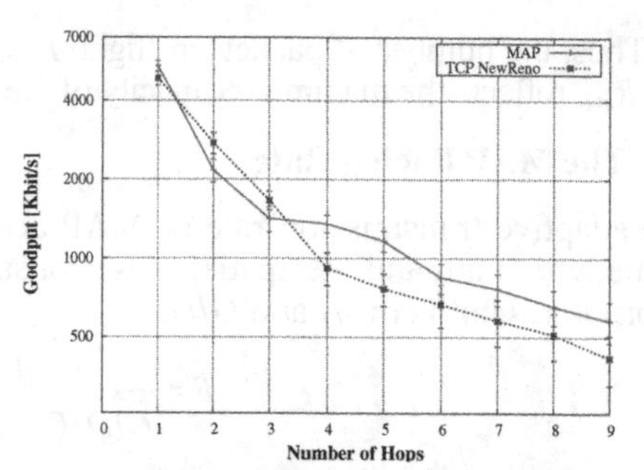

Fig. 5: Wireless chain: Goodput vs. number of hops for wired-to-wireless flow and high link quality

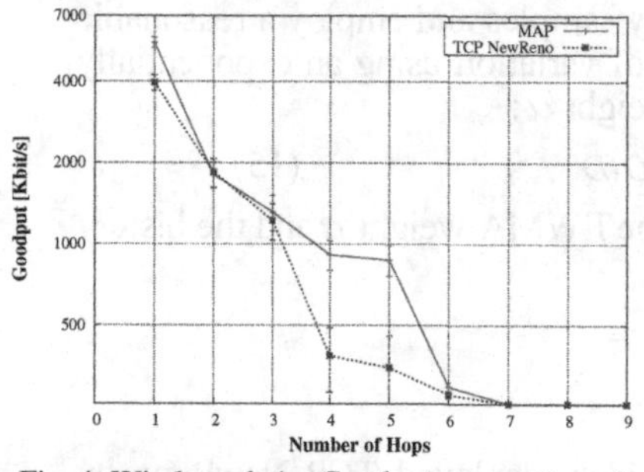

Fig. 4: Wireless chain: Goodput vs. number of hops for wireless-to-wired flow and low link quality

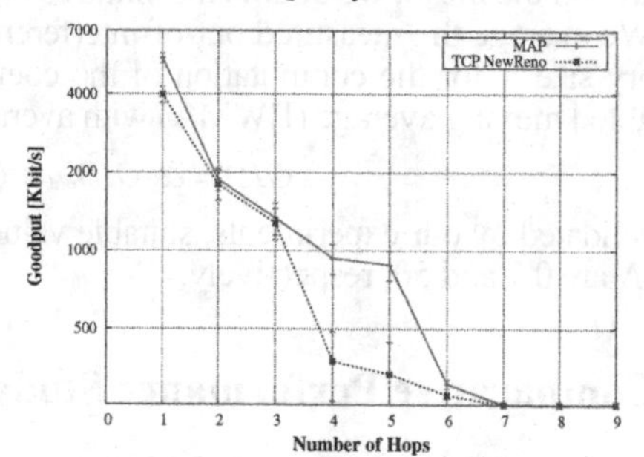

Fig. 6: Wireless chain: Goodput vs. number of hops for wired-to-wireless flow and low link quality

In Figure 3, we observe that the advantage of the MAP scheme evolves for a chain length of 4 hops and above. Specifically, MAP achieves around 46% more goodput than TCP NewReno. Up to a chain length of 3 hops, the goodput of MAP is similar to the goodput of TCP NewReno, with a slight advantage for TCP NewReno at 2 and 3 hops. The reason for such a turning point at 4 hops is the presence of hidden terminals for a chain length above 3 hops. As discussed before, TCP NewReno suffers from such hidden terminals due to its aggressive transmission strategy, whereas MAP takes advantage due to its adaptive pacing rate which reduces hidden terminal effects.

5.2 Concurrent Flows Topology

As a second topology, we consider two concurrent FTP flows running between two wired hosts and a wireless mesh node, as illustrated in Figure 7. This scenario corresponds to the case in reality when a user in the wireless domain starts to simultaneously download content from two hosts in the Internet. In our case, two FTP connections run between the wired source hosts A and B through two mesh gateways (i.e. nodes 1 and 5) to the wireless destination node 3. Obviously, both FTP flows contend for the channel in the wireless part of the network. Our goal is to evaluate the performance of MAP and TCP NewReno in terms of fairness between the competing flows.

We consider the transient behavior of both flows by plotting the goodput of the flows over time. Figures 8 and 9 show the results for MAP and TCP NewReno, respectively. Considering MAP, we see how both flows share the available bandwidth equally over the lifetime of the connections. Since both flows experience similar interference, their cov_{RTT} values are also similar. Thus, according to Eq. 14, the MAP transmission rate is derived such that both flows acquire the same share of the bandwidth.

Opposed to MAP, TCP NewReno suffers from severe unfairness between the competing flows. As Figure 9 shows, during the lifetime of flow 1, it acquires the entire available bandwidth at cost of the completely starved flow 2. Not until about 10 seconds after flow 1 terminates is flow 2 able to take control of the bandwidth. The reason for such delay is the timeout interval of flow 2, which has to expire first before a new transmission attempt is performed.

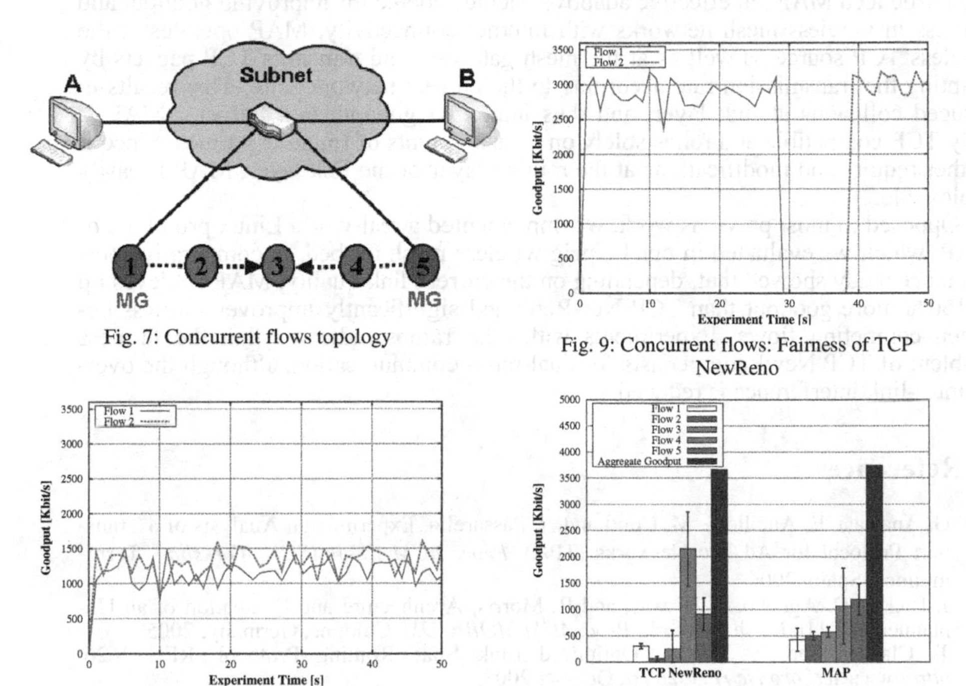

Fig. 7: Concurrent flows topology

Fig. 9: Concurrent flows: Fairness of TCP NewReno

Fig. 8: Concurrent flows: Fairness of MAP

Fig. 10: Random topology: Individual and aggregate goodput for dual-radio communication

5.3 Random Topology

Random node topologies are typically found in community mesh networks such as [2] and are widely deployed in reality. We evaluate MAP and TCP NewReno in such topologies by considering random placements of the testbed's 20 antenna-stations. The 20 antenna-stations are distributed uniformly on a flat area of 2m x 3m such that full connectivity between each pair in the wireless network over one or more hops is granted. We consider 5 FTP flows and 5 different mesh gateways, which are also chosen randomly out of the testbed nodes. Each flow runs from a wired host in the subnet through one mesh gateway to a mesh node in the wireless network. Figure 10 shows the results using dual-radio communication, in which each of the non-overlapping channels 1 and 11 is assigned to a different wireless NIC.

In Figure 10, we see that TCP NewReno penalizes flows 1 to 3 in favor of the other 2 flows. Especially flow 4 acquires most of the available bandwidth. In contrast, MAP achieves more fairness among the competing flows, avoiding the starvation of any flow. The aggregate goodput of MAP and TCP NewReno is similar, since dual-radio communication reduces the effects of hidden terminals due to the reduced interference caused by the non-overlapping channels. Performance results acquired from a cross topology with four concurrent flows are consistent with the above findings. Unfortunately, we have to omit the corresponding curves due to space limitations.

6 Conclusion

We introduced MAP, an effective adaptive pacing scheme for improving goodput and fairness in wireless mesh networks with Internet connectivity. MAP operates at the wireless TCP source as well as at the mesh gateway, and transmits TCP packets by adapting the transmission rate according to the current network state. This results in reduced collisions at link layer, and thus improved goodput and fairness. MAP is fully TCP-compatible and relies solely on measurements of round trip times. Since it further requires no modifications at the routing layer or the link layer, MAP is easily deployable.

Opposed to most previous work, we implemented a real-world Linux prototype of MAP, which we evaluated in our Leipzig wireless mesh testbed. A comparative performance study showed that, depending on the current link quality, MAP achieves up to 150% more goodput than TCP NewReno and significantly improves fairness between competing flows. Experiments with dual radios indicated that the fairness problem of TCP NewReno persists for dual-radio communication, although the overall inter-link interference is reduced.

7 References

1. G. Anastasi, E. Ancillotti, M. Conti and A. Passarella, Experimental Analysis of a Transport Protocol for Ad hoc Networks (TPA), *Proc. ACM PE-WASUN Workshop*, Terromolinos, Spain, 2006.
2. J. Bicket, D. Aguayo, S. Biswas, and R. Morris, Architecture and Evaluation of an Unplanned 802.11b Mesh Network, *Proc. ACM MOBICOM*, Cologne, Germany, 2005.
3. T. Clausen and P. Jacquet, Optimized Link State Routing Protocol, RFC 3626, *http://www.ietf.org/rfc/rfc3626.txt*, October 2003.
4. D. De Couto, D. Aguayo, J. Bicket, and R. Morris, A High-Throughput Path Metric for Multi-Hop Wireless Routing, *Proc. ACM MOBICOM*, San Diego, CA, 2003.
5. S. ElRakabawy, A. Klemm, and C. Lindemann, TCP with Adaptive Pacing for Multihop Wireless Networks, *Proc. ACM MobiHoc*, Urbana-Champaign, IL, 2005.
6. S. ElRakabawy, A. Klemm, and C. Lindemann, TCP with Gateway Adaptive Pacing for Multihop Wireless Networks with Internet Connectivity, *Computer Networks*, 52, 2008.
7. K. Fall and K. Varadhan (Ed.), The ns-2 Manual, Technical Report, The VINT Project, UC Berkeley, LBL, and Xerox PARC, 2007.
8. Z. Fu, P. Zerfos, H. Luo, S. Lu, L. Zhang, and M. Gerla, The Impact of Multihop Wireless Channel on TCP Performance, *IEEE Transactions on Mobile Computing*, Vol. 4, Issue 2, March 2005.
9. V. Gambiroza, B. Sadeghi, and E. Knightly, End-to-End Performance and Fairness in Multihop Wireless Backhaul Networks, *Proc. ACM MOBICOM*, Philadelphia, PA, 2004.

10. T. Gleixner and D. Niehaus, Hrtimers and Beyond: Transforming the Linux Time Subsystems, *Proc. 8th OLS Linux Symposium*, Ottawa, Canada, 2006.
11. A. Haeberlen, E. Flannery, A. Ladd, A. Rudys, D. Wallach and L. Kavraki, Practical Robust Localization over Large-scale 802.11 Wireless Networks, *Proc. ACM MOBICOM*, Philadelphia, PA, 2004.
12. OLSR.ORG Implementation for Linux, *http://www.olsr.org*.
13. Freifunk Mesh Community, *http://start.freifunk.net/*.
14. D. Raychaudhuri, I. Seskar, M. Ott, S. Ganu, K. Ramachandran, H. Kremo, R. Siracusa, H. Liu and M. Singh, Overview of the ORBIT Radio Grid Testbed for Evaluation of Next-Generation Wireless Network Protocols, *Proc. IEEE WCNC*, New Orleans, LA, 2005.
15. S. Saunders, Antennas and Propagation for Wireless Communication Systems, *Wiley & Sons*, May 2007.
16. M. Savoric, H. Karl, M. Schläger, T. Poshwatta, and A. Wolisz, Analysis and performance evaluation of the EFCM common congestion controller for TCP connections, *Computer Networks 49 (2)*, October 2005.
17. B. Scheuermann, C. Lochert, and M. Mauve, Implicit Hop-by-Hop Congestion Control in Wireless Multihop Networks, Ad Hoc Networks 6 (2), April 2008.
18. IEEE Standard for Wireless LAN Medium Access Control (MAC) and Physical Layer (PHY) Specifications, ISO/IEC 8802-11, August 1999.
19. K. Sundaresan, V. Anantharaman, H-Y. Hsieh, R. Sivakumar, ATP: A Reliable Transport Protocol for Ad Hoc Networks, *Transactions on Mobile Computing*, Vol. 4, Issue 6, November 2005.
20. D. Wai, P. Cao, and S. Low, TCP Pacing Revisited, *Proc. IEEE INFOCOM*, Anchorage, AK, USA, 2007.
21. L. Yang, W. Seah, and Q. Yin, Improving Fairness among TCP Flows crossing Wireless Ad Hoc and Wired Networks, *Proc. ACM MobiHoc*, Annapolis, MD, 2003.

Paving the Way Towards Reactive Planar Spanner Construction in Wireless Networks

Hannes Frey[1], Stefan Rührup[2]

[1] University of Paderborn, hannes.frey@uni-paderborn.de
[2] University of Freiburg, ruehrup@informatik.uni-freiburg.de

Abstract. A spanner is a subgraph of a given graph that supports the original graph's shortest path lengths up to a constant factor. Planar spanners and their distributed construction are of particular interest for geographic routing, which is an efficient localized routing scheme for wireless ad hoc and sensor networks. Planarity of the network graph is a key criterion for guaranteed delivery, while the spanner property supports efficiency in terms of path length. We consider the problem of reactive local spanner construction, where a node's local topology is determined on demand. Known message-efficient reactive planarization algorithms do not preserve the spanner property, while reactive spanner constructions with a low message overhead have not been described so far. We introduce the concept of direct planarization which may be an enabler of efficient reactive spanner construction. Given an edge, nodes check for all incident intersecting edges a certain geometric criterion and withdraw the edge if this criterion is not satisfied. We use this concept to derive a generic reactive topology control mechanism and consider two geometric criteria. Simulation results show that direct planarization increases the performance of localized geographic routing by providing shorter paths than existing reactive approaches.

1 Introduction

Wireless ad hoc and sensor networks consist of network nodes which communicate without relying on a given access point infrastructure. Due to physical or regulatory constraints nodes have a limited communication range which often requires a message to be relayed over several intermediate collaborating nodes in order to reach the message destination. Node mobility, node failures, and the dynamic nature of the wireless communication media itself render such networks highly dynamic. In networks with a large number of nodes, setting up a complete routing path from source to destination – either reactively or proactively – becomes impossible. A possible solution to this problem are localized geographic routing algorithms, which perform message forwarding by just taking the current node's, its neighbors', and the destination node's location into account.

There are two basic single-message strategies in geographic routing: *Greedy forwarding* [1] selects a locally optimal neighbor as the next hop, based on criteria such as distance to the destination or deviation from the direction towards the destination. Such greedy strategies fail in case of local minima. The second basic strategy is the so called *face routing* [2], which guarantees delivery and can be applied on its own or as a recovery from local minima in conjunction with greedy forwarding. The idea of face routing is to forward a message along a sequence of adjacent faces of the network graph. The faces are traversed by the message as the nodes forward it along the next edge in counterclockwise order after the previous edge. This strategy needs a planar network graph, i.e. for any two links uv and wx the lines connecting the nodes' positions are at most intersecting in their end points. Planarity of a graph has been shown as a sufficient condition to support delivery guarantees [3].

In general, the network graph resulting from the wireless links among nodes is not planar. Thus, in order to support face routing, a planar graph – also referred to as planar topology – has to be extracted first (see e.g. [2]). Initially, only proactive planar topology control had been considered in the literature. Proactive strategies rely on exchanging control packets among the nodes in order to set up a planar graph regardless if data communication takes place at the same time or not. For nodes that do not participate in the currently ongoing routing tasks, proactive topology control is a waste of resources in terms of energy and communication bandwidth. Due to this observation reactive planar topology control has gained particular interest. In such schemes a node's local view on the topology is constructed on demand only if this node has any messages to forward. Otherwise, no resources are used any longer.

Reactive planar topology control described so far utilized basic geometric structures, which may introduce longer detours in comparison to the underlying network. It is yet preferable to create *graph spanners*, where the length of the shortest path in the constructed topology deviates only by a constant factor from the length of the shortest path in the underlying network. By now it is unclear how to construct such spanners in a reactive way without contacting nodes beyond the one-hop neighborhood. In this work we describe the concept of direct planarization as a possible direction towards this ambitious goal.

In the following section we introduce the concepts used in this work. In Section 3 we discuss related approaches known from the literature. In Section 4 we introduce the concept of direct planarization and list some basic properties. The results are then used in Section 5 to describe a new reactive planar topology control mechanism, and to proof its correctness. This is followed by an empirical study in Section 6 where we compare the topologies obtained by our algorithm with topologies obtained by known reactive schemes. We show how these schemes affect the performance of data communication based on face routing. Finally, in Section 7 we summarize our findings and provide an outlook on future research.

2 Concepts and Notations

We are considering graphs over a finite set V of nodes which are embedded in the two dimensional Euclidean space, i.e., every node has a 2D position and $|uv|$ is the Euclidean distance between the positions of u and v.

Unit Disk Graphs For a given *unit disk radius* R the *unit disk graph* $UDG(V)$ over V contains all edges uv which satisfy $|uv| \leq R$. For a node u we denote the circle with center u and radius R as *unit circle* $C(u)$. In other words, two nodes are connected in the unit disk graph if they are mutually located in the other node's unit circle, by which the transmission region can be modeled.

Planar Graph Constructions Given a set V of 2D nodes, a planar graph can be constructed by global geometric concepts which connect any two nodes if the two nodes' proximity satisfies a certain geometric property, such as the empty region rules used in the following constructions.

The *Relative neighborhood graph* $RNG(V)$ [4] contains all edges uv which satisfy that the intersection of the two circles with center u, center v, and radii $|uv|$ contains no other node (see Fig. 1a). The *Gabriel graph* $GG(V)$ [5] contains all edges uv which satisfy that the smallest circle $C_{GG}(u,v)$ with u and v on its boundary contains no other node (see Fig. 1b). The circle $C_{GG}(u,v)$ is also referred as *Gabriel circle.* The *Delaunay triangulation* $DT(V)$ contains all triangles (u,v,w) which satisfy that the circle $C(u,v,w)$ passing through u, v, and w does not contain any other node (see Fig. 1c). The circle $C(u,v,w)$ is also denoted as *Delaunay circle.*

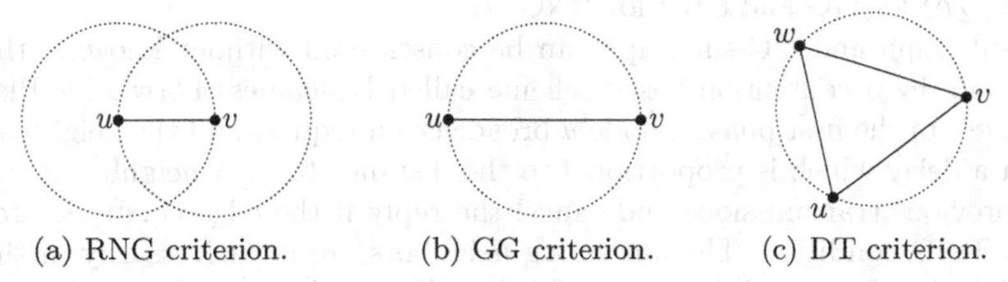

(a) RNG criterion. (b) GG criterion. (c) DT criterion.

Fig. 1: Geometric graph planarization criteria.

Graph Planarization The aforementioned planar graph construction rules can be applied to a given graph in order to remove possibly intersecting edges. This way a RNG or GG subgraph of the unit disk graph ($RNG(V) \cap UDG(V)$ or $GG(V) \cap UDG(V)$) can be constructed locally in the following way [2,6]. Each node u keeps exactly those outgoing edges uv which satisfy that no other unit disk graph neighbor of u violates the relative neighborhood graph or Gabriel graph condition. We are only interested in these localized variants. Following the general literature we use the same notation $RNG(V)$ and $GG(V)$ in order to refer to these localized graph constructions.

In the same way the intersection $DT(V) \cap UDG(V)$ can be considered for Delaunay triangulation. It is easy to construct an example graph which shows that in contrast to $RNG(V)$ and $GG(V)$, this graph can not be constructed in a localized way. As done for $RNG(V)$ and $GG(V)$ we will use $DT(V)$ to refer to the intersection of Delaunay triangulation with the unit disk graph.

Graph Spanners The Euclidean length of a path p is defined as the sum over the Euclidean length of each path edge. Let $sp_G(u,v)$ be the minimum over the Euclidean lengths of all possible paths from u to v in a graph G. The *spanning ratio* of a subgraph $H \subseteq G$ is defined as follows:

$$R_G(H) := \max_{u,v \in S} \frac{sp_H(u,v)}{sp_G(u,v)}$$

A method for constructing a subgraph from a given graph, is denoted to produce a *constant spanner* if there exists a universal constant c such that for any given graph G the spanning ratio of the constructed subgraph $H \subseteq G$ satisfies

$R_G(H) \leq c$. Spanners can also be considered in specific graph families. Within this work we consider so called *unit disk graph spanners*.

Constant spanners are of particular interest for the routing problem since the Euclidean length of the shortest path in the spanner topology will deviate only by a constant factor from the shortest path in the underlying network graph.

3 Related Work

Reactive Planar Non-Spanners Planar subgraph constructions based on Gabriel graph [5] and relative neighborhood graph [4] have the advantage that they can be obtained locally by checking simple geometric conditions using only 1-hop-neighborhood information [2,6]. However, these graphs do not have a constant spanning ratio in the worst case. The spanning ratio of the Gabriel graph is $\Theta(\sqrt{n})$ for GG and $\Theta(n)$ for RNG [7].

RNG-subgraph and GG-subgraph can be constructed without knowing the neighborhood, by a contention-based scheme called Beaconless Forwarder Planarization [8]: In the first phase a node u broadcasts a request and the neighbors reply with a delay which is proportional to the distance to u. A neighbor v can overhear previous transmissions and cancel the reply if the edge (u, v) violates the GG or RNG condition. The answering neighbors are not necessarily in the RNG or GG, therefore possibly wrong selections have to be corrected by protest messages in a second phase. It is shown in [8] that no contention-based scheme can construct GG or RNG subgraphs without protest messages.

Non-Reactive Planar Spanners The Delaunay triangulation is known to be a constant spanner [9,10]. Constructing the Delaunay triangulation in a localized way is not possible since Delaunay circles to be tested for emptiness might get arbitrarily large. However, it is possible to locally construct Delaunay triangulation-like topologies which are constant unit disk graph spanners.

This was first observed in the seminal work where the restricted Delaunay graph (RDG) was introduced [11]. The method consists of two phases. In the first phase each node u computes the Delaunay triangulation $T(u)$ over it's one-hop neighbors. In the second phase nodes exchange their local Delaunay triangulations. Each node u keeps only the edges uv which are in $T(u)$ and which satisfy that there exists no neighbor node w which is connected to u and v and which does not contain uv in it's local Delaunay triangulation $T(w)$.

A follow up publication aimed on reducing the message complexity observed for RDG [12]. While this method significantly reduces the message overhead of RDP when constructing the entire planar topology proactively, it is not clear how the protocol's different phases of constructing and exchanging planarization information can be implemented in an efficient reactive manner.

4 Direct Planarization

The known topology control schemes based on RNG, GG, and DT implicitly obtain a planar graph by keeping only those edges which satisfy a certain geometric property. In the following we describe a scheme which contrary to RNG,

GG, and DT constructs a planar graph by considering edge intersections explicitly. More precisely, we define two different criteria for deciding which one of any two intersecting edges should be removed: one is based on the angles of the quadrilateral enclosing the intersecting edges, the other one is based on Delaunay triangles. We call these variants Angle-based Direct Planarization (ADP) and Delaunay-based Direct Planarization (DDP). Both variants always yield a planar and connected topology when applied to connected unit disk graphs.

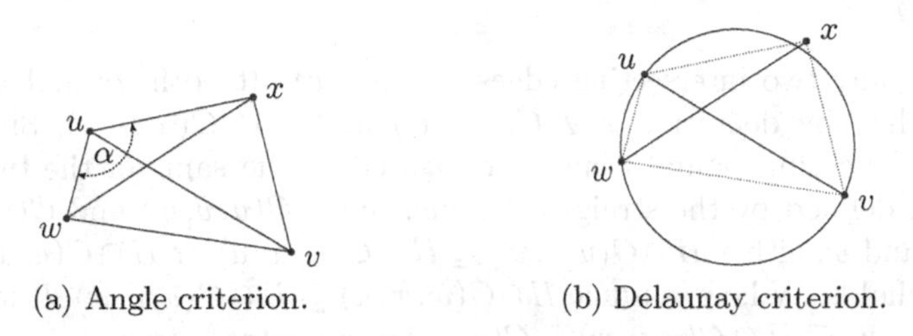

(a) Angle criterion. (b) Delaunay criterion.

Fig. 2: Variants of Direct Planarization. Both will remove edge wx.

4.1 Angle-Based Direct Planarization

Definition 1. *Let $G(V,E)$ be a graph over a finite set V of 2D points. The* Angle-based Direct Planarization *$ADP(V)$ contains an edge $uv \in E$ if for all intersecting edges $wx \in E$ the following condition holds (see Fig. 2a):*

$$\max\{\angle uwv, \angle uxv\} < \max\{\angle wux, \angle wvx\}$$

Theorem 1. *Let $G(V,E)$ be a graph over a finite set V of 2D points. $ADP(V)$ is a planar graph.*

Proof. Assume any two intersecting edges uv and wx in $ADP(V)$. Since both edges are also edges in E we have that uv satisfies $\max\{\angle wux, \angle wvx\} < \max\{\angle uwv, \angle uxv\}$ and that wx satisfies $\max\{\angle uwv, \angle uxv\} < \max\{\angle wux, \angle wvx\}$. It follows $\max\{\angle wux, \angle wvx\} < \max\{\angle wux, \angle wvx\}$, a contradiction. □

Theorem 2. *Let $G(V,E)$ be a graph over a finite set V of 2D points. It holds, $GG(V) \subseteq ADP(V)$.*

Proof. Let uv be be an edge in E which is not in $ADP(V)$. It follows that there exists an edge wx which intersects with uv and which satisfies $\max\{\angle uwv, \angle uxv\} \geq \max\{\angle wux, \angle wvx\}$. W.l.o.g. we assume $\angle uwv = \max\{\angle wux, \angle wvx, \angle uwv, \angle uxv\}$.

Consider the quadrilateral $q = (w, u, x, v)$. Its interior angles sum up to 2π. Thus, $\angle uwv$ being the maximum angle in q satisfies $\angle uwv \geq \frac{\pi}{2}$. It follows that w is lying in the Gabriel circle $C_{GG}(u, v)$. Thus, uv is not an edge of $GG(V)$. □

Corollary 1. *Let $UDG(V)$ be a connected unit disk graph over a finite set V of 2D points. $ADP(V)$ is a connected graph.*

Proof. This follows immediately from Theorem 2 and the fact that GG is connected if the underlying UDG is connected [2]. □

4.2 Delaunay-Based Direct Planarization

Definition 2. *Let $G(V, E)$ be a graph over a finite set V of 2D points. The* Delaunay-based Direct Planarization $DDP(V)$ *contains an edge $uv \in E$ if for all intersecting edges $wx \in E$ node x is not contained in the circle $C(u, v, w)$ (see Fig. 2b).*

Theorem 3. *Let $G(V, E)$ be a graph over a finite set V of 2D points. $DDP(V)$ is a planar graph.*

Proof. Assume any two intersecting edges uv and wx. If both uv and wx are in $DDP(S)$, then by definition $x \notin C(u, v, w)$ and $v \notin C(w, x, u)$. Since uv and wx are intersecting, x and v must be located in the same of the two half planes, say H, defined by the straight line uw. Since $C(u, v, w)$ and $C(w, x, u)$ intersect in u and w, either $H \cap C(u, v, w) \subseteq H \cap C(w, x, u)$ or $H \cap C(w, x, u) \subseteq H \cap C(u, v, w)$ holds. W.l.o.g. assume $H \cap C(w, x, u) \subseteq H \cap C(u, v, w)$.It follows, $x \in H \cap C(w, x, u) \subseteq H \cap C(u, v, w) \subseteq C(u, v, w)$, a contradiction.

Theorem 4. *Let $UDG(V)$ be a unit disk graph over a finite set V of 2D points. It holds, $RDG(V) \subseteq DDP(V)$.*

Proof. Consider any edge uv which is not in $DDP(V)$. We show that uv is not in $RDG(V)$, too. It is sufficient to consider uv being a unit disk graph edge, otherwise it would neither be an edge of $RDG(V)$.

Since uv was removed from $DDP(V)$, there exists an intersecting edge wx such that the circle $C(u, v, w)$ contains x and the circle $C(u, v, x)$ contains w. It follows that at least one of x and y is located in the Gabriel circle $C_{GG}(u, v)$. W.l.o.g. we assume $x \in C_{GG}(u, v)$.

It follows, x is connected to u and v and does not contain uv in it's local Delaunay triangulation, since it's neighbor w is in the Delaunay circle $C(u, v, x)$. Thus, the edge uv will be removed from $RDG(V)$.

Corollary 2. *Let $UDG(V)$ be a connected unit disk graph over a finite set V of 2D points. $DDP(V)$ is a connected constant unit disk graph spanner.*

Proof. This follows from Theorem 4 and the fact that $RDG(V)$ is a connected constant unit disk graph spanner [11]. □

5 Reactive Link Selection

Based on the concept of direct planarization we will now describe a reactive mechanism in order to determine the next link during a face traversal. We assume that nodes know their own and their one hop neighbors' location. Whenever a node receives a message it has to determine the next edge in a reactive manner. A pseudo code description of the following algorithm is given in Table 1.

Assume that node v receives a message from node u. Node v is required to find the edge in counterclockwise direction which satisfies the direct planarization condition. The one-hop neighborhood being the only information, node v will subsequently investigate the links ordered in counterclockwise direction starting from uv. It will stop as soon as the first edge satisfying the direct planarization condition is found and forward the message to the corresponding node.

Checking the planarization condition for a given link vw has to be performed for all edges xy intersecting vw. We use either of the following conditions:

- Angle condition for vw with respect to xy:
  $\max\{\angle vxw, \angle vyw\} < \max\{\angle xvy, \angle xwy\}$
- Delaunay condition for vw with respect to xy:
  $y \notin C(v, w, x)$

Neither node v nor w are always connected to both endpoints of an intersecting edge xy. Therefore, checking the planarization condition has to be performed in a distributed way. We let v broadcast a request to its neighbors, which will respond if the edge vw violates the planarization condition. In order to avoid having all neighbors involved in the message exchange, we use a contention-based scheme which is aborted as soon as the first neighbor reports the violation of the condition.

The contention works as follows: First, node v broadcast a request message $req(v, w)$, which is received by it's one-hop neighbors. Among these neighbors lying in the Gabriel circle $C_{GG}(v, w)$, each node x will set a timer depending on the angle $\alpha := \angle vxw$. When the timer expires, x checks the planarization condition using its one-hop neighborhood information and replies with a block message if the condition is not satisfied. The other nodes can overhear this reply, because they are all located within the Gabriel circle $C_{GG}(v, w)$, and cancel their scheduled replies. After receiving a block message, v will skip vw and retry for the next edge.

The timeout is set such that the neighbors that are most likely to know a violating edge can reply with the minimum delay. This is the case for neighbors with a large value of α. Since only nodes in the Gabriel circle are considered, α is ranging between $\frac{\pi}{2}$ and π. Therefore the timeout t is specified by the following function, which gives $\alpha = \pi$ the minimum timeout 0 and $\alpha = \frac{\pi}{2}$ the maximum timeout $t_{\max}$.

$$t(\alpha) = \frac{2(\pi - \alpha)}{\pi} t_{\max}$$

The whole procedure finally ends when node v has not received any block message for the currently investigated link vw. More precisely, after broadcasting the $req(v, w)$ message, node v waits for the maximum time t_{max}; and if this time elapses without having received a $block(v, w)$ message, a valid next link in counterclockwise direction is found.

Note that at this point we assume a MAC layer which is able to recover from two nodes sending at the same time. In fact two nodes may describe the same angle towards v and w and set the same timeout value. However, adding the above described timeout scheme will render colliding block messages an infrequent event.

The following theorem shows the correctness of the described reactive link selection mechanism.

Event handlers of the requesting node
v - current node
u - previous node
Result: next edge vw in ccw. order satisfying the direct planarization criterion

On_Start_Search:

1: $vw \leftarrow$ first edge in ccw. order from vu
2: **while** vw violates the planarization condition among 1-hop neighbors **do**
3: $vw \leftarrow$ next edge in ccw. order from vw
4: **end while**
5: broadcast $req(v, w)$
6: set timer to t_{max}
7: wait

On_Timeout:

1: return vw as the next hop

On_Block_Message:

1: **while** vw violates the planarization condition among 1-hop neighbors **do**
2: $vw \leftarrow$ next edge in ccw. order from vw
3: **end while**
4: broadcast $req(v, w)$
5: set timer to t_{max}
6: wait

Event handlers of the requested node
vw - requested link
x - receiving node
Result: a block msg. is sent if vw violates the direct planarization criterion and no other block msg. was received

On_Request_Message $req(v, w)$:

1: **if** $x \in C_{GG}(v, w)$ **then**
2: $\alpha = \angle vxw$
3: set timer to $\frac{2(\pi-\alpha)}{\pi} t_{max}$
4: wait
5: **end if**

On_Block_Message:

1: cancel timer

On_Timeout:

1: **for each** neighbor y of x with xy intersects vw **do**
2: **if** planarization condition for vw w.r.t. xy is violated **then**
3: send $block(vw)$
4: break
5: **end if**
6: **end for**

Table 1: Direct Planarization – event handlers of the participating nodes.

Theorem 5. *The described reactive link selection algorithm finds the first edge in $ADP(V)$ or $DDP(V)$, respectively, which is lying next in counterclockwise direction from the previously traversed edge.*

Proof. Let v be the current node, uv be the previously traversed edge, and vw be the first edge in $DP(V)$ which is lying next in counterclockwise direction from vu. For simplicity, we write $DP(V)$, if a statement holds for both variants ADP and DDP. Assume any edge vx in counterclockwise direction after vu but before vw. Since vx is not an edge in $DP(V)$, there exists a link yz which is intersecting vx and which satisfies the planarization condition.

Case 1, ADP: yz satisfies $\max\{\angle vyx, \angle yvz\} \geq \max\{\angle yxz, \angle vzx\}$. The angles of the quadrilateral (v, y, x, z) sum up to 2π. Thus, at least one of the two angles $\angle vyx$ or $\angle vzx$ is greater or equal than $\frac{\pi}{2}$. Thus at least one of the nodes y or z is located in $C_{GG}(v, x)$.

Case 2, DDP: vx does not satisfy $y \notin C(v, x, z)$ and $z \notin C(v, x, y)$. This again implies that at least one of the nodes y or z is located in $C_{GG}(v, x)$.

W.l.o.g. for both ADP and DDP assume node y is located in $C_{GG}(v, x)$. Then, y is a neighbor of v. If z is also a neighbor of v, then node v can check the validity of vx locally and will encounter edge wz which removed the link vx.

If z is not a neighbor of v and if v did not remove vx due to the local check, it will send out a $req(v, x)$ message. Node y will set a timeout which is either cancelled when a $block(v, x)$ message is received or which fires otherwise. In the latter case a $block(v, x)$ will be sent to v due to neighbor y. Thus, v will always remove vx.

It follows, any edge which is not in $DP(V)$ and which is lying in counterclockwise direction after vu but before vw will be removed by the described scheme. Thus, edge vw will always be reached after counterclockwise advancing through the incident edges. For this edge both for node v and for any neighbor node of v, the direct planarization criterion is satisfied; otherwise this would contradict vw being an edge of $DP(V)$. It follows, after timeout t_{max} the node v will use the link vw as the next link for message forwarding. □

6 Simulation Studies

We investigated the planar topologies resulting from existing reactive schemes, i.e., RNG and GG, and the planar topologies resulting from the reactive schemes presented in this work, i.e., ADP and DDP. We are interested in the impact of the planar topology on the performance of face routing in terms of *average dilation* from the shortest path. This parameter is defined as the average number of hops produced by the considered routing algorithm divided by the minimum number of hops required to send a message from source to destination node.

In our simulations nodes were uniformly distributed over a rectangular area of 500×500 length units. The communication range r was set to 100 length units. The network density d, i.e. the average number of neighbor nodes, was varied between 1 and 20. It was controlled by selecting the number n of deployed nodes as $n = \lceil \frac{dA}{R} + 1 \rceil$, with A being the field size $500 \cdot 500$ and $R = \pi r^2$ being the area covered by a node's communication range.

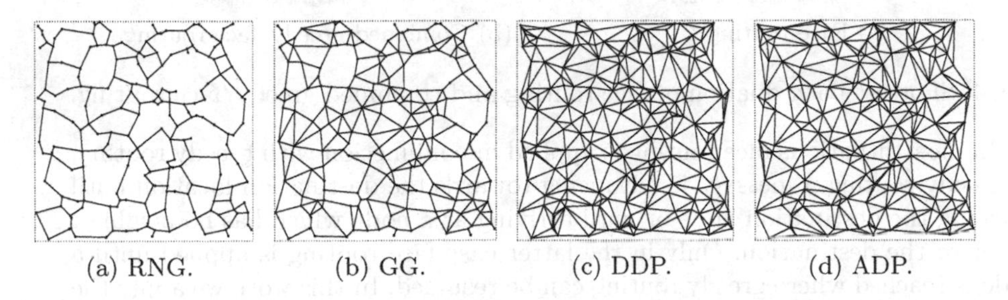

(a) RNG. (b) GG. (c) DDP. (d) ADP.

Fig. 3: Example topologies resulting from 200 randomly placed network nodes.

Figure 3 depicts an example of the discussed topologies over a randomly generated unit disk graph with 200 nodes. The average degree in this case is about 25. The example figures already suggest that direct planarization based on the Delaunay criterion or the angle criterion support better routing performance in terms of hop count when compared to the existing reactive schemes producing the RNG or GG topology. The graphs in the latter case are sparser. Thus, bigger faces have to be traversed in this case, resulting in an increasing number of forwarding steps.

The intuition provided by the example topologies is confirmed by the simulation results on shortest path dilation in Figure 4. In the diagrams each measurement point results from 1000 randomly generated network graphs. In each network graph the different topologies were considered for an arbitrarily selected source destination pair. Source destination pairs being not connected in the underlying unit disk graph were dismissed.

Figure 4a depicts the shortest path dilation of face routing under the considered topologies. There is a considerable improvement when changing from RNG to GG, and also a clear improvement when changing from GG to ADP or DDP. There is no clear difference in face performance when applying face routing under ADP or under DDP. This is also confirmed by the example topologies in Fig. 3 where ADP and DDP look almost the same in a dense network.

The spanning property considered in our theoretical study is defined over the Euclidean distance. However, the simulation results show that under randomly generated unit disk graphs, topologies supporting short paths in the sense of Euclidean distance also support short paths in terms of number of hops.

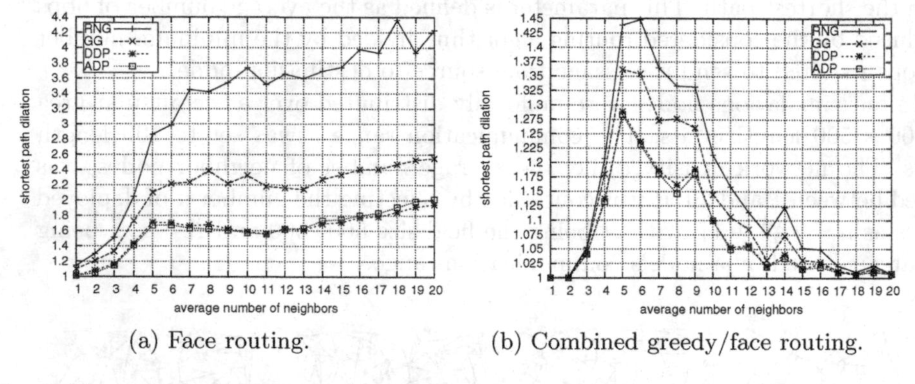

(a) Face routing.

(b) Combined greedy/face routing.

Fig. 4: Shortest path dilation of face routing and combined greedy/face routing.

In most situations face routing is applied in conjunction with greedy routing. In greedy routing a message is advancing towards the destination location until reaching the destination node or until arriving at a node which has no neighbor closer to the destination. Only in the latter case face routing is applied until a node is reached where greedy routing can be resumed. In this work we apply the greedy routing variant, where only nodes closer to the destination are considered and the message is forwarded to the node closest to the destination. Fig. 4b shows the average path dilation of such a combined greedy/face variant.

Again, an improvement can be observed when changing from RNG to GG and from GG to ADP or DDP, while performance under ADP and DDP is about the same. The gain obtained by a better planarization, however, is less dramatic since two concepts are combined here. Whenever the greedy routing part is applied, the planar subgraph construction has no impact. Greedy routing uses any of the current forwarder's neighbor nodes. Especially in dense networks with random node placement the greedy routing paths are close to the shortest possible ones.

For all topologies a maximum in average dilation can be observed for network densities (i.e. the average number of neighbors) of 5 and 6. This is due to the fact that face recovery has the most impact for this "critical density". With low network densities two end nodes being far away from each other are unlikely to be connected by any path. Thus, when arbitrarily selecting a source destination pair until finding one which is connected, such nodes are often connected by paths having a length of a single hop. Since the destination can be reached immediately in such case, the impact of face recovery becomes marginal. When the average number of neighbors increases, greedy routing is almost always successful, thus face routing again has only a marginal influence on the routing performance.

7 Conclusion

In this work we presented our initial findings towards reactive construction of planar spanners in wireless networks. Our work is motivated by the existence of face routing strategies where network planarity is a sufficient condition for their correct operation. Such routing protocols do not require the whole network to be planarized. It is sufficient that a node is able to determine the next planar graph node located in counterclockwise direction from the previously visited node.

We presented the concept of direct planarization and showed by an example algorithm how this concept enables a reactive implementation of graph planarization criteria which have not been described in a reactive setting so far. For both criteria investigated we observed significantly denser topologies than those produced by already known reactive topology control schemes. The spanner property of the Delaunay-based direct planarization follows from already established results, for the angle-based direct planarization the spanner property is not known.

By means of simulation we observed that face routing performance was almost identical in the network topologies ADP and DDP. Both yielded a clear performance improvement of face routing. However, at the moment it appears that this improvement has a price. In the generic direct planarization method described, nodes are required to know their one hop neighborhood information. This is in contrast to those beaconless schemes based on RNG or GG where no information about the neighborhood is required beforehand. However, RNG or GG do not preserve the spanner property. Table 2 summarizes the properties of the discussed schemes.

We believe that finding such schemes which are fully reactive and which produce a network spanner is an interesting, relevant, and challenging research topic. We plan to further investigate the lower bound on message complexity in reactive spanner construction. Moreover, as with all localized planar topology control schemes non unit disk graphs are problematic. We plan to further extend our findings to networks beyond the unit disk graph assumption and beyond an idealized MAC layer. This includes asymmetric and dynamic links as well as message losses or transmission delays due to collisions.

Topology	Reactive Construction	Spanner	Face routing performance
RNG	beaconless	no	bad
GG	beaconless	no	fair
ADP	neighborhood-based	unknown	good
DDP	neighborhood-based	yes	good

Table 2: Summary of the considered planar topologies.

References

1. X. Lin and I. Stojmenović. Location-based localized alternate, disjoint and multi-path routing algorithms for wireless networks. *Journal of Parallel and Distributed Computing*, 63:22–32, 2003.
2. P. Bose, P. Morin, I. Stojmenović, and J. Urrutia. Routing with guaranteed delivery in ad hoc wireless networks. In *3rd ACM Int. Workshop on Discrete Algorithms and Methods for Mobile Computing and Communications (DIAL M 99)*, pages 48–55, August 1999.
3. H. Frey and I. Stojmenović. On delivery guarantees of face and combined greedy-face routing in ad hoc and sensor networks. In *12th Annual Int. Conference on Mobile Computing and Networking (MobiCom'06)*, 2006.
4. G. Toussaint. The relative neighborhood graph of a finite planar set. *Pattern Recognition*, 12(4):261–268, 1980.
5. K. R. Gabriel and R. R. Sokal. A new statistical approach to geographic variation analysis. *Systematic Zoology*, 18:259–278, 1969.
6. B. Karp and H. T. Kung. GPSR: Greedy perimeter stateless routing for wireless networks. In *6th ACM/IEEE Annual Int. Conference on Mobile Computing and Networking (MobiCom'00)*, pages 243–254, August 2000.
7. P. Bose, L. Devroye, W. Evans, and D. Kirkpatrick. On the spanning ratio of gabriel graphs and beta-skeletons. In *Latin American Symposium on Theoretical Informatics (LATIN'02)*, April 2002.
8. H. Kalosha, A. Nayak, S. Rührup, and I. Stojmenović. Select-and-protest-based beaconless georouting with guaranteed delivery in wireless sensor networks. In *27th IEEE Conference on Computer Communications (INFOCOM)*, April 2008.
9. D.P. Dobkin, S.J. Friedman, and K.J. Supowit. Delaunay graphs are almost as good as complete graphs. In *Discrete and Computational Geometry*, 1990.
10. J.M. Keil and C.A. Gutwin. Classes of graphs which approximate the complete euclidean graph. In *Discrete Computational Geometry*, 7, 1992.
11. J. Gao, L.J. Guibas, J. Hershberger, L. Zhang, and A. Zhu. Geometric spanner for routing in mobile networks. In *2nd ACM Int. Symposium on Mobile Ad Hoc Networking and Computing (MobiHoc'01)*, pages 45–55, October 2001.
12. X.-Y. Li, G. Calinescu, and P.-J. Wan. Distributed construction of a planar spanner and routing for ad hoc wireless networks. In *21st Joint Conference of the IEEE Computer and Communications Society (INFOCOM)*, pages 1268–1277, June 2002.

Preventing Service Discovery Cache Reply Storms in Wireless Mesh Networks

Martin Krebs, Karl-Heinz Krempels and Markus Kucay

Department of Computer Science, Informatik 4
RWTH Aachen University, Germany

Abstract. This paper focuses on the problem of controlling service discovery cache reply storms in Wireless Mesh Networks (WMNs). A reply storm could occur if the same redundant service reply is sent from multiple nodes where every node uses a different message sequence number. Currently, this problem cannot be detected by existing approaches which inspect only certain header information. To overcome this problem an application-layer routing is mandatory which inspects also the message body. We describe different message propagation strategies together with our implementation of a service discovery protocol for Wireless Mesh Networks which consists of encapsulated Multicast DNS messages in a new OLSR message type. The measurements performed in the department's wireless mesh testbed are discussed with results at the end.

1 Introduction

Wireless Mesh Networks (WMNs) [1] (see also Fig. 1) are a promising and emerging technology in the direction of future wireless networks. Wireless Mesh Networks are a flexible technology to provide wireless high-speed broadband coverage to areas where the installation of wires is not possible or too costly. Example scenarios are community, emergency, disaster recovery or municipal networks. Automatic service discovery and zero configuration will be a central task in WMNs.
A widely used technique for service discovery is caching. A node with a service cache stores all seen services in a table for a certain lease time as long as the service is valid. If a query for a service occurs, all caches which have this service cached answer with their matching entries to this query. However, if all caches have the same matching services to a query, one simple query could trigger a big avalanche of messages if no control mechanism is applied.
In this paper we propose and discuss different message propagation and reply control strategies for service discovery in WMNs. The algorithms are implemented in our service discovery protocol called OLSR-mDNS [2]. In this approach we apply cross-layer technologies to deliver service discovery messages where DNS based service discovery (DNS-SD) [3] messages are encapsulated in a new Optimized Link State Routing (OLSR) [4] packet to preserve mDNS signalizing phases on the application layer.

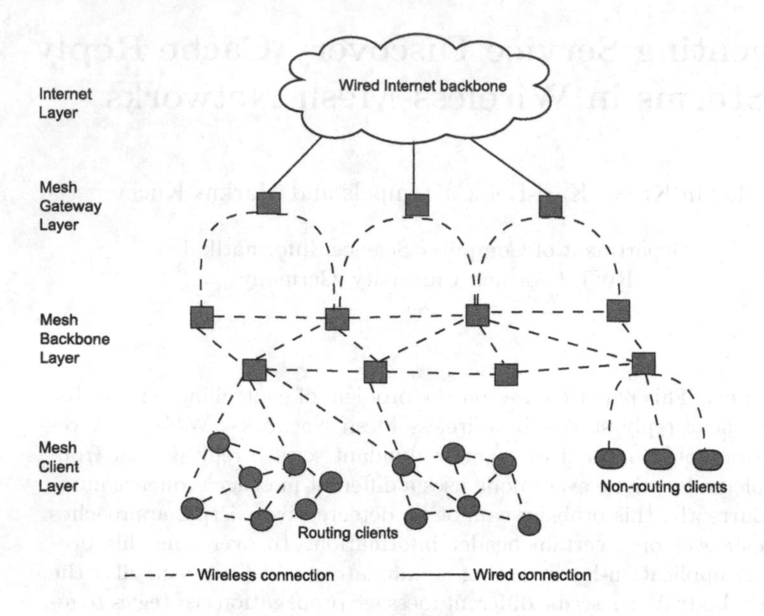

Fig. 1. Wireless Mesh Network Architecture

In OLSR-mDNS service queries and replies are broadcast so that all nodes can overhear all messages. Unicast replies on the reverse route are not very useful and are against the paradigm of mDNS. OLSR broadcast is very efficient, because OLSR heavily aggregates many small messages into larger packet to increase packet efficiency. This paper is organized as follows: In Section 2 we review related work and existing protocols for service discovery. In Section 3 we discuss the cache reply storm problem in Wireless Mesh Networks, before our proposed message propagation strategies are presented in Section 4. Section 5 shortly discusses the wireless mesh testbed. In Section 6 we state the results from our implementation in the testbed, and Section 7 comprises the conclusion.

2 Related Work

On the protocol level a lot of work has been done for service discovery in the Internet, e.g. the Service Location Protocol (SLP) [5], Simple Service Discovery Protocol (SSDP) [6], DNS-based Service Discovery (DNS-SD) [3] together with multicast DNS (mDNS) [7] or Universal Plug and Play (UPnP) [8]. On the application level are the Java-based Jini [9] or UDDI (Universal Description, Discovery and Integration) [10] for web services. These protocols are designed for wired infrastructure networks and are not well suited for Mobile Ad-hoc Networks (MANETs) or even WMNs, since these approaches are directory or simple flooding based.
A lot of work has also been done for service discovery in ad-hoc networks. Konark [11] is a service discovery mechanism on the application side for ad-hoc networks.

One modification to SLP is mSLP [12], where SLP Directory Agents form a mesh structure and exchange service registration states. However, this approach does not scale well in WMNs, because service registration states must be replicated between all servers. This regular replication comes with the cost of a high network load.
Another promising approach seems to be the integration of service discovery mechanisms in a routing protocol which is in general called *cross-layer* design. In many cases the service requests are piggybacked on route request messages. Koodli and Perkins [13] propose to encapsulate service discovery messages in reactive routing algorithms. They describe a service discovery mechanism in on-demand ad-hoc networks along with discovery routes to the service, for example for usage within AODV or DSR.

3 Message Reply Storm

Normally all routing protocols have a mechanism for detecting duplicate messages, like checking the packet or message sequence numbers for duplicates. For example, the Optimized Link State Routing Protocol (OLSR) discards all duplicate packets with the same sequence number to prevent a broadcast storm. However, this mechanism can only prevent exact copies of the same packet from being re-broadcast. This paper does not investigate broadcast storms, because there exists already much research on this topic like [14]. Our intention is to limit service discovery reply storms which we denote as *message reply storm.* A reply storm could occur if the same redundant information is sent from different nodes which all use a different message sequence number. For this reason, a message reply storm is not the same as the broadcast storm problem: A reply storm cannot be detected by routers which inspect only certain header information. To overcome this problem an application-layer routing which inspects also the message body is mandatory.
Here, we differentiate between *active* and *passive* service discovery message reply storm prevention techniques. Active techniques suppress unnecessary messages on the originator node or achieve that nodes send less messages through coordination mechanisms. Suppressed duplicate messages save network resources. Passive techniques act like retention structures which discard already forwarded messages during a given time.

4 Message Propagation Strategies

OLSR implements a mechanism for discarding duplicate packets which occur due to re-broadcasting of the same packet. Exact duplicates of a certain packet are identified by their identical packet and message sequence number. However, this alone is not sufficient. Our proposed message propagation strategies inspect the message content itself and discard also redundant information.
To coordinate emission of reply messages, nodes do not need to be synchronized in advance. The coordination is based on a local backoff timer and the distance

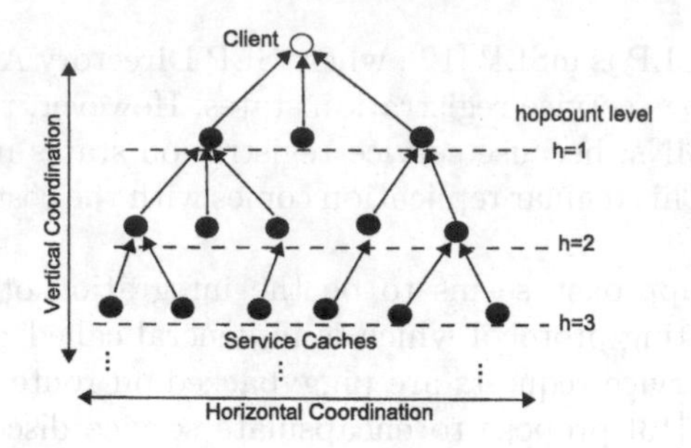

Fig. 2. Coordination of service cache replies

Table 1. Comparison of investigated message propagation strategies

Message propagation strategy	Discard	Suppress	Backoff Timer	Dist. BO Timer
Simple Reply Flooding	No	No	No	No
Discarding Duplicates	Yes	No	No	No
Local Backoff	Yes	Yes	Yes	No
Nearest Nodes Send First (NNSF)	Yes	Yes	Yes	Yes
Farthest Nodes Send First (FNSF)	Yes	Yes	Yes	Yes

to the originator node. This means that the coordination is done on the fly and for each new query message. Nodes from the same hop count level are coordinated with a random backoff time to avoid that all nodes start sending at the same time. Here, we refer to this as horizontal coordination (see Fig. 2).
In the following we present five different message reply control mechanisms namely *Simple Reply Flooding, Discarding Duplicates, Local Backoff, Nearest Nodes Send First (NNSF)* and *Farthest Nodes Send First (FNSF)* for service discovery in Wireless Mesh Networks. Table 1 summarizes the characteristics of the presented message propagation strategies and shows the differences between them.

4.1 Simple Reply Flooding

The *Simple Reply Flooding* mechanism is a straightforward way to propagate service discovery messages. Each node forwards and re-broadcasts all messages it receives as long as the Time-To-Live (TTL) is not zero and the packet sequence number is not duplicate. Duplicate information contents in the message body which arrive from multiple neighbors are always forwarded and never discarded. A node which receives a query answers with all its matching services from the cache. Answers from the local node cache are always sent regardless of already forwarded messages. When a client sends a query, it can limit rebroadcasting with the TTL message field of OLSR to avoid flooding the whole network.

4.2 Discarding Duplicates

The *Discarding Duplicates* strategy is an enhancement for the Simple Flooding strategy. Each mesh router maintains a service forward control hash table H_s.

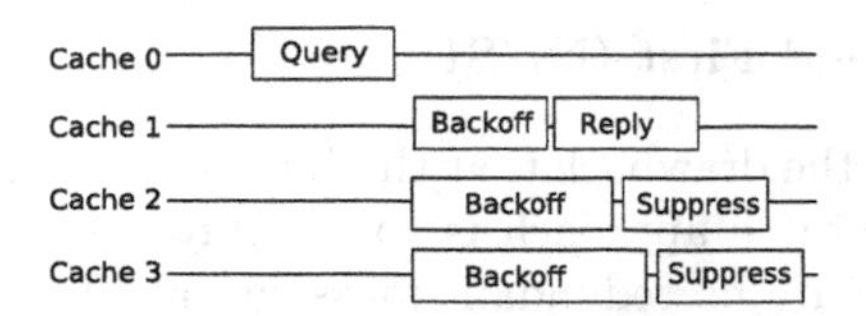

Fig. 3. Simple backoff mechanism

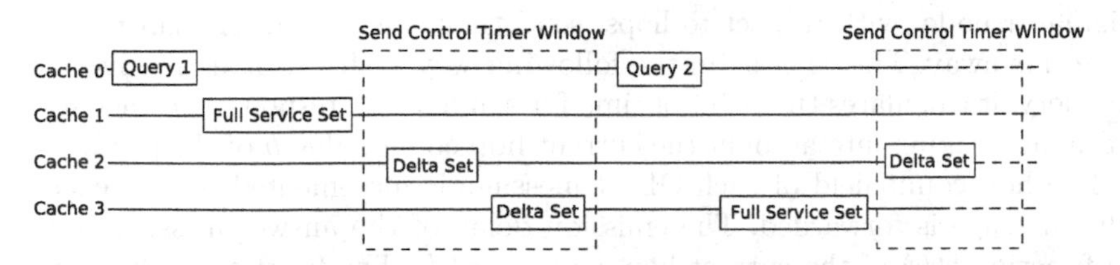

Fig. 4. Delta set mechanism

Every time a node receives a service discovery reply message, it checks whether there is an entry in the hash table with this service. If there is a positive match, the newly received message is discarded, because this means that the service has already been forwarded during the last time. If there is no match in the hash table, the service message is forwarded and a new entry with this service is created in the hash table. A scheduler regularly deletes expired service records in H_s, because the hash values are only valid for a certain forward time. The discarding duplicates strategy is very effective especially in dense scenarios, because there are many redundant replies.

4.3 Local Backoff

One drawback of the Discarding Duplicates strategy is that it only discards messages and does not prevent messages from emission. The general problem still remains: All nodes immediately start sending their reply when they receive a query. To overcome this problem, each node must draw a random backoff time (see Fig. 3) and should only send replies to a certain query which have not yet been sent from other nodes. This is called delta set mechanism (see Fig. 4).
In the *Local Backoff* strategy outgoing answers from the local cache are thus also managed by the hash table in combination with a backoff timer. When a service query arrives at a node, the node draws a random backoff time $t_b \in [0, .., b_{max}]$. A check for a matching entry in the hash table is done two times, the first time before drawing a backoff time and the second time immediately before sending. This has the advantage that unnecessary duplicate information responses from the local node are suppressed. Each suppressed message does not cause unnecessary traffic and saves scarce bandwidth.

4.4 Nearest Nodes Send First (NNSF)

The previous strategy has the drawback that the backoff times are chosen locally by each node. A more suitable approach is to synchronize the reply behavior of the nodes so that there are no redundant messages at all. However, this is a hard task, because all nodes must be synchronized. So we propose a coordination heuristic called *Nearest Nodes Send First (NNSF)*. The nodes which are close to the originator node, with respect to hops, send their answer earlier than nodes which are far away. This is done in the following way: When a node receives a service query, it calculates the point of time for sending the response message by extracting and taking into account the current hop count value h of the received query. The hop count field of each OLSR message is incremented by one each time the message is forwarded. The emission delay of the answer message is a backoff function $b(h)$ of the current hop count level h. The function is the sum of the hop count value h of the service query and a random backoff value x^i_{rand} of node i:

$$b(h) = h + x^i_{rand} \tag{1}$$

4.5 Farthest Nodes Send First (FNSF)

The strategy *Farthest Nodes Send First (FNSF)* is similar to the previously presented NNSF strategy. Here, nodes with a larger hop distance to the querying client send their answers earlier than nodes which have a small hop distance to the originator of the query. This is also done by taking into account the hop count value h of the service request message. Furthermore, the maximum hop count value, here denoted as h_{max} is used. This value can be gained by empirical measurements or information from the local routing table. A check for a matching entry in the hash table is done two times: the first time before drawing a backoff time and the second time immediately before sending. The delay of the answer message is defined as backoff function $b(h)$. The backoff function is constructed with the hop count value h, the global maximum hop count value h_{max} and a random backoff time x^i_{rand} of node i:

$$b(h) = h_{max} - (h + x^i_{rand}) \tag{2}$$

5 Wireless Mesh Testbed

In this section, we first present our wireless mesh testbed, followed by measurements performed in the testbed in the next section. For our measurements we use 39 nodes of our UMIC Wireless Mesh Testbed [15]. The mesh testbed is part of the research excellence cluster Ultra High-Speed Mobile Information and Communication (UMIC) and located at the Department of Computer Science at RWTH Aachen University. The Department complex consists of one four- and two three-story buildings. The wireless mesh routers are distributed over

different offices and floors inside two of the buildings. The routers from number 1 to 25 are located in the first building and routers from number 26 to 39 are located in the second building. The testbed has not yet reached its theoretically possible building coverage limit and is currently in progress to be extended with more nodes.
The mesh routers are single board computers (SBC) based on the WRAP.2E board by PC Engines [16] running on a minimal Ubuntu Linux which boot their OS image over network. Each router consists of two WLAN IEEE 802.11a/b/g interfaces which are built on Atheros AR5213 XR chips, and two omnidirectional antennas. The first WLAN interface is tuned to channel 1 running in ahdemo mode [17] to connect to the mesh network. The second WLAN interface can be run in access point mode and is used for non-routing client access. It also can be tuned to different channels dependent on interferences of other WLAN access points. All routers are also connected with an Ethernet interface for management reasons. Currently, we are running the popular pro-active and table-driven UniK OLSR daemon (OLSRD) [18] in version 0.5.4 as routing algorithm. For more details and performance measurements about our testbed see [19].

6 Measurements

For our measurements we started our OLSR-mDNS plug-in on all wireless mesh routers, which means that every router could act as service cache. Every node also loads a unique service with the name of the router at start-up. All services belong to the same class, which means that one query for this class makes all caches respond with at least one service. A client near router 11 starts a query for the services after stabilization of the OLSR routes. A service discovery query is sent every 30 seconds as encapsulated OLSR packet. For all following measurements we set $h_{max} = 10$, because this was the most suitable value for the maximum hop count we got from experimental results for our testbed topology. An entry in the hash table H_s is valid for five seconds.
The measurement is done after the warm-up phase after each cache has the same services cached. In the following we describe our measurements with regard to hop count, overall message overhead, detailed message overhead and backoff time.

Overall Performance In the first measurement we investigate the overall performance of the proposed strategies. Therefore, 17 nodes are acting as service cache and one node sends a service query every 30 seconds.
Fig. 5(a) shows the reply message overhead and corresponding delay of the strategies Simple Reply Flooding, Local Backoff, FNSF and NNSF. As can be seen, Flooding has the highest number of replies and an average delay. The message overhead and delay for Local Backoff is lower, because fewer message are sent and thus the wireless medium is lesser occupied. As expected, NNSF and FNSF have the smallest message overhead, but are different in message delay. FNSF has a higher delay, because the messages are sent from nodes which are far away.

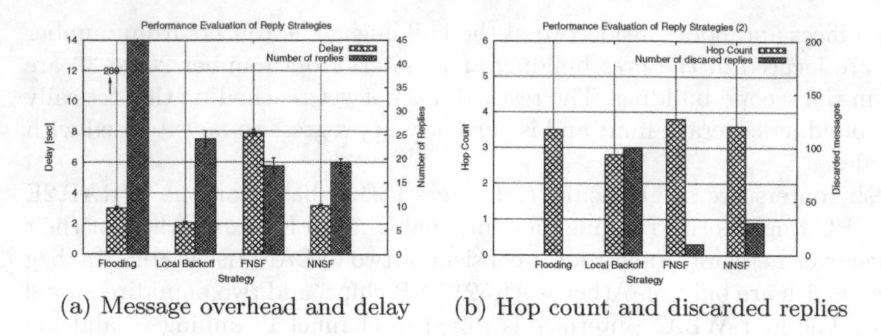

(a) Message overhead and delay (b) Hop count and discarded replies

Fig. 5. Overall performance of investigated strategies

In contrast, FNSF has a smaller delay, but a higher message overhead, because nodes with a small distance reply first. However, more nodes reply, because the backoff interval is too small.
Fig. 5(b) compares the average hop count and number of discarded duplicate messages for the investigated mechanisms. The Simple Reply Flooding strategy has an average hop count value, because all nodes respond regardless of the distance. The Local Backoff mechanism has an average lower hop count, because only some nodes respond regardless of the distance. It has many discarded messages, because there are still too many duplicate replies. NNSF has a low hop count, because near nodes reply, but it has a higher number of discarded messages, because there are still too many collisions in backoff times. FNSF has a high hop count, because far away nodes reply first. It has also a good low number of discarded messages which means that the backoff interval is at least large enough to avoid collisions. However, it comes with the cost of a high delay.

6.1 Detailed Performance Discussion

In the following measurements we investigate the proposed mechanism in detail on each router. Therefore, we now use 39 mesh nodes and one additional client. The detailed message proportion and corresponding backoff times of each router are depicted for Local Backoff (Fig. 6), NNSF (Fig. 7) and finally FNSF (Fig. 8).

Hop Count The first measurement investigates the average hop count of received messages for each router and the corresponding propagation strategy. The average hop count value for the Simple Flooding approach is about 3.5 hops, because all routers respond with their complete service cache and no message is discarded. The average hop count value for the Local Backoff strategy varies between one and five hops, because it depends on the fact which router starts sending at a certain time and which messages are discarded. The value of one hop means that the router gets all answers from its one hop neighbors.

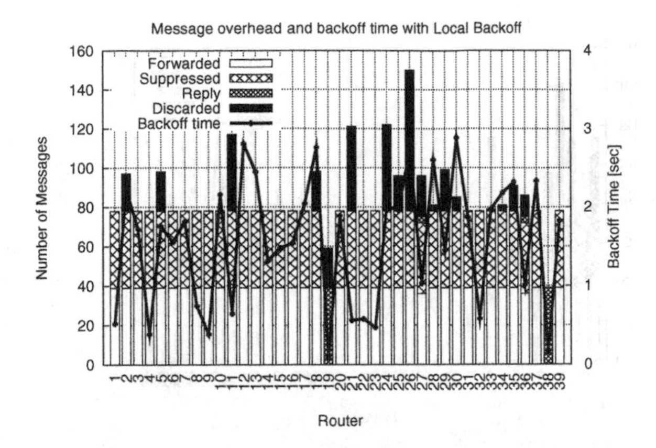

Fig. 6. Detailed message overhead with Local Backoff strategy

The result from the NNSF strategy is more obvious: The routers in the region from where the client originally sent the query receive messages with a low hop count, i.e. routers with a number smaller than 25, because these routers send their answers first. The routers which are far away, receive messages with a higher hop count, i.e. routers with a number larger than 25, because they also get the answers from routers between 1 and 25.
The measurement for FNSF shows a similar result but the other way round: The routers 1 to 25 which are located near the querying client receive messages with a high hop count, because the answers are originated in the region of router 26 to 39. This also means that the routers between 26 and 39 receive messages with a low average hop count value.

Detailed Message Overhead In the next measurement we analyze and compare the message overhead of the strategies *Local Backoff*, *NNSF* and *FNSF* in detail. Therefore, the number of forwarded, suppressed, sent and discarded messages is depicted for each router. Forwarded messages are messages for which there is no entry in the forward control hash table. Discarded messages are the messages which are discarded by the router because of an existing entry in the forward control hash table. Suppressed messages are the messages which are not sent from the local cache because of an existing entry in the forward control hash table.
The detailed message overhead of the Local Backoff strategy shows that the routers 19 and 38 send their complete cache contents while the routers 27 and 36 send only 3 services. This results in a high number of discarded duplicate messages on all other routers because of many duplicate answers. It shows also that 37 routers suppress nearly all of their answers because of already seen answers. Within the NNSF strategy only router 6 sends its full cache contents with 39 services, because it draws the smallest backoff time and therefore wins the competition. Router 4 and router 39 also send their answers, but only with 18 and

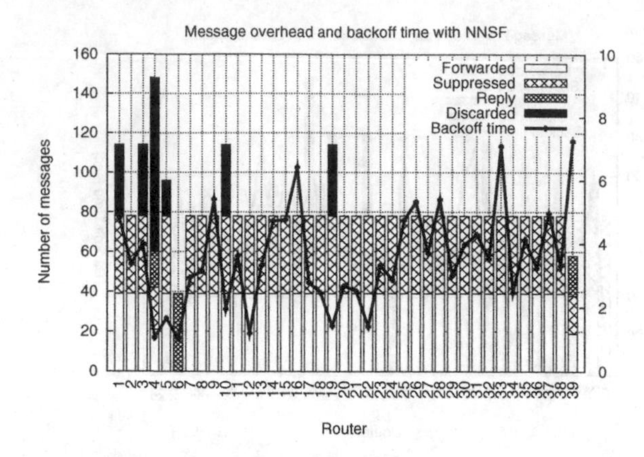

Fig. 7. Detailed message overhead with NNSF strategy

20 services respectively. They only send the answers which were not seen from their point of view. However, there is still a high number of discarded duplicate answers on some routers.
The FNSF strategy shows the best performance compared to Local Backoff and NNSF. Here, only router 29 sends 37 answers, because it draws the smallest backoff time of 5.1 seconds and therefore wins the backoff competition. The routers 1 and 38 send only one answer each which is the delta set to the already propagated 37 services from router 39. In total, there are only 39 services propagated over the network, which means that no duplicate information is sent. Instead of sending any responses, all other routers suppress their unnecessary answers.

Backoff Time In the following measurement we investigate the drawn backoff time of each router for the strategies NNSF and FNSF. In the NNSF strategy the routers which are located near the querying client (1-25) draw a small backoff time. The routers 4 and 6 draw the smallest backoff times and start sending their answers. The far away routers 26-39 draw larger backoff times and do not send answers except for router 39.
In the FNSF strategy routers 1-25 draw a large backoff time, whereas the routers 26-39 draw smaller backoff times. Router 39 draws the smallest value and starts sending first.

7 Conclusion

In this paper we presented and analyzed five different message propagation strategies namely *Simple Reply Flooding, Discarding Duplicates, Local Backoff, Nearest Nodes Send First (NNSF)* and *Farthest Nodes Send First (FNSF)* for service discovery in Wireless Mesh Networks. We showed that simple flooding of service discovery replies is not efficient and that the presented application layer inspection of messages on mesh backbone routers significantly improves the message

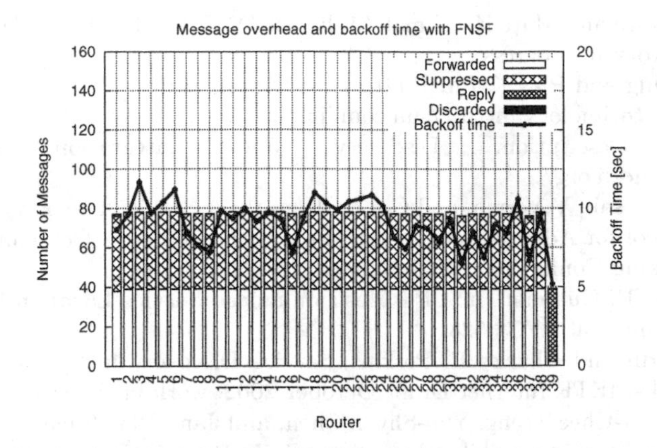

Fig. 8. Detailed message overhead with FNSF strategy

propagation. Furthermore, we implemented these strategies in a service discovery plug-in for OLSRD and presented our measurement results from our testbed. Our measurements showed that a backoff timer is highly required to coordinate the emission of replies from nodes, especially in dense topologies. Our FNSF strategy has the best performance regarding message overhead, but has the drawback of a larger delay, because of larger backoff times. The NNSF strategy has a low delay, but on the downside a higher number of redundant replies.

Acknowledgment

This work was funded by the German National Science Foundation (DFG) within the research excellence cluster Ultra High-Speed Mobile Information and Communication (UMIC).

References

1. Ian F. Akyildiz, Xudong Wang, and Weilin Wang. Wireless mesh networks: a survey. Computer Networks, 47(4):445-487, March 2005.
2. Martin Krebs, Karl-Heinz Krempels, and Markus Kucay. Service Discovery in Wireless Mesh Networks. In Proc. of IEEE Wireless Communications and Networking Conference 2008 (WCNC'08), March 2008.
3. Stuart Cheshire and Marc Krochmal. DNS-Based Service Discovery. IETF Internet Draft, August 2006. work in progress.
4. T. Clausen and P. Jacquet. Optimized Link State Routing Protocol (OLSR). IETF Experimental RFC 3626, October 2003.
5. E. Guttman, C. Perkins, J. Veizades, and M. Day. Service Location Protocol, Version 2. RFC 2608, June 1999.
6. Ting Cai, Paul Leach, Ye Gu, Yaron Y. Goland, and Shivaun Albright. Simple Service Discovery Protocol/1.0. IETF Internet Draft, April 1999. work in progress.

7. Stuart Cheshire and Marc Krochmal. Multicast DNS. IETF Internet Draft, August 2006. work in progress.
8. Universal Plug and Play (UPnP). http://www.upnp.org/.
9. Jini network technology. http://sun.com/jini/.
10. Universal Description, Discovery and Integration (UDDI). http://www.uddi.org/.
11. S. Helal, N. Desaii, V.Verma, and C. Lee. Konark: A Service Discovery and Delivery Protocol for Ad-Hoc Networks. In Proc. IEEE Wireless Communications and Networking Conference (WCNC 2003), March 2003.
12. W. Zhao and E. Guttman. mSLP - Mesh Enhanced Service Location Protocol. IETF Experimental RFC 3528.
13. Rajeev Koodli and Charles E. Perkins. Service Discovery in On-Demand Ad Hoc Networks. IETF Internet Draft, October 2002. work in progress.
14. Sze-Yao Ni, Yu-Chee Tseng, Yuh-Shyan Chen, and Jang-Ping Sheu. The broadcast storm problem in a mobile ad hoc network. In Proc. 5th annual ACM/IEEE international conference on Mobile computing and networking (MobiCom '99), pages 151-162, Seattle, Washington, United States, 1999. ACM Press.
15. UMIC Wireless Mesh Testbed. http://mesh.umic.rwth-aachen.de/.
16. PCEngines. WRAP - Wireless Router Application Platform. http://www.pcengines.ch/wrap.htm.
17. MADWiFi. Multiband Atheros Driver for WiFi. http://madwifi.org/.
18. UniK Optimized Link State Routing Daemon (OLSRD). http://www.olsr.org/.
19. Alexander Zimmermann, Mesut Guenes, Martin Wenig, Sadeq Ali Makram, Ulrich Meis, and Michael Faber. Performance Evaluation of a hybrid Testbed for Wireless Mesh Networks. In Proc. 4th IEEE International Conference on Mobile Ad-hoc and Sensor Systems (MASS'07), October 2007.

Teil II

Standardization and Research – How Do These Two Fit Together?

Bringing ICT Research into Standardisation – What Can Standards Bodies Do?

Kai Jakobs

RWTH Aachen University, Computer Science Dept., Informatik 4, 52074 Aachen

Abstract. This paper aims to provide standards setting bodies with guidelines on how to better incorporate findings from R&D activities into ongoing or future standards projects. Barriers to active participation of R&D people have been identified through a survey of over 500 researchers. Ways how to overcome these barriers, or at least how to lower them, are identified.

1 A Brief Introduction

Standards are a proven mechanism for technology transfer, fostering the diffusion and utilisation of technology. They are also an important aspect of various fields of policy, like innovation, trade and environmental policies, play a vital role in the European market by promoting competitiveness and interoperability of products and services, and serve to protect consumers, health, safety of citizens and employees, and the environment. Standards are, therefore, the bridge between the technical domain and the economic, social and regulatory framework.

The development of new and improved standards requires high quality technical information. This creates a fundamental inter-dependency between the standardisation and research communities. Research can, and should, support the development of new and improved standards through the provision of objective technical information. Standards Setting Bodies (SSBs; this term denotes both formal Standards Developing Organisations like, e.g., ISO, CEN, ETSI, and standards consortia, such as, e.g., W3C), in turn, need to effectively deploy this information.

The need for a closer link from research to standardisation has also been recognised by the European Standards Organisations (ESOs; [1]):

> "In the ICT domain, the link between R&D and standardization is of particular importance; standardization is in a position to leverage the consensus reached within an R&D project .....".

As it currently stands, many publicly funded R&D projects fail to generate any sustainable impact simply because their findings do not make it back into the public domain (from where the funding came in the first place). In many cases, standardisation would be a very appropriate vehicle

2 Improving Standards Through Integration of Research Results

2.1 Motivations and Barriers

Tacit knowledge is crucially important to adequately transfer R&D findings from the lab into the standards committee. Yet, this form of knowledge transfer basically requires R&D staff to contribute to standards setting, and to be present at the meetings. This, however, appears to be problematic. In the following, we will have a brief look at the motivations for, and barriers to, researchers' participation in standards setting.

One can think of various new or improved ways of transferring knowledge from research to standardisation. Yet, to be successful a mandatory pre-requisite must not be ignored – the transfer needs to be mutually beneficial. That is, both the researcher and the corporate research manager will eventually ask "What's in it for me/us?" To come up with answers, SSBs can quote the very real benefits participation in standardisation offers.

With respect to the former, the standards setting arena is a very effective forum for establishing co-operations among researchers, between researchers and industry, and between different industry partners. A recent survey has shown that standards setters show a higher intensity in collaborations than non-standards setters. Moreover, this forum can also serve as a monitor: first-hand knowledge of new developments and personal relations can be gained. These features alone should make participating in standardisation a worthwhile activity for many researchers. Also, at least in the ICT sector well-respected standards setters are very much sought after.

Regarding the latter, participation in standardisation offers the (strategic) prospect of re-shaping existing markets, or of the creation of new ones. In addition, and on a more tactical level, it will give participating organisations the opportunity to influence technology in their favour, which in turn will give them a head start once the standard has been accepted.

Also, over the last couple of years many SSBs, most notably the European bodies, have improved their processes, and/or introduced new ones, to meet their stakeholders' demands. In particular, the new 'lightweight' processes are highly suitable for standards initiatives emerging from (publicly funded) R&D projects with a limited life span. Yet, the barriers to active participation in standards setting as identified by the R&D community suggest that very little has changed in their perceptions of how standardisation works. To overcome these barriers is a major issue since direct participation in standards setting by researchers is crucial as it is the only way to tap into their invaluable tacit knowledge.

Figure 1 shows a list of 'motivators' that could increase researchers' willingness to participate in standards setting. The statements shown were given in response to the question: *"I would consider participating in a standard-setting process ... (please tick the five most important statements)"*.

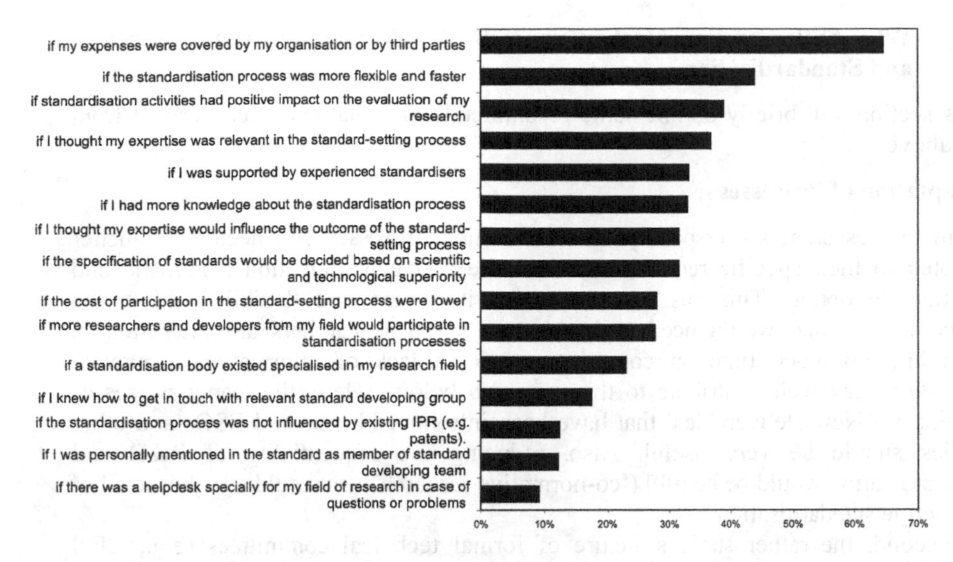

Figure 1: Most efficient incentives for participation in standardisation [2]

According to a survey conducted by the INTEREST project [2], the most important barriers to researchers' participation in standardisation include (each perceived by over 35% of the respondents):

- My expenses are not covered by my organisation or by third parties.
  This is the most important barrier by far. Funding for standards setting activities is rarely (if ever) included in funding for R&D activities. Here, the funding organisations may have to revise their policies, e.g., by also taking into account, through co-funding, the time it takes to turn R&D results into standards. This holds particularly for publicly funded research.
- The standardisation process is not flexible and fast enough.
  Over the last couple of years many SDOs have streamlined their processes and introduced new deliverables that emerge through fairly unbureaucratic, flexible and fast processes. It appears that the SDOs need to better communicate such improvements to their stakeholders.
- Standardisation activities do not have a positive impact on the evaluation of my research.
  It is indeed correct that contributions to standards have little or no impact on a researcher's recognition by his/her peers, and on chances for promotion or for better funding. Closer links between the two communities might help improve this situation.
- My expertise is not relevant in the standards setting process.
  Comments from SDOs suggest that an improved link from R&D to standards setting would be most desirable. This is further highlighted by the current (early 2007) initiative by the ITU-T to improve their links with academia. Here again, this misconception could be clarified by a better communication by the SSBs.

2.2 What SSBs Can Do – Mechanisms to Bridge the Gap Between Research and Standardisation

This section will briefly outline some recommendations that can been derived from the above.

Adaptation of Processes

From the researchers' perspective, standardisation processes will need to be better adapted to their specific requirements to make active participation a realistic and worthwhile option. This has two aspects to it – time and flexibility. First, the processes as such would need to be shorter – few researchers are interested in spending too much time on committee work (a lack of information / relevant education may well contribute to this; see also below). Here, the leaner processes leading to 'New Deliverables' that have been introduced by several ESOs and other bodies should be very useful. Also, reducing the sequentiality of R&D and standardisation would be helpful ('co-normative research'), as would a higher level of pro-active standardisation.

Second, the rather static structure of formal technical committees (e.g., CEN TC/WG, or equivalent) should be extended to accommodate new topics that are not being dealt with by existing technical committees – the necessity to establish a new WG or Work Item before R&D results can be fed into the standardisation system typically implies a considerable delay before work can commence. However, as the creation of a Work Item prior to starting activity is one of the obligations behind the transparency required in the good practices of standardisation, as defined in particular by the WTO, it cannot be omitted. Ways need to be devised that satisfy both the good practices and the researchers' requirements. Related to this are new topics that could be associated with more than one TC; in such situations, additional delays are likely to occur until the TCs involved have come to an agreement. Ad-hoc groups, following the same procedures as 'normal' WGs but (initially) operating outside the TC/WG structure might be a solution here. Here as well, mechanisms like 'Workshops' (CEN) or 'Industry Specification Groups' (ETSI) that deploy a leaner process than formal technical groups and can be also established on an ad-hoc basis are a simple yet efficient tool. Such existing mechanisms, however, need to be better promoted in the research community.

The direct transformation of research results into workable standards will hardly be possible in most cases. Rather, research findings typically need to be complemented by real-world implementation experience (obviously, this does not hold for terminology standards). This could initially be based on 'New Deliverables', revised versions of which that incorporate such experience could then be fed into the 'traditional' process.

Monitoring and Alerting Service

R&D on the one hand, and standardisation on the other, are widely perceived as two entirely distinct and separate activities; the respective communities are largely unconnected. This is one of the major obstacles in the way of a better utilisation of research findings in standards setting. To overcome this problem, an improved flow of information between the communities would be a helpful first step. That is, SSBs need to monitor ongoing R&D initiatives in order to find potentially relevant activities, and to actively 'alert' the R&D community about any needs they have and opportunities they can provide. While this is being done in a limited way, further improvements are of paramount importance. To this end, a dedicated entity (MAM – monitoring, alerting, matching; see below), possibly operated jointly by several SSBs, could serve as a 'gateway' between the communities. In the following, this entity's tasks will be discussed in some more detail.

- Monitoring of R&D Activities
  Learning about current R&D trends and activities is essential for SSBs for several reasons. For one, it will provide information on ongoing activities that are of potential relevance for ongoing standardisation activities. Moreover, incorporating (cutting edge) research findings will help attract researchers, which, in turn, will further improve the technical quality and relevance of the standards. Also, such information may help identify new areas of standardisation, and to initiate activities accordingly. Even with more mature technologies timely knowledge about plans for new projects will offer SSBs the opportunity to incorporate research findings from the outset (this may be important for standards maintenance). R&D organisations are performing similar exercises to identify promising new fields of research and active researchers.
- Alerting of R&D People
  Passive monitoring of ongoing and planned R&D activities is necessary but not sufficient. In addition, mechanisms need to be established to actively inform and alert the research community about ongoing and planned standardisation projects. Researchers are not normally aware of these projects, and such an alerting service would be a suitable way to improve this situation. The important bit here is that alerting needs to go beyond the mere publication of information. Rather, the identified target groups need to be actively informed ('information push').
  Information to be conveyed would have to include a concise description of the technical goals of the standards project, its status and time frame (also indicating whether or not new input could still be incorporated), and any actively solicited contributions from the research side (if any, that is). Administrative information, such as, for example, contact information, a list of members active in the project, and scheduled meetings should also be made available.
- Matching
  Monitoring and alerting will help the standardisation and research communities to learn about ongoing relevant activities in the respective other sector. However, the new entity would be in an ideal position to match SSBs' needs for further research onto activities going on at the R&D side. Subsequently, contact between both groups could be established. For instance, researchers could be invited to present their work at a technical committee meeting, or vice versa; i.e., a technical committee representative could present standardisation activities and discuss future potential co-operation at a project meeting.

Education and Promotion

Education of researchers and research managers about aspects related to standards and standardisation is crucial. If the latter are not aware of the potential benefits of standardisation, researchers and developers will have difficulties obtaining their support for active participation in standards-setting activities, financial or otherwise. Obviously, though, researchers need to be aware of these advantages in the first place.

Apart from raising general awareness of potential benefits education on how, where, and when to participate is essential. Knowing which SSB or committee to address is a major pre-requisite for researchers to effectively join the standardisation process in time. Training researchers in what active participation entails will be the second step.

To actually reach the research community information needs to be actively distributed and made available on easy-to-find web pages. Corporate and universities' Technology Transfer Departments would be natural contact points here.

Some More Specific Suggestions

Numerous additional avenues can be followed to improve the link between standardisation and research. These include, for example,

- Offer individual membership for researchers in SSBs
  While this is being done by several SSBs (most notably by fora and consortia), membership of the ESOs is limited to companies and national bodies, respectively (with the notable exception of CEN workshops). Temporary individual membership would considerably lower the barrier to entry to standardisation for researchers, and would enable them to contribute precisely to those aspects of a standard for which their research is important (i.e., avoid any 'overhead').
- Lobby for greater importance of standards-related aspects in projects' proposals & evaluation
  Judging by the level by which they support standards-setting activities as part of R&D projects, hardly any research funding organisation considers standards as a legitimate and valuable tool for dissemination, or for the production of sustainable results (the EU being half an exception). SSBs need to try and lobby for a higher degree of importance to be assigned to standards aspects in R&D project proposals. This could be achieved, for example, by a dedicated sub-panel evaluating proposals with respect to their potential and importance for ongoing or future standardisation activities – which, in turn, could be partly based on CEN/STAR's (Standardisation and Research) prioritised needs.
- Try to secure dedicated R&D money
  After the 'Standards, measurement and Testing' domain has disappeared from the European Framework Programmes (FPs), normative projects need to compete with others for funding under the individual R&D programmes. For a higher percentage of normative research part of an R&D programme's budget could be managed by ESOs (or SSBs) and spent on projects with a potential for standardisation. In Germany, for example, this could also imply that an SSB is assigned the status of a Project Management Agency.
- Hold co-located standardisation and R&D events
  Scientific conferences are important for researchers from almost all disciplines. Thus, by co-locating standards events (formal technical committee meetings or similar) with major (topically related conferences) would give the opportunity to introduce researchers to the problems and benefits of standards setting. This could also be done through promotional activities such as, for example, dedicated workshops, seminars, or 'taster courses'.
- Co-operate with professional associations

This is related to the above. Co-operation with, for instance, international research umbrella organisations (e.g., IFIP) could simplify the information flow from these societies (i.e., the R&D domain) into standards setting.

- Actively participate in (publicly funded) R&D projects
  SSBs playing an active role as partners in research projects could ensure that any standards-relevant output will be channelled to the appropriate committees or working groups. In fact, in many cases such dissemination activities would, in all likelihood, be the major or even the sole task of the SSB (i.e., no actual research work would be required from the SSBs). Projects suitable for such participation could be identified.
- Forge closer links with academics / tertiary education
  "*The students of today are the stakeholders of tomorrow ....*". (Short) courses on standardisation, joint thesis supervision, internships, etc would all help to expose students to standardisation (something that hardly ever happens in an engineering/management curriculum). Likewise, exchange or personnel (e.g., internships for academics, temporary lectureships for SSB staff) should be considered. Dedicated prizes (like he DIN prize for students) or competitions (like the recent IEC challenge) would also be a useful means to attract students.

The above are only some examples of what could be done to improve the link between research and standardisation. In any case, it will be crucial that the SSBs take the initiative.

3 Some Comments on Current Practice

Many SSBs have developed mechanisms to better link research and the research community to standards setting. In the following, some brief findings from an analysis of 'current practices' will be provided. The Annex provides associated brief descriptions of very different such practices, focussing on DIN and CEN in Europe, and on the IEEE and the IETF at the US/international level.

All but IEEE have dedicated mechanisms in place to provide a link from research to standardisation. Being a professional organisation in the first place, the IEEE Standards Association are benefiting from implicit close links between standards setting and research through IEEE members (typically engineers and computer scientists) also active in standardisation. Obviously, establishing this type of link is a time consuming activity and will hardly be replicable by other SSBs (it might be easier for professional associations to move into standardisation).

The Internet Research Task Force (IRTF) is the 'research arm' of the Internet Society (ISOC). The idea of organising the link from research to standardisation as two partner entities under a common organisational roof is appealing. However, all is not gold that glitters. For one, several of the IRTF's websites appear to be quite outdated. Moreover, between them the current Research Groups have so far only produced four RFCs , only one of which (from 2002) has reached the level of 'Proposed Standard'. Most of the output is in the form of IETF/IRTF-drafts and, primarily, of research papers. This suggests that the traditional publication of research findings is still held in higher esteem than contributions to the standards setting process (even for those that have a higher-than-average interest in standardisation).

DIN is promoting the idea of 'research-phase standardisation'. In principle, this could be a valuable approach to better integrate standardisation and R&D. However, so far it seems that only some publicly funded projects – of which DIN has been a member – have adopted this approach; genuine interest by industry seems to be limited.

CEN/STAR is a CEN Action Group in charge of developing *"a more efficient link between European Cooperative R&D and European standardisation*". However, their means are limited, and they have to cover (too) much ground (all topics addressed by CEN). Thus, their effectiveness could certainly be improved, albeit hardly without additional funding.

CEN workshops are a very suitable mechanism to transfer project findings into something akin to a standard (a 'CEN Workshop Agreement'). However, their value could be further increased if dedicated mechanisms were in place to 'elevate' workshop agreements to full 'European Standard' and/or International Standard level (if so desired).

One major difference and one commonality may be observed between the more 'US-centric' approaches (IEEE and IETF) and the 'euro-centric' ones (DIN and CEN). The former refers to the way the link from R&D to standardisation is organised. IEEE's and IETF's approaches are continuous, and to a high degree based on individual, whether explicit (IETF) or implicit (IEEE). In contrast, both DIN and CEN prefer a more formal, temporary, project-based based approach. Seen from a distance, the latter seems to be more successful (albeit not exactly a raving success either). This holds primarily for the CEN workshops.

All SSBs share the characteristic of a virtually non-existent link from standardisation to R&D. The only (indirect) such link is maintained by CEN/STAR, who keep a list of research needs of CEN's individual TCs. However, CEN can only advise the European Commission's DGs regarding the benefits of their shortlisted proposals. No dedicated funding exists for either co-normative or pre-normative research.

4 Brief Summary and Some Additional Advice

So far, this document has discussed the relevance of adequate links between standardisation and research, and discussed a number of barriers as perceived by researchers. SSBs can do something about some of these barriers, whereas the resolution of others would require the intervention of other entities (e.g., research funding agencies). Also, some comparably easily implemental mechanisms have been identified that should help improve the current situation. Finally, some comments on the current situation have been provided.

The various potential courses of action discussed above have very different time horizons. To get the 'monitoring, alerting, matching' entity up and running may take years, the same holds for the suggested modification of the standards setting processes. In contrast, some of the 'more specific suggestions' can be implemented fairly quickly, e.g., the take-up of lobby work, organisation of co-located standardisation and R&D events, the co-operation with professional associations. It would be advisable to start with some rather more short-term activities and evaluate their outcome before starting any major implementation tasks. In any case, however,

SSBs wishing to implement some of these mechanisms need to be aware that it is not natural for researchers to actively participate in standards setting. Thus, adequate communication of any new mechanisms is crucial.

With a view towards long-lasting and sustainable links between standards setting and research, closer links with academia would be highly advisable. Students of relevant disciplines should be exposed to standards, and learn about the importance of standardisation, fairly early on. With the current switch of many national educational systems to a Bachelor/Master system this means that a course about (ICT) standardisation should be part of the Bachelor curriculum. In this context, co-operation between standards professionals and university lecturers would be most helpful for the development of such a course.

Along similar lines, and definitely not least: SSBs need to be aware that knowledge and research *about* standardisation is as important as research *for* standards setting. Especially ICT standards are becoming increasingly important (just think about the 'Internet of Things'). Therefore, we need to develop an adequate understanding about the various issues surrounding standards and standardisation (their diffusion, adoption, and impact, why they emerge the way they do, how much they cost and what they bring, etc).

5 References

1: Critical issues in ICT Standardization. Discussion paper from the ICT Focus Group for further consideration by ICT Standards Board member organisations. http://www.ictsb.org/ICTSFG/ICTSFG_report_2005-04-27.pdf.

2: D02 – Report on the results of the survey among researchers. http://www.nets.rwth-aachen.de/Interest/D02.pdf.

Teil III

Adaptive Systeme

Query Processing and System-Level Support for Runtime-Adaptive Sensor Networks

Falko Dressler, Rüdiger Kapitza, Michael Daum, Moritz Strübe, Wolfgang Schröder-Preikschat, Reinhard German and Klaus Meyer-Wegener

Dept. of Computer Science, University of Erlangen, Germany
{dressler,rrkapitz,md,moritz.struebe,wosch,german,kmw}@cs.fau.de

Abstract. We present an integrated approach for supporting in-network sensor data processing in dynamic and heterogeneous sensor networks. The concept relies on data stream processing techniques that define and optimize the distribution of queries and their operators. We anticipate a high degree of dynamics and heterogeneity in the network, which is expected to be the case for wildlife monitoring applications. The distribution of operators to individual nodes demands several system level capabilities not available in current sensor node operating systems. In particular, we developed means for replacing software modules, i.e. small applications, on demand and without loss of status information. In order to facilitate this operation, we added a lightweight module support for the Nut/OS system and implemented a new memory management that uses tags for preserving state across module updates and node reboots.

1 Introduction

Sensor networks are being investigated for many application scenarios including precision agriculture, industrial automation, and habitat monitoring. In this paper, we focus on the latter one, i.e. wildlife monitoring, which represents a challenging domain in terms of network dynamics and energy efficiency. Depending on the specific targets to be observed, extreme resource constraints together with requirements for continuous tracking can be found, e.g. for studying small animals such as bats. The application scenario can be roughly described as follows: A number of sensor nodes are distributed (either placed stationary on the ground or tagged to moving animals) to collect sensory data, to aggregate and to process this data according to specific needs of the investigating scientists, and to present the final outcome during the experiment or after its completion.

We believe that user-centric scenario descriptions can be used to balance and define contradicting properties and capabilities in such networks such as monitoring precision vs. scalability vs. energy consumption. We completely rely on network-centric data processing techniques [1], specifically on distributed stream processing [2]. Data stream queries provide means for translating higher-level application requirements into low-level distributed operators. Data stream queries in sensor networks can be strongly influenced by the dynamics of the application domain, e.g. mobile systems and node failures. Furthermore, the environment,

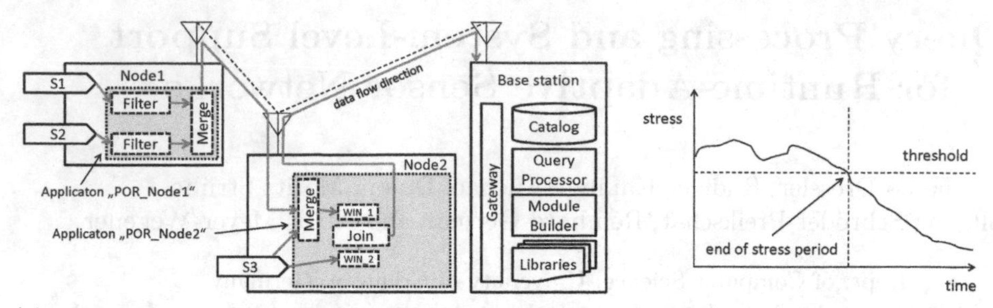

(a) Two sensor nodes executing different queries and base station; shown is the data flow direction

(b) Example scenario: detection of stress and recreation

Fig. 1. Principle scenario description

e.g. day-night-cycle, seasons, and anomalies like earthquakes, introduces additional dynamics. Fortunately, scientists using the sensor network usually get a fine grasp of the application domain and the working behavior of the nodes. They will be able to continuously refine the global queries, which are to be processed by the sensor network. Therefore, data stream systems need to dynamically tailor the queries to the current situation. At the same time, algorithms for self-optimization of data stream queries are being developed, which further increase the demand for frequent updates. Such updates of data stream queries demand for two system level functions: First, sensor nodes need to be able to update the software during run-time, even in case of resource constraints such as limited local flash memory and available communication bandwidth. Secondly, replacement of query operations without loss of status information needs persistent storage of data in volatile memory. Accordingly, we developed an architecture that allows us to reprogram sensor nodes at the OS level and more fine grained on a per-module basis. Furthermore, we developed a new memory management system that allocates memory and associates tags for simplified identification after module replacement or node reboot. We selected the BTnode, a typical sensor node, as our primary hardware. The used operating system is Nut/OS, a non-preemptive, cooperative multi-threaded OS for sensor nodes.

The contributions of this paper can be summarized as follows. We discuss a global query management with separation of queries and node configuration, partitioning of global data stream queries, and mapping of partitions to module descriptions (Section 2). Furthermore, we present developed system level support for node specific linking of modules and replacing the modules during runtime (Sections 3.1–3.4). Finally, we developed a new memory management system with support for tagging memory with names for persistent storage in volatile memory during module replacement and even system reboot (Section 3.5).

2 Distributed Stream Processing

The need for distributed stream processing is apparent as processing nodes and data sinks are distributed. In [2], the Data Stream Management System (DSMS)

Cougar is presented, which deploys distributed queries over a sensor network. We have a similar architecture but different focus. First, we have a heterogeneous network, secondly, we use a different approach to querying, and, thirdly, we are tailoring software that is deployed on each node depending on the specific query.

2.1 A Scenario for Global Query Management

In our scenario, we use sensor nodes that can communicate with each other and may have different sets of sensors, different locations, and different sets of installed modules. An example is depicted in Figure 1a. `Node2` is connected to the base station and has higher energy capacity. `Node1` measures *skin conductivity level* (SCL) with sensor `S1` and *body temperature* (TEMP) with sensor `S2`. `S3` connected to `Node2` delivers *position* (POS) data. The base station processes global queries and configures the nodes, i.e. it maps a partial query to an operator assembly and deploys it on the adequate node. The catalog contains all information (metadata) about nodes, communication paths, configuration, and sets of code fragments that can be composed to modules. Users like behavior scientists want to describe their needs using an abstract query language without considering the sensor network's topology in order to describe a query in a formal way. We assume that the biologists want to find out in which area the observed animals have stress and where they go to for recreation. The fictive stress curve (Figure 1b) shows a threshold that might be reached if the two sensor values exceed certain values. Our query determines the area of recreation as the animal's position at 10 min after the last stress event.

2.2 Global Queries

Many DSMS use SQL-like queries that are fundamentally influenced by considerations about reusing database technologies [3]. Alternatively, some of the early DSMS like Borealis [4] use a box-and-arrow description of data stream queries as it is more intuitive considering the direction of the data flow. Both language families have limited expressiveness, which can be reduced by user-defined aggregates [5] in SQL or by user-defined boxes [6] in DSMS like Borealis.

We are using an extensible abstract query language that is currently being developed in the data management group. A user can define a set of input streams, a sequence of abstract operators, and a set of output streams. Our language keeps the data flow direction and, therefore, it is less declarative than SQL. All operators are either commutative or have a definite position, e.g. number of input streams. Subqueries can be used as input stream. The location of input and output streams, sensors, schema information, and topology is part of the catalog. In our example, we have three sensors that should be merged, if:

- The animal's TEMP is higher than 38 °C and its SCL is greater than 8 Mho.
- The last position of a stress situation (POS) and the position of recreation (POR) (10 min later) are of interest.
- The observation at POR lasts at least 2 min.

```
1 (S1,S2,S3,TIME:$1.filter(SCL>8), $2.filter(TEMP>38), MERGE()),
2 (S3, TIME:MERGE()) :
3    WINDOW(1),JOIN($2.TIME-$1.TIME>10min &&
4    $2.TIME-$1.TIME>12min) :
5 POR
```

$\approx$

```
1 CREATE STREAM POS AS
2   SELECT *,sysdate() as TIME
3     FROM S1[ROWS 1], S2[ROWS 1], S3[ROWS 1]
4     WHERE S1.SCL > 8 AND S2.TEMP > 38;
5 CREATE STREAM POR AS
6   SELECT *
7     FROM POS[ROWS 1], (SELECT *,sysdate() AS TIME FROM S3[ROWS 1]) S3
8     WHERE time_to_min(S3.TIME)-time_to_min(POS.TIME) BETWEEN 10 and 12;
```

Fig. 2. Sample query in the abstract query language and its SQL-like representation

The sample query depicted in Figure 2 has three input streams and one output stream. Further, the query has two subqueries in the input stream list. The first subquery has three abstract operators: one filter operator that selects all interesting SCL values from the first stream, another filter operator that does the same for TEMP values from the second stream, and a ternary merge operator that merges all three streams after filtering the first and the second. The merge operator waits for all input events and creates one element including all inputs. The second subquery simply adds the current time to the sensor value. In our main query, the last items of the two subqueries are joined if the temporal condition is fulfilled. The last items are realized by sliding windows. The main difference between a merge and a join operator is that merge operators use input values only once in the resulting events. As we do not focus on query languages, we also depict the query in a SQL-like notation for a better understanding. The result is not exactly the same, as expiration by window-definitions cannot express that an event should only be delivered once.

2.3 Query Partitioning and Distribution of Operators

The global query goes through the process of partitioning and mapping (Figure 3) in order to define modules that can be deployed on the nodes. Compared to data stream queries in heterogeneous sensor networks, distributed query processing is reasonably well researched. The classical steps can be adapted to the context of stream processing as depicted in Figure 4. Available methods from database systems can be used for "query parsing" and "rule-based optimization". The step "creation of enumerated plans" additionally has to consider the different possibilities of software deployment. A metadata catalog is essential for query processing as it contains all information about data sources, topology of nodes, and even the set of available operators (our query language is extensible).

"Cost estimation" (cost-based optimization) is part of our ongoing work. Thus, we describe a straightforward approach for distributing our sample query. In the scenario (Figures 1a and 2), we have topology information and a description of available sensors. First, a dependency graph of operators is created.

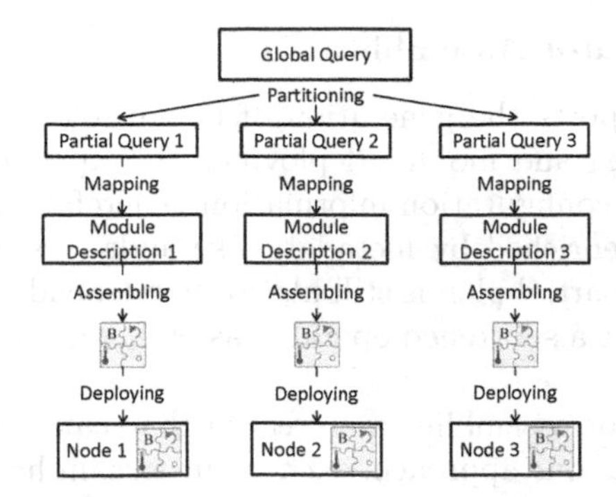

Fig. 3. Mapping of global queries

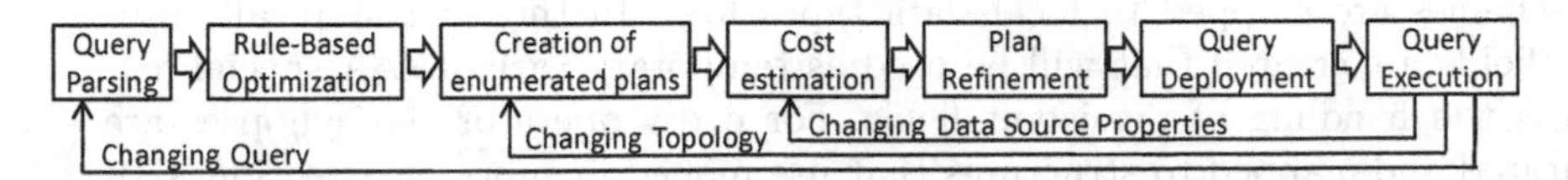

Fig. 4. Steps of query processing and reorganization of queries at run-time

Thus, all subqueries have to be translated first. The first subquery has two filter operators that can be pushed close to the data sources and the ternary merge operator is split into two binary ones. Unlike join operators, the merge operator has always a data rate that is less or equal than its input rate. Therefore, the first binary merge operator is set to the first node. As `S3` is deployed on the second node, `Node1` sends the result of the first merge operator to `Node2` that merges the result with the values of `S3`. The second subquery is processed accordingly. Both subqueries are input streams that are available at `Node2` for the main query. This one has a window operator that refers to both input streams. As there is no other stateful operator, it is only used by the join operator. We have adopted the separation of operator's state (synopsis) and operator that is used by STREAM [7] for our purposes. This is essential for reorganization of queries at run-time. In this paper, we will just take this plan and assume that all node capacities will suffice the needs. Later on, it needs to be compared with alternatives ("plan refinement").

Now, the query plan can be mapped and installed on the nodes ("query deployment"). During "query execution", there might be several reasons for the reorganization of queries. For example, there might be the need for changing a query, e.g. the threshold for the body temperature. In this case, all steps of query processing have to be done, but the topology of nodes is more restrictive as the operators' states have to be considered. Another reason for dynamic reorganization is a changing topology of nodes. In this case, the step "creation of enumerated plans" has to be repeated as other operator distributions lead to valid plans. Furthermore, properties of data sources may change, e.g. the distribution of values. A repetition of "cost estimation" leads to a re-adapted plan. In some cases, it might not be possible to get valid plans without state migration.

2.4 Creation of Operator Assemblies

"Query deployment" supports the generation of deployable code. The system support for module linking and module deployment is explained in Section 3. We separate queries from configuration information. Therefore, the partial plan for each node has to be enriched by metadata like addresses, data rates, and others. At this point, the partial plan is still platform independent. Due to space restrictions, we only depict a shortened operator assembly in form of C-code for `Node2` in Figure 5.

In a first step, operator assemblies are created that can be used in the final deployment process. In our approach, each input stream has a schema that is manipulated by operators. Thus, we provide schemes of input and output streams that are either used internally or for communication with data sinks. All schemes are mapped to local data types first. In the next step, all transient fields are created that will be used as temporary variables. A special feature is the handling of persistent fields. For every operator the synopses are separated and mapped to structures that use named memory (see Section 3.5). The crucial step is mapping the partial plan itself. Operators' predicates like `($2.TIME-$1.TIME>10min && $2.TIME-$1.TIME>12min)` have to be mapped to callback functions. A dependency graph is used to guarantee the right order of operators. There is a template for each operator that is completed by structural information, e.g. variable names. The template for operators like join contains a `for()` loop as the cardinality of the results may be greater than one.

The resulting module (Figure 5) starts with the initialization of streams and sensors. `POR_Node2_OUT_01` stands for one of five `structs` that represent schemas. Templates create the persistent fields for the windows. Name and the size of a window are known, thus, they are not persisted. The main concept of query execution is periodic execution. The "plan refinement" step calculates the length of the sleeping period with metadata.

3 Reprogramming Support

After mapping a global query to a set of sensor nodes, the assigned operator assemblies have to be deployed. The primary system of a sensor node is represented by a kernel containing a scheduler, I/O interfaces, and other system level functions. Additional functionality such as operator assemblies can be added at a later point of time. Besides replacing the entire kernel, we also support modules that can be added, updated, or replaced at run-time. Software updates in sensor networks can be performed at various levels of granularity. For example, the Deluge system [8] propagates software update over an ad hoc sensor network and can switch between several images to run on the sensor nodes. Jeong and Culler [9] studied incremental network (re-)programming with focus on the delivery of software images in sensor networks. We contribute to this domain by investigating techniques to upload and to replace software modules in an efficient way. Despite the fact that there are already two popular micro controller operating systems like SOS and Contiki supporting modularity, none of them fits

```
1  APPLICATION("POR_Node2", stack_size, arg) {
2    // Initialization of Streams
3    LocalSensor POR_Node2_s3 = init_pos_sensor();
4    InputStream POR_Node2_Node1_OUT_01 = init_input("node1");
5    RemoteAddress POR_Client = "base";
6    // Data structures
7    struct POR_Node2_OUT_01 {
8      int struct_size;
9      [...]
10     int time;
11   };
12   [...]
13   // Transient fields
14   POR_Node2_IN_01* in_01;
15   POR_Node2_OUT_01* res_01;
16   [...]
17   // Persistent fields
18   char NAME_POR_Node2_WIN_01[17]="NAME_POR_Node2_WIN_01";
19   int win_size_01 = 1;
20   POR_Node2_OUT_01* win_01 = NutNmemGet(NAME_POR_Node2_WIN_01);
21   if (win_01 == NULL) win_01 = NutNmemCreate(NAME_POR_Node2_WIN_01,
         win_size_01*sizeof(POR_Node2_OUT_01)+sizeof(_WIN_STATE));
22   [...]
23   // Query processing
24   for(;;) {
25     in_01 = getSensorData(POR_Node2_s3);
26     in_02 = getInputStreamData(POR_Node2_Node1_OUT_01;);
27     res_01 = merge(in_01,in_02,"")
28     reorganizeWindow(win_01, res_01);
29     res_02 = merge(in_01, time());
30     reorganizeWindow(win_02, res_02);
31     res_03 = join(&join_resultsize_01, win_01, win_size_01, win_02,
           win_size_02, join_cond_01);
32     for (int i = 0; i < join_resultsize_01 ; i++) {
33       send(POR_Client, res_03[i], sizeof(POR_Node2_OUT_03));
34     }
35     NutSleep(125);
36   }
37 }
```

Fig. 5. Application code for sensor node 2

our demands w.r.t. dynamic module replacement, hardware support, and failure handling [10]. Instead, we chose the Nut/OS operating system as basis for our infrastructure support. In this section, we outline the general process to deploy a module; briefly summarize our implementation platform and finally give details related to the implementation and usage of our reprogramming support.

3.1 Deployment of an Operator Assembly

Figure 6a depicts the necessary steps to successfully deploy an operator assembly. Initially, the deploying node, usually the gateway of the sensor network or an equally powerful mobile system (e.g., a researcher with a laptop), requests the kernel checksum from the target node. We provide such a checksum to identify the kernel to obtain information how it was build to prevent problems related to micro heterogeneity [11]. At this point we anticipate that there is a repository that can be queried using the checksum to get the necessary information

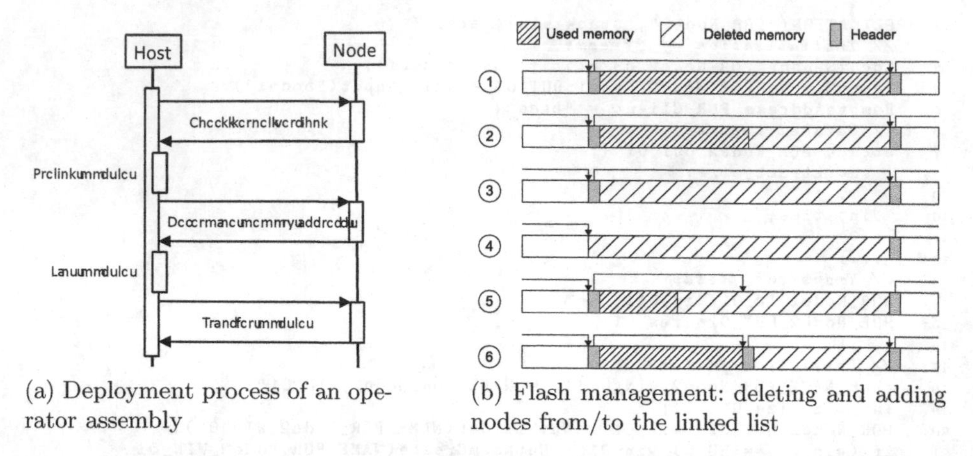

(a) Deployment process of an operator assembly

(b) Flash management: deleting and adding nodes from/to the linked list

Fig. 6. Module-based reprogramming support for operator assemblies

for pre-linking the module (e.g., the symbol table of the kernel). This enables us to link the module against the kernel. After this step, we know the exact size of the module and are able to query the target node for a concrete location to place the module within the flash memory. This is achieved by transmitting the module size to the node that needs this information to find sufficient free program memory space. The module is finalized by linking it again using the provided memory address. Finally, the module is transferred to the node, initialized, and started. The initialization might include the recovery of state provided by a previous version of the operator assembly. This is achieved by supporting *named memory* that enables to store and use variables based on a special memory management library (see Section 3.5). The replacement of the kernel works similar.

3.2 Target Platform

We developed our reprogramming architecture for the BTnode hardware platform developed at the ETH Zurich, which is based on an Atmel ATmega128 micro controller, a RISC processor with 128 KB flash ROM and 4 KB internal SRAM, which is extended to a total of 64 KB SRAM. The Harvard architecture, i.e. program and data memory are addressed independently, uses the flash as program and the SRAM as data memory. Besides programming the flash using an In-System Programmer (ISP), the ATmega128 supports self-programming of the flash memory. The flash is divided into a regular and a boot loader section and can only be programmed from within the boot loader section, which resides in the last 8 KB of the flash. Furthermore, the flash is divided in pages of 256 Byte. Before it is possible to write a page, it has to be erased. Both operations are independently executed and interrupts are not delayed in between. Thus, reprogramming operations need to be synchronized with flash management. During

Field	Description
Application size	Total application size in byte
Application name	Unique application name for identification
Entry function pointer	Needed to start the application
Module start address	Used for consistency checks
Stack size	Enables memory allocation at application start
CRC32 checksum	Determine memory corruptions
Optional flags	E.g., to indicate free space or kernel

Table 1. Header information used for flash memory management

write operations, the code execution is stalled for about 4 ms. This behavior has to be considered as applications may have strict timing assumptions. As operating system we use BTnut, which is build on top of the multi-threaded Nut/OS framework. Nut/OS makes extensive use of dynamic memory management. Opposed to other operating systems including recent versions of TinyOS, a Nut/OS thread does not need any static variables. The stack and heap as well as memory used for thread management are allocated during thread startup. Therefore, it is not necessary for the compiler to know such details at compile time.

3.3 Flash Management

As the flash is normally not used for saving multiple modules and kernel versions, we developed a new flash memory management system. We decided to use a simple linked list of data blocks. Each data block is page aligned and starts with a header that contains information about the block contents and its length. To detect corruption, the header is equipped with a checksum calculated over the contents of the data block. An exception is the kernel. As it must always start with the interrupt vectors, the header is placed behind the interrupt vectors. Kernels, which are saved on flash as a replacement of the original kernel, get an additional header. If a module is saved in a data block, the header also contains information that is needed by the operating system to start the application. This includes the name, the stack size, and a pointer to the entry function of the application. Table 1 summarizes all header fields.

Care was taken to avoid a flash corruption. When data is overwritten, the data is first erased from back to front and then written the opposite way. This allows the bootloader to easily recover data as the old header is kept as long as possible. Otherwise, the next non-empty page must contain a valid header. Figure 6b outlines the usage of the linked list in detail. An application is saved between two other blocks (1). Its header points to the next node. If part of the data is deleted, the linked list is still valid (2). After deleting the block, the header is still pointing to the next block (3). When the header is deleted (4), the list can be recovered by finding the first non-empty page. Writing a new module starts with inserting a new header (5). The pointer points to an empty page. Again, this can be fixed by searching the next non-empty page. After writing the application, the header marking the empty space is written (6).

3.4 Creating Binaries and Flash Management

The binaries of the kernel and the modules need to contain information that is provided only after the linking process, e.g. the size of the binary and the checksum. Instead of adding the header to the final binary, it is added during the build process in order to enable support for tools such as debuggers. The header used for the flash management is added at compile time using compiler attributes to put it into a special section. During linking, the section is placed at the correct location and missing information is added. Symbols are used to replace the name of a function with an address after it is placed at its final address. Similarly, instead of passing an address this technique can be used to pass a variable. The following expression can be used to initialize a variable `foo` with the address of a symbol: `uint16_t foo = (uint16_t)&usersymbol_foo;` When assigning a value to `usersymbol_foo` instead of an address and passing this to the linker, `foo` gets initialized with this value. This approach makes use of the default tool chain and avoids further manipulations.

For the CRC32 calculation, all files are linked twice. For the first linking, the CRC symbol is set to zero. After calculating the CRC32 for the binary image, the files are linked again with the correct CRC. As only 16 Bit pointers are available, the CRC has to be passed to the linker using two symbols, each containing a word of the CRC. If a new kernel was created, its symbol table is extracted and saved in a special directory, using the calculated CRC as an identifier. This symbol table is passed to the linker when creating a module for this specific kernel. This way, an application may access all functions provided by the kernel. Missing functions are taken from libraries that need to be linked to the module.

Flashing is done either by the bootloader (replacing the kernel) or by the kernel (when receiving an application or new kernel). As the flash functions are part of the bootloader, a jump table is used to allow the kernel to access these functions without explicit information about the bootloader. The ATmega128 supports moving the reset vector to the bootloader section. This gives the bootloader complete control after a node reset. When the bootloader starts up, it verifies the flash using the CRCs, if necessary deletes broken modules, and checks whether it finds an updated kernel. To avoid having a corrupted kernel, the bootloader verifies the CRC of the new kernel before deleting the old one. It also makes sure that the new kernel does not overlap with itself when being copied. After copying the kernel, the copied kernel gets verified, before the buffered copy gets deleted to free memory. Finally, the kernel is started.

3.5 Named Memory

In order to recover data saved in SRAM after a reboot, we decided to use a concept similar to shared memory. Shared memory is accessed using a key. Similarly, we decided to use a string to build *named memory.* It is now possible to allocate memory and assign a name to it. Later on, it is possible to get a pointer to this memory using this name – even after the node got rebooted. Named memory is allocated like other managed memory but it is assigned an

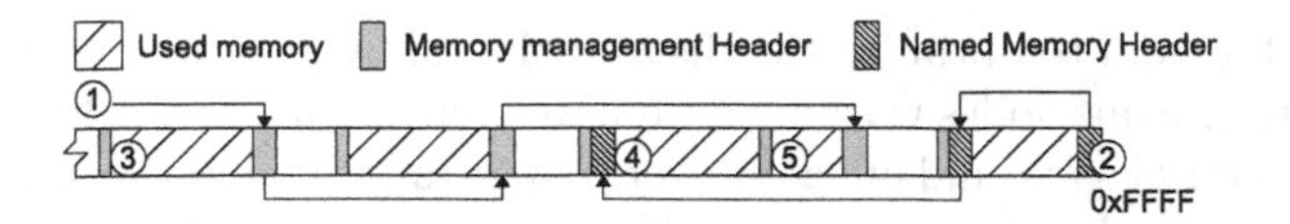

Fig. 7. Named memory

extra header. This header contains the name of the memory block, a pointer to the next named memory block, and a checksum, which is calculated over the header. The root of this linked list is placed at the very end of the memory during the initialization of the managed memory. This way, the probability of a conflicted with a resized data section of the kernel is minimized. During the boot process, the root element and all following headers of the list are verified using their checksums. This does not verify the data itself but it is very unlikely that the memory is modified without touching the headers. Figure 7 shows how the memory is organized when using the concept of named memory. (1) is the linked list of free memory. (2) is the root of the linked list for the named memory located at the very end of the memory. Allocated memory always has a header containing the size of the block (3). (4) shows a named memory block. The memory used for this block is allocated by the normal memory management and, therefore, has its header containing the size. Behind that, the named memory header is saved. Although normally allocated memory is preferably taken from the beginning and named memory from the end, this can still be mixed (5).

3.6 Application Programming Interface

As detailed earlier, Figure 5 shows a shortened listing of a sensor application that has been created in the "query deployment" step of the query processing architecture. The sample code starts with the `APPLICATION` macro, which adds the header to the module that is needed for dynamic deployment and life cycle operations. As parameters, it requires an application name, a stack size, and a pointer to pass arguments to the application.

Besides the declaration of the module, a developer has to decide which parts of the application's state should be preserved across module updates. In the example application, a sliding window should be persistent in case of a module replacement. This is achieved using `NutNmemGet()` and providing the name of the variable (line 19). If a previous version of the module allocated the memory, an address is returned or `NULL` if the variable is not present in the named memory system. In the latter case, the named memory has to be created calling `NutNmemCreate()` supplying the name and the required size (line 20). Finally, `NutNmemFree()` is provided to deallocated memory that is no longer needed.

4 Conclusion

We presented a set of system level support mechanisms for distributed data stream query processing in sensor networks. The concept of data stream processing allows to define and to optimize the distribution of queries and their operators among heterogeneous nodes working in dynamic environments. Additionally, it provides means for elegant and efficient user-centric query definitions. In order to support abstract higher layer query update strategies, the efficient replacement of application modules in individual nodes is necessary. We implemented an update architecture for BTnode sensor nodes running Nut/OS. We demonstrated that it is possible to load and execute modules during runtime. We also developed the concept of *named memory*, a simple way to save and recover the module state, i.e. the content of variables, after a reset or kernel update. Future work includes the state migration between sensor nodes, which is necessary for efficient query optimization w.r.t. metrics like scalability and energy-efficiency.

References

1. Culler, D., Hill, J., Buonadonna, P., Szewczyk, R., Woo, A.: A Network-Centric Approach to Embedded Software for Tiny Devices. In: First International Workshop on Embedded Software (EMSOFT 2001), Tahoe City, CA (October 2001)
2. Gehrke, J., Madden, S.: Query Processing in Sensor Networks. Pervasive Computing, IEEE **3**(1) (January – March 2004) 46–55
3. Babcock, B., Babu, S., Datar, M., Motwani, R., Widom, J.: Models and Issues in Data Stream Systems. In: 21st ACM Symposium on Principles of Database Systems (PODS 2002). (June 2002)
4. Abadi, D.J., Ahmad, Y., Cetintemel, M.B.U., Cherniack, M., Hwang, J.H., Lindner, W., Maskey, A.S., Rasin, A., Ryvkina, E., Tatbul, N., Xing, Y., Zdonik, S.: The Design of the Borealis Stream Processing Engine. In: Conference on Innovative Data Systems Research (CIDR 2005). (January 2005)
5. Law, Y., Wang, H., Zaniolo, C.: Query Languages and Data Models for Database Sequences and Data Streams. In: Thirtieth International Conference on Very Large Data Bases, Toronto, Canada (VLDB 2004). (August – September 2004)
6. Lindner, W., Velke, H., Meyer-Wegener, K.: Data Stream Query Optimization Across System Boundaries of Server and Sensor Network. In: 7th International Conference on Mobile Data Management (MDM 2006). (May 2006)
7. Motwani, R., Widom, J., Arasu, A., Babcock, B., Babu, S., Datar, M., Manku, G., Olston, C., Rosenstein, J., Varma, R.: Query Processing, Resource Management, and Approximation in a Data Stream Management System. In: Conference on Innovative Data Systems Research (CIDR 2003). (January 2003)
8. Chlipala, A., Hui, J., Tolle, G.: Deluge: Data Dissemination for Network Reprogramming at Scale. Technical report, University of California, Berkeley (2004)
9. Jeong, J., Culler, D.: Incremental Network Programming for Wireless Sensors. In: First IEEE International Conference on Sensor and Ad hoc Communications and Networks (IEEE SECON). (June 2004)
10. Dressler, F., Strübe, M., Kapitza, R., Schröder-Preikschat, W.: Dynamic Software Management on BTnode Sensors. In: 4th IEEE/ACM International Conference on Distributed Computing in Sensor Systems (IEEE/ACM DCOSS 2008): IEEE/ACM International Workshop on Sensor Network Engineering (IWSNE 2008), Santorini Island, Greece (June 2008) 9–14
11. Dunkels, A., Finne, N., Eriksson, J., Voigt, T.: Run-time dynamic linking for reprogramming wireless sensor networks. In: 4th ACM Conference on Embedded Networked Sensor Systems (SenSys 2006), Boulder, CO (November 2006) 15–28

SelfWISE: A Framework for Developing Self-Stabilizing Algorithms

Christoph Weyer and Volker Turau

Institute of Telematics, Hamburg University of Technology, Germany

Abstract. This paper introduces SelfWISE, a framework for enabling wireless sensor networks to be programmed in a self-stabilizing manner. The framework eases the formal specification of algorithms by abstracting from low-level details such as wireless channel and hardware-specific characteristics. SelfWISE consists of a language for expressing self-stabilizing algorithms, a runtime environment for simulating algorithms in wireless sensor networks, and supporting tools. The hereby applied transformation of formally described algorithms into the simulation environment preserves the self-stabilizing properties. Development, evaluation, and debugging of self-stabilizing algorithms is considerably facilitated by utilizing SelfWISE.

1 Introduction

The reliability of wireless sensor networks (WSNs) is threatened by several factors such as high fault rates of components, unattended deployment in harsh environments, and disruptions of the wireless channel. Therefore, fault-tolerance is an important requirement for an autonomous operation of WSNs. There are two approaches to fault-tolerance: masking and non-masking. Masking fault-tolerance guarantees that programs continually satisfy their specification in the presence of faults. By way of contrast, non-masking fault-tolerance merely guarantees that when faults stop occurring, program executions converge to states from where programs continually satisfy their specification. Requirements for low energy and cost sensitivity imply that many traditional technics to implement masking fault-tolerance are not adequate for WSNs, leaving non-masking fault-tolerance as the first choice.

A promising technique to realize non-masking fault-tolerance is self-stabilization. A distributed system is self-stabilizing if after transient faults, regardless of their cause, it returns to a legitimate state in a finite number of steps irrespective of the initial state, and the system remains in a legitimate state as long as no new fault occurs [4,11]. It is well known that individual nodes in WSNs may reach arbitrary states after hardware resets and communication errors due to lost or duplicated messages. Thus, self-stabilization is particularly suited for the domain of wireless networks. A tremendous advantage of self-stabilization is that it does not handle individual failures separately. Instead of modeling individual errors that may occur and providing corresponding recovery routines, self-stabilizing systems are based on a description of the error-free system and rules to reach and maintain this state. This avoids the drawback of fault masking approaches that only handle a priori known faults.

These advantages have spurred a lot of research into self-stabilizing algorithms and over the last 20 years, many self-stabilizing algorithms that are of interest for WSNs have been proposed: graph coloring, dominating sets, depth-first trees and spanning trees, see [14] for literature references. However, the majority of the algorithms is based on models not suitable for the constraints of WSNs: shared memory model, central daemon and atomicity. A very general solution for this problem are transformers [8,2,14]. They transform existing algorithms into corresponding algorithms running under weaker assumptions, while preserving the stabilization property. This allows the usage of algorithms in the realm of WSNs.

A serious issue with this approach to fault-tolerance for WSNs is the validation of implementations of self-stabilizing algorithms including the above mentioned transformers. Algorithms and transformers are usually described in pseudo-code and correctness is proved using mathematical techniques. Converting this into executable code for sensor nodes is a challenging task. This is mainly due to the event-based programming style and the limited resources nodes have at their disposal. Verifying distributed programs, which incorporate wireless communication, is difficult and supporting tools are still rare. To tackle this problem this paper introduces the SelfWISE framework. SelfWISE consists of a language for expressing self-stabilizing algorithms, a runtime environment for simulating algorithms in wireless networks, and supporting tools. The SelfWISE language is close to languages used in theoretical works to describe self-stabilizing algorithms. A compiler translates SelfWISE specifications and links them to implementations of the above mentioned transformers. The resulting code is executable on real WSNs. The compiler verifiably preserves the self-stabilization property. Development, evaluation, and debugging of self-stabilizing algorithms is considerably facilitated by utilizing SelfWISE. Hence, it bridges the gap between designing self-stabilizing algorithms and programming sensor network hardware.

2 Self-Stabilization

The majority of programming languages for sensor network applications currently follows an event-based style. This style reflects hardware characteristics, where components have non-blocking interfaces and signal interrupts upon completion of actions. Interrupts are generated by sensors, timers, or message reception. This type of programming seems natural for sensor nodes, but it can complicate program design. Asynchronous events due to state changes, non-blocking calls, and the coordination of multiple events are not trivial to handle. Furthermore, the specification of a distributed algorithm in an event-based language can be rather complex. An alternative paradigm uses a state-based concept relying on an execution model with rule evaluation. Expressing algorithms with rules also matches well the view taken by many developers of distributed algorithms. Self-stabilizing algorithms also follow a style with a state-based foundation.

2.1 Definitions and Notations

A WSN is represented by a graph, in which the n vertices represent the sensor nodes and edges represent bidirectional communication links. Let $G = (V, E)$ be such a graph. A set of local variables defines the state of a node. Let s_i denote the state of node $v_i \in V$. A tuple of local states $(s_1, s_2, \dots, s_n)$ forms a *configuration* of the WSN and defines the global state. An *execution* is a sequence $c_0, c_1, c_2, \dots$ of configurations such that the transition from c_i to c_{i+1} is caused by the execution of an algorithm on a node. Algorithms consist of rules in the form of guarded statements:

$$guard_i \longrightarrow statement_i$$

Guards are Boolean expressions based on the state of a node and the states of its neighbors only (i.e., guards are defined using the local view of a node). The semantics of an algorithm is that whenever a node executes, it executes the statements corresponding to a rule whose guard evaluates to true. Statements can only change the local state. If more than one guard is satisfied, then one of them is chosen non-deterministically. A *move* of a node is the execution of a rule. A rule is called *enabled* if its guard evaluates to true, otherwise it is called *disabled*. A node is called *enabled* if one of its rules is enabled.

The fault-free state of a system is defined by a predicate $\mathcal{P}$ over the global state of the system. A configuration is called *legitimate* relative to $\mathcal{P}$ if it satisfies $\mathcal{P}$. A system is *self-stabilizing* with respect to $\mathcal{P}$ if the following holds:

1. Closure property: A transition always moves a legitimate configuration into another legitimate configuration.
2. Convergence property: An execution starting from any configuration reaches a legitimate configuration within a finite number of transitions.

It is assumed that faults may corrupt the configuration of a system, but not its behavior, i. e., the rules are stored in a fault resilient memory.

The following example illustrates the concept of self-stabilization. The algorithm constructs a spanning tree. In distributed systems, a spanning tree is an very important concept, since it is the basis for complex distributed protocols such as routing or data collection. Several self-stabilizing algorithms for this problem have been proposed [6]. The presented algorithm is according to Dolev et al. [4]. It is a non-uniform algorithm, i.e., it is assumed that one node has been selected to be the root of the tree. The state of a node is described by the variables *dist* and *parent*. The first stores the current distance to the root and the second stores the currently selected parent node. To formally define the rules the following expressions are defined for each vertex v:

$$minN(w, v) \equiv w \in N(v) \wedge \forall x \in N(v) : w.dist \leq x.dist$$
$$minD(v) \equiv \min\{w.dist \mid w \in N(v)\}$$

Here $N(v)$ denotes the set of neighbors of v. Note that $minNeighbor(null, v)$ evaluates to false for every node v. The algorithm consists of two rules. The first rule is only executed by the root node, it sets the variables to 0 resp. *null*. The second rule is executed by all other nodes. Its responsibility is to guarantee that a node always selects a neighboring node as its parent that has the lowest distance to the root. The predicate $\mathcal{P}$ defining the fault-free state for this algorithm is as follows: The directed graph induced by the values of the variable *parent* forms a spanning tree.

Root node: $\neg\,(parent = null \wedge dist = 0)$
$\quad\longrightarrow parent := null,\, dist := 0$
Other node: $\neg\,(minN(parent, v) \wedge dist = minD(v) + 1)$
$\quad\longrightarrow$ choose $w \in N(v)$ with $minN(w, v), parent := w, dist := minD(v) + 1$

Early work on self-stabilizing algorithms relied on the assumption that two neighboring nodes cannot make a move simultaneously. This greatly simplifies the verification of algorithms and also provides a simple means to guarantee the atomicity of reading the states of neighboring nodes. But this assumption is difficult to implement and it is against the spirit of distributed systems since it does not allow for concurrency and scalability. Therefore, different kinds of daemons were introduced:

- Central daemon: At any time only a single enabled node can make a move.
- Synchronous daemon: All enabled nodes make their moves concurrently.
- Distributed daemon: At a given moment, an arbitrary nonempty subset of the enabled nodes makes a move.

Note that an algorithm that is self-stabilizing under a distributed daemon is necessarily self-stabilizing under a central and a synchronous daemon but not vice versa. A daemon is called *fair* if an enabled node is not continuously prevented from making a move. The above described algorithm is self-stabilizing for a fair central daemon.

A very important property of self-stabilizing systems is that they can be built in a layered fashion. This is also referred to as the composition of self-stabilizing algorithms. For example many algorithms are layered on top of a self-stabilizing spanning tree algorithm as proposed above. The idea is rather simple. Let A_1 and A_2 be algorithms such that no variables written by A_2 are used by A_1. The composition of A_1 and A_2 is the algorithm that has all variables and all actions of both algorithms. A_2 begins stabilization only after A_1 has stabilized, i.e., the postcondition of A_1 is the precondition of A_2. The resulting composed algorithm is self-stabilizing with the same properties as the underlying algorithms.

2.2 Self-Stabilizing Algorithms for WSNs

It is well known that WSNs are inherently fault-prone due to the shared wireless communication channel. Often nodes can communicate with each other only with a very low probability. Moreover, node failures due to crashes and energy exhaustion are commonplace. These faults can drive a portion of a WSN to be arbitrarily corrupted and hence to become inconsistent with the rest of the network. Since many of these faults are transient in nature, self-stabilization is an appealing approach to achieve fault-tolerance in WSNs. In particular the fact that they rely on local information is of big advantage. Unfortunately, their usage in WSNs is not straight forward. The problem with the central daemon was already mentioned above. But there are more issues to be resolved: How can a node access the state of a neighbor and how to assure the atomicity of moves?

Many of the arising issues have been addressed in literature. Most of this work is based on the concept of transformers. These are procedures that take as input any self-stabilizing algorithm and produce a semantically equivalent algorithm that works under weaker assumptions. For example Turau and Weyer introduced a transformer that allows to use an algorithm designed for the central daemon with a distributed daemon [14]. The transformed algorithm is self-stabilizing even in case of occasional message losses. The same objective was pursued by other transformers such as Write all with collisions (WAC) [8] or LME which is based on local mutual exclusion [2]. Both transformers prevent the execution of neighboring nodes.

To overcome the limitations of the shared memory model, Herman et al. introduced with the *cached sensornet transformation* (CST) a communication model suitable for WSNs [7]. The basic idea is as follows. Every node has a local cache where it stores the state of each of its neighbors. The evaluation of the guards is based on the data contained in this cache. Each node periodically broadcasts its own state, this way neighboring nodes keep their cache up-to-date in the case of message losses.

3 Related Work

Rule-based languages for programming sensor networks have been proposed by several authors. Rules are usually expressed by guarded statements. In most cases the guards are predicates defined on the state of a node (including its sensors) and its neighbors. The statements are not restricted to local state changes (e.g., messages may be sent). In some proposals the periodicity of evaluating the guards can also be specified [12].

FACTS is a powerful rule-based middleware for sensor networks [13] providing a unified abstraction for communication, execution, and network state management. Guarded statements are defined using so-called facts, which conceptually constitute the state of a node. Statements can change the local facts by altering properties and they can send information to any other node. In a way FACTS operates like a inference engine or a production system in AI. As with many rule-based languages FACTS programs are compiled into an intermediate byte-code, which is executed by a virtual machine. Being more general FACTS can be used to realize self-stabilizing algorithms, but it does not provide the convenience and support provided by SelfWISE (i.e., the abstractions neighborhood is not provided). Furthermore, it follows the concept of a virtual machine, whereas SelfWISE follows a compiler approach. Frank et al. [5] also use a rule-based approach to assign roles to individual nodes in a sensor network. The intention of their work is to facilitate the configuration of a sensor network and their language is geared towards this purpose and therefore not suited to implement self-stabilizing algorithms.

The workings that come closest to SelfWISE are ProSe [1] and DESAL [3]. The intention of ProSe is to simplify the construction and deployment of sensor network protocols. It automates the process of code generation and thereby shields the programmer from low-level details. ProSe provides a language to express guarded command programs that are translated into nesC programs to be executed on the TinyOS platform. The transformation preserves the self-stabilization property by using the WAC model [8]. Compared to ProSe, SelfWISE is a framework supporting general abstractions such as transformation, neighborhood, and composition, which can be bound to concrete realizations.

DESAL is another proposal for a rule-based component specification based on communication by a shared variable abstraction. Periodic scheduling of guarded commands compensates for the lack of event-triggered execution. The expressiveness of the language allows the specification of self-stabilizing algorithms, but it does not provide any support for transformers. An important feature of DESAL is to enable coordinated actuations.

Somehow related is the work of Müllner et al. [9]. They provide a simulation framework to derive fault-tolerance measures for self-stabilizing algorithms. It assists developers during the process of algorithm verification, but does not provide the concept of transformation nor does it support the generation of executable code.

4 SelfWISE

SelfWISE is a framework that facilitates the development and evaluation of self-stabilizing algorithms in wireless sensor networks. The framework can be used for specifying self-stabilizing algorithms and for developing applications running on top of them. The algorithms are specified in a rule-based language by using abstractions provided by the framework. Additionally an interface for accessing the node state from the application exists. This interface can be utilized by application developer for accessing the outcome of a self-stabilizing algorithm. In the case of the spanning tree algorithm a data-gathering application needs the parent node information for sending sensor readings to the root node.

4.1 Overview

The SelfWISE framework is the mediator between the node platform, the self-stabilizing algorithms, and the on-top running application. Three main design goals exist for SelfWISE. First, the framework should provide an abstraction of the low-level details of wireless nodes. Developers of self-stabilizing algorithm must be shielded from hardware-specific characteristics and the properties of the wireless channel. Reusability is the second design goal. Common tasks such as neighborhood management or exchanging node state must be provided by the framework and should not be newly implemented for each algorithm. The last design goal is to ensure the preservation of the self-stabilizing properties of the algorithms in the distributed context by applying appropriate transformations.

In Fig. 1 the overall architecture of the SelfWISE framework is shown. The figure depicts the components that are executed on each node of the network. SelfWISE does not depend on a particular platform. Any platform that supports sending and receiving of packets and handling of timer events can be used. Additional properties that are needed by algorithms, e.g., reading sensor values, are queried in a platform-specific way. All platforms must provide a node identifier to distinguish the origin of the received messages among neighboring nodes. The SelfWISE framework uses these interfaces of the platform and provides an abstraction for the self-stabilizing algorithm and the application.

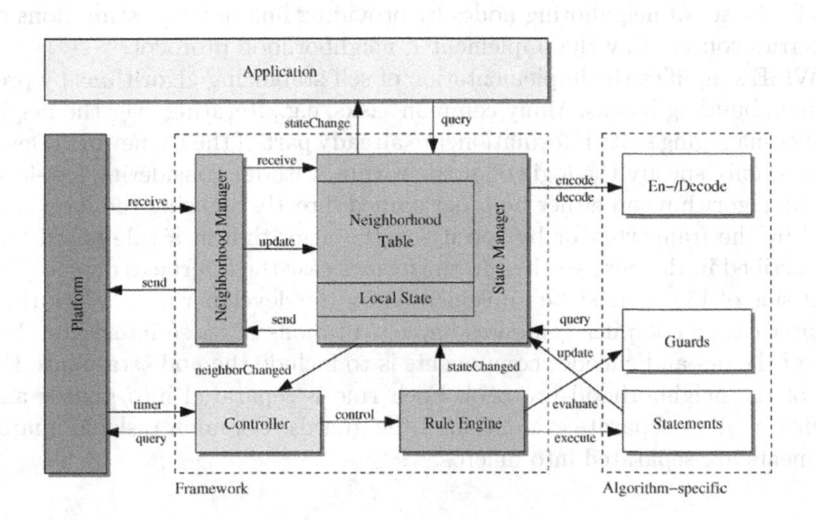

Fig. 1. Architecture of the SelfWISE framework

The controller, rule engine, state manager, and neighborhood manager are the main interfaces of the framework. Implementations of the interfaces are called components. For a single interface different implementations may exist. Alternative components may provide different functionalities. E.g., the neighborhood manager depends on whether the communication protocol stack already provides neighborhood information or a two-hop neighborhood is needed. The controller is responsible for scheduling the execution of the self-stabilizing algorithm and for applying the transformation. For each transformation, a different controller must be implemented. Depending on the transformation, the controller performs its tasks periodically, upon changes within the neighborhood, or in a hybrid way.

The rule engine splits the execution of the algorithm into the guard evaluation phase and the rule execution phase. In the former phase all guards were evaluated in order to check if a node is enabled or not. If a node is enabled the controller decides, based on the used transformation, whether the node performs a move or not. In the first case, the controller initiate the execution of the corresponding statement via the rule engine. The evaluation of the guards and the execution of the statements depend on the local view stored in the state manager. The rule engine is also responsible to ensure atomicity of these actions.

The state manager maintains the state information of the node and of all its neighbors. The rule engine notifies the state manager in case the local node state has changed due to the execution of a statement. Afterwards, the state manager broadcasts the local state via the neighborhood manager. The node state is normally integrated as piggyback data in the existing neighborhood discovery broadcasts. On reception of such a broadcast, the cached values of the neighbor state are updated. The state manager implements the cached sensornet transformation as described in Section 2.2. The neighborhood manager is responsible to identify the set of neighboring nodes by providing link quality estimations or other metrics collected by the implemented neighborhood protocol.

SelfWISE simplifies the implementation of self-stabilizing algorithms by providing main building blocks. Many common tasks, e.g., iterating over the neighborhood or managing state information, are already part of the framework. Developers must only specify the logic of an algorithm, without considering low-level details. An algorithm can either be programmed directly by using the interfaces provided by the framework or by specifying the algorithm in a rule-based language described in the next section. In the former case the interfaces depicted on the right side of Fig. 2 must be implemented by the developer of an algorithm. In the later case a compiler generates implementations of these interfaces. The purpose of the de- and encoder components is to include the node state into the packets of the neighborhood protocol. Each rule is separated into guards and statements to allow separate evaluation of the guards. Common tasks in guards or statements are separated into macros.

4.2 Language

The rule-based language of SelfWISE is restricted to self-stabilizing algorithms. Therefore, no language constructs are allowed that violate this property, i.e., statements can only update the local state and guards have read-only access to the local state and the state of the neighbors as described in Section 2.1. In Fig. 2 the source code of the spanning tree algorithm from Section 2.1 is given. Since the algorithm is non-uniform node identifiers are needed to convert the algorithm into a uniform one. It is assumed that only the root node has node identifier 0. In the following, the main language constructs are presented by means of this example.

The name of an algorithm must be unique within the system, since this name introduces a namespace for variables. This is necessary in the case that more than one algorithm is executed at the same time. In the first block all variables must

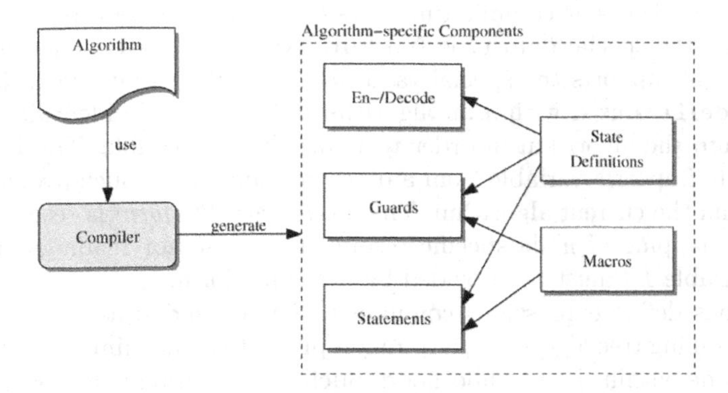

Fig. 2. Compilation process

be declared. After this block, pre-initialized variables are declared, which are initialized at the beginning of every guard evaluation phase. Each rule of an algorithm starts with the keyword **rule** followed by a name. The name of a rule must be unique in the scope of an algorithm and is used for providing debug information. Guards and statements are separated by the token '->'. Guards are evaluated like Boolean expression in programming languages. Statements are simple value assignments to the local state.

```
algorithm SpanningTree;
    public map NodeID Platform.ID as ID;
    public int dist;
    public NodeID parent;
    declare int minD := min(Neighbors v.dist);
rule R1:
     ID = 0 and !(parent = null and dist = 0) ->
         parent := null;
         dist := 0;
rule R2:
     ID != 0 and !(parent in (Neighbors v.ID : v.dist = minD)
            and dist = minD + 1) ->
         parent := choose(Neighbors v.ID : v.dist = minD);
         dist := minD + 1;
```

Fig. 3. Implementation of the spanning tree algorithm

The main differences to a formal definition are that all variables have a visibility and a data type. The visibility of a variable can be private or public. Visibility public means the variable can be read by neighbors. In formal definitions visibility and data types are only implicitly given. Both are added to provide semantic checks at compile time. Besides common data types like integer or Boolean the special data type **NodeId** exists to represent identifiers of nodes. This type supports the special value *null* indicating that the variable is unset. If **NodeID** is used within an algorithm, platform node identifiers must be mapped into the algorithm in order to make them accessible. The keyword **map** is used to import a variable from a different namespace. Such a variable is readable within the current algorithm. The namespace *Platform* is reserved and provides the mapping of node specific resources, e.g., sensor readings or local time. The variable *ID* must be provided by every platform.

Declarations define expressions common to guards and statements. In the case of the spanning tree algorithm, a common property is the minimum distance to the root node within the neighborhood. Such a declaration is accessed like a local variable. This way atomicity is provided, values of such variables do not change between evaluating the guards and executing a statement.

Since self-stabilizing algorithms are based on the local view upon the neighborhood of a node, the states of all neighbors must be accessible. The keyword **Neighbors** provides access to all neighbors of a node. The expression (**Neighbors** v : v.dist $=$ 0) selects all neighbors where the value of the variable *dist* is 0. The semantics of the quantifiers $\forall$ and $\exists$ is supported by combining such sets with the keywords **forall** or **exist**. For example the expression **forall**(**Neighbors** v : v.dist $=$ 0) evaluates to true if the variable *dist* of all neighbors is equal to 0. Besides sets of nodes, sets of values can be created. The expression (**Neighbors** v.dist) creates the set of all values of the variable *dist* within the neighborhood. Such a set can be further constrained. The set of identifiers of nodes where the variable *dist* has the value *minD* is identified by (**Neighbors** v.ID : v.dist $=$ minD). For such sets the operators **min**, **max**, **in**, and **choose** are defined. The **in** operator checks if the operand on left side is contained in the set on the right side. An element is non-deterministically chosen from the set by the **choose** operator.

The SelfWISE framework also supports the composition of self-stabilizing algorithms, as described in Section 2.1. An algorithm can use variables from any other algorithm running in the framework simply by mapping state variables into the local namespace using the same mechanism like mapping node identifiers. If a self-stabilizing algorithm uses the parent state information of the spanning tree algorithm, the statement

private map NodeId SpanningTree.parent **as** myParent;

gives a read-only reference to this variable.

4.3 Run-Time Environment

The run-time environment supports two modi: simulation and real deployment. The simulation environment enhances the rule execution by adding additional trace information for debugging and evaluation purposes. The state of every node in the network is logged over time in order to check that the self-stabilizing algorithm leads to a configuration satisfying predicate $\mathcal{P}$. Additionally, the numbers of moves for each rule are recorded. With this information, an algorithm developer can verify the properties of his algorithm and compare its behavior in different topologies or with other existing solutions.

To integrate self-stabilizing algorithms into applications for wireless sensor networks a standard interface is defined. An event `stateChanged` is fired, whenever the state of the local node or a state of a neighbor has changed. The application can also query the value of all state variables. For accessing algorithm specific state variables, the application must use the state definitions generated by the SelfWISE compiler. The neighborhood information, e.g., link quality or node state, can be accessed via the query interface (see Fig. 1).

4.4 First Prototype

A proof of concept implementation of the SelfWISE framework is accomplished in [10]. The controller implements the randomized round-based transformation proposed in [14]. The main goal of this first prototype was to show that the compilation process and the underlying transformation preserve the self-stabilizing properties of algorithms written for a central daemon in a distributed context.

The prototype was built on top of the TinyOS 2.x platform. One of the main benefits of TinyOS is that it provides a standardized interface for several hardware platforms and an integrated simulator. The SelfWISE interfaces are mapped to nesC interfaces. TOSSIM, the integrated simulator, is used for testing the implementation of the framework. Utilizing the Python binding of TOSSIM enables the framework to simulate the same algorithm under different topologies and start configurations. The compiler employs JavaCC as parser generator.

The memory limitations of wireless sensor nodes make an implementation of the set operations rather difficult, since the number of neighbors is not known a priori. Therefore, all set operations defined by the language are implemented as iterators over the entries of the neighborhood table.

In a first step, self-stabilizing algorithms for finding a maximal independent set, a minimum dominating set, and a spanning tree are implemented with the rule-based language of SelfWISE. All algorithms are self-stabilizing with respect to a central daemon. Simulations where performed with 25 nodes with different packet loss rates. The simulation runs show that the SelfWISE framework preserves the self-stabilizing property. Additionally, the results are comparable to early hand-written transformations. This verifies the quality of the generated transformation of the compiler and the framework is equal to a hand-written version with respect to stabilization. The memory consumption of the framework of around 20 KByte of ROM and 110 Byte of RAM is acceptable for the limited resources in wireless sensor networks.

5 Conclusion

The proposed SelfWISE framework eases the development of self-stabilizing algorithms in the field of wireless sensor networks. The first prototype shows that the rule-based language provides a manageable abstraction for easily transferring theoretical specified self-stabilizing algorithms from literature. The compiler and the transformer of the SelfWISE framework preserve the self-stabilizing property in a distributed context.

The next steps are two-fold. First, the SelfWISE framework will be integrated in a real deployment, in order to evaluate the characteristics and stabilizing properties of several standard algorithms under real conditions. Second, different transformations will be implemented for the SelfWISE framework in order to verify the strengths and weaknesses of existing transformers in different topologies and under different fault models.

References

1. M. Arumugam, L. Wang, and S. S. Kulkarni. A Case Study on Prototyping Power Management Protocols for Sensor Networks. In *Proc. of the 8th Int. Symp. on Stabilization, Safety, and Security of Distributed Systems (SSS'06)*, 2006.
2. J. Beauquier, A. Kumar Datta, M. Gradinariu, and F. Magniette. Self-Stabilizing Local Mutual Exclusion and Daemon Refinement. *Chic. J. Theor. Comput.*, 2002(1), 2002.
3. A. Dalton, W. P. McCartney, and K. Ghosh-Dastidar et al. DESAL$^{\alpha}$: An Implementation of the Dynamic Embedded Sensor-Actuator Language. In *Proc. of the 17th Int. Conf. on Computer Communications and Networks (IC3N'08)*, Washington DC, USA, 2008.
4. S. Dolev. *Self-Stabilization.* MIT Press, Cambridge, MA, USA, 2000.
5. C. Frank and K. Römer. Algorithms for Generic Role Assignment in Wireless Sensor Networks. In *Proc. of the Third ACM Int. Conf. on Embedded Networked Sensor Systems (Sensys'05)*, 2005.
6. F. C. Gärtner. A Survey of Self-Stabilizing Spanning-Tree Construction Algorithms. Technical Report IC/2003/38, Swiss Federal Institute of Technology (EPFL), Lausanne, Switzerland, 2003.
7. T. Herman. Models of Self-Stabilization and Sensor Networks. In *Proc. of the 5th Int. Workshop on Distributed Computing (IWDC'03)*, 2003.
8. S. S. Kulkarni and M. Arumugam. Transformations for Write-All-With-Collision Model. *Comput. Commun.*, 29(2):183–199, 2006.
9. N. Müllner, A. Dhama, and O. Theel. Derivation of Fault-Tolerance Measures of Self-Stabilizing Algorithms by Simulation. In *Proc. of the 41st Annual Simulation Symposium (ANSS'08)*, 2008.
10. K. Pilz. Beschreibungssprache für selbststabilisierende Algorithmen für drahtlose Sensornetze. Diploma thesis, Hamburg University of Technology, Germany, 2008.
11. M. Schneider. Self-Stabilization. *ACM Comput. Surv.*, 25(1):45–67, 1993.
12. S. Sen and R. Cardell-Oliver. A Rule-Based Language for Programming Wireless Sensor Actuator Networks using Frequency and Communication. In *Proc. of the Third Workshop on Embedded Networked Sensors (EmNets'06)*, 2006.
13. K. Terfloth, G. Wittenburg, and J. Schiller. FACTS - A Rule-Based Middleware Architecture for Wireless Sensor Networks. In *Proc. of the First IEEE Int. Conf. on Communication System Software and Middleware (COMSWARE'06)*, 2006.
14. V. Turau and C. Weyer. Fault Tolerance in Wireless Sensor Networks through Self-Stabilization. *Int. J. of Commun. Networks and Distr. Sys.*, 2(1):78–98, 2009.

MASDynamics: Toward Systemic Modeling of Decentralized Agent Coordination

Jan Sudeikat[1] and Wolfgang Renz

Multimedia Systems Laboratory,
Hamburg University of Applied Sciences,
Berliner Tor 7, 20099 Hamburg, Germany
{sudeikat|wr}@informatik.haw-hamburg.de

Abstract. Enabling distributed software systems to purposefully *self–organize*, i.e. to adapt to dynamically changing execution contexts by the collective adjustment of individual components, challenges current development practices. Since the dynamics of self–organizing systems arise from agent coaction, developers cannot directly infer the macroscopic system behavior from established agent design models. This paper plays a part in an ongoing research effort that addresses the provision of self–organizing processes as *design elements*, i.e. reusable patterns of agent interrelations. We propose a *systemic* modeling approach and support the application independent description of (inter–)agent coordination patterns by a domain specific language that allows to map interrelations of agent activity to detailed agent design models. This facilitates the separation of decentralized coordination strategies from domain specific agent implementations and enables development teams to treat nature–inspired coordination strategies, which steer self–organizing dynamics, as design concepts. In addition, we show how this modeling conception provides a declarative programming approach by the automated supplementation of conventional developed agent models with non–linear, inter–agent coordination mechanisms.

1 Introduction

Conceiving complex distributed software systems as Multi–Agent Systems (MAS), i.e. sets of autonomous, pro–active actors, demands the effective coordination of agent activities. The utilization of self–organizing dynamics for the coordination of agent–based applications is a topic of current research [1]. The term *self–organization* refers to physical, biological and social phenomena, where global structures arise from the local interactions of autonomous individuals (e.g. particles, cells, agents, etc.). The underlying dynamics that give rise to these phenomena enable systems to adapt to varying environments and/or to maintain structures while being subject to perturbations. Enabling similar

[1] Jan Sudeikat is doctoral candidate at the Distributed Systems and Information Systems (VSIS) group, Department of Informatics, Faculty of Mathematics, Informatics and Natural Sciences, University of Hamburg, Vogt–Kölln–Str. 30, 22527 Hamburg, Germany, jan.sudeikat@informatik.uni-hamburg.de

dynamics in software engineering contexts promises a novel approach to the design of inherently decentralized, adaptive and robust applications. However, the utilization of self–organizing dynamics is particularly challenging as developers cannot directly infer the macroscopic system dynamics from models of local agent activities.

Since the design of self-organizing applications on the drawing–board is impaired, the bionic *reuses* of nature–inspired coordination *metaphors* [2] and *mechanisms* [3] are dominant development strategies (cf. section 2). Self–organiz-ing applications do not necessarily require the utilization of specialized coordination mechanisms (cf. section 2), but these provide means for non–linear agent interactions, including perturbations and feedbacks, that facilitate the construction of self–regulatory system behaviors. Their utilization as *design patterns* has been argued (e.g. [3]) and coordination frameworks are under active development that support coordination mechanism implementation (cf. section 2.2).

The establishment of self–organizing dynamics can be traced back to (1) *information flows* and (2) the ability of agents to adjust their local activities [4,5]. These information flows and according behavior adjustments establish *causal* influences within agent populations. Self–organization can be observed when agent activities are interrelated and these interrelations enforce feedback loops within agent populations [6,7]. Recently, modeling notions used in research on *System Dynamics* [21] have been transferred to MAS designs in order to provide explicit models of activity interrelations and feedback structures [8,7] (cf. section 3.1). The utilization of this modeling level allows to infer the qualitative dynamic behavior of agent populations from their causal structure [9].

It is an open research question how to support systematic design and development practices for self–organizing MAS. Here, we discuss the utilization of a systemic modeling level to describe nature–inspired coordination schemes in terms of macroscopic agent interrelationships. This modeling level supplements established agent–oriented design approaches and facilitates the separation of agent functionality from coordination schemes. In addition, we present a dedicated Domain Specific Language (DSL) and configuration approach that allows agent developers to *supplement* conventionally designed agent models with means of decentralized agent coordination. Agents serve as *vehicles* for functionality which is carried out autonomously and pro-actively. Developers coordinate agent activities by declaring that specific agent elements are subject to coordination interactions. Agent autonomy is preserved as agent models process the perceived coordination information and chose their course of action.

This paper is structured as follows. In the next section, we outline means to the decentralized coordination of agents (section 2.1) and previous work on encapsulating these means as implementation artifacts (section 2.2). In Section 3, we discuss the modeling of decentralized coordinated MAS by transferring systemic modeling notions to agent–based application designs (3.1) and present the a dedicated DSL (section 3.2) to facilitate model construction and automate agent/mechanism configuration. Finally, the modeling approach is exemplified in section 4 before we conclude and give prospects for future work.

2 Self–Organizing MAS Development

Here, we discuss the construction of adaptive MAS by conceiving the simultaneous, localized adaption of individual agents. This design approach is attractive as it supports adaptivity due to *decentralized* application designs, i.e. in absence of dedicated *controlling* entities [10].

2.1 Engineering Self–Organization by Decentralized Coordination

Developers of decentralized MAS face the challenge to ensure collective phenomena by revising the coaction of agents [11]. A prominent design strategy is the *bionic* reuse of *interaction patterns* that can be observed in physical, biological, and social systems [4]. Figure 1 denotes the conceptual model of applying nature–inspired designs in MAS development. Developers intend that the constructed application (*MAS*), which is composed of *Agent(s)* and *Environment(s)* [12], exhibits a specific macroscopic observable behavior (*System Behavior Space*). Following [9], the space of macroscopic MAS behaviors can be defined in terms of MAS *configurations*, i.e. the sum of agents configurations [13], and the *transitions* between these when agents collectively adjust their behavioral state. Taking inspiration from natural systems, well–known phenomena (*Self–Regulatory Coordination Metaphor*, e.g. ant foraging, insect colony brood sorting, etc. [2,7]) are selected that are known to exhibit the intended dynamical behavior. Metaphors provide patterns of *Agent Activity Interrelations*. These interrelations describe combinations of *Information Flows* and how the received informations are used within agents to adjust their observable behavior (*Behavior Adjustment*) [4]. The adjustment of local agent behaviors are defined in the detailed agent models, based on the specific agent architecture (ranging from purely reactive to purely deliberative). Information flows can be realized by *Direct Information Exchanges*, e.g. between agent components (agent–internal) or by direct communication between agent instances (inter–agent). *Decentralized Coordination Mechanisms* (DCMs) [3,1] (e.g. *pheromones*, *computational fields*, *tags*, etc.; reviewed in [14]) provide means for non–linear agent interactions. These are realized by specific computational techniques (*Computational Technique*; e.g. Tuple Spaces, Token exchange, etc.), that are either *mediated* by MAS environments or provide agents with additional information via *direct* agent interactions, thus supplementing the sensory input to agent instances [12].

The nature of the *design patterns* that support self–organization within MAS is a subject of debate. Pattern/mechanism discussions refer either to the applied computational mechanisms [14,3,1] or their sources of inspiration [2]. We propose to distinguish between *Coordination Metaphors* that describe the intended dynamical system behavior, and the applied (decentralized) *Coordination Mechanisms* which can be used to resemble the detailed interaction mechanisms that were identified in natural self–organizing systems (cf. figure 1). Resolving this ambiguity supports top–down refinement procedures [7].

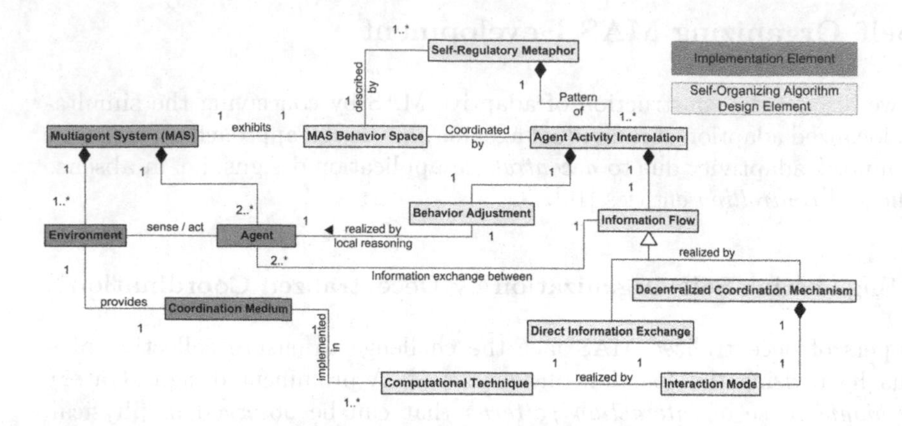

Fig. 1. Conceptual model of self–organizing MAS development.

2.2 Providing Decentralized Coordination Mechanisms as Services

Current DCM definitions serve as MAS analysis and design concepts [15]. The selection of DCMs typically forces development teams to (re–)implement mechanisms within agent execution environments or general purpose coordination frameworks [16]. In [5], a layered architecture has been proposed to provides DCM implementations as (middle–ware) services. This approach combines the coordination architecture presented in [17] and the notion of coordination as development services [18]. Following [17], the utilization of *coordination media* has been tailored to provide DCM implementations. Flows of application specific data are enabled by observing agent execution and (1) *publishing* occurrences of agent–internal events as well as (2) *subscribing* agents to publicly accessible media [18]. Subscribers are notified of the publications from population members by triggering agent–internal events [17,5]. Medium implementations realize the dynamics of coordination mechanisms, possibly by using third–party coordination frameworks and environment models (cf. [5]). This conception is independent from the agent architecture, as the event definitions can range from reactive state machine transitions [17] to deliberative goal / plan adoptions [5]. Agent autonomy is preserved since the publication of events is transparent to the agent, e.g. taking place via *co–efficient* background processing (discussed in [19]). Triggering events in subscribed agents preserves autonomy as well since local agent reasoning decides for the courses of action to take, e.g. to inhibit events that are not appropriate for the current execution context [5].

A prototype implementation has been realized as an add–on to the *Jadex* agent system [5].[1] The separation of agent coordination schemes from agent functionality is supported by a declarative usage interface. Developers document agent models with *annotations* (meta–data information) that describe which agent internal events are subject to coordination and which internal information

[1] http://vsis-www.informatik.uni-hamburg.de/projects/jadex/

(e.g. belief values, goal parameters, etc.) are to be transmitted. The annotations also allow to parametrize DCM realizations by providing *static* parameters, as well as *dynamic* parameters that are evaluated at run–time. E.g. the radius of computational fields can be controlled by computed utility values in the emitting agent to allow the dynamics adjustment of the communication strength [5]. The minimal intrusive usage interface facilitates the exchange and reconfiguration of coordination mechanism implementations without affecting agent implementations (cf. section 4).

3 Modeling and Reuse of Self–Organizing Dynamics

In order to support the conception, reuse and combination of coordination metaphors (cf. section 2.1) in MAS development, we discuss how to model the qualitative dynamics that steer self–organizing dynamics by using system dynamics concepts. A DSL facilitates the reuse of coordination metaphors and enables programming MAS coordination by automating the configuration / annotation of agent models. Consequently, the sources for self–organizing dynamics, namely the inter–agent feedback cycles, become elements of MAS design and can be treated in parallel to established Agent–Oriented Software Engineering (AOSE) development processes [20].

3.1 Systemic Modeling Self–Organizing MAS Dynamics

The establishment of self–organizing dynamics can be traced back to feedback loops within agent populations [6,4] (cf. section 2). Therefore, the explicit modeling of feedback structures, by transferring *system dynamics* modeling concepts [21] to MAS design, has been proposed to describe the requirements on self–organizing MAS [9], design metaphor behaviors [7] as well as MAS organizational dynamics [8]. System dynamics modeling describes the timely behavior of systems in terms of *system properties* and their *causal* relations [21]. System properties describe the accumulative values of system qualities. Causal relations denote the rates of changes of these properties. Causalities denote either positive (additive) or negative (subtractive) influences. Positive influences describe that increases in originating properties enforce that the values of connected properties increase in subsequent time steps. Negative links describe changes in opposite directions, i. e. that increases enforce the decrease in connected properties. Circular causal structures form feedback loops that are either balancing (B; by an odd number of negative links) or reinforcing (R; by an even number of negative links).

Systemic models of MAS dynamics describe the operational state of MAS in terms of accumulative values of organizational concepts (in agreement with [13]), i.e. *role* and *group* occupations [8]. These are widely applied concepts to abstract agent behaviors. *Roles* characterize agent activities within organizational contexts and *groups* partition MAS into sets of individuals that share characteristics, e.g. common goal commitments [22]. A prominent graph-based notation are the so–called *Causal Loop Diagrams* (CLD) [21] that model causalities as edges between property nodes. In [8], this notation has been tailored to model MAS by introducing MAS specific node types and causality semantics. Figure 2 exemplifies the proposed modeling approach and notation in a hypothetical setting. Two agent types (*ProducerA*, *ProducerB*) create instances of *Product* elements. As the number of these agents increases, the number of accumulated products increases as well. This is modeled as a positive causal relation. Products require storage space, therefore reducing the amount available *Storage Capacity* (negative link). Assuming that the number of activated producers is controlled by the storage capacity (positive link), the system exhibits a balancing (negative) feedback loop. The identification of feedback loops and causal relations allows the qualitative examination of the exhibited system behavior by interpreting the relations and examining their mathematical models [21]. E.g. balancing feedbacks are known to enforce s–shaped (a.k.a. goal–seeking) behaviors, as visualized in figure 2 (C) by a system of differential equations.

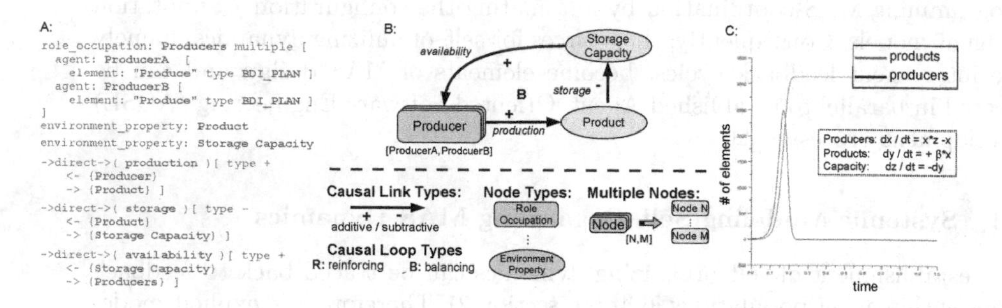

Fig. 2. MASDynamics: DSL (A; cf. section 3.2), graphical notation (B) and exhibited dynamic (C).

3.2 MASDynamics: A Coordination Language

The proposed modeling language supports two modeling levels. First, the description of coordination metaphors is enabled by relating system properties to agent implementations and describing their causalities. Secondly, the realization of causal links by DCMs can be declared and configured (cf. section 3.2).

Modeling Macroscopic MAS Dynamics Figure 3 relates MASDynamics language elements to the conceptual model of self–organizing MAS that was introduced in section 2.1 (top right) and MAS meta–model elements (bottom). Following studies of MAS meta–models (e.g. [23]) and organizational modeling approaches [22], we describe the observable agent behavior by *roles*. The exhibition of roles leads to the execution of *tasks*, e.g. message exchanges or the modification of the MAS environment [23]. The adjustment of agent behaviors is controlled by agent internal *reasoning* that takes input from the agent *knowledge*–base.

MASDynamic (*MASDynamics*) models describe the logical structure of coordination metaphors (*Self–Regulatory Metaphor*) and comprise four kinds of *System Properties.* These macroscopic MAS state can be described by the accumulative values of role occupations (*RoleOccupation*), the number of groups of a certain type (*GroupCount*) and/or the number of participants in specific groups (*GroupMembershipCount*). These properties are connected by causalities (*Causal Link*) that describe the effects of agent interrelations. *Direct* links model effects due to direct information exchanges. Interrelations can also be established by DCM implementations (cf. section 2.1), i.e. exhibit non–linear dynamics (*Decentralized Coordination Link*). The declaration of the later links comprise an optional reference to a *Mechanisms Configuration* that allows to automate the configuration and parametrization of DCM instances.

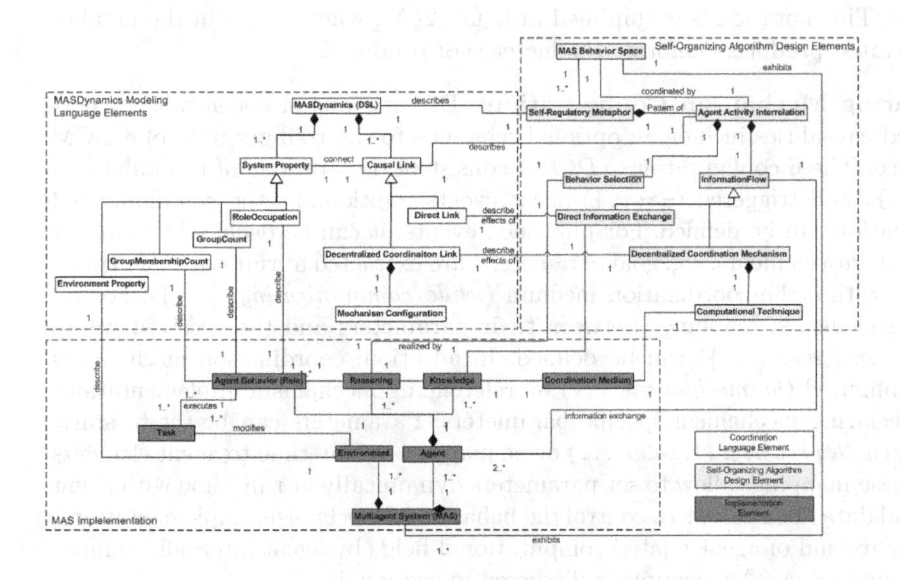

Fig. 3. Coordination modeling language meta model.

MASDynamic models can be specified in XML format. A DSL has been revised[2] to provide a concise notation as well as editing supports (within an eclipse plug–in). The language allows to document coordination schemes and to generate the graphical representations.[3] In addition, the realization of decentralized links can be configured. This allows to encapsulate and reuse coordination schemes in application independent ways.

Following the language meta–model (figure 3), properties are declared by specifying the property type which is separated by a colon and followed by the property name. Optionally, the keyword *multiple* can be specified to de-

[2] using the openArchitectureWare Framework; http://oaw.itemis.de/

[3] using graphviz; http://www.graphviz.org/

note that multiple properties of the specified property exist. Inside the property, agent models can be referenced (agent: *agent_name*) by their model name and an optional list of enclosed agent elements (element: *element_name* type: *element_type_name*). For example in figure 2(A) the amount of activated producer agents is tracked, composed of two agent types that are considered to be activated when the specified plan type is active. State occupations can be refined by an optional condition (*condition:...*) and an optional list of agent elements that inhibit (*inhibited by:...*) state occupations when activated.

Causal links are denoted by the constructs `->direct->( link_name )` and `=>decentral=>( link_name )` to denote direct and decentralized links, respectively. The specification of the link *type* (+/-) is required. Optionally, an interaction rate can be specified to facilitate the generation of simulation models (e.g. discussed in [8]). Links connect lists of publishing (`<-`) and receiving (`->`) properties. This notation is exemplified in figure 2(A), where a rise in the number of activated producers enforces the increase of products.

Declaring Mechanism Configurations Declarations of decentralized coordinated causalities include an optional reference to the configuration of a DCM instance. These configurations (*DCM:*) consist of declarations of the published (`<-{..}`) and triggered (`->{..}`) agent events. Optionally, the communicated information can be defined. For published events, it can be declared that agent internal data elements, e.g. goal parameters, are extracted at run–time and transmitted within the coordination medium (*while communicating:* {...}). For receiving elements, mappings between their parameters and the received values (*while receiving:* {...}) can be defined. In addition, coordination mechanisms are configured (*by mechanism:* ...) by referencing mechanism implementations and declaring mechanism specific parameters. Parameters can be set to static values (*with property:* ... *value* ...) or be mapped at run–time to agent elements [5]. These mappings allow to set parameters dynamically at run–time with agent internal data. This allows to control the behavior of mechanism implementations, e.g. the extend of agent related computational fields by agent internally computed utility values. An example is discussed in section 4.

Self–organized system properties often depend crucially on their (input) parametrization. The declarative configuration and parametrization of patterns of agent activity interrelations as well as the coordination mechanisms facilitates the reuse of coordination strategies, as developers are enabled to save and share them in distinct language files as well as to automate the integration of revised configurations in agent–based applications.

In order to supplement conservatively developed MAS with coordination mechanisms, developers import a generic coordination module and provide a *MASDynamics* configuration file. When agents are initialized, this module (1) looks–up its surrounding agent, (2) extracts the DCM-based coordinations in which the agent participates, (3) loads the DCM-specific implementation(s) of coordination media access and (4) provides the associated mechanisms configuration. After these steps, the loaded set of modules begins to publish / perceive coordination information and influence agents as described in section 2.2.

4 Case Study: Supplementing an Allocation Strategy

The usage of the proposed modeling approach and modeling language is exemplified by supplementing a conservatively developed MAS with a dynamic allocation strategy that takes inspiration from foraging behaviors in *honey bee* societies. Following [24], we examine a cluster of (web–)servers that are allocated to host applications. As the demand of services (e.g. website requests) changes dynamically, it is intended to automate the manual adjustment of static sever allocations by enabling adaptive, autonomous (re–)allocation of server instances. In [24], the dynamic allocation of servers has been approached by resembling the dynamics that honey bee societies exhibit when foraging resources. So–called *scouts* search the environment. The availability of encountered *resources* is communicated along with locally conceivable quality measures (distance to nest, quality of nectar, etc.) are communicated in the nest via so–called *waggle dances.* These are perceived by so–called *foragers* that transport resources to the nest switch to more attractive sites. Figure 4 (A) denotes the systemic requirement of the outlined application (cf. [5] for a detailed discussion of the model refinement). Servers are modeled as agents that are either *associated* (*serving*) to a specific service or are *unbound.* The macroscopic MAS configuration is modeled as the numbers of agents executing these roles. The rate of incoming *jobs* (requests), that are generated by *requesters*, changes dynamically. The system is expected to exhibit two balancing feedback loops. First, the different requests types are to be satisfied (α: negative link). I.e. an increase in requests should enforce the reinforcement of associated servers (α: positive link). Secondly, under-worked servers are to be freed (β: positive link) to allow their recruitment for other allocations (β: negative link).

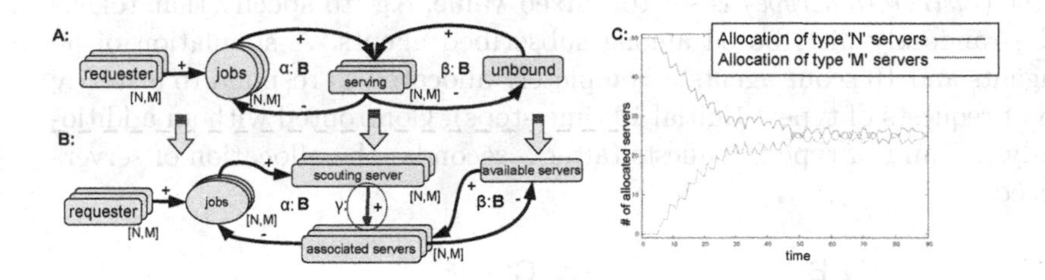

Fig. 4. Case study model [5] and dynamics. A: System requirements. B: Bee–hive inspired coordination dynamics. C: *Responsive* behavior of MAS implementation.

The case study has been implemented in the *Jadex* agent system. It provides an execution environment for agents that follow the *Belief–Desire–Intention* (BDI) architecture [25]. Server agents provide two basic procedural activities, i.e. the abilities (1) to *answer* typed requests and (2) to *change allocations.* A BDI–based design realizes serving activities by plans that are triggered by incoming request messages. The change of allocations is triggered by an agent–internal goal that changes agent registrations in the platform *yellow pages* service (Domain

Facilitator; DF). Foraging agents register to all request types. The agent design is operational, but does not consider self–organizing behaviors. Administrators can manually start and stop agents to set up static server allocations.

The listing 5 (A+B) shows extracts of the MASDynamics model that describes the presented system model given in 4 (B). An environment property (*Jobs*) and three role occupation (*Scout*, *Server*, *Requester*) are specified (listing 5 (A)). E.g. the role *Server* can be played by two agents types (ServerN, ServerM) and denotes the amount of activated server agents. The direct link (*generate*) describes the generation of jobs by requester agents 5 (A). The causality is valid since requesters generate request messages, an increase in requester agents leads to an increase of requests.

In order to allow for the intended dynamic server allocation, it is required to realize a positive causality between scout servers and activated servers, i.e. the activity of scout servers should lead to the recruitment (change of allocation) of servers (4 (B), link: γ). A decentralized coordinated link (*wiggle*) describes the *recruitment* of servers by the communication of Scout agents (listing 5 (B)). This link can be realized non–intrusively by providing the configuration of a DCM. The referenced (*"wiggle_by_token"*) configuration of a token–based coordination mechanism [5] (cf. [14] for a generic discussion of this mechanism type) is outlined in listing listing 5 (C). Occurrences of the plan *advertise* in agents of the type *Scout* are to be published via the token–based mechanism implementation (*deco4mas.mechanism.token.generic.Token*). The value of a plan parameter (*service_type*) is to be transmitted by using a mechanism local identifier (*type*). The serving agent are subscribed to the coordination medium and incoming perceptions trigger the instantiation of the plans (*change_allocation*). A server plan parameter (*service_type*) is set to a transmitted value (referenced with the mechanism internal identifier *type*). Finally, a mechanism specific configuration parameter (*distribution_type*) is set to a fixed value, e.g. to specify that tokens are to be randomly distributed among subscribed agents. A simulation of 50 server agents and 10 scout agents is completely allocated to respond to a steady demand of requests of type 1 (initial 10 time steps). Confronted with an additional steady demand of type 2 requests (after 5 seconds) the allocation of servers is balanced.

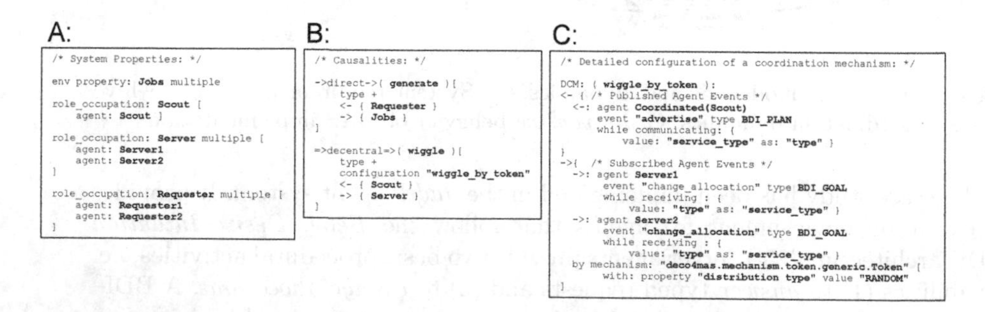

Fig. 5. MASDynamics model excerpt. Declaration of system properties (A), causal links (B) and DCM configuration (C).

5 Conclusions

In order to stimulate the systematic usage of self–organizing design metaphors, i.e. reusable patterns of dynamical processes within agent–based applications, we proposed a *systemic* modeling approach that transfers system dynamics [21] concepts to MAS designs [8]. MASDynamics, a domain specific language supports the modeling of decentralized coordination metaphors for MAS adaptation in terms of agent interrelations and allows developers to align these systemic MAS models with agent implementations. Therefore, coordination metaphors become design elements that can be shared and reused within software producing organizations. Besides the documentation of MAS designs, this alignment enables the automated configuration of decentralized coordination mechanism implementations, following the architecture given in [5].

Future work will address the utilization of causal interrelations as design abstractions for MAS development. Particularly promising is the integration of systemic modeling techniques with AOSE notations and development processes. In addition, it will be examined how models of behavioral interrelations can be used to guide validations of macroscopic MAS behaviors by system simulations.

Acknowledgment

Jan Sudeikat would like to thank the *Distributed Systems and Information Systems* (VSIS) group at Hamburg University, particularly Winfried Lamersdorf, Lars Braubach and Alexander Pokahr for inspiring discussion and encouragement.

References

1. Serugendo, G.D.M., Gleizes, M.P., Karageorgos, A.: Self–organisation and emergence in mas: An overview. In: Informatica. Volume 30. (2006) 45–54
2. Mamei, M., Menezes, R., Tolksdorf, R., Zambonelli, F.: Case studies for self-organization in computer science. J. Syst. Archit. **52** (2006) 443–460
3. DeWolf, T., Holvoet, T.: Decentralised coordination mechanisms as design patterns for self-organising emergent applications. In: Proceedings of the Fourth International Workshop on Engineering Self-Organising Applications. (2006) 40–61
4. Sudeikat, J., Renz, W.: Building Complex Adaptive Systems: On Engineering Self–Organizing Multi–Agent Systems. In: Applications of Complex Adaptive Systems. IGI Global (2008) 229–256
5. Sudeikat, J., Renz, W.: On the encapsulation and reuse of decentralized coordination mechanisms: A layered architecture and design implications. In: Communications of SIWN. Volume 4. (2008) 140–146
6. Parunak, H.V.D., Brueckner, S.: Engineering swarming systems. In: Methodologies and Software Engineering for Agent Systems, Kluwer (2004) 341–376
7. Sudeikat, J., Renz, W.: Toward systemic mas development: Enforcing decentralized self–organization by composition and refinement of archetype dynamics. In: Proceedings of Engineering Environment–Mediated Multiagent Systems. LNCS, Springer (2007)

8. Renz, W., Sudeikat, J.: Modeling feedback within mas: A systemic approach to organizational dynamics. In: Proceedings of the International Workshop on Organised Adaptation in Multi–Agent Systems. (2008)
9. Sudeikat, J., Renz, W.: On expressing and validating requirements for the adaptivity of self–organizing multi–agent systems. System and Information Sciences Notes **2** (2007) 14–19
10. Seebach, H., Ortmeier, F., Reif, W.: Design and construction of organic computing systems. Evolutionary Computation, 2007. CEC 2007. IEEE Congress on (2007) 4215–4221
11. Sudeikat, J., Renz, W.: On the redesign of self–organizing multi–agent systems. International Transactions on Systems Science and Applications **2** (2006) 81–89
12. Gouaich, A., Michel, F.: Towards a unified view of the environment(s) within multi-agent systems. Informatica (Slovenia) **29** (2005) 423–432
13. Lerman, K., Galstyan, A.: A general methodology for mathematical analysis of multiagent systems. USC Inf. Sciences Tech.l Report ISI-TR-529 (2001)
14. DeWolf, T., Holvoet, T.: A catalogue of decentralised coordination mechanisms for designing self-organising emergent applications. Technical Report Report CW 458, Department of Computer Science, K.U. Leuven (2006)
15. DeWolf, T., Holvoet, T.: Towards a methodology for engineering self-organising emergent systems. In: Proceedings of the International Conference on Self-Organization and Adaptation of Multi-agent and Grid Systems. (2005)
16. Gelernter, D., Carriero, N.: Coordination languages and their significance. Commun. ACM **35** (1992) 97–107
17. Singh, M.P.: A customizable coordination service for autonomous agents. In: ATAL '97: Proceedings of the 4th International Workshop on Intelligent Agents IV, Agent Theories, Architectures, and Languages, London, UK, Springer-Verlag (1998) 93–106
18. Viroli, M., Ricci, A.: Instructions-based semantics of agent mediated interaction. In: 3rd International Joint Conference on Autonomous Agents and Multiagent Systems (AAMAS 2004), 19-23 August 2004, New York, NY, USA, IEEE Computer Society (2004) 102–109
19. Sudeikat, J., Renz, W.: Monitoring group behavior in goal–directed agents using co–efficient plan observation. In: Agent-Oriented Software Engineering VII, 7th International Workshop, AOSE 2006, Hakodate, Japan, May 8, 2006, Revised and Invited Papers. (2006)
20. Henderson-Sellers, B., Giorgini, P., eds.: Agent-oriented Methodologies. Idea Group Publishing (2005) ISBN: 1591405815.
21. Sterman, J.D.: Business Dynamics - Systems Thinking and Modeling for a Complex World. McGraw–Hill (2000)
22. Mao, X., Yu, E.: Organizational and social concepts in agent oriented software engineering. In: Agent-Oriented Software Engineering V. Volume 3382 of LNCS., Springer (2004) 1–15
23. Bernon, C., Cossentino, M., Zambonelli, F., Gleizes, M.P., Turci, P., Zambonelli, F.: A study of some multi-agent meta-models. In: Agent-Oriented Software Engineering V. Volume 3382/2005 of LNCS. (2005) 62–77
24. Nakrani, S., Tovey, C.: On honey bees and dynamic server allocation in internet hosting centers. Adaptive Behavior **12** (2004) 223–240
25. Rao, A.S., Georgeff, M.P.: BDI-agents: from theory to practice. In: Proceedings of the First Int. Conference on Multiagent Systems. (1995)

Teil IV

Service-Oriented Computing

Leveraging the BPEL Event Model to Support QoS-aware Process Execution

Farid Zaid, Rainer Berbner and Ralf Steinmetz

Multimedia Communications Lab - KOM, TU Darmstadt, Germany
Email: {Farid.Zaid, Berbner, Ralf.Steinmetz}@kom.tu-darmstadt.de

Abstract. Business processes executed using compositions of distributed Web Services are susceptible to different fault types. The Web Services Business Process Execution Language (BPEL) is widely used to execute such processes. While BPEL provides fault handling mechanisms to handle functional faults like invalid message types, it still lacks a flexible native mechanism to handle non-functional exceptions associated with violations of QoS levels that are typically specified in a governing Service Level Agreement (SLA). In this paper, we present an approach to complement BPEL's fault handling, where expected QoS levels and necessary recovery actions are specified declaratively in form of Event-Condition-Action (ECA) rules. Our main contribution is leveraging BPEL's standard event model which we use as an event space for the created ECA rules. We validate our approach by an extension to an open source BPEL engine.

1 Introduction

One challenge for Service-oriented Architecture (SOA) is to meet the needs of particular processes, not just within the enterprise but across the entire value chain. Research in the context of SOA has shown that the usage of WSDL [8] and SOAP [6] is not sufficient to establish cross-organizational processes in real-world scenarios. Considering Quality of Service (QoS) requirements is crucial for a sustainable success of SOA. Without any guarantee regarding QoS, no enterprise is willing to rely on external Web Services within critical business.

Generally, Quality of Service (QoS) requirements are specified in a Service Level Agreement (SLA) between process partners. The The Web Services Business Process Execution Language (WS-BPEL or shortly BPEL) specification [3] offers support for handling abnormal (functional) situations in form of fault and compensation handlers. However, BPEL has no integrated method to handle QoS degradations, which are more considered as finer non-functional exceptions.

In this paper, we propose an approach that utilizes the BPEL event model to overcome BPEL's limitation in handling QoS exceptions. We also propose to use the Even-Condition-Action (ECA) rules as a logical framework to specify SLA statements and map them to relevant events and recovery actions. The proposed approach leverages BPEL in the following dimensions:

- The approach keeps the alignment with BPEL as a Programming in the Large paradigm. Similar to BPEL's declarative syntax that enables easy mapping of business strategies to corresponding business processes, the ECA rules have a declarative syntax that can be used to express SLA terms in a logical way.
- The approach leaves BPEL's standard syntax intact while reusing BPEL event model to accommodate proposed recovery actions.
- The approach provides explicit separation-of-concerns between the business logic and business control. Thus it is possible to modify existing ECA rules and/or apply new ones without need to modify the process definition or stop running process instances.

This paper is organized as follows: Section 2 describes relevant basic concepts like the BPEL fault handling, the BPEL event model and the ECA rules. Section 3 presents our approach for handling QoS violations. Section 4 sketches our implementation to validate the concept. Section 5 positions our work among existing literature. Finally, Section 6 wraps up our paper.

2 Basic Concepts

2.1 Fault Handling in BPEL

A BPEL process can handle a fault through one or more fault handlers. Within a fault handler, some activities are defined to recover from the fault, possibly reverse the partial (unsuccessful) work of the activity where the fault has occurred, and/or signal a fault message to the client. BPEL faults can be classified in two categories [3]:

- Business faults are application specific faults and occur when an explicit <throw> activity is executed or an <invoke> activity gets a fault as response. Such faults are denoted by the <fault> element within the <operation> declaration of a WSDL definition. A fault has a qualified name (QName) and an associated message type.
- Runtime faults are not user defined and will not appear in the WSDL of a process or a service. The BPEL specification defines standard faults like "uninitializedVariable", "invalidReply", "mismatchedAssignmentFailure", etc. All these faults are typeless, meaning they do not have associated message types.

We focus here on situations related to SLA violation, for example, when the respose time of a service invocation exceeds the threshold specified by a governing SLA. We regard such a situation more as an *exception* rather than a *fault*. The difference is that BPEL deals with an occurring fault as abnormality that leads to unsuccessful completion of the scope/activity, whether that fault is handled or not. However, we see an exception as a finer deviation from normal execution and, if resolved, normal execution may be resumed. Fault is function-related while exception is non-functional.

```
<scope name="BillCreationScope">
 <eventHandlers>
  <onAlarm for="PT5S">
   <throw faultName="createPDF:Timeout"
          faultVariable="faultVar" />
  </onAlarm>
 </eventHandler>
 <invoke partnerLink="pdfConverterPL"
         operation="createPDF"
         portType="pdfConversionPT"
         inputVariable="urlVar"
         outputVariable="pdfVar"/>
</scope>
```

Listing 1.1. Timeout Handling in BPEL

In BPEL, it is possible to raise a timeout exception in an <onAlarm> construct by a <throw> activity and be caught by a <catch> activity. Listing 1.1 shows how a "createPDF:Timeout" fault (or exception in our understanding) is thrown 5 seconds after <invoke> has executed. However, because only one alarm can be activated for each scope at a time, if we want to catch different timeouts, then we must enclose each <invoke> with its own scope, which is a tedious and error-prone task for a process designer.

2.2 BPEL Event Model

Execution of a BPEL process is rich with events that fingerprint each state and transition with useful information. Such information can be used in different scenarios like process audit trailing and coordination of fragmented processes that run on multiple BPEL engines. However, the BPEL specification does not impose any event model on the process execution environment (engine). Therefore, different implementations may have different types of events, and even different event structures [9].

The event model in [9] classifies events according to two different criteria: direction and blocking. The direction indicates the source of the event, which can be the BPEL engine itself or an external entity like another BPEL engine or a coordinator. Blocking events block process instances until an incoming event from an external entity is received that unblocks the particular instance. In the rest of this paper we will use the following definition of a BPEL event.

Definition 1. *For a given BPEL activity A, we define a BPEL event fired by A as the triple e(A, t, s) where t is the time when the event was fired and s is the state entered by A after firing this event.*

Process Events These are triggered as a process instance changes its state as shown in Fig. 1(a). These events are described in detail in [9], however of particular interest to our approach is the *ProcessDeployed* event which is fired whenever a new BPEL process model is deployed into the BPEL engine. This event is not fired for each instance, but rather per process model, therefore we use this event to define variables with process scope, i.e. variables that are accessible from all process instances. The *ProcessInstantiated* event signals when a new process instance is loaded. The *InstanceCompleted* event signals when the process instance finishes successfully. Therefore we can use these last two events to mark overall QoS associated with each process instance.

Activity Events Fig. 1(b) shows the general life cycle events for all BPEL activities. Events at the activity level can be combined to mark QoS metrics for single activities and or scope of activities.

The *ActivityReady* event is fired when an activity becomes ready to execute. This event may be marked optionally as blocking, in this case an incoming *StartActivity* event is needed to start the actual activity execution. When the activity starts execution, it fires an *ActivityExecuting* event. The execution itself depends on the work to be done by that activity, for e.g. an <invoke> activity places a call to a web service, while the <receive> activity waits for an incoming request from another service. If the activity finishes execution successfully, it either fires the *ActivityExecuted* event and enters the *Waiting* state if an event listener is registered, or it fires the *ActivityCompleted* event and enters the *Completed* state directly if no event listener is registered. In the *Waiting* state the activity is blocked and can be only completed by an incoming *CompleteActivity* event. At any state in its life cycle, the activity can change to the *Faulted* state if a fault is encountered in the activity itself or in a preceding activity or when a fault in a child scope is not handled. A faulty situation is signaled via the *ActivityFaulted* event.

Incoming Events External sources like a coordinator of fragmented processes or a monitoring tool can influence a process execution by sending events. The *StartActivity* event causes an activity that is blocked in the *Ready* state to be continued. The *CompleteActivity* event unblocks an activity that is blocked in the *Waiting* state (thus causing the transition to the *Completed* state) or to fire the direct transition from the *Ready* state to the *Completed* state (thus causing an activity to be skipped). The *Continue* event simply unblocks activities [9].

2.3 ECA Rules

ECA Rules form a natural candidate for systems where reactive functionality is needed. Each rule is characterized by the events that can trigger it; once a rule is triggered and its condition holds, then rule action is executed. Rules have languages for event, query, action and condition testing. Each of these languages has metadata and ontology which are associated with a processor [2]. In this paper, we do focus on the paradigm rather than on the specific syntax of the

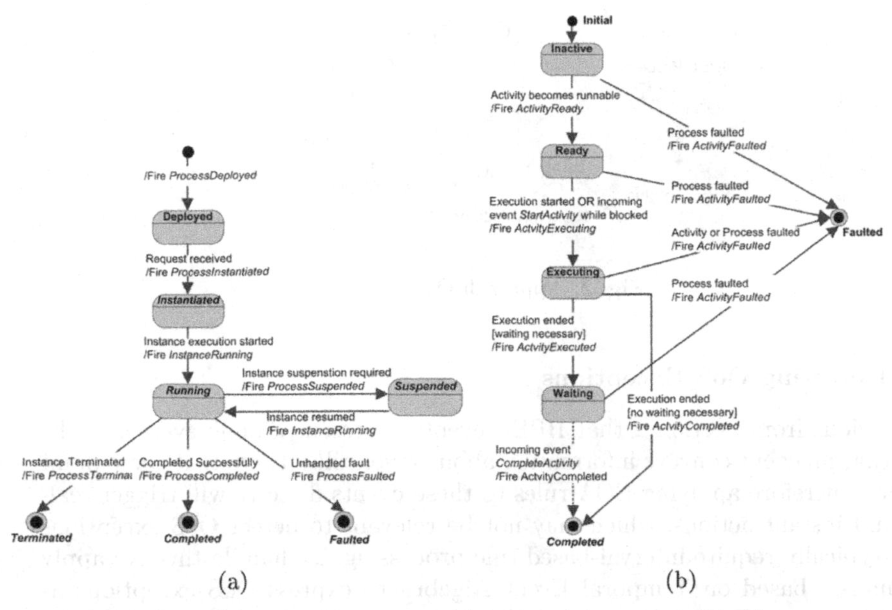

Fig. 1. Process events (a) and activity events (b) [8].

rules. Listing 1.2 shows the pseudo syntax for an ECA rule we will be using in rest of this paper.

```
Rule ruleID
 Event triggering event
 Condition guarding statement
 Action recovery action
```

Listing 1.2. ECA rule pseudo syntax

3 Approach

We propose a flexible and declarative approach to handle QoS exceptions in BPEL processes by applying ECA rules to events generated during a process execution. Fig. 2 shows an overview of the approach. In the Logic Plane, a standard BPEL process will be deployed to a BPEL engine for execution. In the Control Plane, a set of ECA rules are registered with a rule engine (event manager). The BPEL engine sends subscribed events to the rule engine and reacts to recovery actions issued by the rule engine when some rules are triggered.

This clear distinction between logic and control planes permits creation of rules to modify QoS constraints without interrupting running process instances.

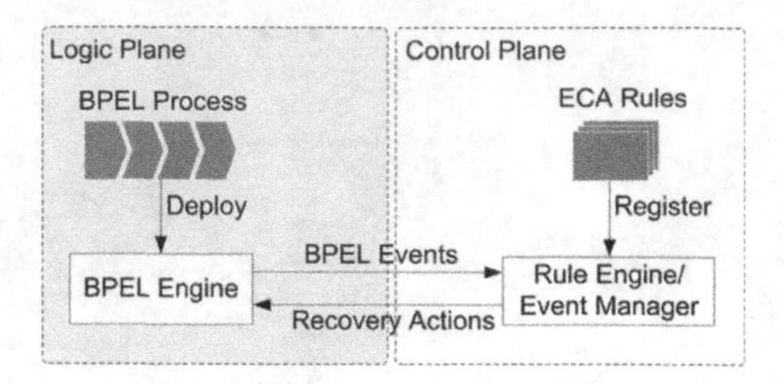

Fig. 2. Approach Overview

3.1 Detecting QoS Exceptions

It is obvious from Section 2 that BPEL events represent atomic events, in the sense that an event conveys information about a volatile situation at some point in time. Therefore applying ECA rules to these events directly will trigger real-time and instant actions, which may not be relevant to detect QoS exceptions which typically require interval-based rule processing. To handle this, we apply a formalism based on Temporal Event Algebra to express QoS exceptions as composite events formed from atomic BPEL events. Then we apply ECA rules to the mapped composite events. Next we show how to detect response time and availability violations from primitive BPEL events.

Response Time Exceptions Listing 1.3 shows the events and rule needed to detect a violation of response time threshold when executing an activity *A*. The rule engine needs to subscribe to two events fired by the invocation activity *A*: event *e1* with type *ActivityExecuting* which marks when *A* starts to execute, and *e2* with type *ActivityExecuted* which marks when *A* finishes execution. We use the temporal event composer *AND THEN* to indicate that the rule *rtRule* triggers each time an *e1* event is followed by *e2* event [2].

```
Subscribe
 e1(invoke(A), t, ActivityExecuting)
 e2(invoke(A), t, ActivityExecuted)
Rule rtRule
 Event e1 AND THEN e2
 Condition (e2.pInstance == e1.pInstance) &&
           (e2.t-e1.t > rtThreshold)
 Action replaceOnNext(A, a1, a2)
```

Listing 1.3. Events and rule to handle a response time exception

We measure the response time as the time elapsed between the two events. Of course, this definition of response time is an approximation of reality as it counts communication delay to the response time of the partner service. The condition component assures that these events are fired within life cycle of the same process instance (pInstance) and that the estimated response time does exceed the threshold value. If the condition holds, the action *replaceOnNext* is executed (explained in Section 3.2).

BPEL's <invoke> activity represents the actual interaction between a process and external services. However, as the event model described earlier applies to all BPEL activities, we can apply similar approach to handle QoS violations for composition activities (constructs). For example, if two invoke activities are composed via a <sequence> construct, then we can use the *ActivityExecuting* and *ActivityExecuted* events fired by the sequence activity to estimate the aggregate response time of the two activities, rather than filtering all events for individual invoke activities.

Availability Exceptions Listing 1.4 shows how different BPEL events can be combined to detect an availability exception. Here, the rule engine subscribes to *e1* event fired from the process where activity *A* is defined. This event is used to to trigger *initRule* that initializes two variables with process-wide scope: *all*, to count the number of times *A* was scheduled for execution, and *failures* to count times of failed executions. The *schedRule* uses event *e1* to increment *all*, while the *failRule* increments *failures* when an *e2 AND THEN e3* pattern occurs. An *e3* event identifies a faulty invocation, which as discussed in Section 2 can have different reasons, therefore the condition part of *failRule* assures that the fault (fault_type) is really related to partner's availability, and is not due to a local reason. When its condition holds, *failRule* will fire the *avEvaluate* which is an internal event we define to trigger the *avRule* rule. This in turn uses the *failures* to *all* ratio to estimate the availability [7].

```
Subscribe
  e1(process(A),t,ProcessDeployed)
  e2(invoke(A), t, ActivityExecuting)
  e3(invoke(A), t, ActivityFaulted)
Rule initRule
  Event e1
  Condition true
  Action all=0, failures=0
Rule schedRule
  Event e2
  Condition true
  Action all++
Rule failRule
  Event e2 AND THEN e3
  Condition (e3.fault_type == remoteFault)
  Action failures++, fire (avEvaluate)
Rule avRule
  Event avEvaluate
  Condition (1-failures/all < avThreshold)
  Action replaceOnNext (A, a1, a2)
```

Listing 1.4. Events and rules to handle availability exception

In contrary to active monitoring, which implies probing partner's availability with periodic pings, the shown mechanism resembles a kind of passive monitoring, which counts the times of successful and unsuccessful processing of requests sent to the partner service.

3.2 Recovery Actions

Basic Actions Actions are recovery commands that attempt to repair process execution in favor of better fulfillment of QoS levels.

As mentioned in Section 2, situations that can be handled by the standard fault handling are excluded here, although our approach can be elaborated to cover such situations. Initially, we identify the following basic actions:

- *Ignore* (A) causes execution of activity A to proceed normally. This is the default action when no QoS deterioration is detected. It steps the activity from *Waiting* state to *Completed* state.
- *Skip* (A) causes execution of activity A to be skipped. It causes the activity to pass over from *READY* state to *Completed* state.
- *ReplaceOnNext* (A, a_1, a_2) instructs activity A to change its binding from partner a_1 to partner a_2 for execution of next process requests (instances). This is useful when a partner service violates QoS levels repeatedly and better be replaced by another service that meets the same functional requirements. This command affects service binding during next process instances and has no effect on current activity state.

Mapping Actions to Event Model The target of an action can be the same activity firing the event that triggered the ECA rule, or it can be another activity. However, external recovery actions should be enacted in such a way that they do not cause conflicts to the states of the executing activities. We make use of the incoming events defined in Section 2 to apply external actions to BPEL activities. However, to preserve consistency of the event model, we assume that an activity enters the *Waiting* state after leaving the *Executing* state. With this assumption, we can map the basic recovery actions to BPEL event model as follows:

- The *Ignore* command is mapped to the *CompleteActivity* incoming event.
- The *Skip* command is mapped to the *Continue* incoming event.
- The *ReplaceOnNext* is mapped to the *StartActivity* incoming event. This command is applied to next execution of the activity and not to current execution.

Another assumption that is specific to applying the *Skip* command is that functional requirements are still met. This implies activity can not be *skipped* if its output parameters form a required input for a successive activity, even if the *Skip* command was issued by a triggered rule.

4 Implementation

To demonstrate our approach, we implemented the Event Manager (EM) as an extension to the ActiveBPEL engine [1]. Consistent with how ActiveBPEL engine manages various functions using managers, EM plugs into the engine by implementing the "IAeManager" interface which defines all methods a manager has to support, most importantly, the create, start, and stop methods. Once EM is created, it registers itself as a listener for following event types:

- AeEngineEvent which marks when a process instance is created, started and terminated.
- AeProcessEvent which marks the different states of a BPEL activity.
- EmDeploymentEvent which is an extra event we defined to signal deployment of new business processes.

EM maintains several registries: an event registry where BPEL events are stored, a rule registry where ECA rules are stored and execution registry where an execution record for each process instance is stored. An execution record is identified by the pInstance as a key, and it accompanies a process instance all through its lifetime and holds information about QoS levels to be monitored and non-functional status of execution for each activity in that process. EM has also an event component which detects event patterns based on a simple event-matching algorithm, a condition component which evaluates condition part of an ECA rule and an action component which applies recovery commands to process execution.

Fig. 3 shows the web frontend we use to manage EM. The "Deployed Processes" pane shows all processes deployed to the engine (information extracted by the deployment event). The "Process Details" pane shows information about the process currently selected in the "Deployed Processes". This information includes a list of invoke activities for that process. In this pane, it is also possible to configure a simple ECA rule per invoke activity. We restrict our proof-of-concept implementation to detecting response time exceptions as it requires less effort to implement. The bottom pane displays breakdown of execution records related to the instances of the selected process. In the example shown, a *replaceOnNext* command causes the "pdfCreate" invoke in second process instance to bind to the backup "pdfConverter2" service, because the response time of the "pdfConverter1" service exceeded the set threshold of 3 seconds. Services "pdfConverter1" and "pdfConverter2" have similar implementations, however they have different response times, which we configured by introducing different artificial delays. This way, we simulated partner services that meet same functional requirements, but with different QoS levels.

To implement the *replaceOnNext* functionality, we modified the AeInvoke Handler which handles invocations of endpoint references on behalf of the business process engine. For each Invoke activity, the handler places a SOAP call (org.apache.axis.client.Call) to the web service located at specified AeEndpointReference address [1]. The address URL can be obtained from two different sources, dependent on the addressing scheme used:

- SERVICE: here the address URL is extracted from the <port> element in the WSDL interface of the target endpoint.
- ADDRESS: here the address URL is retrieved from a WS-Addressing endpoint reference, usually sent by another web service for callback.

We implemented the CurrentBindings class which is a singletone object to store active bindings (i.e. address URL of the partner link) for each invoke activity. The bindings are updated by the replaceOnNext command. The InvokeHandler itself is modified to check first if a binding exists in CurrentBindings. If no binding is available, then one of the two schemes mentioned above will be used to resolve the address URL.

Deployed Processes

BillCreationSubProcess

Process Details

Process Name	Invoke Activity	Response Time Threshold	Action
BillCreationSubProcess	createPDF	3000	Ignore Skip ReplaceOnNext

Event Trace

Process name	Source	Instance	Event Type	Timestamp	Response Time
BillCreationSubProcess	/Process	1	PROCESS_CREATED	1210766325386	
BillCreationSubProcess	/Process	1	READY_TO_EXECUTE	1210766325386	
BillCreationSubProcess	/Process	1	EXECUTING	1210766325402	
BillCreationSubProcess	/Process	1	PROCESS_STARTED	1210766325402	
BillCreationSubProcess	/Invoke [createPDF], by pdfConverter1	1	READY_TO_EXECUTE	1210766325402	
BillCreationSubProcess	/Invoke [createPDF], by pdfConverter1	1	EXECUTING	1210766325402	
BillCreationSubProcess	/Invoke [createPDF], by pdfConverter1	1	EXECUTE_COMPLETE	1210766329468	4066
BillCreationSubProcess	/Process	1	PROCESS_TERMINATED	1210766329510	
BillCreationSubProcess	/Process	2	PROCESS_CREATED	1210766595630	
BillCreationSubProcess	/Process	2	READY_TO_EXECUTE	1210766595630	
BillCreationSubProcess	/Process	2	EXECUTING	1210766595650	
BillCreationSubProcess	/Process	2	PROCESS_STARTED	1210766595650	
BillCreationSubProcess	/Invoke [createPDF], by pdfConverter2	2	READY_TO_EXECUTE	1210766595650	
BillCreationSubProcess	/Invoke [createPDF], by pdfConverter2	2	EXECUTING	1210766595650	
BillCreationSubProcess	/Invoke [createPDF], by pdfConverter2	2	EXECUTE_COMPLETE	1210766598484	2834
BillCreationSubProcess	/Process	2	PROCESS_TERMINATED	1210766598510	

Fig. 3. A snapshot of the Event manager frontend

5 Related Work

In [5], a component-based architecture is proposed to manage execution of process-oriented applications. Binding to a service is performed at runtime, after services are ranked based on their up-to-date QoS attributes.

In [12] SLA conditions are classified in soft and hard constraints. Violation of hard constraints leads to abnormal execution and is handled using constraint violation handlers, while soft constraints violation does not lead to erroneous state and is handled with event handlers. Composite events are detected by applying semantic matching of primitive events. Finally, recovery actions like *replaceBy* and *Retry* are used to fix problems manifested by the fault occurrence.

The authors in [11] follow a top-down approach to annotate a BPEL process with QoS assertions. At the top level, they specify a WSCDL description of the process partners and the messages to be exchanged. The WSCDL descriptor is annotated with references to one or more SLAs at the same level. The SLAs define obligations and guarantees among the participants. The abstract WSDL description is then transformed into executable BPEL processes, while SLAs are transformed to QoS assertions that are directly attached to the corresponding partner links in BPEL to so that they cab be enforced by the BPEL engine.

Similarly, [4] represents dynamic service compositions with BPEL and provides assertions to check if involved services adhere to the contracted QoS levels. Assertions are verified with monitors which can be automaticallly defined as additional services and linked to the composite service.

In [10] also a top-down approach is used, however based on an extensible set of fault handling patterns defined as ECA rules. Before a process is deployed and executed, a generator is used to transform the fault patterns into BPEL code snippets (variables and activities like <if>, <catch>, etc.) that collectively give equivalent fault handling functionality. Although no change to BPEL syntax is needed, the code of transformed fault handlers mixes with code of the process logic and makes process maintenance more difficult. Besides, applying new rules mandates redeployment of the process definition.

In our approach, we also proposed the use of ECA rules as they possess a declarative syntax and map logically to the exception handling problem. However, we keep the creation and processing of these rules independent from process creation and deployment. This means that these rules can be created or edited without need to re-deploy the process definition. This is especially important for processes with long running instances. The key enabler to our approach is BPEL's standard event model which serves as a rich event base for detecting different execution anomalies.

6 Summary and Future Work

We have introduced in this paper an approach that leverages BPEL event model to provide handling of situations that are considered as non-functional exceptions rather than hard functional faults. The approach focuses on separating the business logic from SLA handling, thus enhancing BPEL's fault handling while keeping it intact. A process designer will typically specify ECA rules to handle QoS exceptions such as violations of response time and availability thresholds.

Although we validated the concept with a prototype for basic commands, we still have to address several open issues. Some of these issues are:

- The incorporation of commands that can affect the execution flow. So far, we addressed actions that affect the execution of a single activity, mainly the <invoke> activity.

– Monitoring of other QoS attributes. So far, the proof-of-concept is limited to respose time, due to its ease of implementation.
– We still need to study the computaional complexity of the approach and performance overhead introduced by instrumentation of rule processing.

These questions, once answered will much better outline the flexibility of our approach towards supporting QoS for BPEL processes.

Acknowledgement

Parts of this research have been supported by the German Research Foundation (DFG) within the Research Training Group 1362 "Cooperative, adaptive and responsive monitoring in mixed mode environments".

References

1. The ActiveBPEL Community Edition Engine. http://www.activevos.com/community-open-source.php.
2. J. J. Alferes et al. A First Prototype on Evolution and Behaviour at the XML-Level. Technical report, REWERSE, 2006. http://rewerse.net/deliverables/m30/i5-d5.pdf.
3. A. Alves et al. Web Services Business Process Execution Language Version 2.0. OASIS Standard, 2007. http://docs.oasis-open.org/wsbpel/2.0/OS/wsbpel-v2.0-OS.html.
4. L. Baresi, C. Ghezzi, and S. Guinea. Smart monitors for composed services. In *ICSOC '04. Proceedings of the 2nd international conference on Service oriented computing*, pages 193–202. ACM Press, 2004.
5. R. Berbner, M. Spahn, N. Repp, O. Heckmann, and R. Steinmetz. Heuristics for QoS-aware Web Service Composition. *IEEE International Conference on Web Services (ICWS)*, pages 72–82, Sept. 2006.
6. D. Box et al. Simple Object Access Protocol (SOAP) 1.1. W3C Note, 2000. http://www.w3.org/TR/2000/NOTE-SOAP-20000508/.
7. J. Cardoso, A. Sheth, J. Miller, J. Arnold, and K. Kochut. Quality of Service for Workflows and Web Service Processes. *Journal of Web Semantics*, 1:281–308, Apr. 2004.
8. E. Christensen, F. Curbera, G. Meredith, and S. Weerawarana. Web Services Description Language (WSDL) 1.1. W3C Note, 2001. http://www.w3.org/TR/wsdl.
9. D. Karastoyanova, R. Khalaf, R. Schroth, M. Paluszek, and F. Leymann. BPEL Event Model. Technical report, Universität Stuttgart, 2006.
10. A. Liu, Q. Li, L. Huang, and M. Xiao. A Declarative Approach to Enhancing the Reliability of BPEL Processes. *IEEE International Conference of Web Services (ICWS)*, pages 272–279, Jul. 2007.
11. F. Rosenberg, C. Enzi, A. Michlmayr, C. Platzer, and S. Dustdar. Integrating Quality of Service Aspects in Top-Down Business Process Development Using WS-CDL and WS-BPEL. *Enterprise Distributed Object Computing Conference (EDOC)*, pages 15–15, Oct. 2007.
12. R. Vaculín, K. Wiesner, and K. Sycara. Exception Handling and Recovery of Semantic Web Services. *The Fourth International Conference of Networking and Services (ICNS)*, 0:217–222, Mar. 2008.

Automated Integration of Web Services in BPEL4WS Processes

Steffen Bleul, Diana Comes, Kurt Geihs and Marc Kirchhoff

Distributed Systems Group, University of Kassel, Wilhelmshöher Allee 73, 34121 Kassel

Abstract. In order to fully exploit the potential of dynamic service-oriented architectures based on Web Services we provide a novel self-integration service infrastructure that supports automatic service discovery and reconfiguration for BPEL4WS processes. Our service discovery approach takes into account possible runtime transformations such that a service in a BPEL4WS process can be replaced by a semantically similar service even if service interfaces and message structures do not match. We present the main building blocks of our solution, i.e. a standard-conformant WSDL schema extension called Mediation Contract Extension (MECE), a corresponding semantic discovery algorithm, and a runtime mediation system that generates appropriate XSLT transformations on the fly. Our solution dynamically instantiates mediators to bind services to service processes specified with BPEL4WS.

1 Introduction

Service-oriented architectures (SOA) based on Web Services facilitate dynamic evolution of enterprise applications by run-time service rebinding and reconfiguration. The flexibility of a SOA depends on the ability to add, remove, or update services without interrupting the course of business. However, when introducing a new version of a service or replacing a service by another service from some other service provider, very often there is a change in service interfaces, e.g. operation names are different, and message structures as well as parameter types may change. In such a case, existing client stubs cannot work with the new service and communication will fail.

Our goal is to overcome these limitations and to enable self-integration of services in SOA-based business processes. By the term self-integration we refer to the automatic integration of Web Services into a BPEL4WS [2] service process by an automatic mediation between differing interfaces. This is achieved using semantic matching of Web Services and automatically generated stylesheet transformations based on XSLT [9]. The first step is to evaluate the semantic overlap of corresponding SOAP [7] messages. If the messages share semantically equivalent message elements, then the matching algorithm creates an appropriate transformation. The transformation is performed by mediators that are part of our lifecycle management infrastructure for BPEL4WS processes.

This paper introduces a message mediation approach based on the Mediation Contract Extension (MECE) for WSDL documents [18]. MECE not only allows semantic annotation of syntactic WSDL elements but also presents a novel way for offering Web Services and Semantic Web Services. The main focus of MECE is to enhance the matching success of service offers and requests and also the reuseability of annotations. We do not define a new ontology matching algorithm but show how XSLT transformations can be generated on the fly if a service or its message elements can be successfully matched. We evaluate the perfomance of our system with a large-scale set of service offers.

Furthermore, the presented service mediation solution is embedded in a distributed infrastructure for service management. We divide the tasks of service management, service matching, reconfiguration and monitoring between distributed components implemented as Web Services. The defined interfaces enable the introduction of new matching algorithms or improved service mediation capabilities without the need to redesign a whole middleware. Additionally the infrastructure offers scalability to improve reconfiguration time and to overcome local resource limitations.

This paper presents our approach to the self-integration of Web Services in BPEL4WS processes. In Section 2 we introduce our architectural model and explain the service process lifecycle. Section 3 presents the required main building blocks of self-integration: the MECE semantic annotation of WSDL, a corresponding service discovery algorithm, and the automatic generation of transformations. Section 4 discusses the implementation and our performance evaluation. In Section 5 we compare related work. The paper closes with conclusions in Section 6.

2 Self-Integration

BPEL4WS provides a language for the formal specification of business processes and interaction protocols. A BPEL4WS process typically consists of a number of Web Services that collectively provide the business process. Our objective is to develop a methodology and a software infrastructure that service process architects can use to automate the management of BPEL4WS processes. In general, our new infrastructure for BPEL4WS substantially reduces the need for manual administration. It is an important step towards a service management system that acts autonomously and offers self-management and self-optimization functionality.

Our self-integration approach requires appropriate semantic information as well as mediators that perform transformations. The additional cost is to prepare once a semantic annotation of the message elements inside the WSDL [8] description of a Web Service according to our new MECE schema and using OWL [14]. Based on the semantic annotations our semantic service discovery algorithm enables semantic matchmaking and ranking [16, 5, 6]. In addition to runtime transformation of messages with XSLT, our system is able to integrate also user-defined value conversion functions by means of additional software *plug-ins*.

Figure 1 illustrates our approach. Services and service processes are available when their interface descriptions, formulated in WSDL, or orchestrations, formulated in BPEL4WS, are registered in the Service Registry. The Service Registry is the only manually administered component in our model. Services and orchestrations are no longer available as soon as their interface descriptions are removed from the registry. A service description is also removed when the Monitoring System detects and throws faults. In our model we also include deployment and undeployment of BPEL4WS instances. We assume that for all registered BPEL4WS documents the system must deploy at least one running instance. Furthermore, there must be at least one service match for each service request inside a BPEL4WS document. Otherwise, the process instance must be undeployed and wait for newly registered service offers.

The central part of our self-integration system is the Integration Manager. The Integration Manager processes the following steps:

1. **Service discovery**: The WSDL files of the BPEL4WS specification represent requested services that are matched against the service offers. A matching score is

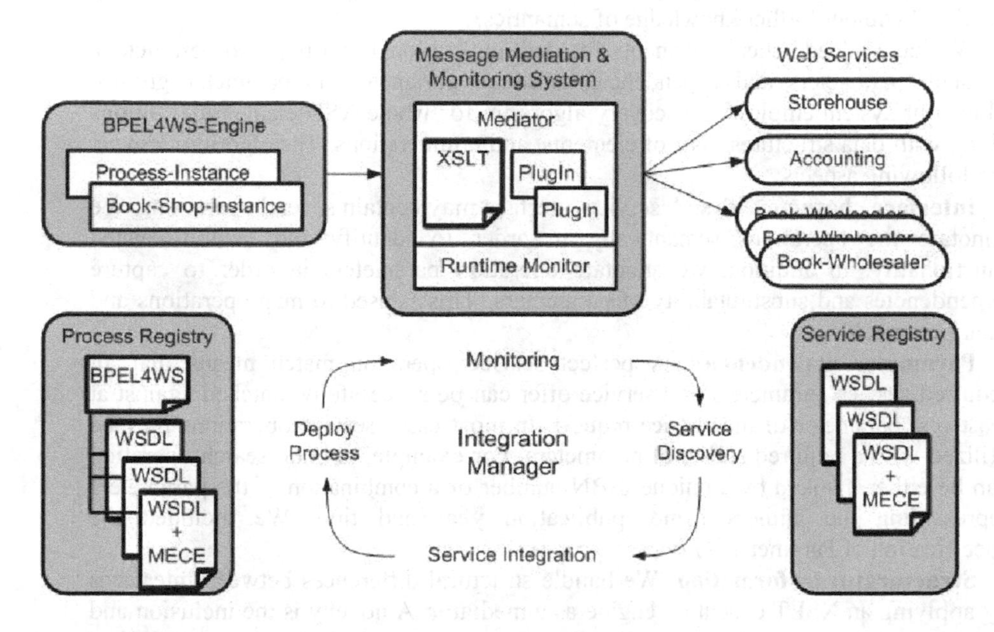

Figure 1: Self-Integration for BPEL Processes.

   calculated [18] and the services are ranked by their matching score.
2. **Service integration**: The discovery algorithm generates XSLT documents for successful matches. Furthermore, the algorithm produces a list of mediator plug-ins which are necessary to convert values. Both the XSLT documents and the plug-in list are used for runtime configuration of the message mediation system.
3. **Process Deployment**: The process will be deployed on the BPEL4WS engine and the service endpoint references are adjusted such that the engine invokes endpoints of mediators instead of direct invocation of the participating Web Services.
4. **Monitoring**: The system removes service descriptions automatically when the monitors discover faulty or failed services. In this case the manager starts anew by discovering services.

In the following we will use an example scenario to explain our approach. It is a BPEL4WS process representing a book shop which uses two services: a *storehouse service* for checking the availability of books contained in a customer's shopping cart; an *accounting service* for the creation of bills.

3 Automatic Message Transformation for Web Services

One foundation of our approach is MECE, the Mediation Contract Extension for WSDL. First of all, MECE enables semantic annotation of XSD type definitions. The MECE syntactic features are not expressed using ontologies and can be easily specified without further knowledge of semantics.

We have added schema elements for defining optional and required parameters, constant parameters and dependencies between parameters in parameter groups. Thus, our system employs a discovery algorithm for whole XSD element definitions along with data structures, lists of elements, and enumerations. The algorithm covers the following aspects:

Interface characteristics: A service interface may contain several operations. We annotate the operations semantically in order to identify and exploit related functionality. In addition, we annotate operation parameters in order to capture dependencies and substitutability of parameters. This is used to map operations and their parameters.

Parameter dependencies: A perfect service operation match means that all required service parameters of a service offer can be successfully matched against at least one parameter of the service request. In most cases service operations may be utilized with a required subset of parameters. For example, a book search operation can be either invoked by a unique ISBN number or a combination of the parameters representing the authors name, publication year and title. We included the specification of Parameters Groups.

Structural transformation: We handle structural differences between interfaces by applying an XSLT execution engine as a mediator. A novelty is the inclusion and matching of array bounds in case the client message may request an upper bound of subelements in order to avoid buffer overflow. In this context the MECE specification can also include sorting criteria on XSD-Elements, e.g. descending order in respect to a book price.

Content transformation: Message parameter values have a data type and may represent some quantity that has a type and a unit. XSLT cannot be used for content transformation of message values. Thus, we provide a flexible plug-in mechanism for converting values which is considered and integrated at runtime by the matching algorithm. Furthermore, we also dynamically build plug-in compositions for stepwise transformation over several plug-ins.

3.1 Semantic Extension of WSDL

MECE integrates as a new section in the WSDL with its own document root. We can add semantic information to WSDL elements without invalidating the WSDL documents. Apart from the automatic message transformation, this information may serve as an additional documentation of Web Service interfaces. A Web Service is described by a set of operations, for each of which we define a semantic extension. A message is divided into *parts* which are defined by *XSD elements*. The expressiveness of XSD allows specifying message elements with a simple value or a structured element with subelements. Arrays and enumerations may also be part of a schema definition.

Each element may be semantically annotated. In addition to considering input and output parts, we can do reasoning over the whole message structure as illustrated in the example on the right hand side in Figure 3. The example shows an informal representation of the response message of a book wholesaler search service. The message has the following structure:

- On the outer level the response message is an array of elements. The array represents a list of Book-Infos.
- The next level is a structure of elements with simple values, i.e. ISBN number, title, author, and year, as well as shipment data. This structure represents the data of a single Book-Info.
- The substructure called Shipment contains information about the price of the book and the shipping costs.

In our extension, elements are represented by a tuple of concepts representing the type, data type, and a unit. Figure 2 shows an example: On the left side we have an excerpt of the client's response message definition. The client expects an element BookPrice whereas the interface of the server returns an element named Price. We reference both elements in the respective extension sections and annotate them with the appropriate concepts, as defined in the domain ontologies. In our approach we use the Ontology Web Language (OWL) to specify concepts of domain ontologies.

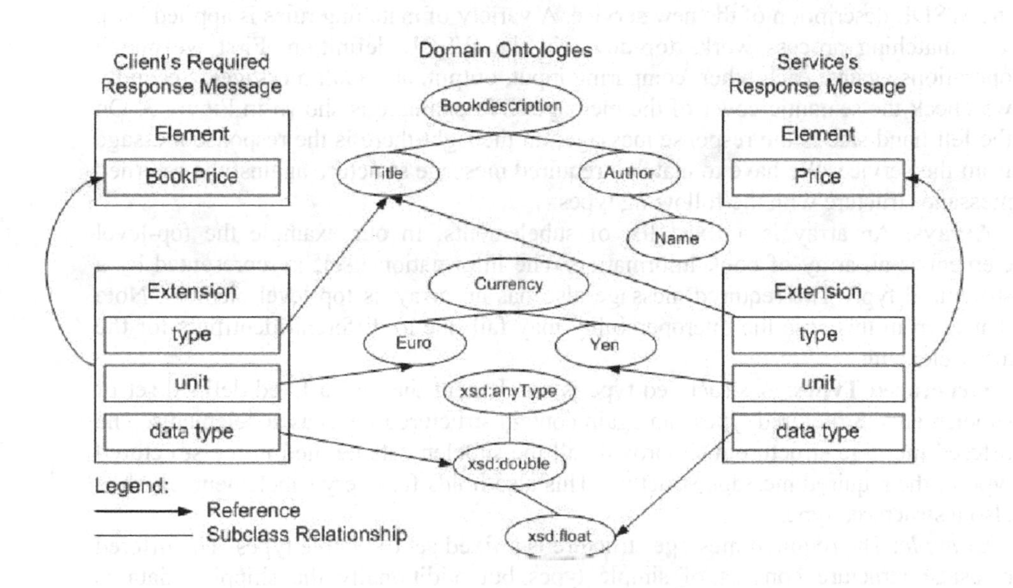

Figure 2: Annotation of an XSD Element.

In order to annotate the elements we use three domain ontologies. The upper ontology represents concepts from the *BookDescription* area. The concept *Title* is referenced by the *type* element of our extension. Both definitions reference this

concept, and despite of different identifiers we have a semantic equivalence between both elements.
The next ontology defines concepts of the *Currency* domain. It is used to express the pricing units. While the client's pricing is based on the currency *Euro*, the service returns the price in *Yen*. Here we have a semantic mismatch which requires matchmaking (see Section 3.2). The last step is the annotation of the data type of the element; here we use a type ontology which is directly related to the XSD type hierarchy. In this example the client's pricing is expressed by a *double* whereas the server returns the price as a *float*. The semantic cover of the two messages can now be evaluated by our matching algorithm.

3.2 Semantic Service Discovery

Semantic Service Discovery is provided by an algorithm which looks up a service that offers a desired functionality. In principle we apply input/output matching of service operations, as described in [6]. With respect to this approach, we are not only looking for a required functionality but we are also interested whether the client can actually invoke the service. This is an issue of interoperability between client and service. As already mentioned, we have a mediation system which can transform SOAP messages and convert content by means of plug-ins. This is considered already in the service matching process. In the following we explain the key elements of the matching process and give some examples.

The WDSL description of the service as expected by the client is compared against the WSDL description of the new service. A variety of matching rules is applied [18]. The matching process works top-down in the WSDL definition. First we match operations against each other, comparing input, output, and fault messages. Secondly we check the semantic cover of the messages. An example is shown in Figure 3. On the left hand side is the response message; on the right there is the response message from the service. We have to match a required message structure against the returned message structure with the following types:

Arrays: An array is a fixed list of subelements. In our example the top-level element is an array of book information. The information itself is represented by a structured type. The required message also has an array as top-level element. Note that even in this case the interoperability may fail due to different identifiers for the array elements.

Structured Types: A structured type is an element that has a fixed defined set of subelements. Structured types can again contain structured types as subelements. The offered message structure must provide all the subelements defined in the structured type in the required message structure. This also holds for every subelement which is also a structured type.

Example: The required message structure is a fixed set of simple types. The offered message structure consists of simple types but additionally the shipping data is embedded into another structured type *Shipment*.

Enumerations: An enumeration is a fixed set of simple types. The offered message structure must not have more enumerated elements than the requested message structure. All elements of the offered message structure must be semantically related to all elements of the requested message structure.

Example: The genre of the book may be represented by an enumeration. While the requested enumeration may contain the genres romance, fantasy, and research, the offered enumeration must not contain more or any other apart from these three genres.

Simple Types: A simple type is an element with a value. The offered simple type must contain a related semantic type with the appropriate unit and a compatible data type. Here we refer to the example in Figure 3. The requested simple type is on the left side and requires as its value a *Price* in the unit *Euro* expressed by the data type *double*. The offered simple type offers the semantic equivalent type but in the unit *Yen* and is expressed by the data type *float*.

On the lowest level we have the matching of simple types, achieved by matching the semantic concepts for their type, unit, and data type. We define the specialization relationship between two concepts A and B of an ontology as the predicate *subsumes*(A,B). The evaluation of the *subsumes*(A,B) is true when concept A is an equivalent or a subsumption of concept B. In this case the type annotated with concept B is an equivalent or a specialization of the parameter annotated with the concept A. In other words, the type annotated by concept B matches to the type annotated by concept A or an inheritance of A.

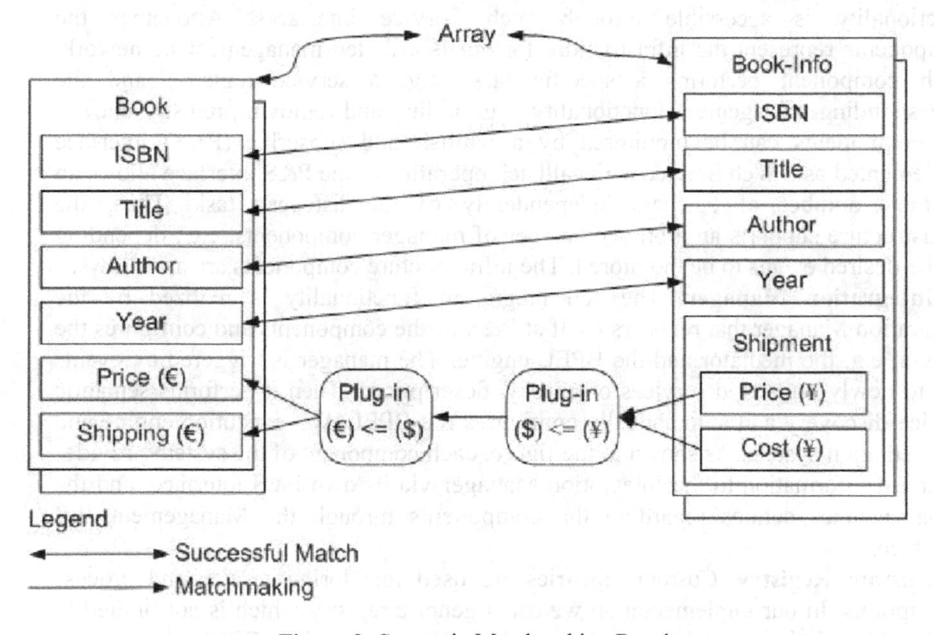

Figure 3: Semantic Matchmaking Result.

Additionally, we calculate the semantic distance between concept A and B. The semantic distance is 0 for equivalent concepts, $+\infty$ for mismatches and +1 for each inheritance step. The sum of the semantic distance of all successfully matched parameters is the ranking score for a service operation or $+\infty$ if a request cannot suffice all required parameters. The sum of the ranking scores for all service operations is the ranking score for a service or +∞ if the service does not offer all requested service operations.

After matching all simple types of the two message structures we get the following result. Successful matches are represented by arrows. Both message structures have arrays as their top-level elements. The arrayed book information shares a semantic cover because the offered message structure nearly offers all the elements of the required message. Finally, we have discovered the necessary elements but now we discover a mismatch of units for the value of *Price*, *Shipping*, and *Cost*. At this point matchmaking comes into play. If units and data types do not match, we need content conversion. This conversion is done by plug-ins at runtime. In our example in Figure 3, we are in need of two currency conversion plug-ins. The first one converts from Yen to Dollar and the next one converts from Dollar to Euro.

4 Implementation

All of the described features have been implemented in a service management prototype based on Web Services. The prototype implements the components illustrated in Figure 1. It is implemented as a set of distributed components whose functionality is accessible through Web Service interfaces. Altogether the components represent the infrastructure for our distributed management framework. Each component performs a specific task, e.g. a service registry, and the corresponding management functionality, e.g. adding and removing registry entries. All components can be monitored by a publish and subscribe (P&S) interface implemented as a Web Service with callback operations. The P&S interface allows an arbitrary number of listeners independently of the listener's task. Thus, the infrastructure supports an arbtirary number of manager components, e.g., depending on the desired events to be monitored. The infrastructure components are as follows:

Integration Manager: The self-integration functionality is realized by the Integration Manager that registers itself at P&S of the components and configures the system, e.g. the mediator and the BPEL engine. The manager is triggered by events due to newly registered services or process descriptions. Then it performs semantic service discovery and automatically configures the BPEL4WS execution engine and the mediation system. As shown in the figure, each component of the system provides feedback information to the Integration Manager via its own P&S interface, and the manager takes actions regarding the components through the Management WS Interface.

Custom Registry: Custom registries are used for storing service and process descriptions. In our implementation we use a generic registry which is not limited to WSDL descriptions only, i.e. we can also store ontologies, BPEL deployment archives as well as configurations as files. Additionally, we can relate corresponding documents to each other. In this way a service ranking can be stored in relation to a service request and therefore reused. The registry entries can be managed through a WS interface and new entries are reported to listeners.

BPEL4WS-Engine: We use an Oracle BPEL4WS execution engine for the deployment and management of BPEL processes [17]. We have implemented a Web

Service interface which offers the necessary operations and is generic in respect to alternative BPEL execution engines.

Jetty Web Server: Our Message Mediation & Monitoring System is realized with the Jetty Web Server. Each mediator is implemented as a Java Servlet, and every mediator can be controlled and configured by a management WS interface. We have chosen a Web Server-based solution because it offers the necessary performance required by Web Service proxies for handling and transforming multiple concurrent invocations of Web Services. Additionally, it reports any faults between client and service. This will usually lead to a reconfiguration with alternative services.

4.1 Performance

A detailed performance study of our system is beyond the scope of this paper; it is forthcoming in a separate report. Nevertheless, we want to give some performance insights here. The test system is a Pentium 4 computer with 3Ghz and 2 GB memory running a Java Virtual Machine with 1 GB allocated memory. The test case scenario includes Plug-In discovery, XSLT generation and deployment of a mediator. The service discovery system has been tested with a single service request on up to 1000 similar service offers. As a result, we have a mean matching and XSLT creation time of 300 milliseconds per offer. Thus, if there are 50 service offers we can successfully deploy a mediator for the best matching result after about 15 seconds. The response time grows linear with the given configuration up to 3000 service offers. This limit is due to memory consumption as for the sake of a fast system response we keep the requests, offers and previous results in memory. Here, the scalability of our distributed infrastructure can be improved by balancing service offers between several server instances. Also multicore processors can greatly enhance the multithreading architecture. Thus, a more detailed system evaluation taking these system configurations into account is under way.

Even more promising is the stress test of our runtime mediation system. We have instantiated a single mediator on our test system and scaled the size of results for a simulated book search service in order to measure time consumption of runtime mediation in respect to the message size. Each book result adds 742 bytes to the SOAP response message as a set of XML nodes. The mediator is running on the same test system and responsible for currency conversion of the book price by executing integrated Plug-Ins and performing the XSLT tranformation of the SOAP message, as described above. A substantial difference between direct invocation of the Web Service and indirect invocation with our mediator between client and service becomes apparent with a response message carrying about 30000 book results and a message size of nearly 21 megabytes. The direct invocation needs 1,8 seconds and the mediated invocation 3,6 seconds. Again, we notice a linear growth and measure a mediated invocation time of nearly 7,2 seconds for a single 42 megabytes large SOAP message with 60000 book results. The current limit for a 1 GB JVM is a response message with 120000 book results and 20 concurrent client invocations on the same mediator. It has turned out that memory consumption for the XSLT transformation is the real limitation of our mediator system, but this can be mitigated by using multiple mediation servers on different machines.

5 Related Work

Several projects have dealt already with semantic annotations for services and Semantic Web Services. The most prominent ones are OWL-S [12] and WSMO [15]. Likewise, several semantic extensions for WSDL are available, e.g. WSDL-S [11] and SAWSDL [10].

OWL-S is an OWL domain ontology for Web Services. It describes the structure, composition, and protocol of a Web Service. The messages are described by a reference to elements inside the WSDL definition. However, the OWL-S ontology does not define a domain ontology for parameters and does not extend beyond the definition of WSDL parts. The ontology lacks the definition of fault messages, and it does not include a matching algorithm. Existing matching algorithms [6, 3, 4] do not match whole data structures, let alone handle ad hoc generation of XSLT.

Service mediation is a key element in the WSMO Semantic Web Services framework. It not only defines message mediation but also mediation between ontologies. If the mapping of parameters is manually specified, the system generates code for runtime mediation. Unlike our system, WSMO lacks support for a fully automatic mediation. It offers logic components for content transformation but does not apply semantic service discovery using a stepwise transformation of data types and units. Overall, the WSMO framework can mediate without manual administration but requires fixed, pre-configured transformation instructions, e.g. in XSLT.

WSDL-S and SAWSDL both define a schema extension of WSDL for semantic annotation. Whereas WSDL-S is directly related to OWL-S and therefore OWL ontologies, SAWSDL is a more general approach [13]. In WSDL-S additional attributes reference concepts in an OWL-S document, while in SAWSDL there is the process of uplifting and downlifting. Uplifting is the process of transforming the message's into an ontology or another semantic representation. The reasoner works and transforms on the ontology level which is then converted back to the required message format.

SAWSDL profits from semantic reasoning on ontologies but does not define a general matching algorithm. Furthermore, uplifting or downlifting for ontologies is done by manually specified transformation descriptions. SAWSDL is complementary to our approach as we only consider subclass relationship in our matching algorithm.

Several mediation systems evolved in the context of the Semantic Web Service Challenge [17]. The task of this challenge is to develop ontologies and systems for service mediation in respect to a problem definition. A successful implementation can solve one or more aspects of the challenge scenarios. These systems already accomplish behavior mediation and also to some degree ad-hoc invocation of Web Services. Behavior mediation is an important aspect in service mediation and will be considered in future work. In this paper we focus on a sophisticated extension for WSDL, support for transformation generation, and a performant mediation and binding system working with standard technologies.

In summary, our approach advances the state of the art in several ways: Firstly, we provide a complete and fully automatic service integration approach ranging from service registration over semantic service matching to runtime mediation. Secondly, we focus on complete service processes specified in BPEL4WS.

6 Conclusions

Among the key advantages of a SOA are flexibility and dynamicity. When business processes are modeled as a structured collection of loosely-coupled services, new business logic, in the form of Web Services, may be integrated dynamically in order to adapt the business process to changing conditions of the environment. Thus, SOA and Web Services are considered cornerstones of the "adaptive enterprise". However, even with a language like BPEL4WS process specifications depend on statically specified Web Service interfaces. Thus, some of the flexibility of a SOA is lost if there is no support for automated service evolution without time-consuming manual adjustments in case of changing interfaces.

In this paper we have presented a solution for self-integration of Web Services in BPEL4WS processes. This self-integration is based on semantically and syntactically extended WSDL service descriptions that conform to the WSDL standard. The extended WSDL documents are instrumental for the matching of service requests and offers, whereby various sophisticated transformation and conversion possibilities are considered. In case of a successful match, the required transformations are generated automatically. In addition, available plug-ins for value conversions may be arranged and deployed such that a stepwise transformation of values may be done on the fly. Thus, syntactically different message formats and type incompatibilities can be solved in a convenient, yet powerful way.

We have shown the viability of our approach with a prototype implementation based on Web Services. The performance study so far revealed fast, reliable and scalable service matching and runtime mediation even for large-scale test sets. We have already proceeded to enhance the usability of our approach by implementing user and administatrion interfaces for both the MECE annotation and the matching and mediation system. In our future work we will not only perform further performance studies but also adapt our approach for service compositions and behavior mediation. In this case the mediator will be able to split and merge SOAP messages to provide seperate access to input and output parameters for heterogenous Web Services in different states.

References

1. Automatic Service Brokering in Service oriented Architectures, Project Homepage. URL: http://www.vs.uni-kassel.de/research/ADDO/.
2. Tony Andrews, Francisco Curbera, Hitesh Dholakia, Yaron Goland, Johannes Klein, Frank Leymann, Kevin Liu, Dieter Roller, Doug Smith, Satish Thatte, Ivana Trickovic, and Sanjiva Weerawarana. *BPEL4WS, Business Process Execution Language for Web Services Version 1.1*. IBM, 2003.
3. Steffen Bleul, Thomas Weise, and Kurt Geihs. Large-Scale Service Composition in Semantic Service Discovery. In *IEEE Joint Conference on E-Commerce Technology(CEC ' 06)and Enterprise Computing, E-Commerce and E-Services(EEE ' 06)*, pages 427–429. IEEE Computer Society, June 2006.
4. Steffen Bleul, ThomasWeise, and Kurt Geihs. Making a Fast Semantic Service Composition System Faster. In IEEE Joint Conference on E-Commerce Technology(CEC ' 07)and Enterprise Computing, E-Commerce and E-Services(EEE ' 07), pages 517–520. IEEE Computer Society, 2007.

5. Steffen Bleul, Michael Zapf, and Kurt Geihs. Automatic Service Process Administration by Semantic Service Discovery. In 7th International Conference on New Technologies of Distributed Systems, Marrakech, Maroc, June 2007
6. Steffen Bleul, Michael Zapf, and Kurt Geihs. Flexible Automatic Service Brokering for SOAs. In Proceedings on 10 th IFIP / IEEE Symposium on Integrated Management (IM2007), Munich, Germany, May 2007.
7. Don Box, David Ehnebuske, Gopal Kakivaya, Andrew Layman, Noah Mendelsohn, Henrik Frystyk Nielsen, Satish Thatte, and Dave Winer. Simple Object Access Protocol (SOAP) 1.1. W3C Note NOTE-SOAP-20000508, World Wide Web Consortium, May 2000.
8. Erik Christensen, Francisco Curbera, Greg Meredith, and Sanjiva Weerawarana. Web Services Description Language (WSDL) 1.1. W3c note, World Wide Web Consortium, March 2001.
9. James Clark. XSL Transformations (XSLT). W3c:rec, W3C, November 1999. http://www.w3.org/TR/1999/REC-xslt-19991116.
10. Jacek Kopecký, Tomas Vitvar, Carine Bournez, and Joel Farrell. SAWSDL: Semantic Annotations for WSDL and XML Schema. IEEE Internet Computing, 11(6):60–67, 2007.
11. Ke Li, Kunal Verma, Ranjit Mulye, Reiman Rabbani, John A. Miller, and Amit P. Sheth. Designing Semantic Web Processes: The WSDL-S Approach. In Jorge Cardoso and Amit P. Sheth, editors, Semantic Web Services, Processes and Applications, volume 3 of Semantic Web And Beyond Computing for Human Experience, pages 161–193. Springer, 2006.
12. David Martin, Mark Burstein, and Grit Denker et al. OWL-S, OWL-based Web Service Ontology, 2004. URL: http://www.daml.org/services/owl-s/1.1/.
13. David Martin, Massimo Paolucci, and Matthias Wagner. Bringing Semantic Annotations to Web Services: OWL-S from the SAWSDL Perspective. In Karl Aberer, Key-Sun Choi, Natasha Noy, Dean Allemang, Kyung-Il Lee, Lyndon J B Nixon, Jennifer Golbeck, Peter Mika, Diana Maynard, Guus Schreiber, and Philippe Cudré-Mauroux, editors, Proceedings of the 6th International Semantic Web Conference and 2nd Asian Semantic Web Conference (ISWC/ASWC2007), Busan, South Korea, volume 4825 of LNCS, pages 337–350, Springer.
14. Deborah L. Mcguinness and Frank van Harmelen. OWL Web Ontology Language Overview. W3c note, World Wide Web Consortium, February 2004.
15. Dumitru Roman, Uwe Keller, Holger Lausen, Jos de Bruijn, Rubén Lara, Michael Stollberg,Axel Polleres, Cristina Feier, Cristoph Bussler, and Dieter Fensel. Wsmo - web service modeling ontology. In DERI Working Draft 14, volume 1, pages 77–106, BG Amsterdam, 2005. Digital Enterprise Research Institute (DERI), IOS Press.
16. Thomas Weise, Steffen Bleul, and Kurt Geihs. Web Service Composition Systems for the Web Service Challenge - A Detailed Review. Technical Report 34-2007111919638, November 2007. Permanent Identifier: urn:nbn:de:hebis:34-2007111919638.
17. SWS – Challenge on Automating Web Services Mediation, Choreography and Discovery. Challenge Homepage, September 2008. URL: http://sws-challenge.org/
18. Marc Kirchhoff. Automatische Nachrichtentransformation für semantische Web Services. Diploma thesis, Distributed System Group Kassel, December 2007, Kassel.

Dynamic Message Routing Using Processes

Thorsten Scheibler, Dimka Karastoyanova, Frank Leymann

IAAS, Universität Stuttgart, Universitätsstr. 38, 70569 Stuttgart
{scheibler, karastoyanova, leymann}@iaas.uni-stuttgart.de

Abstract. The *Enterprise Service Bus (ESB)* is composable middleware that provides applications with services such as message routing and transformation, service composition, dynamic discovery, transactional support, coordination, security features, and others. In an ESB supporting SOAP message exchange, routing algorithms typically follow the sequential SOAP message processing model, where SOAP headers are the main artefacts used to specify the message route and the processing of the payload by intermediaries along that route. This model supports neither alternative nor parallel message routes. In the case of a failing intermediary node this leads to a failure in the message delivery. Moreover, the execution order of services on SOAP message payloads at the intermediaries cannot be prescribed. In this paper, we demonstrate how these deficiencies of the SOAP message processing model can be addressed. We introduce an approach that allows for specifying SOAP message routing logic in terms of BPEL processes. We show that parallel and alternative routes for SOAP messages can be modelled and executed, and the order of services that process a message at intermediaries can be predefined to accommodate the correct processing sequence as required by the concrete application domain. Features like dynamic discovery of services and flexible service composition are leveraged to enable flexible SOAP message routing.

1 Introduction

Services provide a powerful abstraction that renders a heterogeneous system homogeneous and thus facilitates application integration. Services expose functionality as abstract endpoints and are described in a platform and programming language independent manner. The binding to transport protocols and serialization formats is held separate from the interface descriptions to enable configurability and maintain loose coupling. The *Service Oriented Architecture (SOA)* embodies the service-orientation as its major principle. It reflects the natural evolution in architectural styles towards enabling seamless integration. The middleware for SOA is the so-called *(Enterprise) Service Bus (ESB)* [3] or shortly the Bus. The ESB is composable middleware that supports messaging as the basic communication paradigm.

The Web Service technology [12] is the only available SOA implementation that enjoys a great support by industry and academia. To enable interoperability, most software vendors support *SOAP* [6] since it is the standard messaging format and message processing model recommended to enable interoperability among *Web services (WS)*. The WS interfaces are described in *WSDL (Web Service Description*

Language) [7]. Therefore it is a prerequisite for the existing ESB implementations to support WSDL and SOAP.

The SOAP specification defines a model for processing SOAP messages on the message path that may involve multiple intermediaries and different transport protocols with different *Quality of Service (QoS)* characteristics between them. This is considered one of the greatest advantages of SOAP. The intermediaries relay the SOAP messages and may also perform additional functionality like encryption, logging, addressing and others using the so-called *additional services*. This is enabled by the SOAP message headers that also serve as an extension mechanism to the standard SOAP message processing.

The routing of SOAP messages from one intermediary to another is not addressed in the SOAP specification. Existing approaches however have the following disadvantages: (a) the sequence in which the additional services at an intermediary should be performed is not specified, which in some application cases is of great importance (e.g. decryption should be done before processing parts of the message on behalf of an additional service); (b) parallel execution of message processing tasks is not supported; (c) reliable processing and delivery of messages in the case of failing nodes is not guaranteed.

In this paper we present an approach that applies the process-based approach to tackle these disadvantages. Since *BPEL (Business Process Execution Language)* [2] is the standard for Web Service composition, it is only natural to apply it as a process description language; however, any other service composition language would suit the same purposes equally. In general, the approach boils down to mapping the SOAP message route to a BPEL process, where each node on the message path is represented in terms of a WS interaction activity in the BPEL process. The BPEL process is therefore driving the choice of the next intermediary on the SOAP message path. Apart from addressing the above open issues, BPEL, and in particular the existing extensions for flexibility and adaptation, can be exploited to enable a very powerful approach for SOAP routing. Since service composition is considered a part of the infrastructure services of an ESB, and hence BPEL engines are inseparable components of an ESB, the approach could easily be enabled for use on any existing ESB implementation. The approach has been implemented as a proof-of-concept prototype as an extension to an existing ESB implementation and a BPEL engine.

The paper is organized as follows. We start with an overview of the problem domain and discuss in detail the unsolved issues in SOAP routing. We also summarize the features and advantages of BPEL. Then the details about the actual approach are presented. We discuss future research directions and present our conclusions at the end of the paper.

2 Problem Statement and Motivation

This section presents the state-of-the-art in message routing and identifies the deficiencies of the current approaches when applied for routing SOAP messages. It therefore motivates the approach we present later in this paper. For the purpose of completeness we make an overview of BPEL, which we employ in this work.

2.1 SOAP Processing Model

SOAP [6] defines a standardized XML-based message format, a set of rules that describe how services should process a message and a mechanism to bind SOAP messages to different network transport protocols. SOAP messages are transferred from an origin (*initial sender*) to a destination (*ultimate receiver*) via potentially multiple SOAP processing nodes (*intermediaries*) (see Fig. 1). The transport protocol used along the path can be different between any two nodes on the message path, which provides an enormous advantage and is in the sense of composable middleware. On the other hand, QoS characteristics of the transport protocol influence the type of message delivery. Messages themselves consist of two parts: a header and a body. The body of a SOAP message is directed to the ultimate receiver of a message and contains the actual message payload. SOAP supports multiple encodings for the message payload. The header part of a message comprises metadata, primarily directed to the SOAP intermediaries along the message path. Intermediaries can be addressed by so called roles. Certain SOAP headers define how a message or parts of a message are to be processed by the intermediaries according to the SOAP processing model; these are the so-called additional services. However, the processing model does not specify in which order these header fields have to be processed at an intermediary. This may contradict the demands of the supported application domain and security measures. Sometimes, there are no dependencies among the additional services supported by the intermediaries for a SOAP message, which allows for optimized routing to multiple intermediaries, which may perform the work in parallel. This is not excluded by the SOAP processing model but the currently used routing mechanisms do not support parallelism.

In most cases, a static route is predefined and message processing is performed sequentially by the specified intermediary nodes. Upon failure of a node fault handling mechanism must be in place to tackle these faults. This concern is not addressed by the SOAP specification and hence the reliability of the SOAP message delivery is not guaranteed, as long as the message delivery is not guaranteed by the transport protocol implementation.

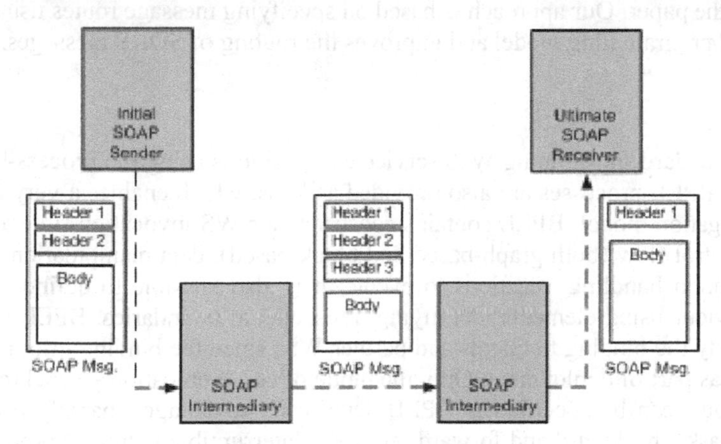

Fig. 1. SOAP processing model

2.2 Open Issues in SOAP Routing

The mechanisms for routing SOAP messages are considered out of scope of the SOAP specification since they are implementation specific. There have been attempts to standardize such mechanism and the most prominent ones are WS-Routing [9], WS-Referral [10], and WS-Addressing [8, 12].

The WS-Routing specification defines a format for defining a fixed SOAP message route between initial sender and ultimate receiver using message headers. It also allows for intermediaries to include additional nodes on the SOAP message path. WS-Referral is another specification meant for use in combination with WS-Routing and had the goal to enable flexible changes in the SOAP message route. Even though the use of additional services is enabled at each node, the sequence of processing the message headers cannot be controlled.

The WS-Addressing [8] specification defines a model and format for describing service endpoints in a technology independent manner; this is done through the so-called *endpoint references (EPR)* [8]. It also specifies the rules for serializing the information contained in an EPR into a SOAP message. Since an EPR contains the address of a service endpoint, once included into a SOAP message it can be used to identify the next node to process the message on the routing path. Each intermediary can set the endpoint address appropriately and thus prescribe the routing path. However, each of the intermediaries needs to have knowledge of the appropriate message path, which requires extensive configuration of the intermediaries with routing rules. This approach is followed by the Apache Synapse project [11].

With the existing solutions it is not yet possible (i) to define SOAP message routes with alternative or parallel processing of messages at multiple nodes at the same time. Additionally, (ii) the sequence of message processing by additional services at intermediaries cannot be predefined, even though it is required for the correct execution of applications in multiple scenarios. (iii) The fact that message routes are predefined and allow no parallelism and branching results also in fault-intolerance, since reaction to failures at nodes on the message path is not supported.

These disadvantages define the problem we address with the approach presented in the rest of the paper. Our approach is based on specifying message routes using the process-based programming model and improves the routing of SOAP messages.

2.3 BPEL

BPEL is the standard for defining Web service compositions using the process-based approach. All BPEL processes are also provided as WSs, which enables a very flexible WS aggregation model. BPEL contains constructs for WS invocation (interaction activities), control flow (both graph-based and block-based), data manipulation, fault and compensation handling, reactions to events; it is also possible to define all-or-nothing behaviour using elements identifying transactional boundaries. BPEL per se does not specify the binding to clients and partner WSs since the binding information is considered as part of deployment. Only the mode of communication – synchronous or asynchronous, can be specified in BPEL. Due to its advantages, namely parallel execution of tasks, backward and forward recovery, interruptible nature of processes, flexibility in WS aggregation through abstraction from concrete service endpoints, and improved configurability (due to deployment), BPEL is being successfully applied. Due to the advantages of the process-based approach in general and BPEL in particular, in this work we utilize BPEL to enable flexible, reliable SOAP routing (see section 3).

3 Dynamic Message Routing Using Processes

A typical routing route consists of various nodes connected by message flows. The flow can be split after certain activities and can be joined before other activities. This is similar to workflows where activities are connected by control connectors and the control flow can be split and joined. Thus, business processes are predestined to describe and execute routing logic. In our work we use BPEL for serializing the routing information and executing the actual message routing.

We distinguish two fundamentally different approaches for SOAP message routing regarding the way the routing information is made available: (i) the routing information is shipped with each message to each intermediary node, or (ii) the routing information is stored separately from the message and is accessed each time a SOAP message arrives at an intermediary.

In the case of shipping the routing information with the message, the message is self-contained, but increases in size and therefore the overhead for communication increases as well. Another drawback is that an intermediary has to be able to understand and execute (BPEL) processes. This is often not plausible because it requires a certain infrastructure which may not be offered by intermediaries. Moreover, the current state of the BPEL process instance, i.e. the progress of routing, has to be piggy-backed in the message. Hence, the BPEL process together with the status has to be serialized. Until now, no standard exists to describe how such information can be serialized in a platform-independent manner.

In contrast, the second alternative has no major impact on the SOAP intermediary. As the BPEL process is not shipped with the message, while only a pointer to the BPEL file is stored within the SOAP header, the intermediary does not need to understand and execute BPEL, and the message itself remains small. Because of these advantages we argue for the centralized routing approach, i.e. the SOAP messages routing is driven by a BPEL process that is not executed at the intermediaries, but rather centrally on a BPEL engine on the ESB (see Figure 2).

The routing process is executed on a BPEL engine provided as a service on the ESB. To enable this approach, the SOAP processing model has to be extended as follows: (i) a new header field including routing information has to be introduced, and (ii) this header has to be executed before all other headers (see Section 4 for details). Moreover, (iii) a new protocol has to be introduced to specify the interaction between each SOAP intermediary processing the routing header and the "central" BPEL engine where the routing process and the status is stored and executed.

This approach is not limited to a single workflow engine. It is possible to split the routing process into several processes, each executed on a different workflow engine; additionally, in general it is a common practice to use an infrastructure that can run the engines in such a way that a single-point-of-failure is non-existent (e.g. on a cluster). Here the term "centralized" stands for the fact that the SOAP nodes communicate with an external engine instead of processing the routing logic themselves. The approach (a) enables specification of alternative and parallel paths in the message routing programs, (b) provides a mechanism for ordering the processing of message headers at the intermediaries and thus allows for ordering of the execution of additional services at the intermediary SOAP processors, and (c) fosters reliability of the message delivery in a technology independent manner by enabling fault handling in case that nodes on the route fail. All these features allow for the flexibility needed by applications. The approach utilizes the principles of composable middleware and maintains the standard-based approach for extending specifications and bus implementations.

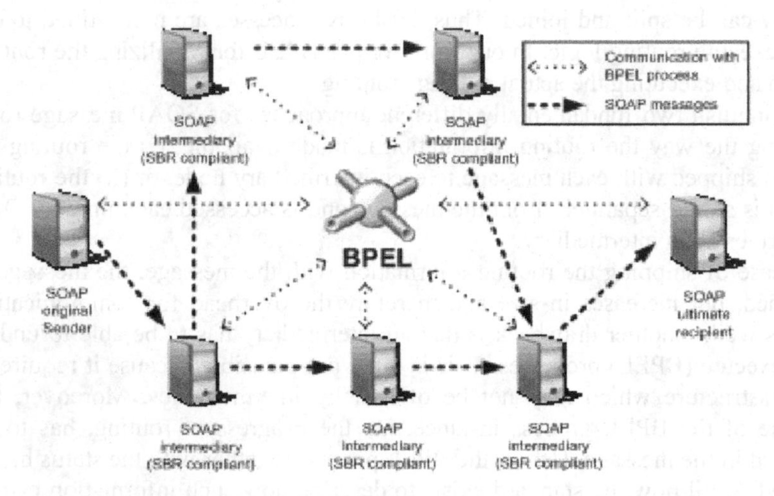

Fig. 2. Overview of SOAP BPEL Routing with centralized Routing Logic

4 SOAP BPEL Routing (SBR)

The mechanism for process-based routing within the SOAP processing model we propose in this work is illustrated in Figure 2. As mentioned in the previous section, apart from the routing logic, the additional routing information is needed and is incorporated in SOAP header fields (Section 4.1). Additionally, a mechanism and communication protocol between an intermediary and the workflow engine needs to be devised (Section 4.2), as well as an overall routing protocol (Section 4.2).

4.1 Header Information

The header block of SOAP messages needs to be extended so that routing using BPEL processes can be performed by SOAP intermediaries. The following information is required: The EPR of the routing process must be included since the routing is performed by a central BPEL process and it the intermediaries need to communicate with it. For correlation the process ID reflecting the process instance and the current routing status are needed. Because a message can traverse various parallel routing paths we need a message path ID. It is also needed to correlate requests sent to concrete process instance on the BPEL engine. The header must also include information about which services in which order have to be processed at an intermediary together with an optional part with the path IDs to be aggregated, and the address (EPR) of the aggregation service. The field *messageId* enables the definite correlation of a message to a routing process instance. The optional fields *replyTo* and *faultTo* specify the URIs of the ultimate receiver and the service to which possible faults have to be sent. The field *relatesTo* indicates the connection to a message sent earlier (see Figure 3).

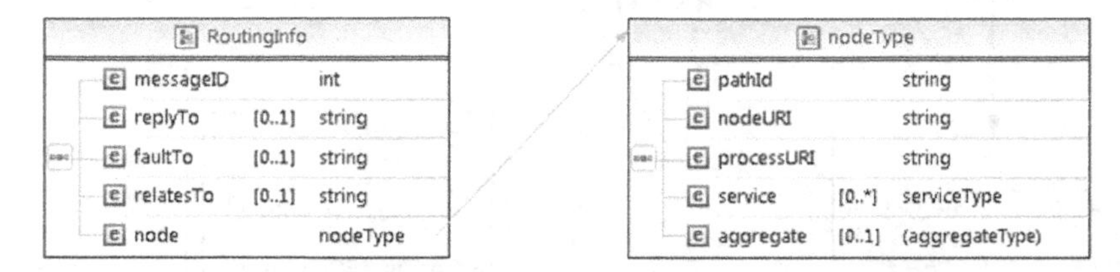

Fig. 3. Routing Header (in XSD)

4.2 Protocol Between Intermediary and Process

Since the routing logic is described in BPEL it is therefore rendered as a Web service, accompanied by a WSDL file describing the service interface. Each SOAP node (initial sender, intermediary, ultimate receiver) sends a *RoutingRequest* message to the BPEL engine, i.e. the Web service reflecting the process, to get the needed routing information (see Figure 4). The correlation of request message and process instance is handled by a correlation set including a system-wide unique *messageID* and a unique *pathID*. With the help of these fields the engine can identify which running process instance is requested and which receiving element within the instance the message has to be sent to.

The answer including the routing information is sent to the SOAP node as a *RoutingResponse* message. The routing information contains a list of nodes to which the message has to be sent next. Each node is addressed by a URI and is optionally assigned a list of services to be processed at the node. Furthermore, a URI of the routing process to be contacted by each subsequent node and the path ID of the message flow is contained. Merging of several parts is enabled by the aggregate list and the name of the aggregation service.

4.3 Detailed Routing Protocol

To set up and process the additional header fields a new protocol has to be introduced (see Figure 4). The initial sender (SBR compliant) gets a message to be sent from a client. The first step is to contact the Web service representing the routing logic (i.e. a BPEL process) to obtain the data needed for the first routing step. Afterwards the sender constructs the SBR header fields based on the response from the routing logic. The elements *massageID*, *pathID*, *nodeID*, and *processURI* are set. If the application wants to establish a request-response communication (i.e. the ultimate recipient has to respond to the application) the header field *replyTo* has to be set with the appropriate URI. The node responsible for collecting error messages is identified by its URI in the *faultTo* element. After the construction of the SBR header the SOAP message is transmitted to the recipient listed at the *nodeURI* element. If the routing logic specifies to send the message to a set of nodes, a message is created for each and every recipient according to the routing information and is transmitted to them.

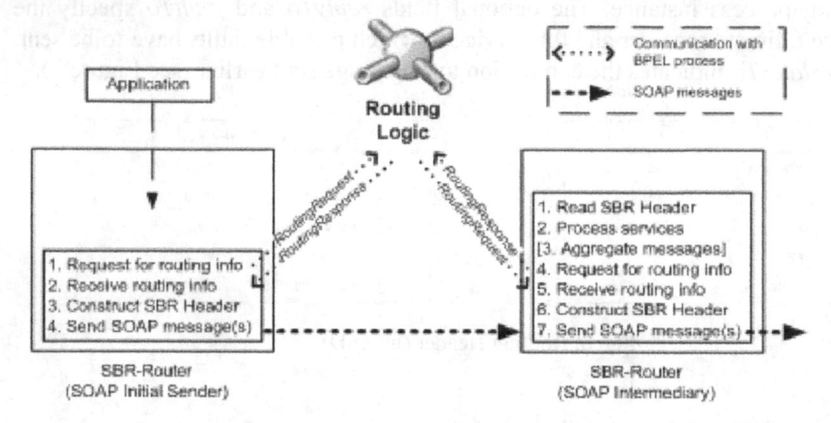

Fig. 4. Routing Protocol in Detail

After a SOAP intermediary receives a message it has to read and interpret the SBR header. Note that for these purposes the header attribute *mustUnderstand* has to be set to true. According to the information included in the *service* element, the node has to process the message using all listed additional services. These services (i.e. roles) are installed on the SOAP node according to the SOAP processing model. After processing the message content the intermediary may have to aggregate incoming messages if the appropriate SBR header field is set. The aggregation service is also installed on the SOAP node. Upon completed aggregation, the intermediary contacts the routing process, collects the routing information, and constructs the SBR header as stated above. Afterwards, the SOAP message is sent to the next intermediaries.

If the intermediary is the ultimate recipient (there is only one ultimate recipient) the mechanism is similar: first, the message content is processed according to the header fields, and second, the routing logic is contacted. If the logic responds with an empty *routeTo* field, the sender is thus the ultimate recipient. In this case, the node transfers the message to its application. If the element *replyTo* is set, the message is sent to the specified URI.

Special cases of the routing protocol are nodes where the outgoing message path is split or the incoming message paths are joined. Two different scenarios exist for splitting a message: (a) the whole message is copied and transferred over different message paths where all intermediaries can change arbitrary parts in the copies; (b) the message is split into different parts and these parts are sent to parallel processing steps. The parts do not have to be necessarily non-overlapping. Both alternatives leads to different problems to be solved at join nodes (where the different message paths lead to one node) and the messages have to be aggregated. The former approach requires aggregating of the different copies of a message. The algorithm is complex and not always deterministic if same parts of the messages are changed in parallel.

Otherwise the aggregation can be easily processed. The aggregation of messages is also straightforward for the latter approach if the message split is disjunctive. Problems can occur, if a message is split non-disjunctively or if for example similar parts are added to the message by nodes on parallel message paths. Currently, the implementation only allows the approach that routes copies of whole messages.

4.4 Example Scenario for SBR

To illustrate SBR on a practical basis, we present a scenario with a simple routing process (see Figure 5). We do not show the BPEL and WSDL files in detail but explain how the SOAP message header represents the routing information. The process specifies a routing route which starts at router 1 as the first message processing node. Afterwards the message is copied and sent to router 2 and 3 in parallel. After the nodes represented by router 2 and 4 finished their work, two messages are sent to router 5. This node is responsible for aggregating these two incoming, correlated messages into a single message. After processing the message at router 5 the resulting message is sent to the connected application.

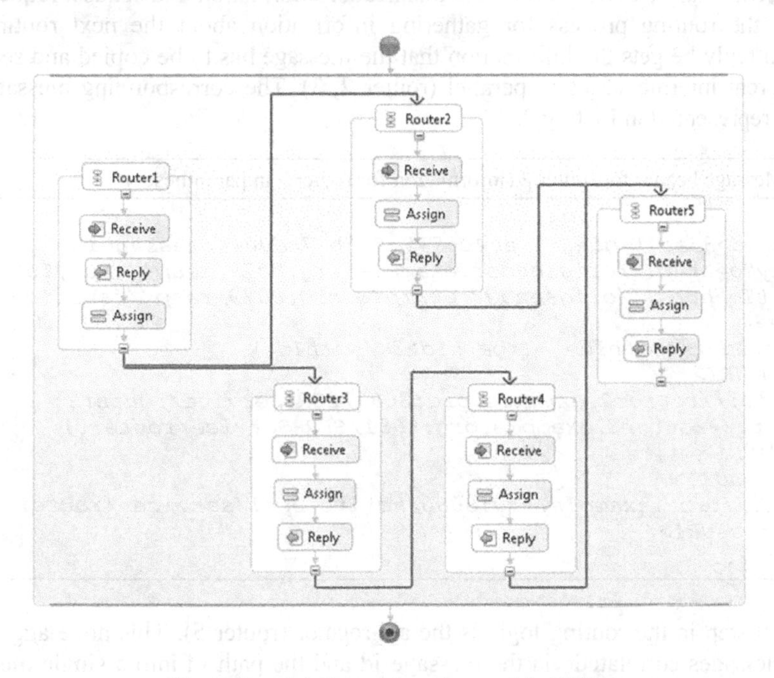

Fig. 5. Routing Protocol represented in BPEL

Initially, the origin sender constructs the SOAP message header with which the first intermediary of the routing logic has to work (Listing 1). This header includes all data necessary for identifying the message (messageId and pathId), the next intermediary (nodeURI), and data for referencing the routing process (processURI). For the sake of simplicity the service elements, indicating the real processing of message content, are left out. The header is included into the message by the initial sender, and afterwards sent to the intermediary identified by the nodeURI element.

Listing 1. SOAP message router of origin sender

```
<ns1:RoutingInfo soapenv:mustUnderstand="1"
  xmlns:ns1="urn:iaas.uni-stuttgart.de/proposals/sbr/2006/08"
  xmlns:soapenv="http://schemas.xmlsoap.org/soap/envelope/">
  <messageId>33ea4f-d5eg41-ab4ca5-5efa3b-7cd901</messageId>
  <replyTo>http://origsender.example.org:8079/resp</replyTo>
  <faultTo>http://origsender.example.org:8079/resp</faultTo>
  <node>
    <pathId>1</pathId>
    <nodeURI>
      http://router1.example.org:8081/SBR-Router/RoutingService
    </nodeURI>
    <processURI>
      http://proc.example.org:8080/active-bpel/services/route1
    </processURI>
  </node> ...
```

The next intermediary (router1) processes this header information and sends a request message to the routing process for gathering information about the next routing step(s). As a reply he gets the information that the message has to be copied and sent to two different intermediaries in parallel (router 2, 3). The corresponding message headers are represented in Listing 2.

Listing 2. Message header for router 2 (information for router 3 in parentheses)

```
...
 <messageId>33ea4f-d5eg41-ab4ca5-5efa3b-7cd901</messageId>
   <replyTo>http://origsender.example.org:8079/resp</replyTo>
   <faultTo>http://origsender.example.org:8079/resp</faultTo>
   <node>
     <pathId>2</pathId>  (<pathId>3</pathId>)
     <nodeURI>
       http://router2.example.org:8081/SBR-Service/router2
     (http://router3.example.org:8081/SBR-Service/router3)
   </nodeURI>
   <processURI>
     http://proc.example.org:8080/active-bpel/services/route1
   </processURI>
 </node> ...
```

An important step in the routing logic is the aggregator (router 5). This node aggregates two messages correlated via the message id and the path id into a single message. The aggregator is not processing the content but rather constructs a result message for the ultimate receiver application. The header fields of messages arriving at the aggregator are similar to those in Listing 1 but also include aggregation information (see Listing 3).

Listing 3. Message header for aggregator

```
...
<aggregate>
    <pathID>2</pathId><pathID>3</pathId>
</aggregate>
...
```

5 Discussion and Future Work

The approach for SOAP message routing using BPEL can be improved further. In particular, currently we disallow the splitting of messages along the routing path in the present implementation, and if two nodes need to process the same message in parallel, each of them gets a copy of the whole message. This might lead to inconsistencies and irreconcilable messages. When splitting messages the necessity of correlation of the results becomes obvious. Correlation of messages to the appropriate process instances is supported by BPEL and the BPEL engines; however the correlation information has to be carried in the SOAP messages, which is supported by the newly introduced header fields. Aggregation of messages needs also to be modelled in the routing process. Fault handling and compensation are mechanisms provided by the process-based approach to enable correct completion of the processes. These can be employed for enabling the reliability of SOAP message routing. Fault handling and compensation logic needs to be included into the BPEL processes. For this some additional extensions to the messages exchanged between the intermediaries and the BPEL engine are needed. In particular, the intermediary must provide the EPR of a compensating service. Addressing these issues is part of our future work.

The routing processes can be rendered even more flexible. The EPRs of the SOAP intermediaries can be discovered dynamically during execution of the routing logic using a mechanism for dynamic binding developed in our previous work; this is the "find and bind" mechanism [5] and has been implemented as an extension to the bus implementation incorporated into the ActiveBPEL[1] engine. This mechanism can also be applied as a fault handling mechanism when nodes on the routing path fail. Parameterisation of the BPEL logic can enable adaptation, as presented in [5], and can be leveraged in SOAP message routing processes during their execution. Semantic information in terms of ontologies can also be employed for the description of the SOAP processors to be discovered by the routing logic [1].

Routing of messages has to be specified while modelling enterprise application integration (EAI) scenarios with EAI patterns [13] (e.g. Routing Slip pattern). Such patterns can be parameterized and automatically transformed into executable BPEL code [4]. The BPEL routing code can natively be executed by the middleware.

In order to support the automatic generation of BPEL processes for routing we plan to develop a special purpose graphical modelling tool. The tool will exploit the one-to-one correspondence between the BPEL process and the routing graph.

[1] ActiveBPEL Engine. http://www.activevos.com/community-open-source.php

6 Conclusions

In this paper we introduced an approach that facilitates the routing of SOAP messages using business processes. BPEL is used to model and actually execute routing logic, whereas the SOAP intermediaries are guided by the BPEL process and thus can send the message to the next dynamically selected processing node. For this purpose, in order to represent the routing information, extensions to the SOAP processing model with additional header fields were necessary. We also specified and implemented an additional communication protocol between the SOAP processor and the BPEL engine that executes the routing process. We have shown that the suggested approach enhances existing approaches for routing SOAP messages with features like parallelism and branching. Furthermore, the reliability of SOAP message processing is improved, since BPEL supports fault and compensation handling, as well as dynamic binding of services during runtime which all address the problem with failing SOAP nodes.

7 References[2]

1. Karastoyanova, D. et al.: Semantic Service Bus: Architecture and Implementation of a Next Generation Middleware. In Proceedings of SEIW 2007 at ICDE 2007.
2. OASIS: WS-BPEL Version 2.0. http://docs.oasis-open.org/wsbpel/2.0/CS01/wsbpel-v2.0-CS01.html.
3. Chappell, D.: Enterprise Service Bus. O'Reilly Media, Inc., 2004.
4. Scheibler, T., Leymann, F.: A Framework for Executable Enterprise Application Integration Patterns. Enterprise Interoperability III. Springer, 2008.
5. Karastoyanova, D. et al.: An Approach to Parameterizing Web Service Flows. ICSoC2005.
6. SOAP Version 1.2. 2007. http://www.w3.org/TR/soap/.
7. W3C: WSDL 1.1. http://www.w3.org/wsdl/.
8. W3C: Web Service Addressing (WS-Addressing). http://www.w3.org/Submission/ws-addressing/
9. Nielsen, H. F., Thatte, S.: WS-Routing. 2001. http://msdn.microsoft.com/en-us/library/ms951249.aspx.
10. Nielsen, H. et al.: WS-Referral. 2001. http://msdn.microsoft.com/library/default.asp?url=/library/en-us/dnglobspec/html/ws-referral.asp.
11. Apache Synapse Enterprise Service Bus (ESB). http://incubator.apache.org/synapse/.
12. Weerawarana, S. et al.: Web Services Platform Architecture: SOAP, WSDL, WS-Policy, WS-Addressing, WS-BPEL, WS-Reliable Messaging, and More. Prentice Hall PTR, 2005.
13. Hohpe, G., Woolf, B.: Enterprise Integration Patterns: Designing, Building, and Deploying Messaging Solutions. Addison-Wesley Professional, 2003.

[2] Links' validity checked on 09/10/2008.

Abstract User Interfaces for Mobile Processes

Sonja Zaplata, Ante Vilenica, Dirk Bade, Christian P. Kunze

Distributed Systems and Information Systems,
Computer Science Department, University of Hamburg,
Vogt-Kölln-Str. 30, 22527 Hamburg, Germany

Abstract. An important focus of recent business process management systems is on the distributed, self-contained and even disconnected execution of processes involving mobile devices. Such an execution context leads to the class of *mobile processes* which are able to migrate between mobile and stationary devices in order to share functionalities and resources provided by the entire (mobile) environment. However, both the description and the execution of tasks which involve *interactions of mobile users* still require the executing device and its context to be known in advance in order to come up with a suitable user interface. Since this seems not appropriate for such decentralized and highly dynamic mobile processes, this work focuses on the integration of manual tasks on the respective ad-hoc creation of user interfaces at runtime. As an important prerequisite for that, this paper first presents an *abstract and modality-independent interaction model* to support the development and execution of *user-centric* mobile processes. Furthermore, the paper describes a prototype implementation for a corresponding system infrastructure component based on a service-oriented execution module, and, finally, shows its integration into the *DEMAC* (*Distributed Environment for Mobility-Aware Computing*) middleware.

1 Introduction

Current mobile applications and middleware platforms are evolving into a main driving factor for *pervasive systems*. Main advantages of such environments include the use of context information for increased awareness of highly dynamic vicinities and adapting to those accordingly. Since the use of mobile devices spreads increasingly, such context-aware systems also become increasingly interesting for the execution of distributed business processes (e.g. [4, 9]). In difference to traditional approaches in this field, the concept of *mobile processes* [5] focuses on the cooperation among devices in a mobile vicinity. A mobile process therefore represents a goal-oriented composition of services which can migrate to other (mobile or stationary) devices in order to share the functionality provided by these nodes. Figure 1 shows an (abstract) mobile process migrating between three devices in dependence of the discovered context. As long as the process engine of a device is able to bind local or remote services to the activities of the process instance, it is responsible for its execution. However, in cases of failures or lack of respective resources the engine has to find other devices in order to transfer the remaining process, its state and control flow to one of them. Due to the opportunity to execute the mobile process in different execu-

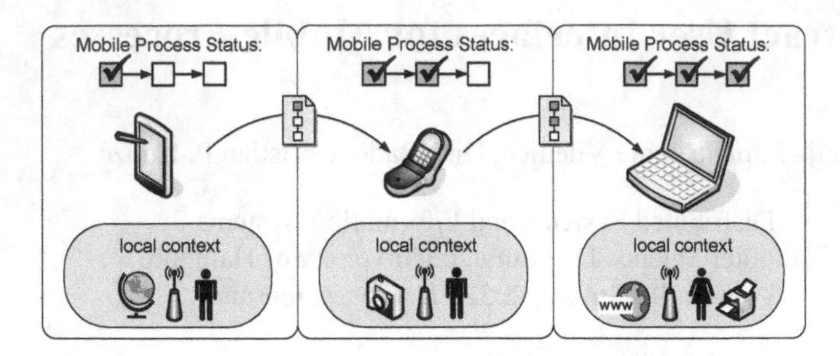

Figure 1 Context-based Cooperation: Mobile Process Execution [6]

tion contexts, this strategy avoids bottlenecks resulting from missing resources and thereby increases the probability of a successful execution [6].

Within a mobile process, activities containing (automated) applications are integrated in a single process description holding the relevant data and the current status of the process instance. The activities within such a process are identified by *abstract service classes* to refer to applications and services in a technology-independent way. This is necessary since the type of services and applications provided in the actual execution environment cannot be determined at design time – but results from the available resources and technologies during runtime. Furthermore, a mobile process can involve arbitrary tasks and heterogeneous devices – and therefore also different contexts which cannot be foreseen in advance [5,6]. Examples for such contexts are different service qualities, different network connections, and different device characteristics such as processing power, memory capacity or display size and resolution.

Depending on the type of the mobile device, also a particular set of interaction modalities is supported. Devices such as built-in car navigation systems mostly support voice output only, whereas a simple pager can only present short text messages. Other devices such as PDAs and notebooks use combined modalities (e.g. for a video-conference), and finally input-only devices such as RFID-readers are not able to present output data by themselves but have to be connected to additional hardware (e.g. a monitor). Due to this heterogeneity, there is also a great variety of possible user interfaces, so interactive tasks still have to be developed platform-dependent with a priori knowledge about the specific device and its current context.

Because of these circumstances, mobile processes are so far only realized to execute automated services. But, primary due to the fact that users carry mobile devices in order to *interact* with them, manual tasks and interactive applications play a very important role. Relevant applications for mobile processes include user notification, confirmation of activities, or the manual handling of errors occurring during process execution. A supporting middleware platform therefore also needs an abstract, modality- and platform-independent user interface model and an interaction execution module to (automatically) tailor the user interface to a specific platform at runtime. Accordingly, this paper analyses the integration of user interactions to enable the development of *user-centric* mobile processes.

The following sections of the paper summarize relevant requirements and analyse whether existing approaches can be applied to the identified problems. After a brief review of existing systems (section 3), section 4 presents the developed approach for an abstract interface model. Section 5 evaluates this approach by reporting on the development, the integration, and the scenario-based application of such user interfaces. Finally, section 6 concludes the paper with a summary and a brief outline of future work.

2 User Interactions for Mobile Processes: Requirement Analysis

The main goal of mobile processes is to support an autonomous cooperation to share mobile resources between mobile and stationary devices. As many of such processes are running in the background, an appropriate interaction module needs to emerge explicitly in case a new user interaction is required. Consequently, the interface description has to be specified within the mobile process in order to be able to migrate from one device to another – abstracting from particular interaction modalities, platforms, contexts and other device properties [5]. The descriptions must thus be *capable of being integrated into existing process description languages* and allow for *data exchange* with superordinated data flow constructs to enable control flow decisions based on data entered or automatically processed in previous (automated or manual) activities.

Since for such mobile processes all participating devices are determined at runtime, the type and the characteristics of the device which will actually execute the interactive activity cannot be predicted in advance. This means, the specific user interaction cannot be customized to the executing device, but rather depends on the resources available in the mobile vicinity. An adequate modality- and platform-independent approach for the specification of such user interfaces therefore leads to increased requirements resulting from the heterogeneity as well as from the limitations of mobile systems, e.g. restricted capacity of memory, computing power and electricity [6, 12]. Consequently, the interaction model should ideally *abstract from specific interaction modalities*, such that the most adequate one can be picked at runtime. However, in individual cases, a *specific interface modality is preferred* or even has to be fixed (e.g. viewing a picture is impossible without visual output). This means that not only the user interaction is dependent on the mobile device but also the selection of an appropriate mobile participant depends on the required interaction modality.

Finally, due to limited connectivity and relatively high costs of mobile data transfer, the process interaction model should *support disconnected execution*. This means that the execution environment must be able to process interface descriptions *without a durable connection to a central server* or to any other device. At the same time, both the description and the processing module have to be designed *considering memory capacity limitations of mobile devices*. Because of this trade-off, an approach should ideally respect both flexibility and dynamism requirements. This means, it should be possible to integrate user interactlos within the mobile process in order to allow disconnected operation as well as to externalize task descriptions in order to load them at runtime, e.g. in case the mobile device has not enough capacity to store large data or it needs up-to-date information.

3 Existing Approaches

A number of research efforts have already addressed some of the requirements for realising system environments related to this work. This section briefly reviews some of these activities and analyses their respective influence, feasibility and drawbacks to be considered in an enhanced approach for mobile processes.

For the overall architecture of a mobile process management system, one of the key questions is whether to use a *thin* or a *fat client* solution. Several workflow systems exist for either of these architectures, most of them also considering user interactions. To present a user interface, thin client approaches most commonly use a locally installed internet browser to exchange information with servers in the backend using stateless HTTP or WAP protocols. Most popular technologies involve *HTML/WML*, *XForms*, *Adobe Flash* or *Java Applets* to describe visual interaction elements. Furthermore, *Ajax* (Asynchronous JavaScript and XML) is used (e.g. in *Google Gears*) to provide a richer user experience as this technology allows to partially update the user interface by asynchronously fetching new information from a server in response to interaction events. Nevertheless - because of the inherent characteristic of decentralised mobile processes - such approaches which require a centralised infrastructure have several drawbacks in general:

- Thin clients require a stable network connection to exchange information with servers, which, however, is often neither possible nor preferable (e.g. considering costs or energy consumption).
- Interaction possibilities are constrained to the elements of HTML or WML as mobile devices cannot be assumed to support browser technologies like Flash or Java applets.
- Application development is more difficult as the responsibility for managing user sessions and dealing with unreliable network connections shifts from the client to the server side.

In contrast to that, a fat client does not necessarily need to be connected to a server all the time. Instead, the whole application as well as its data is stored directly on the device, user input is processed locally and a network connection is only used to communicate results or to receive new tasks. Even fully decentralized operation is possible as data may directly be exchanged between multiple (mobile) devices. This way, applications may run independently of a network connection and sessions may be stored directly on the local device. Once a network connection is available, results may be sent back to a server or to other clients for further processing. The notion of a *rich client* takes the idea of a fat client yet another step further, as a rich client is not only designed for one dedicated task, but allows arbitrary tasks to be executed. This is often accomplished by an open, plug-in oriented and hence extensible architecture. Moreover, such architecture promotes the adaptation for different user requirements and device capabilities.

There are several corresponding fat/rich client workflow engines available. For example, the architecture presented by Pajunen [9] describes a fully service-based workflow engine, running on mobile devices. For interaction, HTML pages and forms are used and the user's input is wrapped in SOAP messages and forwarded to a local WS-BPEL workflow engine managing the control flow of the process. As another example, the *Active Forms* [10] runtime environment addresses the integration of arbitrary applications into an XHTML- or mobile forms-based user interface. User tasks are described using WS-BPEL and executed by a lightweight workflow engine to orchestrate user interactions spanning multiple applications. However, several major drawbacks can be identified for these solutions in general:

- Web-based markup languages for rendering user interfaces such as XHTML, VoiceXML, etc. constraint interaction possibilities to a specific modality and do not allow arbitrary combinations.
- Business process execution languages which require static endpoint references (e.g. WS-BPEL) are inappropriate for inter-device processes in dynamic (mobile) environments as service providers need to be known in advance.
- Common extensions for user interfaces in process execution languages (e.g. *BPEL4People* [1], or *WS-HumanTask* [2]) mostly concentrate on the specification of manual human-oriented tasks, but lack the possibility to describe a user interface in detail.

In summary, existing approaches either require a centralized infrastructure and/or lack the possibility of processing a rich description language for interactive processes. Considering languages for this purpose, approaches can be classified into *abstract* and *model-based descriptions*. The *User Interface Modelling Language* (*UIML*) [8], for example, is a representative of the abstract description family. UIML allows defining interface elements in an abstract – device independent – way, but lacks a mapping to concrete presentation components as well as the integration of control flow logic. As another example, the *Extensible User Interface Language (XUL)* [3] is not – in contrast to UIML – transformed to a specific language, but interpreted at runtime. It is used by Mozilla's application suite to create user interfaces and is interpreted by the Gecko Rendering Engine at runtime. But as XUL can only describe graphical user interfaces, it is bound to the visual modality.

A further abstraction level is introduced by the class of *model-based interface approaches*. A popular example is the *ConcurTaskTree* (CTT) model [11] which specifies hierarchically ordered user tasks organized in a tree structure. The tree's root represents the overall task of the user in a platform-independent way, e.g. a confirmation task. The leaves of the tree structure represent the interaction components of the user interface which are necessary to fulfil this task, e.g. presenting the text to be confirmed and collecting the user's input. Although CTT thus allows designing dependencies between interface presentations, it lacks sufficient support to model data and control flow. For instance, it cannot be specified that the output of an interface should be dependent on the data values entered in a previous interface. Furthermore it is not possible to specify non-functional requirements to determine a particular behaviour of a user interface. However, CTT considers the heterogeneity of platforms and allows specifying multimodal interaction methods, which proves to be most suitable to form the basis of an abstract interface language for mobile processes. The enhanced approach based on CTT is therefore presented in the following.

4 A CCT-based Interface Model for Mobile Processes

The most important function of a user interface is to present information and to capture the input of the user. Therefore, user interaction components can be characterized as (data) containers, having a set of input data which can be accessed by the user via one or more interaction modalities, and having a set of output data, which can be referenced as the result of the user interaction. The proposed abstract description language to model user interactions is therefore defined as an XML-Schema consisting of three main artifacts: One represents the description of the user's task and the respective interface specification. The other two artifacts are needed to specify the control flow and the data flow allowing the integration into existing process description languages.

In order to deal with the heterogeneity of mobile devices and to enable an efficient development of user interfaces, an instance of such a user interface description is developed only *once* and is automatically transformed into an *arbitrary number* of platform-dependent representations at runtime (cp. figure 2), taking into account the specific capabilities of each platform and also the current context of the user.

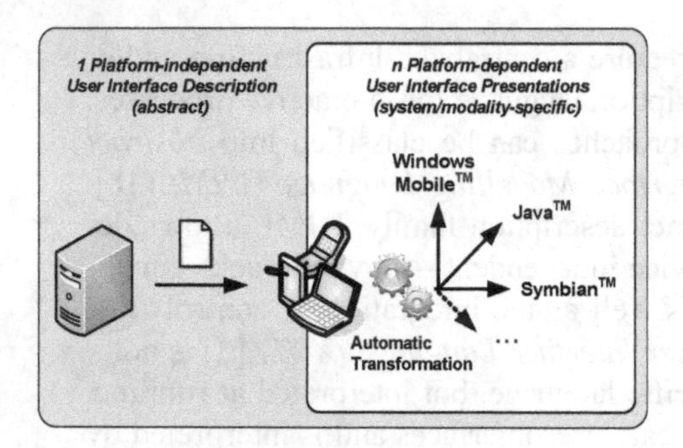

Figure 2 Schematic Diagram of the Platform-independent Model

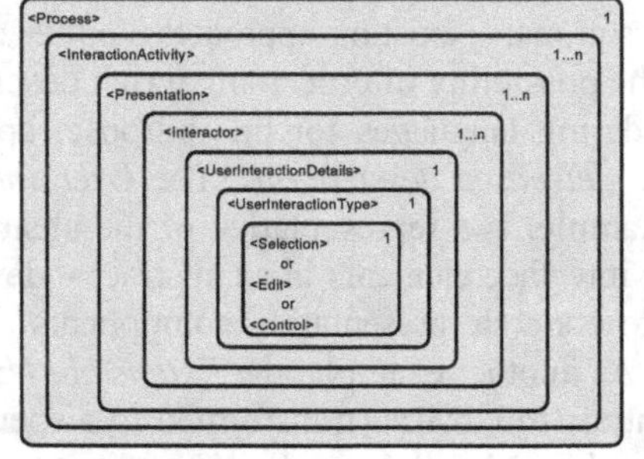

Figure 3 Artefacts of the Abstract User Interface Model

4.1 Abstract Interaction Components for User Interfaces

Resulting from the analysis of existing approaches as presented in section 3, abstract interaction components are based on CTT. The interaction components themselves have been adopted, but have been redesigned in order to ease and enrich the platform-independent description. Furthermore, the model was enhanced to express non-functional requirements as well as stylesheets to define a specific modality-dependent representation if needed. The hierarchy of the abstract interaction components is depicted in figure 3. Herein, *Presentation* denotes a single user interface, which consists of a number of interaction components called *Interactors*. An *Interactor* represents the root element of an abstract interaction component and could for instance be mapped to a *TextField* using the visual modality or a *Prompt* using the audio modality. The concrete functionality of an *Interactor* is specified by its child elements, which are grouped by the *UserInteractionType* into the basic user interface elements *Selection, Edit* and *Control*. The *Selection* element is responsible for data elements that can only be selected but not edited, whereas *Edit* also allows data manipulation. The *Control* element is used to navigate within user interfaces or to activate actions, e.g. it can be used to switch between different *Presentations*. Key concept within the abstract description of interaction components is the use of descriptive attributes. These attributes characterize the intended behaviour of an element in a platform-independent way, e.g. a *Selection* can be defined as a *SingleSelection* (meaning only one item can be selected) or as a *MultipleSelection* (allowing the selection of an arbitrary number of items). Furthermore, the expected cardinality of items can be specified to enable the most appropriate representation, e.g. a *SingleSelection* with a high cardinality may be transformed to a *ChoiceGroup* realized as a *Popup* using the visual modality whereas it may be transformed to a number of dialogs using the audio modality. Furthermore, the abstract description may contain a preferred modality and a fallback, if the modality is not available on the mobile device (not depicted).

4.2 Control Flow and Data Flow Components

As mentioned above, the platform-independent model also contains artefacts to describe the control flow and data flow between several user interfaces. With this approach, the proposed model is able to support a micro as well as a macro perspective on user interactions, so called *User Interaction Processes.*

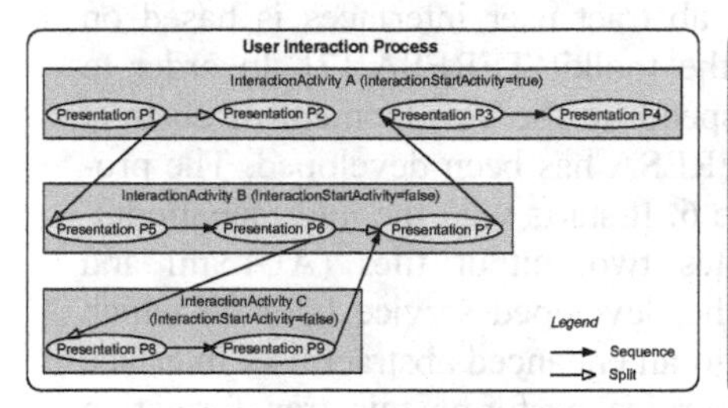

Figure 4 Micro Perspective on User Interactions

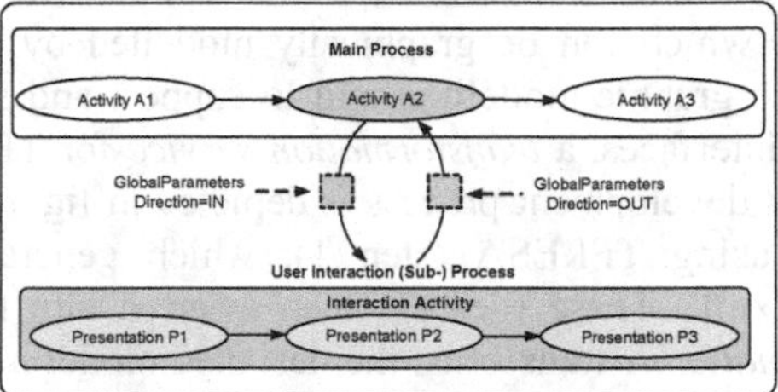

Figure 5 Macro Perspective on User Interactions

The former perspective describes a situation where the interaction process is used as a separate stand-alone service and therefore has to maintain the control flow and data flow itself. Figure 4 depicts such a stand-alone interaction service, which itself consists of a few subprocesses, called *InteractionActivities,* being connected via standard control flow elements such as *Sequence, Loop* or *Split* (cp. [13]). It is characteristic for the micro perspective that the service does not depend on other components to process the data and control flow. In contrast to this, the macro perspective characterizes a situation where control flow and data flow is (mainly) maintained by a superordinate process. Thus, the interaction process is only called when user interaction is needed. This perspective is depicted in figure 5 where *Activity A2* of the main process calls a user interaction (sub)-process. Selected parameters are passed to the subprocess and (the same or other parameters) are expected to be returned. Using the macro perspective with multiple *Presentations* requires a more powerful interaction processing module, but avoids to interrupt the interaction processing in case of several follow-up interfaces as usual for more complex interactions. Alternatively, the interaction can consist of a single *Presentation* only, so that the control flow is returned to the parent process after each interface presentation. This variant allows the realization of more simple interaction processing modules (only responsible for single interface interpretation and representation) and is therefore also suitable for less powerful devices. Being able to support these two perspectives enables developers to tailor interaction processes to specific applications by deciding which functionality should reside inside the interaction process and which functionality should be provided by the superordinated process. This flexibility therefore also allows a combination of user interactions and automated services.

5 User Interface Development, Integration and Realisation

To evaluate the developed interaction model, this section gives a brief overview of its overall applicability. Therefore, support for the development process using an existing tool is presented first, followed by the integration into the DEMAC middleware and the execution of a selected example application. Finally, experiences with the prototype realisation as well as usability aspects are discussed.

5.1 Modelling Abstract User Interfaces with TERESA

As mentioned above, the proposed model for abstract user interfaces is based on CTT, which can be graphically modelled by the toolkit TERESA [7]. In order to enable graphic modelling and to support and speed up the development of abstract user interfaces, a *transformation service* for TERESA has been developed. The proposed development process is depicted in figure 6. It starts with the interface modelling using TERESA (step 1), which generates two output files (AUI.xml and CTT.xml). These files are then inserted into the developed service (step 2) which *automatically* transforms the designed model into an enhanced abstract user interface description (step 3). Since the intermediary service performs this transformation automatically, it allows the developer to use TERESA as a graphical development tool to design abstract user interfaces for mobile processes, making it unnecessary to learn the syntax of the abstract description language.

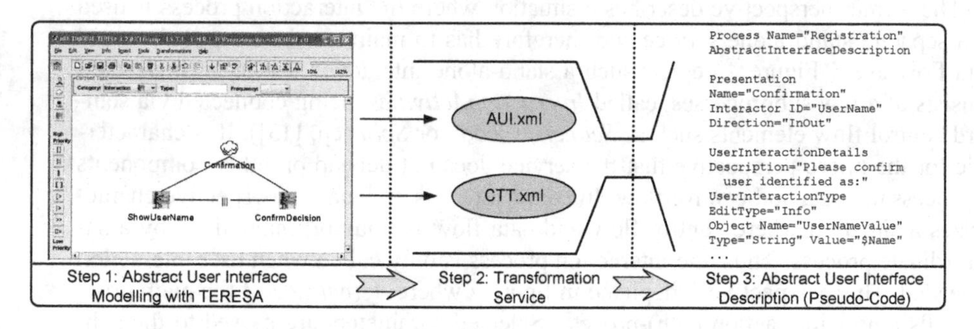

Figure 6 Development of Abstract User Interfaces

5.2 Integration with the DEMAC Process Management System

Mobile processes can be executed by a distributed execution engine such as realized in the *DEMAC* (*Distributed Environment for Mobility-Aware Computing*) project (cp. [5,6]). The respective mobile process management system uses the XPDL-based meta-description language DPDL (*DEMAC Process Description Language)* to describe the sequence of activities as well as the user's and application's non-functional demands (cp. [5,13]). Figure 7 shows the most relevant elements of the DPDL metamodel, consisting of native XPDL elements and enhancements for process migration, e.g. abovementioned non-functional requirements (modelled as *Strategies*). As shown in the figure, the abstract interface descriptions can be attached to the *workflow relevant data* without changing the structure of the process description language but inheriting existing constructs. The module which interprets the interface description is installed as an ordinary application. Thus, whenever user interaction becomes necessary, the application is called by the processes' control flow and presents the required user interface. In conjunction with the definition of non-functional requirements, this architecture also allows executing user-prioritised modalities automatically.

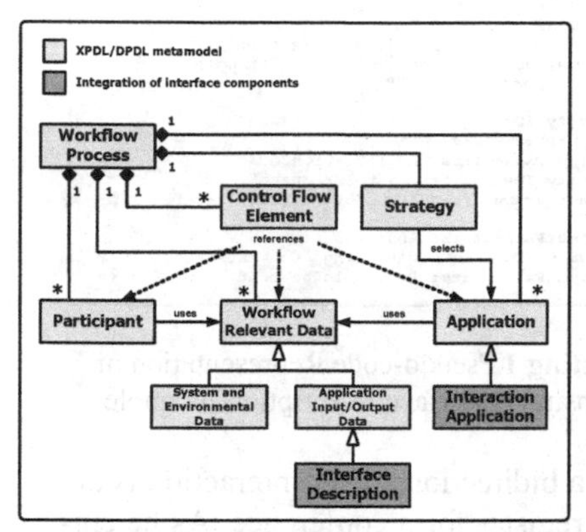

Figure 7 Integration of Interface Components into XPDL-derived Language

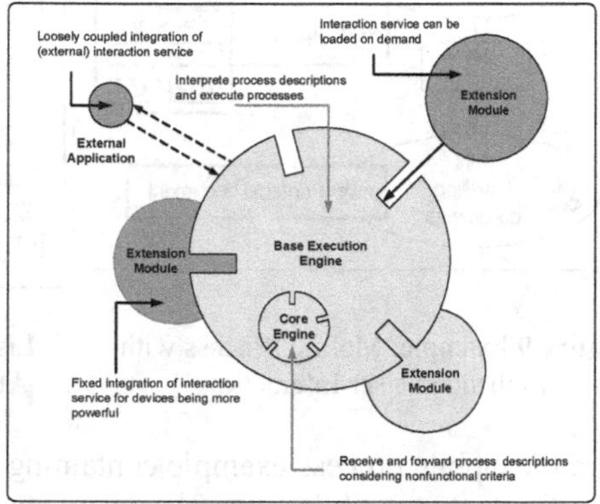

Figure 8 Schematic Diagram of the DEMAC Workflow Engine (cp. [5])

To support a large range of mobile devices with different capabilities, the corresponding *mobile process execution* engine is structured modularly. A core engine module supports the migration of processes and a base execution engine is responsible for executing the control flow of the mobile process and to bind functional services to the processes' activities (cp. figure 8). The interaction module can either be installed as a fixed part of the process engine, as an extension module or as an external service component which is only activated in case a user interaction is needed, e.g. to save memory space. Due to this loose coupling strategy, the interaction module can easily be switched off, exchanged and e.g. substituted by a module for another interaction modality if applicable. However, due to its abstract structure and its independence from superordinated control flow mechanisms and process management systems, the interface description can also be applied to other process description languages such as WS-BPEL or native XPDL and their corresponding execution modules.

5.3 Example Application Implementation

As motivated in section 1, there are several application areas for user interactions within mobile processes. Most relevantly, unidirectional interactions (presenting either output or input interfaces) and bidirectional interactions (combining output and input interfaces) can be integrated and combined to realize directives, notifications or confirmations addressed to the mobile user.

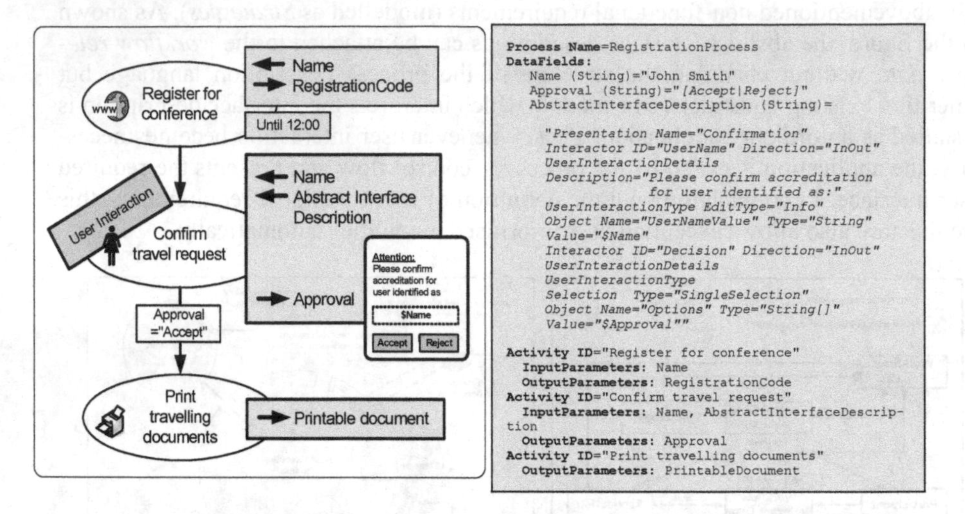


```
Process Name=RegistrationProcess
DataFields:
  Name (String)="John Smith"
  Approval (String)="[Accept|Reject]"
  AbstractInterfaceDescription (String)=

    "Presentation Name="Confirmation"
    Interactor ID="UserName" Direction="InOut"
    UserInteractionDetails
    Description="Please confirm accreditation
         for user identified as:"
    UserInteractionType EditType="Info"
    Object Name="UserNameValue" Type="String"
    Value="$Name"
    Interactor ID="Decision" Direction="InOut"
    UserInteractionDetails
    UserInteractionType
    Selection  Type="SingleSelection"
    Object Name="Options" Type="String[]"
    Value="$Approval""

Activity ID="Register for conference"
  InputParameters: Name
  OutputParameters: RegistrationCode
Activity ID="Confirm travel request"
  InputParameters: Name, AbstractInterfaceDescrip-
tion
  OutputParameters: Approval
Activity ID="Print travelling documents"
  OutputParameters: PrintableDocument
```

Figure 9 Example: Mobile Process with Embedded User Interaction

Listing 1 Pseudo-code Representation of Abstract Interface Description Example

A simple mobile process example containing a bidirectional user interaction is depicted in figure 9: A mobile researcher wants to register for a conference. As he currently does not have an internet connection to directly access the registration service and registration has to be done until a specified deadline, he initiates a mobile process to potentially use the resources of other devices in his vicinity to get his accreditation in time. Assumed that his request has been confirmed by the researcher's supervisor, the resulting travelling documents can be obtained in printable format (e.g. PDF). The graphical representation of the mobile process (figure 9) shows two service invocations (*Register for conference, Print travelling documents*) and a manual activity (*Confirm travelling request*). Attached to the activities, the required context (Internet access, special person, printer), non-functional parameters (the deadline condition) as well as the input and output data of each task are shown. As to see, the abstract interface is embedded inside the mobile processes' data container, holding the description of the elements and attributes to build an appropriate interface at runtime. Listing 1 shows a selected part of the mobile process containing the abstract interface description of the *Confirm travel request* activity as modelled with TERESA (cp. section 5.1).

For the actual execution, there are now several possibilities: Still assuming the researcher's mobile device is not able to handle the registration request, the process migrates to another (more capable) device and calls the registration service. Following, as mobile processes allow the specification of concrete participants (persons, devices or generic roles), the required person to execute the upcoming task is selected. The mobile process could therefore either migrate to the supervisor's device and present the confirmation task locally or - if applicable - invoke the respective interaction module from remote. Using the abstract description of the user interface, the interaction module decides about the modality in dependence of the current context. If, e.g. the supervisor is currently within a meeting, the confirmation is presented as a textual dialog. However, if she is driving a vehicle, audio output and automatic speech recognition are applied. Furthermore, if the interaction activity requires a particular interface modality or has to consider other non-functional aspects (e.g. display resolution) the DEMAC core engine searches for an adequate device to invoke this task, e.g. preferring the supervisor's notebook instead of her mobile phone.

5.4 Prototypical Implementation and Usability Evaluation

The interaction module receives and interprets the abstract interface description and transforms it into a device-specific representation. Except for its standard interfaces for integrating the process management system it can be realized as a device-specific component involving arbitrary sub-modules, e.g. to provide different interaction modalities. The prototypical implementation used in the DEMAC project is developed for conventional PDAs (using J2ME's CDC Personal Profile and visual modality only) and for modern sub-notebooks (using Java Standard Edition with voice output and automatic speech recognition). Without support for mobile processes, the interaction module can additionally be used as a standalone application for mobile phones, using the J2ME CLDC MIDP 2.0 profile (cp. [12]).

The respective mapping decision as well as the transformation process is transparent to the user. However, resulting from the scarcity of resources in mobile environments, the usability of the automatically generated interfaces mostly depends on the complexity of the desired artefacts and the capabilities of the platform actually used. Simple output interactions (e.g. directives or notifications) can be presented in a very consistent way over both modalities by presenting either a textual info screen or by using synthesised voice reading the message to be presented. Nevertheless, more complicated interface descriptions which require the user's input are sometimes affected by a vendor-specific interpretation of concrete interaction objects. Therefore, at least visual user interfaces differ slightly from device to device. With respect to the layout of output components this is not a usability problem, whereas the vendor-specific mapping of navigation keys and menu placements in some cases hinders an intuitive navigation (e.g. using left and right buttons for back- and forward navigation). Considering the audio modality, usability is strongly influenced by the quality of speech recognition software and hardware (e.g. microphones). For instance, within the realised example bad recordings or insufficient interpretations of spoken words sometimes lead to wrong decisions in the confirmation activity. However, the fall-back to the (more unambiguous) visual modality helps to deal with such problems in a reliable way.

6 Conclusion and Future Work

This paper introduces an abstract model to describe *modality-independent user interfaces* for mobile processes, enabling user interactions even for distributed tasks which involve several heterogeneous devices. Depending on the actual context and on the characteristics of the respective mobile device detected at runtime, the most appropriate way of interaction can thus be chosen dynamically. Moreover, the possibility to describe human tasks in a very abstract way relieves process designers from considering the system-specific behaviour of each executing device and its possible context.

In order to avoid problems caused by the cooperation of multiple heterogeneous devices using different modalities, future work will address the processing of data resulting from a user's input. A platform-independent representation of a user's input data may be necessary to ensure this information can be reused as output data in follow-up activities on devices with different modalities. In addition, use cases containing cross-modality interactions shall be analysed to further evaluate and advance the approach.

References

[1] Agrawal et al., BPEL4People Specification 1.0, Active Endpoints, Adobe Systems, BEA Systems, IBM, Oracle, SAP, 2007.

[2] Agrawal et al.: WS-HumanTask Specification 1.0, Active Endpoints, Adobe Systems, BEA Systems, IBM, Oracle, SAP, 2007.

[3] Goodger, Hickson, Hyatt, Waterson: XML User Interface Language (XUL) 1.0, Specification, http://www.mozilla.org/projects/xul/xul.html, Mozilla Foundation, 2007.

[4] Hackmann, Haitjema, Gill, Roman: Sliver: A BPEL Workflow Process Execution Engine for Mobile Devices, in: Proceedings of 4th International Conference on Service Oriented Computing (ICSOC), pages 503-508, Springer Verlag, 2006.

[5] Kunze, Zaplata, Lamersdorf: Mobile Processes: Enhancing Cooperation in Distributed Mobile Environments, in: Journal of Computers, 2(1):1-11, 2007

[6] Kunze, Zaplata, Turjalei, Lamersdorf: Enabling Context-based Cooperation: A Generic Context Model and Management System, in: Business Information Systems (BIS), 2008.

[7] Mori, Paterno, Santoro: Design and Development of Multidevice User Interfaces through Multiple Logical Descriptions. In: IEEE Transactions on Software Engineering 30(8): 507–520, 2004.

[8] OASIS: User Interface Modelling Language (UIML), Specification, Organization for the Advancement of Structured Information Standards, 2007.

[9] Pajunen, Chande: Developing Workflow Engine for Mobile Devices, in: Proceedings of the 11th Enterprise Distributed Object Computing Conference (EDOC), 2007.

[10] Pajunen, Chande: ActiveForms: A Runtime for Mobile Application Forms, in: Proceedings of the International Conference on the Management of Mobile Business, page 9, IEEE Computer Society, 2007.

[11] Paterno: Model-based Design and Evaluation of Interactive Applications, Springer-Verlag, 2007

[12] Satyanarayanan: Fundamental Challenges in Mobile Computing, in: Proceedings of the 15th ACM Symposium on Principles of Distributed Computing, 1996.

[13] WfMC: XML Process Definition Language, Version 2.0. Specification, Workflow Management Coalition, 2005.

Teil V
Leistungsbewertung

A New Service Curve Model to Deal with Non-FIFO Systems

Jens B. Schmitt, Nicos Gollan, Ivan Martinovic

Distributed Computer Systems Lab (DISCO), University of Kaiserslautern, Germany

Abstract. In this paper, delay bounds in data flow systems with non-FIFO service disciplines are explored. It is shown that conventional network calculus definitions of a service curve are not satisfying under the assumption of non-FIFO service. Either the definition is too strict to allow for a concatenation and consequent beneficial end-to-end analysis, or it is too loose and thus results in infinite delay bounds. Hence, a new definition is proposed and demonstrated to achieve both finite delay bounds and a concatenation of systems resulting in a favourable end-to-end analysis. In particular, we show that the celebrated pay bursts only once phenomenon is retained under non-FIFO service.
Keywords: Network calculus, non-FIFO, pay bursts only once, concatenation property.

1 Introduction

1.1 Motivation

Network calculus is a min-plus system theory for deterministic queuing systems [10]. The important concept of service curve was introduced in [3,6]. The service curve based approach facilitates the efficient analysis of tandem queues where a linear scaling of performance bounds in the number of traversed queues as well as the so-called pay bursts only once phenomenon is achieved [10].

Network calculus has found numerous applications, most prominently in the Internet's Quality of Service proposals IntServ and DiffServ, but also in other scenarios like wireless sensor networks [8,13], switched Ethernets [15], Systems-on-Chip (SoC) [2], or even to speed-up simulations [7]. Hence, besides queueing theory it has been accepted as a valuable methodology.

However, with respect to a single flow it is common in network calculus analyses to assume that *FIFO scheduling* is applied. This is restrictive, since for many real systems this assumption cannot always be made: In several studies of Internet traffic it has been shown that packet reordering is a frequent event (see for example [1]). According to these studies this is due to a growing amount of parallelism on a global (use of multiple paths) as well as on a local (device) level. In particular, for scalability reasons routers often contain a complex multi-stage switching fabric which cannot ensure to preserve the order of arrivals at its output. Furthermore, the use of link aggregation, where multiple physical lines are aggregated into a single virtual link, may often lead to non-FIFO behavior.

Also, in wireless networks, reordering of packets is a frequent phenomenon due to the use of retransmissions and sliding window protocols to recover from transmission failures. As a last example, let us mention wireless sensor networks in which packet scheduling decisions may be based on the data values contained in the packets following a data-centric paradigm. Under such circumstances hardly anything may be assumed about the scheduling order, let alone FIFO behaviour.

So, from an application perspective there is enough demand to warrant an investigation on how network calculus can be extended towards the analysis of non-FIFO systems. Immediate questions that come up are:

- Can existing network calculus concepts be carried over to the non-FIFO case?
- Is an efficient end-to-end analysis still possible?
- What is the cost in terms of performance bounds compared to pure FIFO systems?

1.2 Related Work

To the best of our knowledge, there is amazingly little existing work on the treatment of non-FIFO systems in the context of network calculus. Remarkably, in his pioneering paper [5], Cruz briefly showed how to derive a delay bound for a single work-conserving server under a general scheduling assumption (comprising any non-FIFO behaviour) based on the observation that the maximum backlogged period can be bounded given that traffic is regulated. Similar results can also be found in [4]. Yet, the multiple node case is not treated in these.

In [9], Le Boudec and Charny investigate a non-FIFO version of the Packet Scale Rate Guarantee (PSRG) node model as used in DiffServ's Expedited Forwarding definition. They show that for a single node case the delay bound from the FIFO case still applies while it does not for a specific two node case. They leave more general concatenation scenarios for further study.

The most directly related work to ours was done by Rizzo and Le Boudec [11]. They investigate delay bounds for non-FIFO guaranteed rate nodes and show that a previously derived delay bound is not valid in the non-FIFO case (against common belief). Furthermore, they derive a new delay bound based on network calculus results. Their delay bound does not exhibit the nice pay bursts only once phenomenon any more. Based on sample path arguments they argue that their bound is tight and thus conclude "pay bursts only once does not hold for non-FIFO guaranteed rate nodes". By contrast, in this paper we show that non-FIFO systems still possess a concatenation property and that Rizzo and Le Boudec's conclusion is not valid in the general case (their tightness proof contains a simplifying assumption which however is crucial and does restrict generality, for details see [12]).

In [14], we dealt with the problem of computing tight delay bounds for a network of arbitrary (non-FIFO) *aggregate multiplexers*. Yet, in that work we still made a FIFO-per-microflow assumption, meaning that we allow arbitrary interleaving of packets from several flows, but do not change the order in which packets of any given flow are handled.

2 Preliminaries on Network Calculus

As network calculus is built around the notion of cumulative functions for input and output flows of data, the set $\mathcal{F}$ of real-valued, non-negative, and wide-sense increasing functions passing through the origin plays a major role. In particular, the input function $F(t)$ and the output function $F'(t)$, which cumulatively count the number of bits that are input to, respectively output from, a system $\mathcal{S}$, are in $\mathcal{F}$. Throughout the paper, we assume in- and output functions to be continuous in time and space. Note that this is not a general limitation as there exist transformations between discrete and continuous models [10]. There are two important min-plus algebraic operators:

Definition 1. *(Min-plus Convolution and Deconvolution) The min-plus convolution and deconvolution of two functions $f, g \in \mathcal{F}$ are defined to be*

$$(f \otimes g)(t) = \inf_{0 \le s \le t} \{f(t-s) + g(s)\},$$

$$(f \oslash g)(t) = \sup_{u \ge 0} \{f(t+u) - g(u)\}.$$

Let us now turn to the performance characteristics of flows which can be bounded by network calculus means:

Definition 2. *(Backlog and Virtual Delay) Assume a flow with input function F that traverses a system $\mathcal{S}$ resulting in the output function F'. The* backlog *of the flow at time t is defined as*

$$b(t) = F(t) - F'(t).$$

Assuming FIFO *delivery, the* virtual delay *for a bit input at time t is defined as*

$$vd(t) = \inf \{\tau \ge 0 : F(t) \le F'(t+\tau)\}.$$

Next, the arrival and departure processes specified by input and output functions are bounded based on the central network calculus concepts of arrival and service curves:

Definition 3. *(Arrival Curve) Given a flow with input function F, a function $\alpha \in \mathcal{F}$ is an arrival curve for F iff*

$$\forall t, s \ge 0, s \le t : F(t) - F(t-s) \le \alpha(s) \Leftrightarrow F = F \otimes \alpha.$$

A typical example of an arrival curve is given by an affine arrival curve $\gamma_{r,b}(t) = b + rt$, $t > 0$ and $\gamma_{r,b}(t) = 0$, $t \le 0$, which corresponds to token-bucket traffic regulation.

Definition 4. *(Service Curve – SC) If the service provided by a system $\mathcal{S}$ for a given input function F results in an output function F' we say that $\mathcal{S}$ offers a service curve β iff*

$$F' \ge F \otimes \beta.$$

For continuous functions F and β this is equivalent to the following condition

$$\forall t : \exists s : F'(t) \ge F(s) + \beta(t-s).$$

A typical example of a service curve is given by a so-called rate-latency function $\beta_{R,T}(t) = R(t-T) \cdot 1_{\{t>T\}}$, where $1_{\{cond\}}$ is 1 if the condition *cond* is satisfied and 0 otherwise.

A number of systems fulfill a stricter definition of service curve [10], which is useful as it permits certain derivations that are not feasible under the more general service curve model:

Definition 5. *(Strict Service Curve – S^2C) Let $\beta \in \mathcal{F}$. System $\mathcal{S}$ offers a* strict *service curve β to a flow, if during any backlogged period of duration u the output of the flow is at least equal to $\beta(u)$. A backlogged period of duration u at time t is defined by the fact that $\forall s \in (t-u, t] : b(s) > 0$.*

Note that any node satisfying S^2C also satisfies SC, but not the other way around. For example, nodes operating under a delay-based scheduler and guaranteeing that a work unit arriving at any time t will not leave the node later than $t+T$ for some fixed $T > 0$, are known to provide a service curve $\delta_T = \infty \cdot 1_{\{t>T\}}$ [10]. Yet, such a variable latency node does not provide δ_T as a *strict* service curve. In fact, it does not provide any strict service curve apart from the trivial case $\beta = 0$.

Using those concepts it is possible to derive *tight* performance bounds on backlog, *virtual* delay and output:

Theorem 1. *(Performance Bounds) Consider a system $\mathcal{S}$ that offers a service curve β. Assume a flow F traversing the system has an arrival curve α. Then we obtain the following performance bounds:*

$$\text{backlog: } \forall t : b(t) \leq (\alpha \oslash \beta)(0) =: v(\alpha, \beta),$$
$$\text{virtual delay: } \forall t : vd(t) \leq \inf\{t \geq 0 : (\alpha \oslash \beta)(-t) \leq 0\} =: h(\alpha, \beta),$$
$$\text{output (arrival curve } \alpha' \text{ for } F'\text{): } \alpha' = \alpha \oslash \beta.$$

One of the strongest results of network calculus is the concatenation theorem that enables us to investigate tandems of systems as if they were single systems:

Theorem 2. *(Concatenation Theorem for Tandem Systems) Consider a flow that traverses a tandem of systems $\mathcal{S}_1$ and $\mathcal{S}_2$. Assume that $\mathcal{S}_i$ offers a service curve β_i to the flow. Then the concatenation of the two systems offers a service curve $\beta_1 \otimes \beta_2$ to the flow.*

Using the concatenation theorem, it is ensured that an end-to-end analysis of a tandem of servers still achieves tight performance bounds, which in general is not the case for an iterative per-node application of Theorem 1.

3 Why Conventional Network Calculus Does Not Work Well for Non-FIFO Systems

Our goal is to depart from the FIFO assumption under which the bound on the virtual delay in Theorem 1 can be computed. Hence, we are interested in bounding the *real* delay which is simply defined as follows:

Definition 6. *Assume a flow with input function F that traverses a system $\mathcal{S}$ resulting in the output function F'. The* real delay *for a bit input at time t and output at time t' is defined as*

$$rd(t) = t' - t.$$

Note that $rd(t)$ can be in any relation to $vd(t)$ ($<, >, =$). However, any scheduling order other than FIFO results in an increase of the bound for the real delay (obviously, $\forall t : vd(t) = rd(t)$ under FIFO):

Theorem 3. *(FIFO is Best-Case Scheduling) With respect to the worst-case real delay, FIFO scheduling is the best scheduling order as there is no other scheduling order that achieves a lower worst-case real delay.* [1]

So, in a certain sense it could be considered a logical break for a worst-case analysis methodology to assume FIFO scheduling as this actually constitutes a best-case assumption. This can be seen as a further motivation for making no restrictive assumptions on the scheduling order.

As mentioned in the previous section, one basically has two general options for node modelling: SC and S^2C.

3.1 Using Service Curves (SC) for Non-FIFO Systems

As the SC definition bears the advantages that many systems belong to that class and that it possesses a concatenation property, it is worthwhile an attempt to apply it also in the case of non-FIFO systems. Yet, the following example shows that it is impossible to bound the real delay in non-FIFO systems based solely on the SC definition:

Example 1. Assume a single node system $\mathcal{S}$ which offers a rate-latency service curve $\beta = \beta_{2,1}$ to a flow F which is constrained by an affine arrival curve $\alpha = \gamma_{1,1}$. Now assume the flow to be greedy, that means $F = \alpha$ and the server to be lazy, that means $F' = F \otimes \beta$. Thus, we obtain

$$\begin{aligned} F' &= \alpha \otimes \beta = \gamma_{1,1} \otimes \beta_{2,1} = \gamma_{1,1} \otimes \gamma_{1,1} \otimes \delta_T \\ &= (\gamma_{1,1} \wedge \gamma_{1,1}) \otimes \delta_T = \gamma_{1,1} \otimes \delta_T < \gamma_{1,1} = F. \end{aligned}$$

Hence, $\forall t \geq 0 : F'(t) < F(t)$, or equivalently, $\forall t \geq 0 : b(t) > 0$, which means the system remains backlogged at all times and a certain work unit can be forever in the system under these circumstances. Thus, the real delay of that work unit is unbounded. Note that using the standard FIFO assumption, we can of course bound the virtual delay of the system by $\forall t \geq 0 : vd(t) \leq \frac{3}{2}$.

From this example, we see that the SC property is too weak as a concept for analysing non-FIFO systems.

---

[1] Due to space limitations and for the sake of readability, the proofs of this theorem and of all following theorems can be found in [12].

3.2 Using Strict Service Curves (S^2C) for Non-FIFO Systems

Since, the SC property is too weak in order to derive a delay bound without a FIFO assumption on the system's scheduling order, it is interesting to investigate whether S^2C can deal with that situation. In fact, as was already shown by Cruz [5] (and can also be found in [4] (Lemma 1.3.2)), the intersection point between an arrival and a *strict* service curve constitutes a bound on the length of the maximum backlogged period and thus also a bound on the real delay for such a system:

Theorem 4. *(Real Delay Bound for Single S^2C Node) Consider a system $\mathcal{S}$ that offers a strict service curve β. Assume a flow F traversing the system has an arrival curve α. Then we obtain the following bound on the real delay:*

$$rd(t) \leq \sup\{s \geq 0 : \alpha(s) \geq \beta(s)\} =: i(\alpha, \beta).$$

So, the situation has improved in comparison to the SC case: Based on the single node result one can conceive, for the multiple node case, an iterative application of Theorem 4 together with the output bound from Theorem 1. More specifically, if n S^2C non-FIFO nodes, each providing a strict service curve $\beta_j, j = 1, \ldots, n$, are to be traversed by an α-constrained flow then a bound on the real delay can be calculated as

$$rd(t) \leq \sum_{j=1}^{n} i(\alpha \oslash \bigotimes_{k=1}^{j-1} \beta_k, \beta_j).$$

Setting for example $\beta_j = \beta_{R,T}, j = 1, \ldots, n$ and $\alpha = \gamma_{r,b}$ this results in

$$rd(t) \leq \frac{n(b + RT) + \frac{n}{2}(n-1)rT}{R - r} \tag{1}$$

Here, we see the typical drawback of additive bounding methods, with the burst of the traffic being paid n times as well as a quadratic scaling of the bound in the number of nodes [10]. The key to avoid this behaviour is to perform an end-to-end analysis based on the concatenation theorem. Yet, as we demonstrate in the next example S^2C does not possess such a concatenation property.

Example 2. (S^2C Possesses No Concatenation Property) Assume two systems $\mathcal{S}_1$ and $\mathcal{S}_2$, both providing a strict rate-latency service curve $\beta^i = \beta_{1,1}, i = 1, 2$, which are traversed in sequence by a flow F. Let F_1' and F_2' be the output functions from $\mathcal{S}_1$ and $\mathcal{S}_2$, respectively. As a candidate strict service curve for the composite system, we consider $\beta^{1,2} = \beta^1 \otimes \beta^2 = \beta_{1,2}$.

We now construct a backlogged period $[t_1, t_2]$ of the composite system such that

$$F_2'(t_2) - F_1'(t_1) < \beta^{1,2}(t_2 - t_1).$$

thereby showing that $\beta^{1,2}$ is not a strict service curve for the composite system:

Let $t_1 = 0$ and $t_2 = 3$ and assume the following behaviour of the input and output function

$$F(t) = \begin{cases} \epsilon, & 0 < t < 2 \\ 2\epsilon, & 2 \leq t \leq 3 \end{cases} \quad F_1'(t) = \begin{cases} 0, & 0 \leq t \leq 1 \\ \epsilon, & 1 < t \leq 3 \end{cases} \quad F_2'(t) = \begin{cases} 0, & 0 \leq t \leq 2 \\ \epsilon, & 2 < t \leq 3 \end{cases},$$

with any $\epsilon > 0$. It is easy to check that the composite system is continuously backlogged during $[0, 3]$ as well as that each individual system is not violating its strict service curve property. Nevertheless, for any choice of $\epsilon < 1$ we obtain

$$F_2'(3) - F_2'(0) = \epsilon < \beta^{1,2}(3) = 1,$$

which shows that $\beta^{1,2}$ is not S^2C for the composite system (while, of course, being SC for it). In fact, extending the example appropriately it can be shown that the only strict service curve that can be guaranteed by the composite system is the trivial case $\beta = 0$. This can be seen by making ϵ arbitrarily small and alternating between backlogged and idle periods of the individual systems sufficiently often. Another way to view this, is that the backlogged period of a composite system cannot be bounded based on the individual systems providing a strict service curve.

So, from this discussion we can conclude that S^2C is too strict as a concept in order to allow for tight bounds under the non-FIFO assumption, since it possesses no concatenation property for the multiple node case.

The bottom line of this section is that we need a new node model: It should allow for calculating a bound on the real delay and, yet, also have a concatenation property in order to avoid loose additive bounds.

4 Introducing a New Service Curve Model: Sufficiently Strict Service Curve

In this section, we introduce a new node model that allows to bound the delay over a tandem of non-FIFO systems well as it possesses a concatenation property. Central to the new service curve definition is the notion of a *maximum dwell period*.

Definition 7. *(Maximum Dwell Period) The maximum dwell period at time t, denoted as $D(t)$, is the length of the interval $[t^0(t), t]$, i.e., $D(t) = t - t^0(t)$, where $t^0(t)$ is the arrival time of the oldest work unit in the system at time t under* all possible *scheduling orders. If the system is empty at time t, then by definition $t^0(t) = t$ and $D(t) = 0$.*

For a single node with a simple buffer, the maximum dwell period at time t equals the backlogged period at time t; consequently, $t^0(t)$ equals the start of the last backlogged period. The scheduling order that achieves the maximum dwell period for such a simple buffer is LIFO. However, the maximum dwell period of more complex systems can be shorter than the backlogged period of the system, which for complex systems is generally unbounded (see Section 3.2, Example 2).

Furthermore, note that the maximum dwell period is always within a backlogged period of the system, even if the system is not employing the scheduling order leading to the maximum dwell period. This can be understood by assuming that each work unit is time-stamped at entrance to the system and observing that exchanging those time stamps between work units always allows to achieve the maximum dwell period without affecting the length of the backlogged period of the system.

Using the notion of the maximum dwell period, the new service curve definition can be introduced:

Definition 8. *(S^3C) Given a system S with input function F and output function F', $\beta \in \mathcal{F}$ is a* sufficiently strict service curve *(S^3C) if for any $t \geq 0$ it applies that*

$$F'(t) \geq F(t - D(t)) + \beta(D(t)).$$

Before we apply that definition, let us discuss its relation with the other node models.

Remark 1. (Relation with Other Node Models) We have the following implications respectively non-implications:

$$S^2C \Rightarrow S^3C \Rightarrow SC$$
$$SC \not\Rightarrow S^3C \not\Rightarrow S^2C$$

These relations can be readily checked:

1. $S^2C \Rightarrow S^3C$ can be seen from the fact that the maximum dwell period is certainly within a backlogged period of the system.
2. $S^3C \Rightarrow SC$ can be seen from the fact that the required existence of time s in the definition of SC is fixed in the S^2C definition to be $t - D(t)$.
3. $SC \not\Rightarrow S^3C$ is obvious, because it does not have to apply that $s = t - D(t)$.
4. $S^3C \not\Rightarrow S^2C$ is obvious, because S^3C makes no statement for arbitrary backlogged periods, but only for the specific backlogged periods $[t - D(t), t]$.

Since S^2C implies S^3C, all schedulers known to deliver strict service curves also deliver sufficiently strict service curves. Hence, S^3C is not too restricting as a node model. Even more so, note that S^3C also applies for delay-based schedulers which guarantee any work unit to be served within a time period T after their arrival, because such a node can be abstracted as providing a sufficiently strict service curve δ_T. This can be understood by realising that at a given time t any work unit that entered the system before $t - D(t)$ must have left the system again (for any scheduling order). Formally,

$$\forall \epsilon > 0 : F'(t) \geq F(t - D(t) - \epsilon).$$

As we assume F to be continuous and because $D(t) \leq T$ according to the guarantee of a delay-based scheduler, this translates into

$$F'(t) \geq F(t - D(t)) = F(t - D(t)) + \delta_T(D(t)),$$

which constitutes δ_T as a sufficiently strict service curve for a delay-based scheduling node. Note that the node does not have to be FIFO, though its non-FIFO behaviour is restricted due to the delay guarantee: basically, a reordering can actually only lead to scheduling work units ahead of their deadline. On the other hand, if a delay-based scheduling node is abstracted as providing δ_T as SC, then it must be assumed FIFO to calculate its delay bound.

As we show in the next two theorems, the S^3C definition achieves for non-FIFO systems the two attractive features known from conventional network calculus with FIFO systems: a concatenation property and a bound on the delay, yet now on the real instead of the virtual delay.

Theorem 5. *(Concatenation Theorem for Tandem S^3C Systems) Consider a flow with input function F that traverses a tandem of systems $\mathcal{S}_1$ and $\mathcal{S}_2$. Assume that $\mathcal{S}_i$ offers a sufficiently strict service curve β_i, $i = 1, 2$ to the flow. Then the concatenation of the two systems offers a sufficiently strict service curve $\beta_1 \otimes \beta_2$ to the flow F.*

(Real Delay Bound for an S^3C System) Consider a system $\mathcal{S}$ that offers a sufficiently strict service curve β. Assume a flow F traversing the system has an arrival curve α. Then we obtain the following bound on the real delay:

$$rd(t) \leq \sup\{s \geq 0 : \alpha(s) \geq \beta(s)\} = i(\alpha, \beta).$$

By combining the results from Theorem 5 and 5, we can, for the multiple node case involving n non-FIFO nodes, each providing an S^3C $\beta_j, j = 1, \ldots, n$, which are traversed by an α-constrained flow, derive a bound on the real delay as

$$rd(t) \leq i(\alpha, \bigotimes_{j=1}^{n} \beta_j).$$

Looking at the same special case as in Section 3.2, i.e., $\beta_j = \beta_{R,T}$ and $\alpha = \gamma_{r,b}$, we obtain the following bound on the real delay

$$rd(t) \leq \frac{b + nRT}{R - r}, \tag{2}$$

which improves considerably on the additive bound based on S^2C from Section 3.2. We can perceive again the pay burst only once principle as the burst term appears only once as well as a linear scaling in the number of nodes. We provide some more quantitative observations in Section 5.

The delay bound argues over the maximum dwell period, under more knowledge about the non-FIFOness it could possibly be improved. Such an approach should parallel the characteristic that under FIFO scheduling the horizontal deviation actually allows to tighten the delay bound. We leave this for further study.

Other performance bounds besides the delay bound and further results, like output bound, backlog bound, etc., can be carried over from conventional network calculus as S^3C implies SC. In fact, it is only the delay bound that is sensitive on the scheduling order. However, often in applications the delay bound is also the figure of most interest.

5 Numerical Experiments

To give some feeling for the improvements achievable by using the S^3C-based end-to-end analysis compared to an additive bounding based on S^2C we provide some numerical experiments. In addition, we demonstrate what cost is incurred for releasing the FIFO assumption. For these numerical experiments we use simple settings: as arrival curve for the flow to be analysed we assume a token bucket $\gamma_{r,b}$ where we set $r = 10[Mbps]$ and $b = 5[Mb]$ unless we vary the rate r to achieve a certain utilization; for the service curves of the nodes to be traversed we use a rate-latency function $\beta_{R,T}$ with $R = 20[Mbps]$ and $T = 0.01[s]$. Unless we use the number of nodes as a primary factor in the experiments we assume $n = 10$ nodes to be traversed by the flow under investigation.

5.1 Comparison of Different Service Curve Models

In this first set of numerical experiments we investigate how end-to-end (S^3C) and additive (S^2C) analysis compare to each other. In Figure 1(a) the two methods are shown for a varying number of nodes (from 2 to 20), based on equations (1) and (2). To emphasize the quadratic scaling of the S^2C-based method we also provide results for the same experiment with a larger number of nodes to be traversed (up to 100) in Figure 1(b). In both graphs it is obvious that the end-to-end analysis facilitated by the S^3C definition is highly superior and scales linearly with the number of nodes.

A different view on the relative performance of S^3C- and S^2C-based bounding methods is provided in Figure 1(c). Here, the acceptable utilizations for a given delay bound are shown for both methods. This information can be used for admission control purposes. Again, as can be clearly seen, the S^3C-based method outperforms the S^2C-based method by far, especially for lower delay bounds.

5.2 FIFO vs. Non-FIFO Delay Bounds

In the next set of numerical experiments, we investigate the cost of releasing the FIFO assumption in terms of delay bounds. For that purpose, we vary the utilization by increasing the sustained rate of the traffic flow under investigation (while at the same time scaling the bucket depth accordingly). As we can observe from Figure 1(d), only for higher utilizations there is a significant difference between the FIFO and non-FIFO delay bounds (at least for the S^3C case). The bottom line is that only for highly utilized systems it is necessary to enforce a

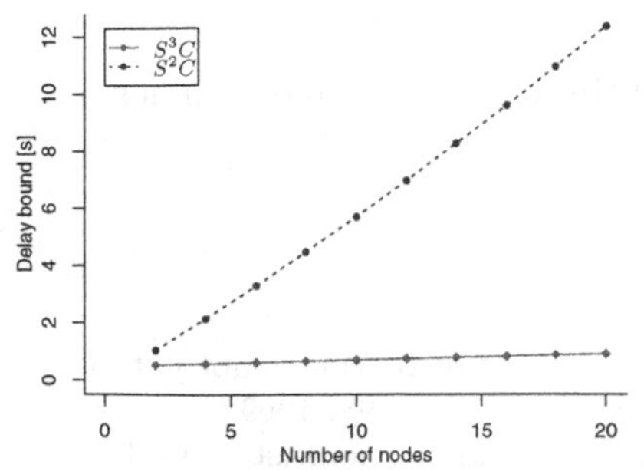

(a) Delay bounds under different service curve models.

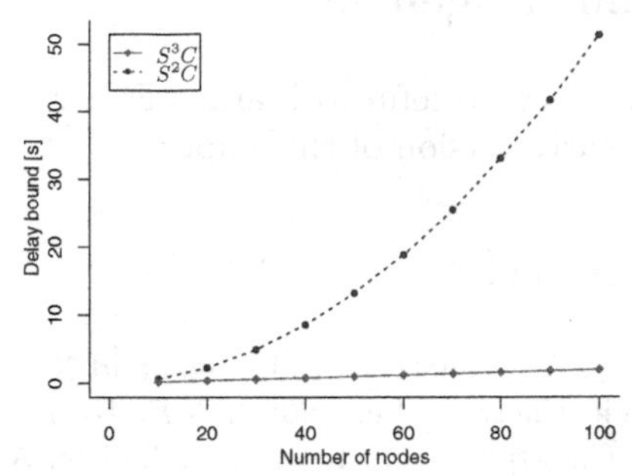

(b) Exposing the quadratic scaling of the additive bound based on S^2C.

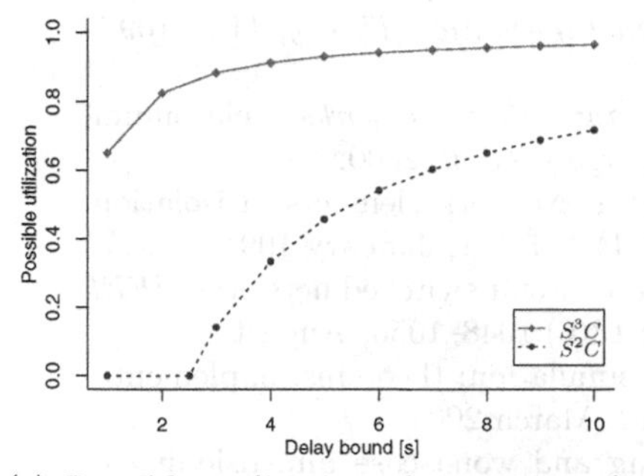

(c) Possible utilizations for a target delay bound under S^2C and S^3C.

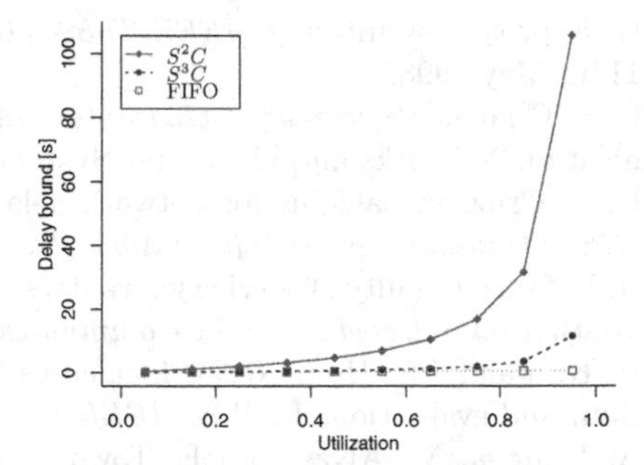

(d) FIFO vs. non-FIFO delay bounds depending on the utilization.

Fig. 1. Comparison of S^3C to other analysis methods under different metrics. Subfigures (a) and (b) show results for 50% utilization.

FIFO behaviour, as far as delay bounds are concerned. For systems with lower utilizations, optimizations such as for example link aggregation or multi-stage switching fabrics do not incur a high cost in terms of worst-case delay bounds.

6 Conclusion

In this paper, it was our goal to extend the scope of network calculus towards non-FIFO systems, as non-FIFO behaviour is a reality in many networking scenarios. It turned out that existing service curve definitions are not satisfying under non-FIFO scheduling: they are either too loose to enable any bounding or too strict to allow for an efficient end-to-end analysis. Therefore, we introduced a new service curve definition, S^3C, which allows to bound the delay and at the same time enables an end-to-end analysis. By numerical examples, we showed that the new analysis based on S^3C is far superior to existing methods. S^3C allows to recover the pay bursts only once phenomenon for non-FIFO systems, which had been disputed to be valid under non-FIFO scheduling in literature.

Acknowledgements

We are very grateful to Markus Fidler for insightful discussions and comments on an early version of this paper.

References

1. J. C. R. Bennett, C. Partridge, and N. Shectman. Packet reordering is not pathological network behavior. *IEEE/ACM Trans. Netw.*, 7(6):789–798, 1999.
2. S. Chakraborty, S. Kuenzli, L. Thiele, A. Herkersdorf, and P. Sagmeister. Performance evaluation of network processor architectures: Combining simulation with analytical estimation. *Computer Networks*, 42(5):641–665, 2003.
3. C.-S. Chang. On deterministic traffic regulation and service guarantees: A systematic approach by filtering. *IEEE Transactions on Information Theory*, 44(3):1097–1110, May 1998.
4. C.-S. Chang. *Performance Guarantees in Communication Networks.* Telecommunication Networks and Computer Systems. Springer-Verlag, 2000.
5. R. L. Cruz. A calculus for network delay, Part I: Network elements in isolation. *IEEE Transactions on Information Theory*, 37(1):114–131, January 1991.
6. R. L. Cruz. Quality of service guarantees in virtual circuit switched networks. *IEEE Journal on Selected Areas in Communications*, 13(6):1048–1056, August 1995.
7. H. Kim and J.C. Hou. Network calculus based simulation: theorems, implementation, and evaluation. In *Proc. IEEE INFOCOM*, March 2004.
8. A. Koubaa, M. Alves, and E. Tovar. Modeling and worst-case dimensioning of cluster-tree wireless sensor networks. In *Proc. 27th IEEE International Real-Time Systems Symposium (RTSS'06)*, pages 412–421, Rio de Janeiro, Brazil, 2006. IEEE Computer Society.
9. J.-Y. Le Boudec and A. Charny. Packet scale rate guarantee for non-fifo nodes. In *Proc. IEEE INFOCOM*, pages 23–26, June 2002.
10. J.-Y. Le Boudec and P. Thiran. *Network Calculus A Theory of Deterministic Queuing Systems for the Internet.* Number 2050 in Lecture Notes in Computer Science. Springer-Verlag, Berlin, Germany, 2001.
11. G. Rizzo and J.-Y. Le Boudec. Pay bursts only once does not hold for non-fifo guaranteed rate nodes. *Performance Evaluation*, 62(1-4):366–381, 2005.
12. J. Schmitt, N. Gollan, and I. Martinovic. End-to-end worst case analysis of non-fifo systems. Technical Report 370/08, University of Kaiserslautern, Germany, August 2008. http://disco.informatik.uni-kl.de/publications/SGM08-1.pdf.
13. J. Schmitt and U. Roedig. Sensor network calculus - a framework for worst case analysis. In *Proc. Distributed Computing on Sensor Systems (DCOSS)*, pages 141–154, June 2005.
14. J. Schmitt, F. Zdarsky, and M. Fidler. Delay bounds under arbitrary aggregate multiplexing: When network calculus leaves you in the lurch... In *Proc. IEEE INFOCOM*, April 2008.
15. T. Skeie, S. Johannessen, and O. Holmeide. Timeliness of real-time IP communication in switched industrial ethernet networks. *IEEE Transactions on Industrial Informatics*, 2(1):25–39, February 2006.

Providing Probabilistic Latency Bounds for Dynamic Publish/Subscribe Systems

M. Adnan Tariq, Boris Koldehofe, Gerald G. Koch and Kurt Rothermel

IPVS – Distributed Systems, Universität Stuttgart
{firstname.lastname}@ipvs.uni-stuttgart.de

Abstract. In the context of large decentralized many-to-many communication systems it is impractical to provide realistic and hard bounds for certain QoS metrics including latency bounds. Nevertheless, many applications can yield better performance if such bounds hold with a given probability. In this paper we show how probabilistic latency bounds can be applied in the context of publish/subscribe. We present an algorithm for maintaining individual probabilistic latency bounds in a highly dynamic environment for a large number of subscribers. The algorithm consists of an adaptive dissemination algorithm as well as a cluster partitioning scheme. Together they ensure i) adaptation to the individual latency requirements of subscribers under dynamically changing system properties, and ii) scalability by determining appropriate clusters according to available publishers in the system.

1 Introduction

Publish/subscribe is a well-known and popular communication paradigm for building distributed applications such as stock exchange, traffic monitoring or person tracking. It provides a decoupling of producers of information, called publishers, from consumers of information, called subscribers. Without knowledge of the actual source of information, subscribers specify their interests in the form of subscriptions and are notified about the corresponding published events.

In the past, most research has focused on providing expressive and scalable publish/subscribe systems. However, innovative Internet applications such as distributed online games have other requirements like time bounded processing and delivery of events. Moreover, in business applications, complex event processing [13] may be used to perform the transition from basic events, e.g. sensor readings, to complex events that match the semantics of the application, e.g. the detection of a fire. If such transitions need to be performed in a timely manner, delayed events may not only be useless, but also lead to wrong computations by the application.

Reserving resources along the communication links can guarantee end-to-end QoS between subscribers and publishers [5]. However, this is not always viable since reservation protocols are typically not available on a global scale and reservation in the context of heterogeneous network environments is even harder.

An alternative approach is to observe the behavior of the underlay and then provide a QoS bound with a probabilistic reliability derived from the observations. This reliability depends on the value chosen for the QoS bound and its probability distribution.

Although the characteristics of the underlay may change dynamically over time and so affect the probabilistic reliability, providing probabilistic bounds is still useful in three ways. First, the end-to-end latency distribution can be fairly stable, e.g. in the Internet it can be modeled with a certain probability distribution with small variation [8,17]. Second, probabilistic reliability allows the system to overstep a given QoS bound to a determined extent while not violating the agreement with the user. Third, even a small reduction of the demanded probabilistic reliability yields a better probabilistic bound and, with this, a significant performance improvement. For instance, assuming that the probability distribution of message latency is stable, one can derive that an event will be propagated within 200*ms* with a probability of 95%, while a more useful latency bound of 100*ms* can be achieved with a probability of 90%.

In this paper we address how end-to-end latency requirements of individual subscribers in a content-based publish/subscribe context can be satisfied by accounting for the latency distribution of communication links. We propose an algorithm that adapts to the requirements of subscribers and maximizes the set of subscribers and publishers it can support. First, we introduce an event dissemination algorithm in a restricted content-based model with constraints on the set of publishers that adapts to dynamic changes in the underlay (cf. Section 3). Then we show how to generalize the algorithm to match the content-based publish/subscribe model by providing a clustering scheme (cf. Section 4). We also present an experimental evaluation (cf . Section 5) of the algorithm performance under dynamic behavior.

2 Probabilistic Latency Bounds in Content-Based Publish/Subscribe

We consider the content-based publish/subscribe model of communication in a distributed system consisting of an unbounded and dynamic set of peers. We assume that peers can leave or join arbitrarily often and they can fail temporarily or permanently. Furthermore, we assume that the underlying communication environment is heterogeneous with different link properties related to delay and bandwidth; however each peer is connected to the network through a single interface. Each peer is assumed to have a unique identity, which can be used to establish a logical point-to-point connection, forming an overlay network. Logical links are created and maintained by a probabilistic membership service such as [16], which helps peers to bootstrap and prevents the partitioning of the network. On top of the membership service, peers are organized in a single spanning tree, where the links of the spanning tree are embedded within the links of the membership service overlay.

Peers contribute in the publish/subscribe system in one of two roles: publishers or subscribers. Publishers serve as information sources and the publish/subscribe overlay ensures that subscribers receive all the relevant messages. According to the content-based publish/subscribe model, an event consists of a set of attributes and associated values. We use Ω to denote the set of all attributes that exist in the system. Each publisher p periodically propagates an advertisement $Adv(p) \subseteq \Omega$. Thereby p announces potential future events with any desired attribute set taken from the set $PS_{Adv}^{-\emptyset}(p) := PS_{Adv}(p) - \{\emptyset\}$, with $PS_{Adv}(p)$ being the power set of $Adv(p)$. For example, a publisher p with $Adv(p) = \{temperature, humidity\}$ can publish events consisting of $\{temperature\}$, $\{humidity\}$ or $\{temperature, humidity\}$. Subscribers issue subscriptions which are expressed as a conjunction over ranges of attribute values, e.g. $(color = red \wedge temperature \in [20,25])$. Beyond typical content-based publish/subscribe systems, subscribers can specify upper latency bounds with their subscriptions, together with a minimum probability that these bounds are met.

Peers observe two QoS metrics: traffic (in terms of bandwidth) and latency. Each peer maintains a traffic specification of its network interface, which specifies the number of event messages that can be propagated per time unit. Traffic specifications place constraints on the creation of overlay links. Let $T_S(n)$ and $T_C(n)$ denote the traffic specification and the current traffic characteristics of peer n, respectively, and let $r(n,s)$ specify the message rate for any new connection to peer s. Then, peer n will accept the new connection only if $T_C(n) + r(n,s) \leq T_S(n)$ is satisfied. Latency is modeled probabilistically in our system: each peer maintains information about the latency distribution for each of its overlay links, assuming that all messages are of similar size. In practice, information about the latency distribution and traffic characteristics can be collected by relying on cross-layer sampling services [15].

In addition to latency characteristics of overlay links to neighbors, each subscriber peer also maintains information about the latency distribution of end-to-end paths to distant peers, which we call *path latency characteristics* (*plc*). Subscribers maintain their *plc* recursively: after receiving the *plc* of a direct predecessor n in the spanning tree, a subscriber s combines it with latency characteristics of the overlay link between n and s, and notifies its successors on the tree about its updated *plc*.

A subscriber can use the path latency characteristics to determine the validity of its *latency specification* (i.e. probabilistic upper latency bound) for an end-to-end path to a publisher, like the one shown in *Figure* 1. If the latency characteristics fail to match the individual latency specification, the subscriber has to take steps to increase the *plc*. Our approach fulfills the individual latency specifications of subscribers by placing them at an appropriate position with respect to relevant publishers in the overlay network.

Satisfaction of latency specifications in content-based publish/subscribe in a scalable manner is highly challenging. First, providing an optimal solution to satisfy the QoS demands of all subscribers with the same interest in the presence of traffic constraints is NP hard and is known as "delay-constraint minimum cost routing" problem [14]. Second, in publish/subscribe systems, the selectivity of subscriptions (i.e. the ratio of the total number of events that match the subscription) can vary widely. Less selective subscribers should obviously be placed before more selective ones, but at the same time peers with low traffic specifications should be behind subscribers with high specifications. A trade-off is necessary if subscribers with high traffic specifications are highly selective or subscribers with low specifications are less selective. Third, one must also consider that multiple publishers' trees may be embedded in the same overlay network and hence a subscriber may need to consider placement with respect to many publishers.

In this paper we approach these challenges by looking first at the constraints on subscriber selectivity by extending Siena's content-based routing [6]. We propose adaptation mechanisms that maximize the number of satisfied subscribers. In a first step, we

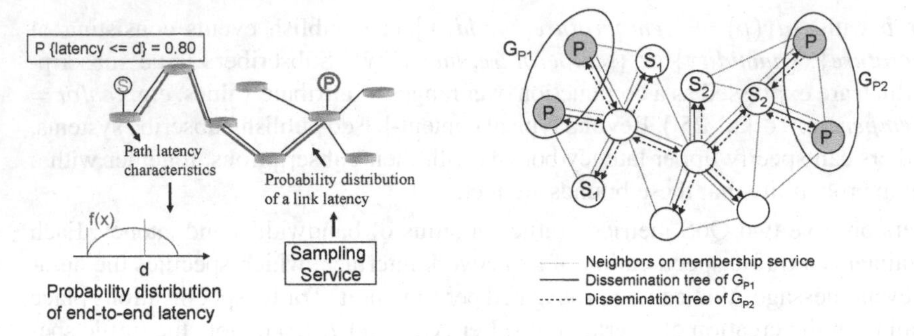

Fig. 1. QoS Model

Fig. 2. Spanning trees created on top of membership service with embedded dissemination trees

impose constraints on the advertisements of publishers in order to reduce the multiple-publisher problem. Finally, we release these constraints and propose an approach to group publishers in clusters according to their advertisements and this way tackle the multiple-publisher problem.

3 Adaptation to Probabilistic Latency Requirements

In a first approach to adapt publish/subscribes system to probabilistic latency specifications we introduce the constraint that publishers have either completely overlapping or disjoint advertisements, i.e., the set of publishers can be partitioned into disjoint groups of publishers $G_P = \{p_1, p_2, \ldots, p_m\}$ so that $\forall p_i, p_j \in G_P : Adv(p_i) \subseteq Adv(p_j) \vee Adv(p_j) \subseteq Adv(p_i)$. Hence, publications that match a subscription s are issued by a single group of publishers further denoted as $G_P(s)$. We write $s \prec G_P(s)$ to denote that s can be satisfied by $G_P(s)$. We assume that each subscriber has only one subscription and hence will not differentiate between the terms subscriber and subscription.

We now present an adaptive algorithm that maximizes the number of subscribers whose latency specifications can be satisfied without violating their traffic constraints. The algorithm, on top of the spanning tree, maintains a separate dissemination tree for each group of publishers G_p (cf. Figure 2). To construct the dissemination tree and to match events with subscriptions, we extend Siena [6] approach to take into account the *path latency characteristics* (*plc*) for a publisher. A dissemination tree is created by a publisher flooding its advertisement along the spanning tree. Each advertisement includes the *plc* with respect to the publisher. A peer that receives an advertisement sets up the path for the dissemination tree, updates the *plc* and forwards the advertisement along with the updated *plc* down the dissemination tree.

In the following we show how to adapt the dissemination trees by relying on two strategies. The *reactive adaption* uses local adaptations, to find an appropriate position for each subscriber in its relevant dissemination tree such that its individual latency specification is met. The *proactive adaptation* periodically runs an optimization algorithm and tries to enhance the dissemination trees, so that a large number of subscribers can be satisfied.

Algorithm 1 Placement Strategies

Require: A subscriber s whose latency specification $l(s)$ should be satisfied
Ensure: Peer n which can satisfy the latency specification of s.

1: noOfTries $\leftarrow 0$ // Number of tries to find a suitable position
2: childForInsertion [ ] $\leftarrow \emptyset$
3: **for all** $n \in N(s)$ **do** // $N(s) = \{n \in Neighbors \mid (s,n) \notin SpanningTree\}$
4: **if** $(T_S(n) - T_C(n) > r(n,s)) \wedge (l(s) =$ satisfied $)$ **then**
5: create link (n,s) on spanning tree and remove existing link.
6: **break**
7: **for all** $z_i \in \{z_m, z_{m-1}, \ldots z_0 | z_m = Grandparent(s) \wedge \forall_i\ z_{i-1} = parent(z_i) \wedge z_0 \in G_P\}$ **do**
8: **if** $l(s)$ = satisfied **then**
9: **if** $T_S(z_i) - T_C(z_i) > r(z_i,s)$ **then**
10: connect to z_i
11: **else** // Try to insert s between z_i and one of its children
12: **for all** $k_i \in K$ **do** // $K = \{k_i | k_i \in child(z_i)\}$
13: **if** $\neg(k_i \prec G_p(s)) \wedge \neg(subtree(k_i) \prec G_p(s))$ **then**
14: childForInsertion $\leftarrow k_i$ // insertion is always possible
15: **else if** $k_i \prec G_p(s) \wedge \neg(subtree(k_i) \prec G_p(s))$ **then**
16: if subscription of k_i is not violated then childForInsertion $\leftarrow k_i$
17: **else** // $subtree(k_i) \prec G_p(s)$
18: childForInsertion $\leftarrow k_i$ (insert with probability)
19: **if** $|$childForInsertion$| > 0$ **then** // more than one child can be used for insertion
20: Select child with more selective subscription and low traffic specs ($T_S(k_i)$)
21: add links (z_i,s) and (s,k_i) and remove (z_i,k_i)
22: If $T_C(s) + r(s,k_i) > T_S(s)$ then s will leave one of its children to the existing parent
23: **break**
24: **if** $l(s) \neq$ satisfied **then**
25: noOfTries++
26: backoff for noOfTries $*\Delta T$ seconds
27: Start from random location

3.1 Reactive and Proactive Adaptations

A new subscriber s arriving in the system, or an existing subscriber (because of dynamic behavior such as the crash or departure of a parent node, or changes in the *plc*), triggers the reactive algorithm to find a new position within the dissemination tree of $G_P(s)$. The reactive algorithm uses the following placement strategies (cf. *Algorithm* 1):

Local transformation (*lines 3-6*): If changes to the underlying QoS violate the latency specification, peers first try to connect to another parent among their neighbors of the member service overlay.

Bottom-up strategy (*lines 7-22*): If the local transformation is unsuccessful, then the subscriber needs to connect to a suitable parent higher in the dissemination tree, i.e. closer to the publishers. The subscriber s follows the reverse path formed by the advertisements. Once a suitable parent z_i is found, s will connect directly, if the traffic specification of z_i allows. Otherwise, s tries to be inserted between z_i and one of its child peers k_i.

If the peers in the subtree of k_i are subscribed for $G_p(s)$ (*lines 17-18*), then s is inserted probabilistically. The reason is that the number and latency specification of the subscribers are not locally available, so the changes in the link behavior may trigger a lot of simultaneous adaptations, which may clutter the network. The probability of insertion decreases with the number of unsuccessful tries performed by s to find an

Algorithm 2 Proactive Algorithm

Require: Peer n performing proactive algorithm.

1: childToPromote [] $\leftarrow \emptyset$
2: $V = \{G_{p1}, G_{p2} \cdots G_{pm} | \forall_k \, k \in child(n) \wedge k \; is \; subscriber \Rightarrow G_p(k) \in V\}$
3: **for all** $v_i \in V$ **do**
4: **for all** $k_i \in K$ **do** // $K = \{k_i \in child(n) \wedge k_i \prec v_i\}$
5: $W(k_i) =$ Assign weight according to selectivity of subscription and traffic specs $T_S(k_i)$
6: **if** $\forall_{k_j \in K, j<i} \, W(k_i) > W(k_j)$ **then**
7: childToPromote[v_i] = k_i
8: **for all** $k_i \in$ childToPromote **do**
9: promoteToParent(k_i,z_i) // Performs bottom-up strategy (*Algorithm* 1) to connect to parent

appropriate position and with the level of node k_i in the dissemination tree (details are in Section 3.2).

Random Connect (*lines 23-26*): If the latency specification of s cannot be satisfied after reaching one of the publishers, it will perform an exponential backoff and tries to find its position by connecting to a random peer. However, s leaves the existing parent only when a suitable peer is found that can satisfy its latency specifications.

The *proactive algorithm* runs periodically and pushes the subscribers with good traffic specifications and less selective subscriptions near the publishers. The goal is to improve the overall quality of the dissemination tree so that more subscribers with their individual latency specifications can be satisfied. The algorithm is performed by every non-leaf peer for the immediate child subscribers on each dissemination tree (cf. *Algorithm* 2).

3.2 Algorithm Properties

The algorithm design addresses two issues: compliance to individual latency specifications and scalability.

Clearly, latency specifications can only be fulfilled if there exists a suitable position for the peer in the overlay. In cases where an individual subscription can be fulfilled by a large number of neighbors there is a high chance to find an appropriate position by performing the local adaptation strategy. If such neighbors are not at hand, the bottom-up strategy is of benefit, since peers closer to the publishers can satisfy higher requirements. Nevertheless, it is possible that a subscriber will not be able to satisfy its latency specification. In this case the random selection ensures that it will eventually find a suitable position.

Scalability is related to the number of satisfied subscribers, the overhead of message forwarding and finally the cost of performing adaptations. Latency specifications of a large number of subscribers can be satisfied because the proactive maintenance yields fat trees, where subscribers with good traffic specifications are pushed close to the publishers. Furthermore, the notification forwarding overhead is reduced by the placing subscribers near their relevant publishers, saving intermediate peers from forwarding irrelevant notifications. The subscription forwarding overhead is reduced by placing less selective subscriptions close to the relevant publishers.

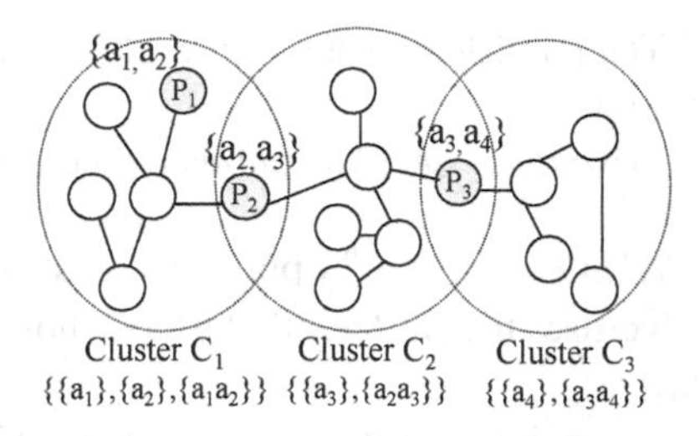

Fig. 3. Cluster management for a system with four attributes $\Omega = \{a_1, a_2, a_3, a_4\}$ and three publishers. $PS^{-\emptyset}_{Adv}(p_2) = \{\{a_2\}, \{a_3\}, \{a_2, a_3\}\}$, so p_2 publishes notifications with attribute $\{a_2\}$ in C_1 and with attributes $\{\{a_3\}, \{a_2, a_3\}\}$ in C_2.

Another important aspect is the cost of performing adaptations. The application of a bottom-up strategy and local transformation reduce the management overhead of the peers higher in the dissemination tree. Furthermore, the algorithm reduces the number of concurrent adaptations during failures: a subscriber s whose latency specification is violated first tries to find a position satisfying also all the relevant subscribers in its subtree. A probabilistic approach is used, which balances two factors—the position of the subscriber in the dissemination tree and the number of unsuccessful attempts and is given by $e^{-level(s)*noOfTries/(Normalizationparameter)}$. The higher the subscriber is located in the tree, the higher is the probability to move to a position that satisfies all peers in its subtree and prevents the start of many simultaneous adaptation algorithms. However, simulation results have shown that due to saturation near the publishers the subscriber higher in the tree may not be successful, so the number of tries should be limited.

4 Cluster Management

In this section, we extend the adaptive dissemination algorithm of Section 3 to match the requirements of a generic publish/subscribe system without constraints on publishers. This implies that the advertisements of different publishers overlap, and a subscription can be satisfied by more than one publisher's group (the multi-publisher problem). In the following we present how clustering of publishers leads to an appropriate number of groups with which publishers as well as subscribers need to be associated.

Let C be a cluster of publishers and let CS_C denote the set of all attribute sets that are published in the cluster. CS_C determines the potential subscribers of the cluster. In *Figure* 3, for example, cluster C_1 has $CS_{C_1} = \{\{a_1\}, \{a_2\}, \{a_1, a_2\}\}$, and subscribers with subscriptions consisting of either of these attribute sets will join C_1.

The basic idea is to prevent the presence of these attribute sets in additional clusters, so that subscribers will not have to be associated with multiple clusters and thus preserve scalability for subscribers. Therefore, the cluster management algorithm has to consider the intersections of $PS^{-\emptyset}_{Adv}$ of publishers rather than $Adv(p)$. Let $M := \{C_1, C_2, ...\}$ be the set of all clusters currently in the system. The cluster management algorithm preserves the invariant that the attribute sets of all clusters $C \in M$ are disjoint, i.e. $\forall C_i, C_j \in M : i \neq j \Rightarrow CS_{C_i} \cap CS_{C_j} = \emptyset$. When a publisher p arrives in the system, the overlap between its $PS^{-\emptyset}_{Adv}(p)$ and all CS_{C_i} in M is calculated. The following cases are distinguished:

No overlap with any CS_C: The publisher creates a new cluster C_{new} with $CS_{C_{new}} = PS_{Adv}^{-\emptyset}(p)$ and advertises the cluster.

$PS_{Adv}^{-\emptyset}(p)$ is included in an existing cluster: The publisher merges in the corresponding cluster.

Existing clusters are included in $PS_{Adv}^{-\emptyset}(p)$: The publisher creates a new cluster C_{new} with $CS_{C_{new}} = PS_{Adv}^{-\emptyset}(p)$ and advertises the cluster; all clusters whose CS_C is a subset of $PS_{Adv}^{-\emptyset}(p)$ merge in the new cluster.

Partial overlap: The publisher joins every cluster whose CS_C overlaps with $PS_{Adv}^{-\emptyset}(p)$, and for the remaining elements of $PS_{Adv}^{-\emptyset}$ it creates a new cluster $CS_{C_{new}} = PS_{Adv}^{-\emptyset}(p) - \bigcup_i CS_{C_i}$. Joining a cluster C means that p publishes events with an attribute set from the intersection $CS_C \cap PS_{Adv}^{-\emptyset}(p)$ exclusively in cluster C. The publisher with the most general advertisement (i.e. that has the highest share in the CS_C of the cluster) becomes the cluster head.

With the resulting clustering, a subscription can always be satisfied by publishers of just one single cluster, and we can directly apply the adaptive dissemination algorithm of *Section 3* to each cluster. However, if each publishers p would select the attributes in $Adv(p)$ uniformly at random from Ω, a large set of publishers can create many disjoint clusters, each cluster only serving a small fraction of the involved publishers' $PS_{Adv}^{-\emptyset}(p)$. This is beneficial for subscribers because clusters publish only a small variety of events and subscribers receive only a small amount of false positives (i.e. events that do not match their individual subscription). Publishers, however, might have to be associated with a high number of small clusters.

Since the number of clusters to which a publisher might have to connect grows exponentially with $|Adv(p)|$, we use an inherent property of the cluster management algorithm to ensure scalability: It merges a pair of clusters C_1 and C_2, if CS_{C_1} contains CS_{C_2} or vice versa. If a publisher p realizes that it has to connect to a large number of clusters, it generalizes its advertisement by adding an appropriate attribute to $Adv(p)$ so that another cluster can merge in the newly created cluster of p. This way, the arrival of a new publisher does not result in a growth of $|M|$ in the system. Of course, the effect of this solution has to be balanced with the subscribers' interest that clusters have a small CS_C in order to limit the number of false positives. This can be achieved with a threshold for the number of clusters that p has to connect, before the solution is applied, and by changing the number of attributes that p is allowed to assume in order to generalize its $Adv(p)$. For further scalability, cluster heads do not advertise CS_C which is often a large proper subset of $PS_{Adv}^{-\emptyset}(p)$. Instead, the cluster head advertises its $Adv(p)$ together with the sets that are in $PS_{Adv}^{-\emptyset}(p)$ but excluded from CS_C. The exclusion of a set amounts to the exclusion of its power set so that the exclusion information in an advertisement is kept rather small, and the algorithm's tendency to merge clusters also prevents the exclusion of too many subsets.

5 Evaluation

This section evaluates the self-adaptation algorithm with respect to convergence and stability in the presence of failures and churn, using metrics similar to [2]. The evaluations were performed using PeerSim [12], a large-scale P2P simulator.

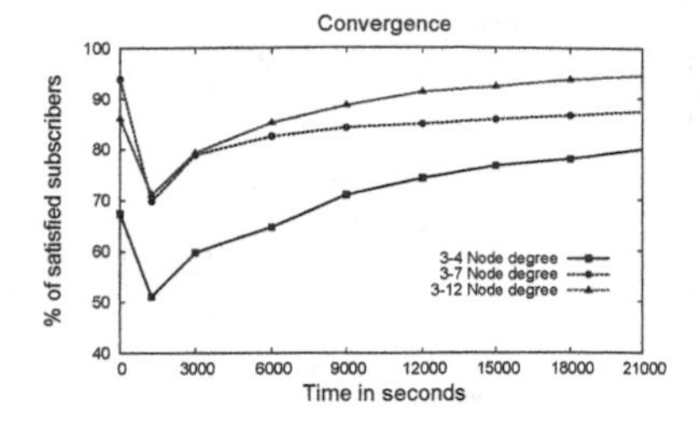

Fig. 4. Convergence

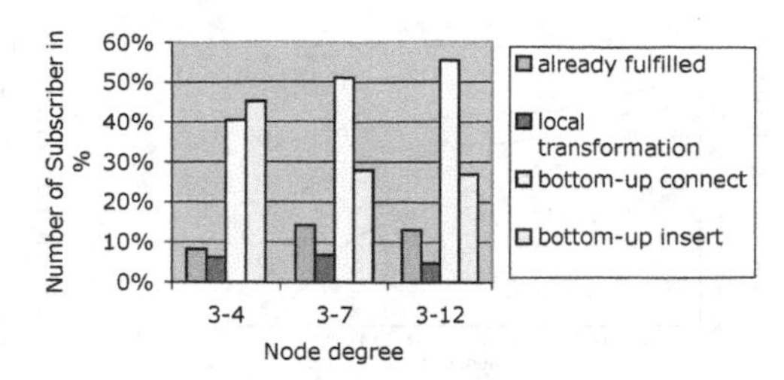

Fig. 5. Adaptations

No routing protocol was implemented at the underlay level. Instead, latencies between the routers were assigned based on the King [10] methodology, which estimates the latency between any pair of Internet hosts by measuring the latency between nearby authoritative DNS servers. The latencies between the routers are in the range $[1,500]$ms with reliability factor of 90% to 100%.

All the simulations are performed for $1,024$ peers. The number of neighbors on the underlying membership service is assigned randomly between 10 to 15. The initial delay for the *Random Connect* strategy is 3 seconds and the delay for *proactive algorithm* is 5 seconds. The latency requirements from the subscribers are in the range [120, 260]ms with low probabilities. For simplicity, the traffic characteristics of a peer is simulated by the node degree.

5.1 Algorithm Convergence

We analyze the algorithm's behavior to converge in a limited number of adaptations under static conditions. Convergence means that if the number of subscribers with individual latency requirements remains constant, the system will eventually converge to a stable state where a considerably large percentage of the subscribers is satisfied and no more adaptations are performed. We evaluated the algorithm with different traffic specifications of peers, i.e with possible node degrees in $[3,4]$, $[3,7]$ and $[3,12]$, with all other parameters left unchanged. Starting with 10 publishers with disjoint advertisements, a new peer chosen uniformly at random (among the 1024 peers), subscribed with its individual latency requirements at each simulation step until all $1,024$ peers in the system were either subscribers or publishers. Figure 4 shows the convergence behavior of the algorithm with respect to traffic specifications of peers. The lower percentage of satisfied subscribers in the first 1,024 simulation steps is due to the fact that new subscribers are constantly arriving in the system and are not immediately satisfied. Figure 4 also shows the effect of traffic specifications on the satisfaction of subscribers: as peers with high traffic specifications are pushed up by the proactive algorithm, the dissemination tree becomes fat and hence more subscribers can be satisfied. Figure 5 shows the percentage of subscribers (out of the total number of satisfied subscribers) satisfied by each adaptation strategy. Only $8-14\%$ of the subscribers are satisfied without any adaptation, which shows the effectiveness of the algorithm in increasing the number of satisfied subscribers. Similarly, low traffic specifications result in more insertions during the bottom-up strategy as visible in the case of a node degree $[3,4]$.

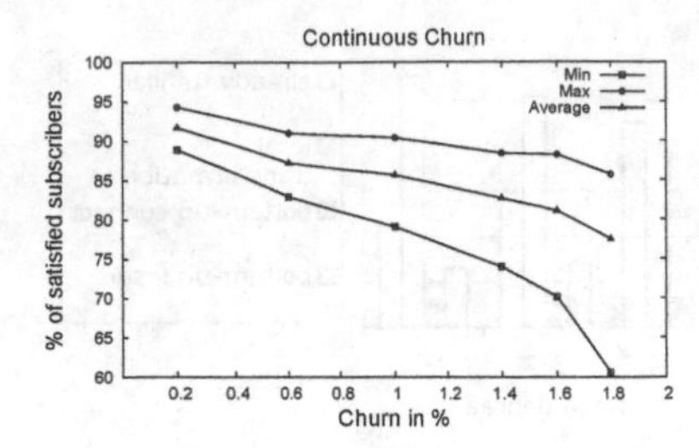

Fig. 6. Continuous churn

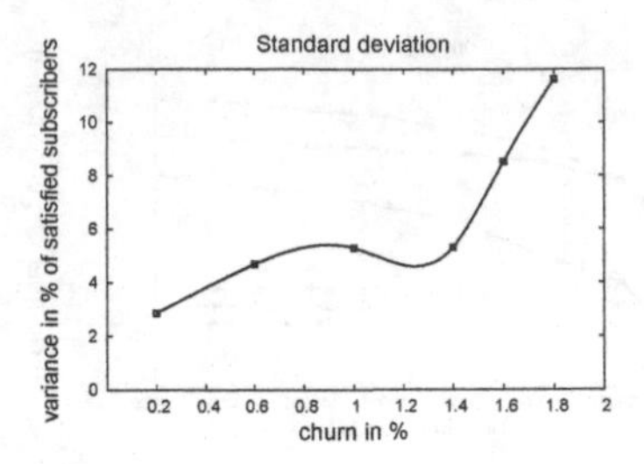

Fig. 7. Standard deviation for continuous churn

5.2 Algorithm Stability

We have evaluated the algorithm's reaction to the dynamic changes in the system state and its convergence to a stable state.

Continuous churn: Simulations were performed with peers having a node degree in [3,7]. In each simulation, 512 subscribers were pushed into the system and the system was allowed to converge to a stable state. Afterwards, continuous churn was introduced in the system. The percentage of churn was relative to the total of all peers in the system, e.g. a churn of 1.8% means that at every simulation step, 9 peers subscribed to and 9 peers unsubscribed from the system. Figure 6 shows the minimum, average and maximum percentage of satisfied subscribers in the system with increasing churn. Figure 7 shows the corresponding standard deviation, which gives an indication about the stability of the system. It is evident from the figures, that at higher churn rate the system is more unstable, because a higher number of potential subscribers are looking for a position. The reason being that the subscribers who canceled their subscriptions are still in the system occupying their previous positions, which makes it difficult for the new subscribers to find the position.

Massive churn: This scenario evaluates the behavior of the algorithm in the case of sudden rapid churn. The simulation settings were the same as in above experiments. Figure 8 shows that there is no relation between the percentage of churn and the course of the corresponding curve. For example, a curve with higher rapid churn might converge faster than others. The reason is that the algorithm relies on random interaction between peers and hence may converge to a different state on different runs. However, the system can tolerate and recover from massive occurrence of churn gracefully.

Further measurements on continuous and massive failures shows similar results. These results are omitted due to space constraints.

6 Related Work

Over the last decade many content-based publish/subscribe systems [6,9,11,3] have evolved. Most systems focus on increased scalability of the system by reducing the cost of subscription forwarding and event matching. Clustering has also been identified as a technique to achieve scalability [4,1,7]. Clustering of subscribers can be achieved in two ways, either based on similarity of subscriptions or by partitioning the event

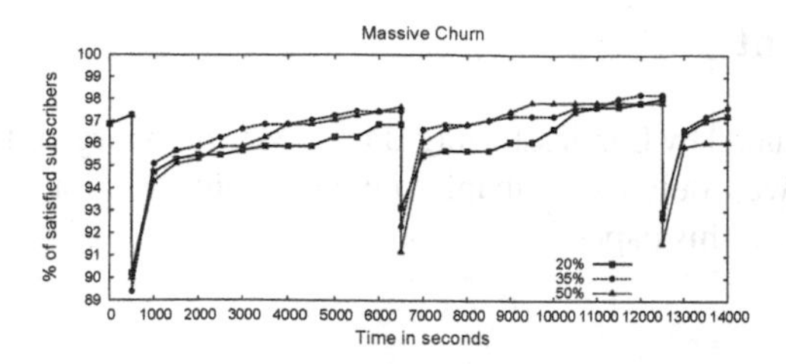

Fig. 8. Massive churn

space. Kyra [4] partitions the event space into clusters, brokers are assigned to each cluster and subscriptions are moved to relevant brokers. However, their approach is not dynamic, and when a broker joins or leaves, the whole partitioning needs to be recomputed. Additionally, no event partitioning criteria is specified. In [7], a direct mapping of the containment graph of subscriptions is mapped to a tree structure. This results in as many trees as there are subscriptions that are not contained in any other subscription. Similarly, [1] builds a tree for every attribute of the event space, and a subscriber can join any tree for which it has specified an attribute filter. Publishers publish to each tree with a matching attribute, which results in a huge number of unnecessary messages on each tree. Apart from the stated drawbacks, none of the approaches address issues related to QoS fulfillment.

Although it is easy to add QoS semantics into subscriptions [5], only few systems actually cope with satisfying QoS specifications in a decoupled environment like publish/subscribe, but rather deal with QoS as a metric for performance comparisons. To the best of our knowledge only two systems address issues related to satisfying individual latency requirements of subscribers. Indiqos [5] addresses delay requirements of individual subscribers, but relies on network reservation protocols, which limits its scalability. In [17] bounded delays on event delivery by employing message scheduling strategies at each broker are considered. They use a QoS model similar to ours. However, a static broker topology is assumed.

7 Conclusion

In this paper we have shown, in the context of pub/sub, how to deal with probabilistic latency bounds in large dynamic network environments. In particular, we apply subscription-centered adaptation to ensure an appropriate arrangement of subscriptions with various selectivity and to maintain high-capacity dissemination trees. Additionally, scalability is ensured by a publication centric clustering of the overlay. The evaluation shows that the algorithm performs well with respect to the fulfillment of individual latency specifications and is robust in a very dynamic setting. The described algorithm is currently practically applied to support a gaming application, in SpoVNet [15] project.

In the future, we will extend our partitioning schemes to reducing the management overhead due to advertisements. Moreover, we plan to investigate the impact of further QoS metrics and possible synergies with the current adaptation schemes.

8 Acknowledgment

This work is partially funded by Landesstiftung Baden-Württemberg under the initiative BW-FIT. Furthermore, we would like to thank Manuela Antonovic for her contributions towards the initial ideas of this paper.

References

1. E. Anceaume, A. K. Datta, M. Gradinariu, G. Simon, and A. Virgillito. Dps: Self-* dynamic reliable content-based publish/subscribe system. Technical report, IRISA, France, 2004.
2. Roberto Baldoni, Roberto Beraldi, Leonardo Querzoni, and Antonino Virgillito. Efficient publish/subscribe through a self-organizing broker overlay and its application to SIENA. *The Computer Journal*, 50:444–459, 2007.
3. Jorge A. Briones, Boris Koldehofe, and Kurt Rothermel. SPINE: Publish/subscribe for Wireless Mesh Networks through self-managed intersecting paths. In *International Conference on Innovative Internet Community Systems*. IEEE Computer Society, June 2008.
4. Fengyun Cao and Jaswinder Pal Singh. Efficient event routing in content-based publish-subscribe service networks. In *INFOCOM*, 2004.
5. Nuno Carvalho, Filipe Araujo, and Luis Rodrigues. Scalable QoS-based event routing in publish-subscribe systems. In *Proceedings of the Fourth IEEE International Symposium on Network Computing and Applications*. IEEE Computer Society, 2005.
6. Antonio Carzaniga, David S. Rosenblum, and Alexander L. Wolf. Design and evaluation of a wide-area event notification service. *ACM Transactions on Computer Systems*, 2001.
7. Raphaël Chand and Pascal Felber. Semantic peer-to-peer overlays for publish/subscribe networks. In *Euro-Par*, pages 1194–1204, 2005.
8. A Corlett, D.I. Pullin, and S. Sargood. Statistics of one-way internet packet delays. Presentation at 53rd IETF, March 2002.
9. Ludger Fiege, Mariano Cilia, Gero Mühl, and Alejandro Buchmann. Publish-subscribe grows up: Support for management, visibility control, and heterogeneity. *IEEE Internet Computing*, 10:48–55, 2006.
10. Krishna P. Gummadi, Stefan Saroiu, and Steven D. Gribble. King: estimating latency between arbitrary internet end hosts. 2002.
11. Abhishek Gupta, Ozgur D. Sahin, Divyakant Agrawal, and Amr El Abbadi. Meghdoot: Content-based publish/subscribe over p2p networks. In *Intl. Middleware Conference*, 2004.
12. Márk Jelasity, Alberto Montresor, Gian Paolo Jesi, and Spyros Voulgaris. Peersim: A peer-to-peer simulator. http://peersim.sourceforge.net/.
13. David C. Luckham. *The Power of Events: An Introduction to Complex Event Processing in Distributed Enterprise Systems*. Addison-Wesley Longman Publishing Co., Inc., 2001.
14. Ariel Orda and Er Sprintson. QoS Routing: the precomputation perspective. In *Infocom*, 2000.
15. The SpoVNet Consortium. Spontaneous Virtual Networks: On the road towards the Internet's Next Generation. *it - Information Technology*, 50(6), December 2008.
16. Spyros Voulgaris, Daniela Gavidia, and Maarten van Steen. Cyclon: Inexpensive membership management for unstructured P2P overlays. *J. Network Syst. Manage.*, 2005.
17. Jinling Wang, Jiannong Cao, Jing Li, and Jie Wu. Achieving bounded delay on message delivery in publish/subscribe systems. In *International Conference on Parallel Processing*, 2006.

Traffic, Structure and Locality Characteristics of the Web's Most Popular Services' Home Pages

Joachim Charzinski

Nokia Siemens Networks, Munich, Germany
j.charzinski@ieee.org

Abstract. Web pages have drastically evolved from single files with some links to very complex structures consisting of a multitude of elements which the user's Web browser dynamically collects from a widely distributed crowd of servers. Analyzing active traffic measurements of the home pages to the 100 most popular services in the United States, this paper reveals that services nowadays show a large variation in characteristic measures such as the number of elements on a page, the amount of bytes a page consists of, and even the number and logical locations of servers contacted.

1 Introduction

1.1 Evolution of Web Applications

In the beginning of the World Wide Web (the Web), web pages were highly localized and had a simple structure: one page was equal to one file retrieved by a client from one server. The main progress over previous systems such as file distribution via FTP (file transfer protocol) was that documents now included links that allowed directly following references, which essentially created a network of documents (a "Web") as a logical overlay on the Internet. In the meantime, not only have web pages changed their shapes to include images and frames, but the whole service structure of the Web has changed. Some Web sites nowadays include a high number of external elements from many different services. They also delegate hosting of many of their own files to CDNs (contents distribution networks) that reduce latency between client and server for frequently accessed, semi-static contents. Under the keyword of "Web 2.0", the "mashup" way of composing Web services has appeared, allowing a Web site to make the user's browser access not only external elements such as embedded images or frames, but also raw data via Web APIs. The input data obtained via an API can be combined by applications running on the Web client, such as Flash, JavaScript or Java applications, or by applications running on the Web server(s) (see Fig. 1). Note that the latter cannot be observed by client side traffic measurements as used in this paper.

The locality and connection characteristics of Web traffic have an impact on a variety of network issues. The dimensioning of middleboxes such as NATs (network address translators) or firewalls directly depends on the number of

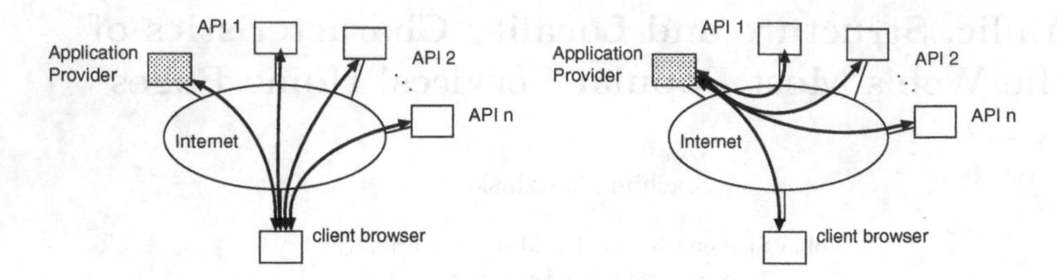

Fig. 1. Principal connectivity architecture of a client-side mashup (left) and a server-side mashup (right).

simultaneous connections to be expected per client connected. The viability of explicit quality of service (QoS) support or strict packet filter configurations for selected Web applications is severely restricted by the the complexity of the traffic required to display some of the most relevant Web pages. The changes in Web and Web page structures have to be reflected by Web traffic models in order to allow for correct performance evaluations by mathematical analysis or simulation, e.g. in the area of cacheing forwarding table lookups in routers or setting up on-demand lower layer connections to bypass routers.

1.2 Related Work

Crovella and Krishnamurthy [1] have written a comprehensive book on Internet Measurement, including passive and active measurement approaches and the most important findings in traffic characterization. Traffic characteristics and topology properties of new applications like peer-to-peer based services have been analyzed by numerous authors, e.g. in [2], but to the author's knowledge, there is no measurement study on the locality of Internet Web services and mash-up traffic yet.

Geographic locality has been studied recently in some publications. Fonseca et al. [3] focused on caching and location of proxies. Lakhina et al. [4] study the geographic locations of Internet nodes, Autonomous Systems and links. Spring et al. [5] give a good overview of methods to analyze the Internet's network structure and topology.

In a previous study [6], the author investigated the service and locality structure of popular Web services and selected mashup sites, analyzing application properties and logical locations such as domain ownership and routing towards the large number of different servers that make up a single Internet service such as *google maps, weather.com* or *myspace.com.* The study in [6] was based on active measurements that included following links on the site beyond the main page, which made the results somewhat difficult to repeat. In contrast, in this paper site usage is restricted to the sites' home pages, but in turn the number of sites investigated is increased from 25 to 100, and more Web page properties such as the number of elements, element sizes and a more detailed analysis of Web technologies (POST requests, secure connections, mashup mechanisms) have been analyzed.

1.3 Overview of the Paper

This paper is organized as follows: In Sec. 2, the measurement method and details are documented. The home page characteristics observed by the measurements are presented in Sec. 3, and an analysis of passive service popularity (i.e., how often is a specific service used by other sites) is included in Sec. 4.

2 Measurement Method

The evaluations in Sec. 3 and 4 are based on client-side measurements of actively initiated Internet traffic. All traffic from and to a client machine was observed, but the traffic between different Internet servers caused by a client request could not be seen.

While *passive observations* have the advantage of representing users' browsing habits and preferences and yielding high statistical significance from large sample sizes, it is impossible to extract per-site or per-click data from those traces. Also, such measurements cannot be replicated in detail.

In order to obtain replicable results per site, we chose an approach of *actively initiated observations* similar to [7,8] in this paper. Unlike classical *active measurements* on the Internet, e.g. [9], which generate Internet Protocol traffic on level and observe metrics related to delay, loss or path through the network, actively initiated observations of Web traffic use a defined set of URLs to make a browser download everything that is required to display the corresponding Web pages.

In this paper, the URLs to visit were selected to be the top 100 US sites as listed by the Alexa [10] Web statistics service. Alexa ranks Web sites based on popularity among a large number of users that have installed Alexa's toolbar in their browsers. This list of URLs includes a mixture of search, news, trading, contents sharing, adult services and social networking sites.

In contrast to [6], only the home pages on the URL list were visited and no further browsing on the sites was performed. For each site on the URL list, a Web browser was started with empty cache and cookies list, and all traffic between the client computer and the network was traced. After the page had fully loaded (or had been loading for more than one minute, to limit the effect of quasi-streaming services on some sites), the browser was closed and a new browser process and trace file started for the next URL. This process was mostly automated using scripts on a Linux machine running kernel 2.6.25 and using firefox 3 as Web browser. A 6 Mbit/s downstream and 640 kbit/s upstream DSL connection from Arcor in Germany was used to access the Internet.

From those complete traffic traces (one file per home page visited), the following *direct* characteristics were derived:

- number of bytes received from the network
- number of connections opened

- number of different servers contacted
- number of network prefixes (NPs) the servers' IP addresses were located in. For a given server IP address, the corresponding NP was determined by selecting the longest matching prefix from the OIX route-views BGP table [11].
- number of Autonomous System Numbers (ASNs). Similar to the NP analysis, the target ASN was read out of the OIX BGP table [11].
- number of different organizations contacted. For each IP address contacted, the corresponding DNS lookup in the trace was analyzed. If none was found, a reverse DNS lookup was performed. If that also did not yield a result, the NS pointer for the corresponding network prefix was looked up. The resulting DNS SLDs (domain name system second level domains) were taken to be representative for different organizations.
- number of GET and POST requests. This number could only be analyzed for non-encrypted connections. Secure HTTP (https) connections were recorded separately and counted as one GET request in the corresponding graphs. As all sites using https also used plain HTTP connections and most sites carried most traffic on unencrypted connections, this approach seemed more appropriate than separating out results for the https connections.

In addition, across all trace files an *indirect* characteristic was derived, indicating in how many home pages requests to each of the externally contacted services (as represented by their DNS SLDs) were included. For each of those externally contacted services, also the number of different NPs and ASNs observed in the 100 trace files were recorded.

Fig. 2 visualizes different views underlying the locality evaluations mentioned above. Clients collect data from multiple Web servers (Fig. 2 a.). Those servers are part of different AS networks (autonomous systems) and reached through different entries in the BGP routing tables (Fig. 2 b.), listed as NPs (network prefixes) in the following. The servers and networks belong to different organizations (Fig. 2 c.) and are located in different places of the world (Fig. 2 d.). The organizational relations are approximately represented by DNS second level domains (SLDs). The actual geographical location of servers is not considered in this paper.

3 Home Page Characteristics

The main traffic characteristics of the top 100 sites investigated are summarized in Tab. 1 in terms of minimum value, average and maximum value observed per site. The "Bytes" column indicates the number of downstream bytes received from the servers, including all HTTP, TCP and IP protocol overhead. The "Conn." column counts the number of connections opened until the Web page has finally loaded in the web browser (or a timeout of one minute occurred). The "Hosts" column gives the number of different (based on IP addresses) servers contacted when loading a page. The number of HTTP GET and POST requests

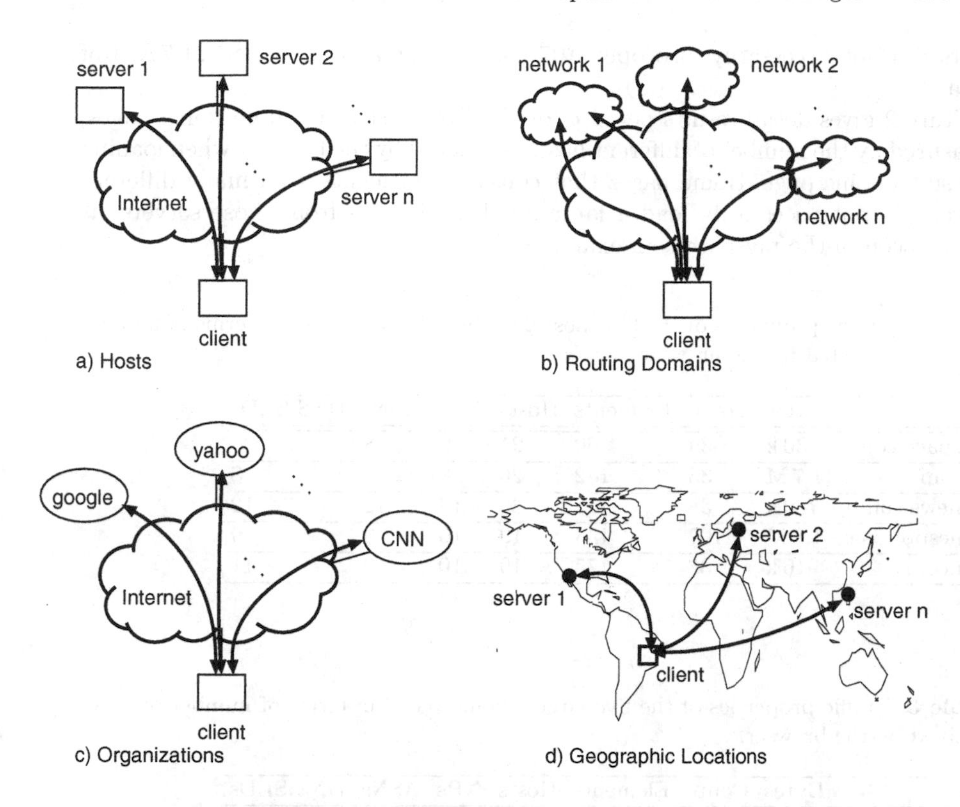

Fig. 2. Different notions of locality for services as seen by the Web client.

is counted in the "Elements" column. Encrypted connections (https) are counted as one GET request, as the HTTP contents of those connections could not be analyzed. The "NPs" and "ASNs" columns indicate the number of different BGP routing table prefixes and autonomous system numbers seen when looking for best matches of the servers' IP addresses in the BGP routing table. The "DNS SLDs" column counts the number of different DNS second level domains the server IP addresses resolve to.

Table 1. Minimum, average and maximum of the traffic and locality properties per Web site.

	Bytes	Conn.	Hosts	Elements	NPs	ASNs	DNS SLDs
min.	943	1	1	2	1	1	1
average	600 k	22.94	8.24	62.18	5.65	5.04	5.15
max.	11.7 M	107	21	284	14	13	15

Note that the minimum and maximum indications per column are independent of one another, i.e., the site that made the browser contact 21 different hosts did not necessarily also open 107 connections and download 11.7 MB of data.

Tab. 2 gives detail results per site for the five most distributed home pages, measured by the number of different hosts contacted by the browser when loading the site's home page. Home pages that consist of elements from many different servers do not necessarily load a large number of bytes from those servers, as can be seen in the myspace.com example.

Table 2. Traffic properties of the five most distributed home pages in terms of number of hosts contacted by the browser.

Site	Bytes	Conn.	Elements	Hosts	NPs	ASNs	DNS SLDs
myspace.com	330 k	34	60	21	9	8	8
go.com	11.7 M	35	142	20	8	8	8
foxnews.com	780 k	38	112	20	13	12	12
gamespot.com	1.8 M	107	133	19	10	9	9
cnn.com	916 k	38	175	19	10	9	11

Table 3. Traffic properties of the five largest home pages in terms of number of bytes received by the browser.

Site	Bytes	Conn.	Elements	Hosts	NPs	ASNs	DNS SLDs
go.com	11.7 M	35	142	20	8	8	8
xtube.com	5.5 M	52	284	9	5	3	5
imeem.com	1.9 M	32	43	13	5	5	6
gamespot.com	1.8 M	107	133	19	10	9	9
nba.com	1.6 M	15	154	5	4	4	4

Neither do pages that cause the browser to load a large number of bytes necessarily also contact a large number of hosts, as can be seen in the example of nba.com in Tab. 3. Note that there are adult and gaming sites with objectionable contents included in the results tables, which is why the author recommends the automated scripting approach for research. Quite a number of sites show videos on their home pages, which explains the very large amount of traffic received by the browser in those cases. In one case even a continuous sequence of videos was observed where after the end of one video, a subsequent video was loaded and played.

At the other end of the spectrum, there are also some very traffic conscious sites among the top 100 Web sites most popular in the United States. The first entry in Tab. 4 (msplinks.com) actually does not display any contents because the site is only intended for providing links to myspace.com pages. The rest of the sites listed in Tab. 4 manage to display a useful home page with less than 25 kB of downstream traffic. But even those quite frugal home pages cause the browser

Table 4. Traffic properties of the five smallest home pages in terms of number of bytes received by the browser.

Site	Bytes	Conn.	Elements	Hosts	NPs	ASNs	DNS SLDs
msplinks.com	943	1	2	1	1	1	1
craigslist.org	10081	6	6	1	1	1	1
live.com	18971	6	8	3	3	3	3
google.com	21947	3	5	2	1	1	1
orkut.com	22121	7	7	4	4	2	2

to open multiple connections to multiple hosts. Note that the firefox browser downloads two items also for the practically empty home page of msplinks.com because besides the actual HTML code for the homepage, a request is made for `/favicon.ico` to display in the browser's URL field.

Fig. 3 gives the rank distributions of the properties introduced above. Again, rank distributions are displayed per measure, i.e., the page with the 10th most connections is not necessarily the same as the site with the 10th most hosts or Network Prefixes. The rank distribution of the number of connections per home page in Fig. 3 (left) indicates that only 10 % of the sites actually have home pages which cause the browser to open 40 connections or more, although one of the top 100 sites most popular in the U.S. caused the browser to open as many as 107 connections. The other 90 % of sites show an almost uniform distribution between 1 and 40 connections. The vertical axis zoom-in in Fig. 3 (right) reveals that the rank distributions of the number of network prefixes, autonomous systems and DNS second level domains contacted are almost identical, varying between one and 10–15.

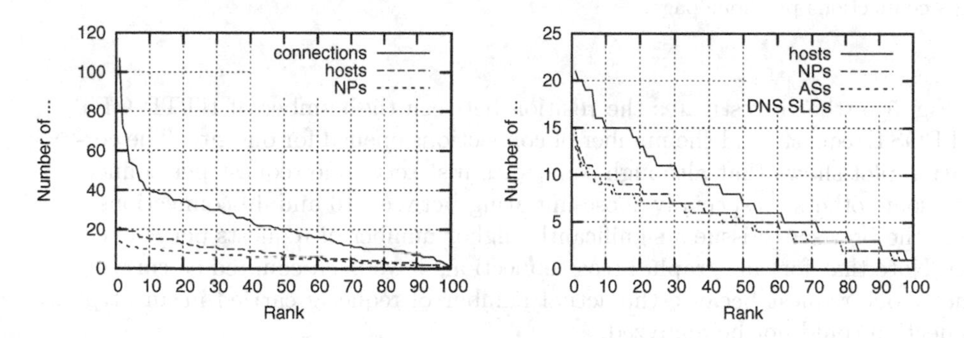

Fig. 3. Rank distributions of number of connections, hosts, network prefixes, Autonomous Systems and DNS SLDs contacted per site.

One possible explanation for the large number of hosts contacted by many sites lies in the combination of Web site developers' interest in providing fast loading performance and the restriction put forward in RFC2616 [12, sec. 8.1.4], which suggests that a browser should not open more than two connections to the same server in parallel. Therefore, to accelerate downloads of multiple elements from the same organization, it is useful to distribute them among multiple servers. This hypothesis is also backed by the fact that on average there are 1.5 hosts contacted per network (NP, AS or SLD).

Complementing the connection level analysis of Fig. 3, Fig. 4 shows the rank distributions for the number of HTTP POST requests and https connections per page. Only a few sites out of the 100 tested sites employ POST requests (11) or https (10). The largest number of HTTP POST requests observed for one home page was 5 whereas one site (chase.com) caused the browser to initiate as many as 46 https connections. Most of the sites using https only used https for one or a few connections out of a larger number of total connections.

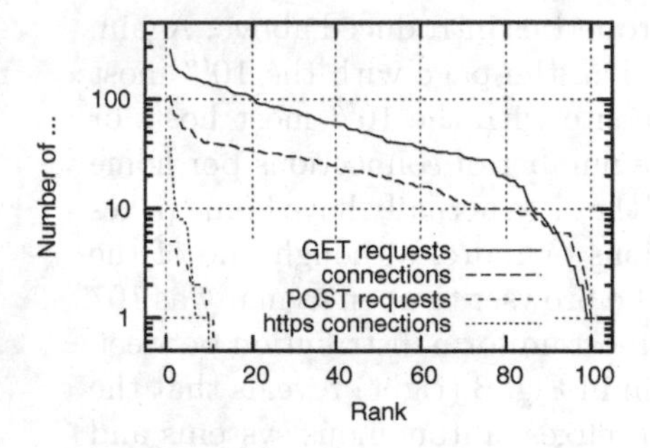

Fig. 4. Rank distributions of number of GET requests, number of connections, number of POST requests and number of https connections per homepage.

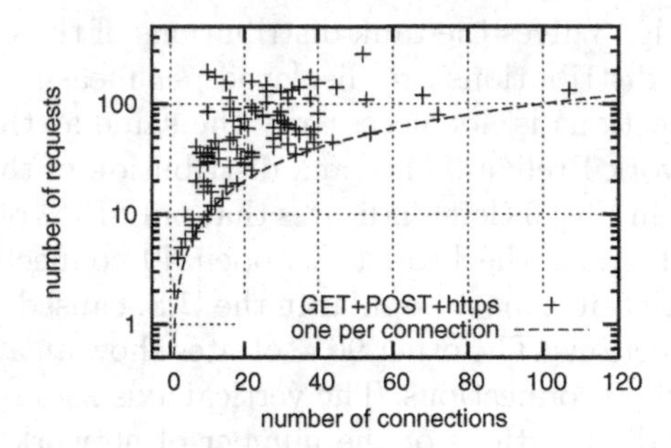

Fig. 5. Correlation between number of connections and number of requests on a homepage.

Fig. 5 further investigates the relation between the number of HTTP GET and POST requests and the number of connections opened for one site. The correlation plot shows that although some sites just serve one request per connection, some others – especially those initiating between 10 and 40 connections – cause the browser to issue a significantly higher number of requests per connection. Note that for this graph, https connections have been counted as carrying exactly one request because the actual number of requests carried in an https connection could not be analyzed.

Fig. 6 further analyzes the correlations between the numbers of hosts contacted and the number of connections established or bytes received (left) as well as the number of different ASs hosting the servers (right). It can be seen that the pages containing elements from only a few (less than around 7) servers also tend to open fewer connections and download less traffic volume whereas for pages with elements from more servers the number of connections initiated and number of bytes received is rather independent of the number of servers contacted.

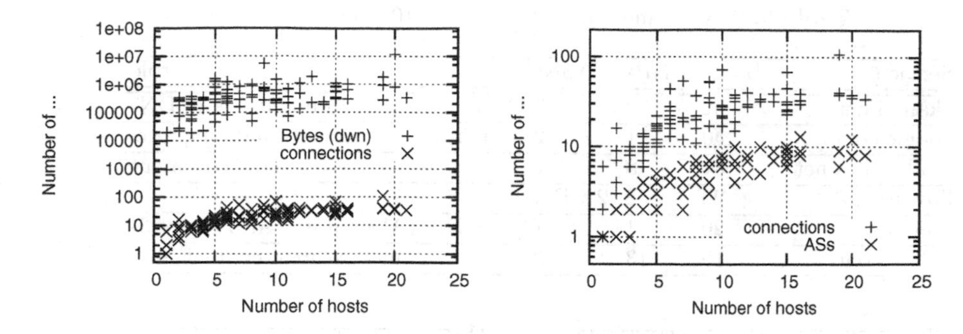

Fig. 6. Correlation between number of hosts connected when visiting a site and number of connections opened, number of bytes downloaded and number of ASs connected.

A look at the lower cloud of marks in Fig. 6 (right) suggests that the correlation between the number of servers contacted and the number of ASs disappears less quickly than that with the number of connections for increasing number of hosts.

4 Helper Services

In this section, the combination of all traces is evaluated to obtain observations not only from the perspective of pages using external services but also from the perspective of external services which are used by the sites' home pages.

Tab. 5 lists the most used external services: the content distribution network Akamai is used by 62 % of the top 100 sites most popular in the U.S., followed by search and advertisement giant Google (40 %) and advertisement service provider Doubleclick (31 %). As Akamai is specialized in bringing contents close to the end user (in the case case of this study, some Akamai servers were seen as being part of the access provider Arcor's network), the Akamai servers contacted are located in only three different ASs with three different network prefixes. On the other hand, Yahoo servers were contacted in 9 different ASs reached via 13 different network prefixes. Note that although different prefixes for the same AS very often result in the same next hop in core routing tables, examples from the OIX BGP table [11] show that the best BGP paths for different prefixes belonging to the same AS network do differ.

Note also that there is a residual difference between DNS SLDs and legal entities which could not be consolidated automatically, as there are some services which employ multiple DNS SLDs such as ebay.com and ebayrtm.com or att.net and att.com.

Fig. 7 (left) shows the rank distribution of usage from the point of view of the services being included. Similar to many other popularity distributions, also this distribution shows a long tail, at least over the two orders of magnitude that could be observed among the 180 services included by the 100 home pages investigated in this study.

Table 5. Services most used by the top 100 home pages.

Service	Usage	NPs	ASNs	role
akamai.net	62	3	3	Content distribution network (CDN)
google.com	40	11	2	search, advertisement, mapping, etc.
doubleclick.net	31	8	2	advertisement
llnw.net	20	2	2	CDN
gtei.net	20	1	1	CDN (Akamai hosted by Level3)
yahoo.com	19	13	9	mail, search, content, etc.

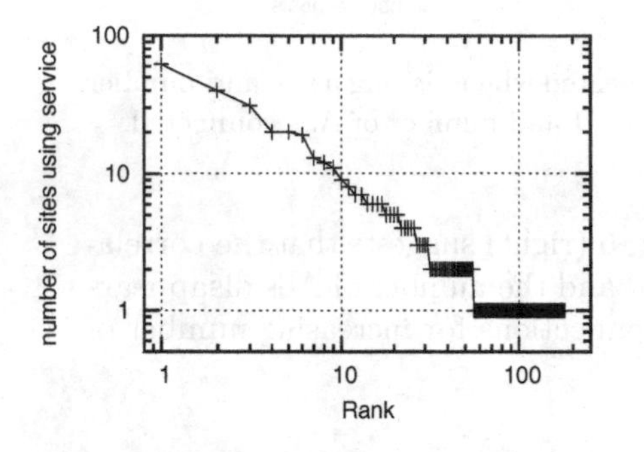

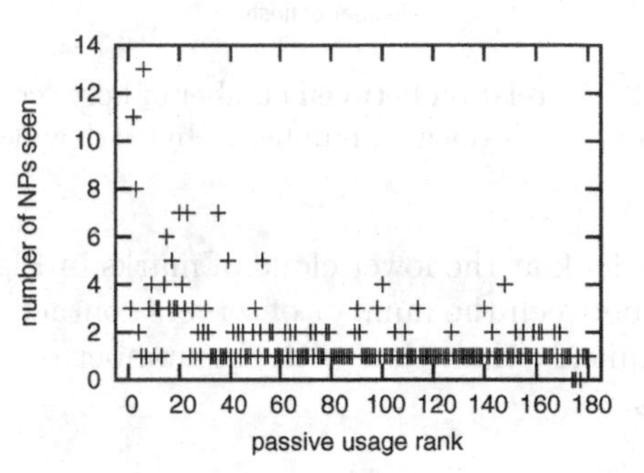

Fig. 7. Rank distribution of number of sites using a service (left) and correlation between passive usage rank and number of network prefixes (NP) seen for the service (right).

Fig. 7 (right) takes an additional look at the correlation between passive usage rank (how popular is the service to be included by others) and the number of network prefixes seen for the services. It can be observed that although on the full scale of popularity there are services whose servers are all located within a single network prefix, there are also services operating in multiple different network prefixes. The frequency of occurrence of multiple NPs per service as well as the degree of non-locality decreases with decreasing popularity of a service.

5 Conclusions

In this paper, the home pages of the 100 Web sites most popular in the USA have been investigated with respect to several network traffic related characteristics such as the number of different servers and their logical locations and affiliations. Not only in terms of its transport infrastructure but also as a service structure, the Internet respectively the World Wide Web has turned into a highly distributed structure.

The restriction to the sites' home pages could have severely limited the complexity of the observed traffic but a comparison with results for more extended browsing sessions on some of the same set of sites in [6] shows that many of the sites already exhibit a large degree of distribution on their home page.

This study found that many of the most popular Web sites have home pages whose contents is a combination of a wide distribution of external services. On the other hand, there are a few more traffic conscious services that offer a lean home page which can be loaded with only a few connections to a small number of hosts, downloading only 10–20 kBytes.

Among the external services utilized by many sites are contents distribution (Akamai), advertisement (Google and Doublecklick) and embedded search functionalities (Google).

The fact that Web pages nowadays consist of elements from a multitude of servers in different networks and organizations has consequences for quality of service design (no use setting up a single reservation per client session), security configuration (hundreds of services need to be admitted to allow full functionality of a Web site), availability (a page only loads properly if all of the embedded elements are available and the respective servers can be reached) and traffic modeling, e.g. for the number of ports in use at the same time on a network address translation device.

Further work on this topic will need to include measurements from multiple client sites, extended site sessions beyond home pages, performance effects of the CDNs and the effect of browser properties and local cacheing on traffic characteristics.

References

1. Mark Crovella and Balachander Krishnamurthy. *Internet Measurement: Infrastructure, Traffic and Applications.* John Wiley and Sons, Inc, 2006.
2. Kurt Tutschku and Phuoc Tran-Gia. Traffic characteristics and performance evaluation of peer-to-peer systems. In Klaus Wehrle Ralf Steinmetz, editor, *Peer-to-Peer-Systems and Applications.* Springer, 2005.
3. Rodrigo Fonseca, Virgílio Almeida, and Mark Crovella. Locality in a web of streams. *Communications of the ACM*, 48(1):82–88, January 2005.
4. Anukool Lakhina, John W. Byers, Mark Crovella, and Ibrahim Matta. On the geographic location of internet resources. *IEEE Journal on Selected Areas in Communications, Special Issue on Internet and WWW Measurement, Mapping, and Modeling*, 2003.
5. Neil Spring, David Wetherall, and Thomas Anderson. Reverse engineering the internet. In *2nd workshop on hot topics in networks*, Nov. 2003.
6. Joachim Charzinski. Locality Analysis of Today's Internet Web Services. In *Proc. 19th ITC Specialist Seminar, Berlin, Germany*, Oct 2008.
7. Paul Barford and Mark Crovella. Measuring Web Performance in the Wide Area. *ACM Performance Evaluation Review*, 27(2):37–48, August 1999.
8. Balachander Krishnamurthy and C. E. Wills. Analyzing factors that influence end-to-end Web performance. *Computer Networks*, 33(1):17–32, 2000.
9. Jean-Chrysostome Bolot. End-to-end packet delay and loss behavior in the internet. In *SIGCOMM '93: Conference proceedings on Communications architectures, protocols and applications*, pages 289–298, New York, NY, USA, 1993. ACM.
10. Alexa: most popular US web sites. available at http://www.alexa.com/site/ds/top_sites? cc=US&ts_mode=country&lang=none, visited June 16, 2008.

11. OIX Route Views. http://archive.routeviews.org/oix-route-views/2008.05/, visited 28. May 2008.
12. R. Fielding et al. Hypertext Transfer Protocol – HTTP/1.1 . IETF RFC 2616, http://www.ietf.org/rfc/rfc2616.txt, 1999.

Seamless Dynamic Reconfiguration of Flow Meters: Requirements and Solutions

Tobias Limmer and Falko Dressler

Computer Networks and Communication Systems, University of Erlangen,
Martensstr. 3, 91058 Erlangen, Germany
{limmer,dressler}@informatik.uni-erlangen.de

Abstract. In this paper, we investigate the need for seamless dynamic reconfiguration of flow meters. Flow monitoring has become a primary measurement approach for various network management and security applications. Sampling and filtering techniques are usually employed in order to cope with the increasing bandwidth in today's backbone networks. Additionally, low level analysis features can be used if CPU and memory resources are available. Obviously, the configuration of such algorithms depends on the (estimated) network load. In case of changing traffic pattern or varying demands on the flow analyzers, this configuration needs to be updated. Hereby it is essential to lose as little information, i.e. packet or flow data, as possible. We contribute to this domain by presenting an architecture for seamless reconfiguration without information loss, which we integrated into the monitoring toolkit Vermont. Additionally, we integrated support for situation awareness using module specific resource sensors. In a number of experiments, we evaluated the performance of Vermont and similar flow monitors.

1 Introduction

Flow monitoring is becoming a dominant metering technique in professionally managed networks. Mainly, there are two reasons for network providers to measure their network traffic. First, the amount of transferred data is monitored for accounting purposes. All monitored packets are assigned to single IP addresses or specific subnets and aggregated to customer-related records, which contain information about the IP traffic. Secondly, the area of security also makes use of network monitoring: intrusion detection, attack detection, scan detection and forensic analysis are just a few application domains [1].

Usually, flow monitoring is performed using statically deployed monitors with predefined configuration settings. This procedure has two drawbacks. First, the configuration of sampling algorithms and filters must be defined for a medium load scenario. Thus, resources are waisted in case of low network load (it would be possible to inspect all packets instead of a subset) and in case of extreme load, the monitor will not be able to process all packets, which leads to nondeterministic packet drops. In order to adapt it to changing network conditions, reconfiguration of the monitor, e.g modifying the packet sampling rate, would be needed.

Secondly, in the security context, often high speed networks are scanned for anomalies, as processing of more detailed network data would be computationally too expensive. If anomalies are detected, usually single hosts or subnetworks are involved. For more information about the cause of the anomaly, a detailed analysis of the subnetwork's traffic is required. Again, dynamic reconfiguration of the network sensors to supply detailed data about the affected subnetwork is an adequate solution.

We analyzed the capabilities of state-of-the-art flow meters for their capabilities to provide such reconfiguration. We discovered that there is no direct way for such parameter updates nor for adding new functionality during runtime. Usually, the monitor needs to be stopped, (re-)configured, and started again. This leads to information loss during the reconfiguration process.

Based on all these observations, we developed a novel architecture for seamless dynamic reconfiguration and integrated it into our monitoring toolkit Vermont [2].[1] In order to achieve the desired behavior, we extended the modular structure of Vermont to add internal queues between all modules. Using these queues, it is possible to change the modules' organization, to add and to remove modules without stopping all monitoring and processing activities. Without loss of generality, in this paper, we concentrate on flow monitoring for network security purposes because the requirements are covering all problem domains of other applications as well.

In this paper, we first analyze the characteristics of flow monitoring with respect to adaptive configuration of parameters, e.g. the sampling rate, or the complete update of the monitoring functionality (Section 2). We not only integrated our developed reconfiguration architecture in Vermont (Section 3.2) but also added means for situation awareness based on integrated sensors that provide information about the current resource utilization of Vermont modules (Section 3.3). In several experiments, we analyzed the performance of Vermont in comparison with other flow meters. The main focus was the monitoring performance during reconfiguration tasks (Section 4).

2 Overview and Problem Statement

2.1 Flow Monitoring

Flows are sets of IP packets sharing common properties. A flow record contains information about a specific flow. In most applications, a typical configuration would be using the IP 5-tuple *<source IP, dest IP, source port, dest port, protocol>* as flow keys, i.e. attributes describing the flow. Furthermore, relevant statistical data can be added such as the flow start and end times or the number of bytes of all packets belonging to the flow. Several protocols are available to efficiently transfer flow records. Most of the state-of-the-art flow meters support either Netflow.v9 or Internet Protocol Flow Information Export (IPFIX). The latter one was standardized by the IETF in RFC 5101 [3]. Both protocols support

[1] `http://vermont.berlios.de/` and `http://www.history-project.de/`

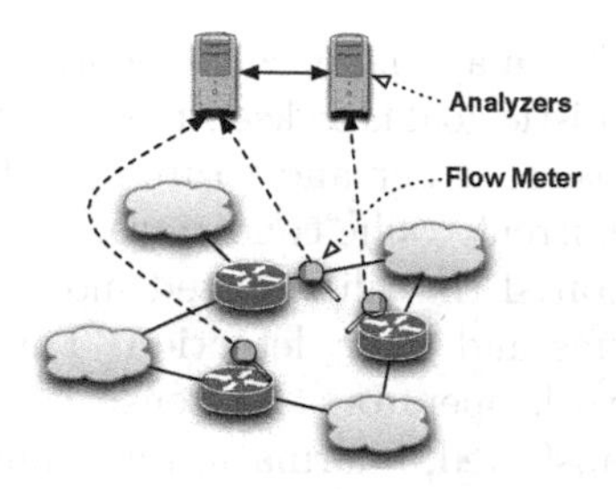

Fig. 1. Example of a distributed monitoring system for integrated attack detection

variable configurations: so called template records are transmitted that describe the structure and content of flow records. Flow records are exported regularly according to predefined timeouts. The active timeout describes the maximum time a flow record is kept in cache and the passive timeout is used if no more packets are received for the particular flow.

2.2 Requirements in the Security Domain

Attack detection methodologies require input data with different levels of detail. On the one hand, there are systems available that operate on raw packet data including full payload for a detailed analysis of the monitored traffic. On the other hand, systems process summarized data that contains e.g. aggregated information about traffic volumes for subnets.

We assume an attack detection system that comprises flow monitors that are directly attached to the observed network links, and analyzers that process the collected flow data in order to detect attacks or intrusions. The flow data may have different levels of detail. Figure 1 shows an overview of the architecture. Flow monitors can be chained to support flow aggregation. Multiple hierarchically structured flow aggregators are also a topic of the IPFIX working group [4]. The depicted analyzers may execute different algorithms ranging from attack detection to application identification. Besides simple anomaly detection methods like top-N lists, more intelligent traffic summaries [5] or horizontal portscan detection [6] could be supported. Many application identification methods are also based on IP header data as available in flows [7–9].

2.3 Challenges

Today's backbone networks maintain high data rates, where it is only possible to get sampled flow statistics for further analysis. Due to the nature of less accurate information, the detection of security incidents becomes more difficult. Similarly, detected anomalies require further inspection of suspicious hosts and connections. The monitoring infrastructure needs to provide more detailed information of potentially malicious traffic. To achieve this, the configuration of the flow meters needs to be temporarily adapted. Furthermore, even normal traffic behavior changes over time. This may influence the load of different modules in the detection system. The idealistic goal is to keep the monitoring system always as effective as possible, thus, there is demand to update the parameters of the flow meters according to the current traffic conditions.

Rajab et al. [10] demonstrated that distributed monitoring decreases time between the outbreak of worms and their detection. This suggests a collaboration between different network operators. As sensitive information between those entities must not be transferred, information exchange should be held at a possible minimum. The best way is to reduce the level of detail of transferred information at the cost of less accurate attack detection. Only in specific cases, the level of detail may be increased in a well-controlled manner. Finally, direct attacks on monitoring infrastructures may cause the equipment to fail and create holes in accounting and performance logs, or security-related incidents may not be detected. Current networking equipment, especially in the area of flow monitoring, offers only limited capabilities for reconfiguration if it detects overload and its monitoring functionality may be impaired.

All these scenarios suggest a dynamic solution for flow aggregation: a network of sensors tries to deliver exactly the data that is needed for efficient traffic analysis by the detection algorithms.

3 Dynamic Reconfiguration

In this section, we will describe the basic concepts of our monitoring toolkit Vermont. We continue with the developed architecture for seamless reconfiguration, which has been specifically designed for Vermont. However, the basic principles can easily be adapted for other flow meters as well. Finally, we briefly cover the capabilities of Vermont to detect the resource consumption of currently running modules to support situation-aware reconfiguration steps.

3.1 Vermont

Vermont is an open-source monitoring toolkit capable of processing Netflow.v9 and IPFIX conforming flow data. It has been developed in collaboration with the University of Tübingen. The application runs on Linux and derivatives of BSD. It can receive and process raw packets via Packet Capturing (PCAP) (up to 1 GBit/s) as well as IPFIX/Netflow.v9 flow data. Supported data formats for export are IPFIX, Packet Sampling (PSAMP), and Intrusion Detection Message Exchange Format (IDMEF). The following modules are available:

- *Importers* capture raw data via PCAP, receive Netflow.v9 and IPFIX flow data via UDP and Stream Control Transmission Protocol (SCTP)
- *Samplers and filters* provide sampling algorithms and packet filter definitions
- *Exporters* export data using IPFIX, PSAMP, or IDMEF
- *Aggregators* aggregate incoming data according to customizable rules
- *Analyzers* detect anomalies in flows and output IDMEF events

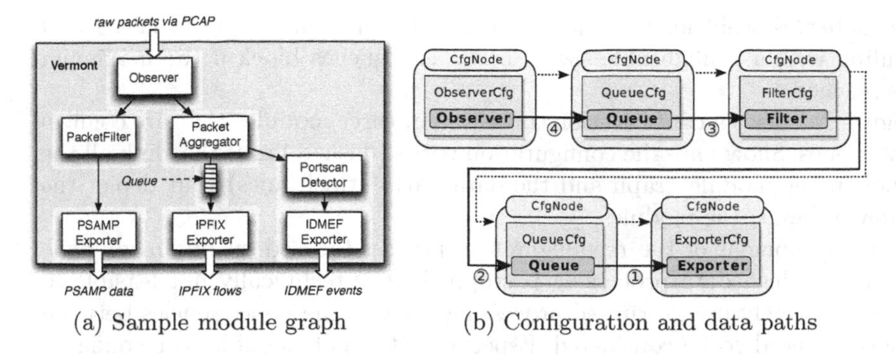

(a) Sample module graph (b) Configuration and data paths

Fig. 2. Vermont module configuration

Modules can be linked in almost any combination: only the input and output data type of linked modules need to be compatible. Modules may also have more than one succeeding and preceding module. Figure 2a shows an example for an arrangement of several modules. In this configuration, Vermont captures packets using PCAP, filters these packets and exports the selected PSAMP records. A second branch aggregates flows, which, in turn, are exported using IPFIX and analyzed in a portscan detector, respectively.

3.2 Reconfiguration

A special feature of Vermont is its support for dynamic reconfiguration of the module structure. Linked modules in Vermont correspond to a directed acyclic graph and operate independently from each other.

The idea is to support updates of the configuration file and to reconfigure Vermont accordingly at runtime. For this reconfiguration, Vermont computes the differences between the old and new configuration. Unique IDs are used to identify the modules. Vermont always tries to reuse existing modules in order to allow keeping state information and to speed up the reconfiguration process. If the configuration of an existing module has been changed, Vermont tries to reuse it and applies updates on-the-fly. If it is not possible to reuse a module, a new one is created. Examples are aggregator modules: for aggregation configurations, no on-the-fly reconfiguration is allowed because the used hash tables need to be rebuilt. Thus, all stored flows need to be exported and sent to the subsequent module in the module graph. This ensures as little flow data loss as possible. This process is repeated for each module until instances for all new modules are created. Modules are reconnected according to the new configuration and started in reverse topological order as depicted by the numbers in Figure 2b.

If modules do not have any asynchronous tasks to perform, they may be executed synchronously using a single thread. If, on the other hand, Vermont runs on a multicore machine, the software can be configured to use multiple threads, at most one per module. Asynchronous execution of modules causes lags in the processing time, so Vermont may use queues between modules to compensate this problem. The queues can be fully customized, but usually FIFO scheduling with a configurable size is used. The queues block if the maximum size is reached.

Figure 2b shows a configuration consisting of three modules that are connected by queues. Shown are the configuration paths (dashed lines) that link all the modules in the module graph and the data paths (thick lines) that depict the data flow between the modules.

The development of the reconfiguration process focused on minimizing the time during which data processing is stopped. It is technically not feasible to provide completely uninterrupted processing because the dependencies between the modules need to be considered. Especially, it is not possible to reconfigure the module graph without stopping the modules that need to be re-ordered in the graph. We minimized the module's outage by preparing new modules before the processing is stopped. Additionally, the shutdown of old modules is performed after the new configuration is completed and started.

We achieved downtimes smaller than 5 ms using this method. On a link transferring 1 GBit/s, this timeout could result in a data loss of about 650 KByte. Vermont is able to buffer this data during the reconfiguration process using the memory-mapped PCAP library.[2] For our tests, this buffer was set to 64 MByte.

3.3 Situation Awareness

Dynamic adaptation to current traffic data rates and corresponding load on flow meters does not only depend on seamless reconfiguration, but also on the ability to identify and, in the best case, anticipate bottlenecks in the monitoring hierarchy. We implemented sensors inside Vermont to retrieve information about the current load of the system. Each module offers standard measurement values like CPU utilization and memory requirements. Additionally, module-specific data is monitored, e.g. the current packet rate or the queue size. This information is an essential requirement for algorithms that try to balance load among multiple flow aggregation nodes. Based on the data coming from the sensors, it is possible to move a task to a different system that still has unused capacities.

Figure 3 shows example statistics from the aggregator's hash table that were collected over one day: the black line shows the total number of entries inside the hash table, the blue line shows the number of entries that shared a single bucket with other entries inside the hash table. Multi-entry buckets considerably slow down the lookup of entries in a hash table, as they are implemented as linked lists. In our example, the hash table offered a total of 256 Kbuckets, but at the time of 800 min a DDoS attack occurred on the monitored link and the number of entries exceeded the hash table's capacity by far. This is a typical case for a DoS attack against the flow meter and should be evaded by monitoring the module load and adequate reconfiguration.

---

[2] `http://public.lanl.gov/cpw/`

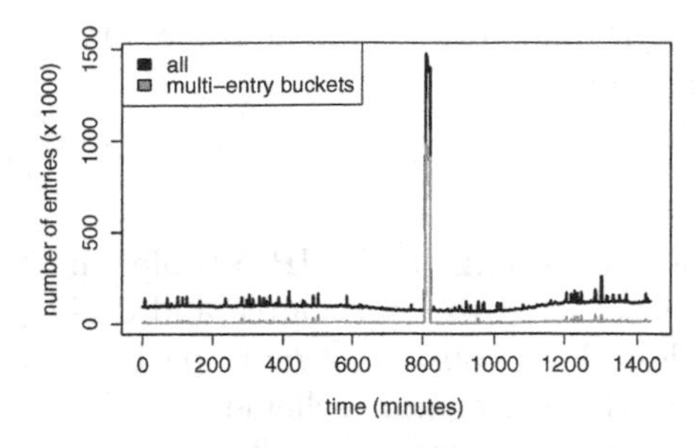

Fig. 3. Hash table size

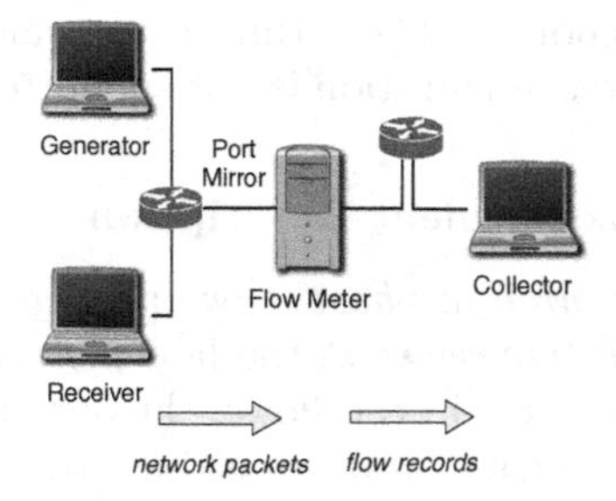

Fig. 4. Testbed setup

4 Performance Measurements

4.1 Test Setup

In this section, we analyze the reconfiguration performance of Vermont and compare it to the performance of typical flow meters. We set up a testbed for these experiments in which the different flow monitors are tested with artificial traffic as well as with real traffic. Figure 4 shows the structure of the test setup. We used a dedicated PC for generating traffic, which, in turn, was forwarded to the system under test. The forwarding was performed using a mirror port on a layer-2 switch. The flow meters exported their data on a separate network interface to a flow collector, which logged the received flows for later analysis. Care was taken to deactivate all unneeded functions of the systems, including the switches, for more deterministic results.

For performance comparison, we used a Cisco Catalyst 6500 router running IOS firmware version R12.2 SXF. It supports basic flow aggregation for routed traffic using a "NetFlow cache", which exports Netflow.v5/v9 data. More flexible configuration options are offered by the feature called "NetFlow aggregation". It uses an additional NetFlow cache table in the switch called "Aggregation cache" which has aggregated flow statistics of the monitored traffic. Different aggregation schemes like "source prefix" (aggregation according to source IP address), "destination prefix" (destination IP address), "prefix-port" (both IP addresses and ports), "prefix" (both IP addresses) and more are supported, and for each aggregation scheme several collectors of the flow data may be specified. The parameters for the timeout of active and inactive flows are specified in minutes and seconds, respectively. So the minimum timeout for active flows is 1 min and for inactive flows 1 s.

Another popular flow meter is nProbe (Netflow probe), an open source Netflow.v5/v9 and IPFIX probe. Similar to Vermont's basic functionality, it captures packets on an Ethernet network, aggregates the packets to flows, and exports them. The main focus of nProbe is its efficiency to support fast flow aggregation in software. Attributes of exported flows are fully configurable. According to the documentation, aggregation is performed identically to Vermont: incoming packets are inserted into a hash table, which in turn is regularly checked for flows to be exported. Those timeouts are also configurable on the command-line. On-the-fly reconfiguration is not supported by nProbe.

4.2 Experiment Description

In *configuration phase 1*, we aggregated flows according to the IP 5-tuple. In *configuration phase 2*, the flow meters were instructed to omit source and destination ports in the flows, thus producing less flows containing more packets. These two configuration settings are similar to the aggregation schemes "prefix-port" and "prefix" provided by the Cisco router and ensure that different rules must be used for aggregation. Parameters controlling the timeout for inactive and active flows were set to 10 s and 60 s, respectively. Both nProbe and Vermont were configured to use a scan / export interval of 10 s for the internal hash table. The testing process involved the following steps:

1. start collector and flow meter using *configuration setting 1*
2. start traffic generator
3. reconfigure flow meter for *configuration setting 2*
4. wait until flow meter finished sending flows to collector

Reconfiguration of Vermont was performed as described in Section 3.2. We ensured that the other tools were reconfigured in as little time as possible: nProbe does not explicitly support dynamic reconfiguration, so we executed nProbe using the settings of *configuration phase 1*, terminated the process using the `SIGINT` signal at reconfiguration time, and immediately restarted the process. The Cisco router was reconfigured using an already established `telnet` connection: old flow aggregator settings were shut down and then the new scheme was activated by transmitting the corresponding commands to the machine.

We generated two different types of traffic for the test: artificially generated traffic, where all packets shared almost identical properties, and real-world traffic. As our goal was to test traffic losses caused by reconfiguration, we only generated low data rates, so that none of the flow meters got overloaded. For generating artificial traffic, we used the Network Packet Generator (Npag) tool. It produced TCP packets with constant source and destination IP, constant source port, no payload and the destination port was uniformly distributed in a specified range. Additionally, we used `tcpdump` and `tcpreplay`[3] to record traffic from a LAN and to replay the traffic to the flow meter, respectively, so that the flow meters processed almost identical traffic. The network dump had a length of 71 s. It counted 150 608 packets in total and had an average data rate of 11.69 MBit/s or 2111 packets/s. The traffic was generated for a total of 60 s. Reconfiguration was performed 30 s after the traffic generator was started.

4.3 Further Issues

If the flow meter is reconfigured or stopped, all cached flow information needs to be exported. In the best case, already processed data records are exported

[3] `http://www.tcpdump.org/` and `http://tcpreplay.synfin.net/`

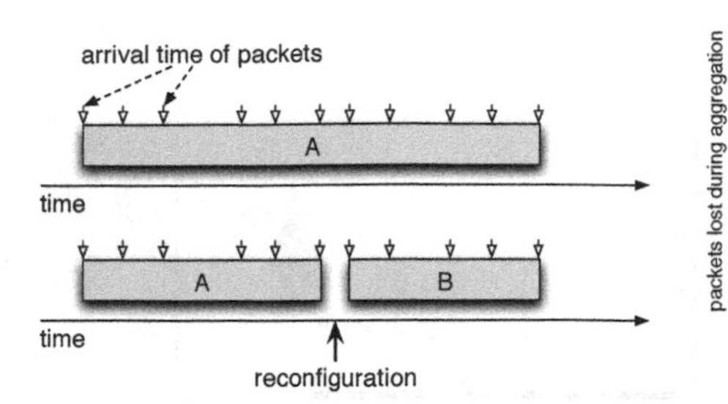

Fig. 5. Flow splitting problem

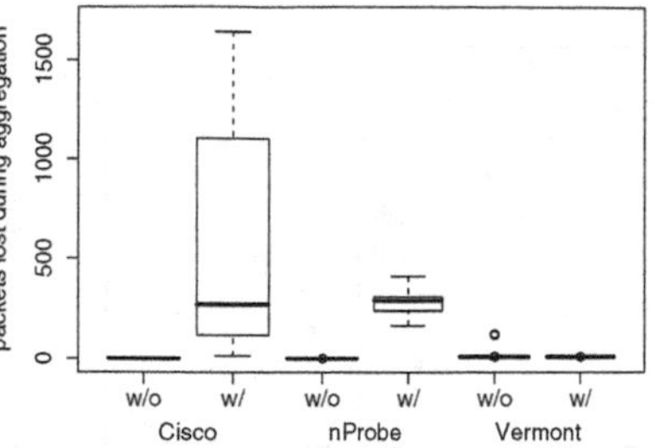

Fig. 6. Packet loss for `tcpdump` traffic

immediately after reconfiguration. Simultaneously, newly arriving packets are processed using the new configuration and exported with a new flow description. This ensures that all packets are reported using the configuration that was valid at reception time and minimizes time until flow data is sent to the collector. A side-effect of this immediate configuration switching is that flows are split into two parts. An example is depicted in Figure 5. On the upper part, a flow is shown matching configuration `A`. If reconfiguration is performed during the lifetime of the flow (lower part), the flow is being split. This effect is unavoidable, as otherwise the aggregator would not follow its configuration semantics. Depending on the configuration, it will not be possible to join both parts at the collector.

4.4 Results and Discussion

In the following, we present selected results of our experiments. Primarily, we focus on the packet loss caused by reconfiguration. Furthermore, we investigate the flow export times of the different flow meters with and without reconfiguration.

Packet Loss We compared the number of packets contained in all flow records exported by the flow meter with the number of packets sent by the traffic generator. The results are depicted in Figure 6 using boxplots: a box is drawn from the first quartile to the third quartile, and the median is marked with a thick line. Additional whiskers extend from the edges of the box towards the minimum and maximum of the data set. For this experiment, we used `tcpreplay` for testing the system with real-world traffic. For all the systems, two box plots are displayed without and with reconfiguration. We performed 30 test runs for statistical validity and to identify outliers. Without reconfiguration, all flow meters performed very well with almost no packet loss. With reconfiguration, only Vermont shows the loss rate close to zero, whereas Cisco and nProbe kept much higher loss rates – an average downtime of 130 ms was observed. nProbe needs to be completely restarted for reconfiguration. Thus, there is a short time period in which no packets can be recorded. This explains nProbe's loss of roughly 300 packets. The Cisco router performed much worse losing about 550 packets on average. The high variance cannot be explained without deeper insights into the internal flow processing.

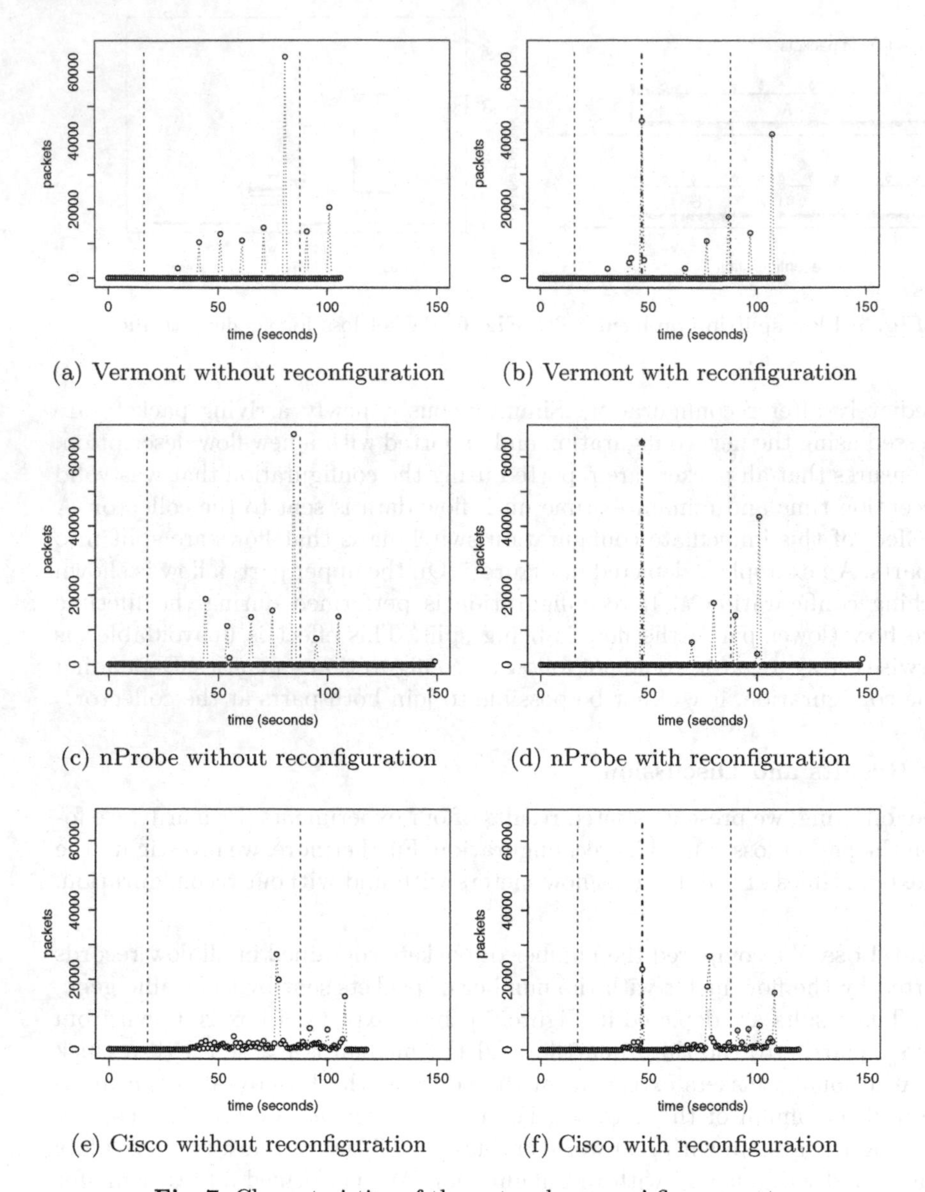

(a) Vermont without reconfiguration (b) Vermont with reconfiguration

(c) nProbe without reconfiguration (d) nProbe with reconfiguration

(e) Cisco without reconfiguration (f) Cisco with reconfiguration

Fig. 7. Characteristics of the network sensors' flow export

Flow Export Times All generated flow records were logged by the collector including a time stamp recording the time of reception. This way, we were able to relate the start and end times of the flow, i.e. when it was monitored by the flow meter, to the time when the flow record was exported. Figures 7a–7f show such relations: the start and end times of traffic generation are marked by the dashed vertical lines. In all figures with reconfiguration, a vertical bar at 30 s after start time indicates the switch from *configuration phase 1* to *configuration phase 2*. The dotted lines with markers show the amount of packets contained in flows that were sent to the collector, displayed at the time of reception at the collector. All figures show the captured, real-world traffic replayed by `tcpreplay`. The same tests were performed with artificial traffic and confirmed the presented results.

For Vermont, the results without reconfiguration are shown in Figure 7a. It can clearly be seen that Vermont was configured to check its aggregation hash table every 10 s and then immediately export the expired flows to the collector. The high spike at 80 s is caused by the active timeout of 60 s, thus, all active flows are contained in the corresponding flow records. nProbe uses almost the same aggregation technique as Vermont. Thus, Figure 7c does not show many differences. Interesting is the small spike at 150 s, where the last flow records were exported. According to the configuration, this export comes much too late, as no flows should be active after stopping the traffic generator. Passive flows were to be cached for 10 s and at most 1 s was waited until records were exported. Figure 7e shows that the Cisco router uses a different aggregation scheme compared to the software-based flow meters. Flows were not exported in regular intervals, but continuously after their expiry. First flows were exported 10 s after traffic generation started. The spike at 80 s corresponds to the configuration settings (see Vermont and nProbe).

For reconfiguration, Vermont shows the expected outcome in Figure 7b. All flows are exported at reconfiguration time and the succeeding exports show regular behavior. The same applies to nProbe, including the aforementioned spike at 150 s that is not conform to the configuration (Figure 7d). The Cisco router shows an interesting behavior depicted in Figure 7f. There is a spike in the graph that shows the expected peak at reconfiguration time, but there are less packets exported compared to Vermont or nProbe. Additionally, there is a spike 60 s after start that seems to be roughly as high as the spike in Figure 7e at the same time. These spikes are caused by exported active flows and should not show the same values as all cached data should have been exported at reconfiguration. We concluded, that the Cisco router does only export passive flows at reconfiguration time and continues caching all active flows that are exported at the same time as they would have been without reconfiguration. This means, that flows monitored during *configuration phase 1* are exported using the settings of *configuration phase 2*. This behavior is weird because exported data can not associated to the correct phase.

5 Conclusion

We demonstrated the need for seamless dynamic reconfiguration of flow meters for various application fields. Based on this motivation, we presented a new solution for this issue: the flow monitor Vermont, which offers a modular structure that is optimized to guarantee short reconfiguration times and offers in-depth self-monitoring capabilities for situation-aware reconfiguration decisions. In our performance tests, which included the software-based flow aggregator nProbe and a high-end Cisco router, we showed that currently available flow meters do not offer the needed reconfiguration performance. Typically, an average downtime of 130 ms was observed in which all incoming packets were dropped and not reported to the flow collector. For complex hierarchical analysis systems, reconfiguration procedures should be seamless without noticeable data loss. The implemented architecture showed its advantages during this test. Due to its modular, data flow oriented structure, the overhead of a reconfiguration process can be kept at a minimum – no packet loss has been observed.

Acknowledgments

The authors would like to thank Christoph Sommer for his work on Vermont and his standardization efforts, and Peter Baumann for the implementation of the basic reconfiguration concept within Vermont.

References

1. Carle, G., Dressler, F., Kemmerer, R.A., König, H., Kruegel, C., Laskov, P.: Manifesto - Perspectives Workshop: Network Attack Detection and Defense. In: Dagstuhl Perspectives Workshop 08102 - Network Attack Detection and Defense 2008, Schloss Dagstuhl, Wadern, Germany (March 2008)
2. Lampert, R.T., Sommer, C., Münz, G., Dressler, F.: Vermont - A Versatile Monitoring Toolkit Using IPFIX/PSAMP. In: IEEE/IST Workshop on Monitoring, Attack Detection and Mitigation (MonAM 2006), Tübingen, Germany, IEEE (September 2006) 62–65
3. Claise, B.: Specification of the IP Flow Information Export (IPFIX) Protocol for the Exchange of IP Traffic Flow Information. RFC 5101, IETF (January 2008)
4. Kobayashi, A., Nishida, H., Sommer, C., Dressler, F., Stephan, E., Claise, B.: IPFIX Mediation: Problem Statement. Internet-Draft (work in progress) draft-ietf-ipfix-mediators-problem-statement-00.txt, IETF (May 2008)
5. Estan, C., Savage, S., Varghese, G.: Automatically Inferring Patterns of Resource Consumption in Network Traffic. In: ACM SIGCOMM 2003, Karlsruhe, Germany, ACM (August 2003) 137–148
6. Jung, J., Paxson, V., Berger, A.W., lakrishnan, H.B.: Fast Portscan Detection Using Sequential Hypothesis Testing. In: IEEE Symposium on Security and Privacy, Berkeley/Oakland, CA (May 2004)
7. Bernaille, L., Teixeira, R.: Early Application Identification. In: 2nd International Conference On Emerging Networking Experiments And Technologies (CoNext 2006), Lisboa, Portugal (December 2006)
8. Crotti, M., Dusi, M., Gringoli, F., Salgarelli, L.: Traffic Classification Through Simple Statistical Fingerprinting. ACM Computer Communication Review (CCR) **37**(1) (January 2007) 5–16
9. Wagner, A., Dübendorfer, T., Hämmerle, L., Plattner, B.: Identifying P2P Heavy-Hitters from Network-Flow Data. In: 2nd CERT Workshop on Flow Analysis (FloCon 2005), Pittsburgh, Pennsylvania (September 2005)
10. Rajab, M.A., Monrose, F., Terzis, A.: On the Effectiveness of Distributed Worm Monitoring. In: 14th USENIX Security Symposium, Baltimore, MD (July 2005)

Teil VI

Sicherheit

Towards the Design of Unexploitable Construction Mechanisms for Multiple-Tree Based P2P Streaming Systems

Michael Brinkmeier[2], Mathias Fischer[1], Sascha Grau[2] and Guenter Schaefer[1]

[1] Telematics and Computer Networks, TU Ilmenau
[2] Automata and Formal Languages, TU Ilmenau

Abstract. In peer-to-peer based live streaming systems, a great number of participants have to cooperate to efficiently and reliably distribute a continuous flow of data. Each receiving peer in return provides its resources to the system. Since these systems operate in a completely distributed manner, it is of particular importance, to prevent malicious members from harvesting important topology information or influencing the streaming system to their needs. In this article, we analyze potential attack methods on multiple-tree-based P2P streaming systems, discuss important design decisions to constrain the impact of malicious behaviour, and we introduce the new concept of peer testaments. By analyzing existing systems, we show that so far only few attention has been given to the design of unexploitable construction mechanisms. Based on the identified design decisions, we propose a novel streaming system and evaluate it by exposing it to different types of internal attackers. Our results show that these attackers have to spend large effort to reach relevant positions in the streaming topology and that their bandwidth contribution far outnumbers the damage they achieve.

1 Introduction

In recent years, peer-to-peer (P2P) based Application Layer Multicast (ALM) live streaming systems have become a major topic of interest, both in research and practical application. In such a system, a continuous flow of data - the stream - is distributed from a source node to a great number of peers by utilizing their resources for redistributing the stream to other peers. A major advantage of such a design is that the number of participants can grow independently of the source's upload bandwidth.

ALM systems are commonly classified into pull and push approaches. Push approaches create and maintain an explicit topology for content distribution, whereas in pull approaches every node explicitly requests each part of the stream at other participating nodes. So, pull approaches require to preload the stream well in advance of the playout, which causes relatively high delays. Therefore, they are out of scope of this article and the main emphasis is put on push-based approaches, which organize their participants in a *topology* of one or more spanning trees, each rooted at the source node. If multiple trees are used, the source divides the stream into equally sized substreams called *stripes* and distributes each one via its own tree, thereby removing bottlenecks and improving resilience. Thus, by using Multiple Description Coding or Forward Error Correction methods, it is possible to compensate the loss of one or several stripes.

Consequently, each peer takes part in every tree and automatically receives each stripe from a node one step closer to the source, which is called *parent* or *predecessor*. Equivalently, it redistributes one or more stripes to its *children*. The set of all nodes transitively receiving data from a peer is its *successor set*. Generally, we will say that a node is on a *low level* in a certain tree, if it is located far away from the source.

In order to construct and maintain such topologies, a distributed mechanism is required, especially since the set of participants is highly dynamic, because of joining and leaving nodes (the so-called *node churn*). Elementary operations of such a mechanism are *bootstrapping*, that is the way nodes join the system, and *repairing* of trees after the announced or unannounced exit of nodes. Furthermore, multiple kinds of optimizations like balancing and flattening of the trees, as well as bandwidth and timing optimizations are commonly implemented.

All these actions are performed by the participants using a common strategy. Since topology maintenance always influences the position and hence the size of a node's successor set, it is important to design all mechanisms in such a way, that they cannot be exploited by malicious participants for conducting attacks against the distribution mechanism.

In a first step, this article collects basic properties of attacks on push-based streaming systems in section 2. Our main contribution is given in section 3 by discussing building blocks for unexploitable construction mechanisms for push-based ALM streaming systems, including the new concept of *peer testaments*. Current streaming systems are classified and analyzed in section 4 according to the proposed building blocks, revealing that most of them provide no effective defense against internal attackers. So, in section 5 we propose a streaming system that includes an unexploitable topology construction mechanism, which gets experimentally analyzed in section 6. Section 7 summarizes our findings and gives an outlook on future work.

2 Attacks Against P2P Streaming Topologies

There are two basic types of attackers, the *external* and the *internal* one. An *external attacker* can only observe and attack the system from outside. Thus, it may issue attacks on participating nodes without being sanctioned by the system, allowing aggressive approaches. In general, we assume, that an external attacker can take down a specific node by issuing a DOS attack against it, or triggering some other effect which removes it from the system. The main limitation of an external attacker is the fact, that it has to gather information by eavesdropping the communications between nodes, which can be restricted by using cryptographic protocols.

Unless an external attacker can gather a lot of information about the system, an *internal* attacker is more powerful, especially if combined with an external component. In the following, we specifically concentrate on variations of *sleeper attacks* with additional capabilities, covering a wide range of possible attack scenarios, since many attacker models can be reduced to a sleeper attack.

The *sleeper attack* is one of the most basic attacks. The attacker controls a set of *agents*, which participate in the system. In addition, they may communicate with each other or with a central authority, guiding the attack. The agents join the system in the same way ordinary nodes do, and start participating. In this way, they can easily use all procedures and protocols that the system provides.

In a *passive* sleeper attack, these agents simply wait until a certain condition is met and then an attack is triggered. The point in time at which this happens, may be chosen in many ways. Either the agents attempt to reach certain relevant positions in the topology, or they just collect information and try to identify important nodes or even the (possibly concealed) source itself. The second aim is basically equivalent to the first, since usually the source can be identified by a node that reaches a specific position. Hence we may assume, that an attack is triggered as soon as the positions of the agents satisfy specific conditions.

How the agents (or the controlling authority) decide whether their current positions are 'important', mainly depends on the signalling procedure of the particular P2P streaming approach. If, for example, the system provides its participants with informations about the number of other nodes depending on their service (ie. their number of successors) or even the IDs of these nodes, the attacker can calculate the exact damage it can cause at any given time. Hence, it may simply trigger the attack, as soon as a given bound is reached. In other situations, the position of a node may correlate with the time it was in the system. In these cases, the attacker may simply wait for a specific time to pass and then has a good chance that his agents may cause a given damage.

If the attacker decides or assumes, that the agents have reached good positions, it can trigger an attack. This might be a simple disruption, caused by all agents leaving the system at the same time. Optionally, the agents may not leave the system completely, but reduce their bandwidth, such that the quality of service for nodes depending on them decreases significantly. Another way to disrupt the service is a coordinated attack on specific nodes, which were previously identified by the agents. These attacks can either be issued by the agents themselves, risking their discovery and possible sanctions like exclusion, or by an assisting external attacker, leaving the agents concealed. Furthermore, the agents can provoke damage with a *resource-consuming attack*, during which a large number of agents try to connect to the same node with the goal of preventing the target from forwarding the stream to other participants. This is a variation of a DOS attack, consuming the bandwidth of a specific node.

Alternatively, the agents may start to *pollute* the system by inserting corrupted data into the stream. Successors may detect the pollution (e.g. by verifying cryptographic signatures on the stream data) and try to reconnect to the system, possibly leading to a massive reconstruction and a decrease in the quality of service. This *Pollution attack* can have the same effects as the failure of the agents or the attack on specific nodes.

In addition to simply cooperating with the streaming system, the agents may pursue their task to reach relevant positions more *actively.* For example, in surprisingly many streaming systems, peers can promote themselves to more important positions. They are often even rewarded for taking on more responsibility, with the goal to inhibit freeriders.

A second way for the agents to gain importance is to lie about their performance, making them seemingly better than other peers. This misinformation may lead to a 'false promotion', since the other nodes assume, that the agent is the best possible choice for an important position. Or they may try to attract peers to become their children, increasing their number of successors. Third, they might support each other, eg. by recommending other agents for promotion or giving them high reputations. Fourth, they can become aggressive in advance by attacking other peers in their surroundings, provoking an (at least local) reconstruction of the topology, thereby giving them the chance of reaching a better position. As above, these supporting attacks might be conducted by an external assistant, preventing the discovery of the agents.

One important parameter of sleeper attacks is the degree of cooperation between agents. The agents may be completely independent from each other, preventing coordinated attacks – except if a global synchronized clock is used. Or they may communicate via an external authority, allowing a coordinated attack and the simultaneous collection of information from all agents. The costs and modalities of communicating with the coordinating authority can be used to model some specific types of attacks. For example the Sybil attack [Dou02], in which agents are logical instances of the same physical node, may be modeled by assuming, that the coordinator has at every time the knowledge of every agent.

In contrast to an external attack, an internal attacker supports the attacked system for a while. Hence, the *efficiency* of an internal attack can be measured by the quotient of the caused damage and the invested cost. Let X be a set of nodes, which we assume to be agents or attacked due to the information, the agents gathered. An estimate for the damage caused by the attack at time T is the number of successors of the nodes in X at time T summed up over all stripes, i.e. $\text{damage}(X,T) = \sum_{i=1}^{k} \text{succ}_{i,T}(X)$, where $\text{succ}_{i,T}(X)$ is the number of nodes that are successor of at least one vertex in X in stripe i at time T. The cost invested by the attacker can be measured by the total bandwidth, that his agents provided over the time, i.e. $\text{bandwidth}(X,T) = \sum_{t=1}^{T} \sum_{v \in X} \text{fanout}(v,t)$, where $\text{fanout}(v,t)$ is the bandwidth that vertex v provided at time t. The *efficiency* of an internal attack if given by the quotient of the caused damage and the invested bandwidth, ie. $\text{efficiency}(X) = \frac{\text{damage}(X)}{\text{bandwidth}(X)}$. Using this measure, the vulnerability of different systems against a specific attack can be compared, with a higher value indicating a lower resilience. Alternatively, different attack strategies on the same system can be compared.

3 Requirements for Manipulation-Proof Construction Mechanisms

The basic principle of manipulation secure topology management mechanisms is *mistrust* in all participating nodes. In such a mistrustful system, every node is suspected to be malicious, is therefore provided with the minimum required topology information and has to proof its reliability, e.g. by long-term cooperation, before being considered for taking over responsibility.

When implementing this idea in a functional P2P streaming system, a list of requirements for key design decisions arises, that concern the direction of the distribution of topology information as well as repair mechanisms, choosing the right nodes for node promotion, and bootstrapping issues.

3.1 Distribution of Topology Information

To build both efficient and reliable streaming topologies, it is necessary to make a certain degree of topology information available to the participating nodes. Examples for such information reach from the numbers of stripes/nodes/successors over the IDs of nodes in relevant positions to a complete snapshot of the current topology. Of course, it would also be possible to build topologies without any more information than the IDs of nodes in a local neighborhood, however the resulting topologies can become rather inefficient or unstable.

On the one hand, there is a trade-off between supporting topology management decisions with more information, and on the other hand providing malicious agents with the same data, which allows more effective attacks. Hence, all information distributed should at least have a local character, such that it is related only to limited regions of the topology and is only available to nodes from such regions. A typical example is the successor number of a node and its children, allowing important tree balancing operations. Without an estimate on the total node number, a prediction of the own importance in a topology is not possible.

In addition to the kind of information to be distributed, the direction of information flow is equally important. Clearly, a concentration of knowledge near to the source is advantageous compared to a distribution towards the tree leafs. This way the number of involved nodes is minimized and their reliability must have been previously certified in some way. A related rule in the design process must be the strict separation of stripe-related information. So, data describing the role of a node in the distribution tree of a certain stripe should not allow conclusions about its role in other stripe trees. This is necessary, since a node being a predecessor in one stripe and hence receiving such information, may be on very low levels in other stripes. Thus, without a separation, the source-directed information flow would be violated.

3.2 Locality of Repair Mechanisms

As soon as the failure of a relaying node is detected, appropriate topology repair mechanisms have to be performed. Especially, a substitute node from a lower level has to be found. Here, we can again choose between different alternatives. At first, a repair mechanism considering nodes from the whole topology seems to be desirable. This way, a node from a completely different subtree could take over the role of the failed one. Thereby, the node profiting from the failure would not belong to the direct neighborhood of the failed node, thus making attacks on direct predecessors worthless.

However, without a coordinator with global topology knowledge, such a system has a number of major drawbacks. First, the substitute node has to be chosen, possibly involving a high number of other nodes, each of questionable trust. Additionally, due to long communication paths, such a mechanism will imply long repair times which are furthermore dependent on the total number of topology nodes (the time may grow at least logarithmically with the number of nodes). At last, the substitute node has to be replaced in its old position, too, raising questions of convergence and the undesirable property that local failures propagate through the whole topology.

Therefore, a local repair method in which the substitute node is chosen among the children of the failed one, is preferable. This way restricts the repairs to the subtree rooted at the failed node. Furthermore, the risk that disabling a predecessor gives a chance to advance in the topology can partially be mitigated by one of the reliability estimation mechanisms described later.

3.3 Initiative of Repair Actions

The first nodes noticing the failure of a node v, are its direct children and its predecessor (the exact order depends on the streaming system). Which of them initiates the repair is another important design decision. In many systems the initiative lies at the children; they either exit and rejoin the system or they try to attach to their grandfather. The first variant has to be discouraged, since it leads to unbalanced trees and requires a number of global rebalancing operations.

The second variant depends on regular updates on the grandfather's ID from each parent to its children. Clearly, this reveals a lot of topology information to possibly unreliable nodes. Furthermore, during the reconnection process the grandfather has to decide which of its affected grandchildren shall now take over the role as head of the complete subtree that was formerly lead by the failed node. Since the grandfather has no knowledge about the number and quality of its grandchildren as well as to shorten repair times, it will be tempted to choose the first candidate arriving. Clearly, an attacker disabling its own predecessor has a timing advantage over its siblings.

Thus, regularly distributing child information to the predecessor and assigning repair initiative to it, seems more appropriate. In this case, nodes detecting a parent failure have to wait for a certain time threshold before acting on themselves. Meanwhile, their grandfather chooses a new child node from its grandchildren based on the information formerly sent by the failed node (additionally ignoring connection requests of its grandchildren). When communicating this decision to the involved nodes, the grandparent should authenticate itself, e.g. by using a secret of the dead parent, which has been sent upwards before.

Of course, rebalancing and capacity-based adjustments of the topology are still necessary. However, they will be restricted to the subtree in which the damage occured.

3.4 Decision Process for Node Promotion and Degradation

Whenever higher topology positions shall be assigned or nodes are chosen to be dropped to lower levels, the decision process is based on different properties of the available candidates. Once again, a trade-off between efficiency and reliability may occur. Typically compared key factors include available bandwidth, successor number, participation time and the effort a node has already invested in stream distribution. If available, the latter can be estimated by a trust or reputation system.

Independent from the decision which of these properties are considered, it is important to prevent candidates from lying, which requires some kind of proof. Depending on the checked property, this may be done by demonstration in response to some kind of challenge. Examples for such a procedure are bandwidth-tests or cryptographic puzzles for a successor estimation [RSS07]. Another kind of proof is to present witnesses, by direct communication or by forwarding cryptographically secured testimonies, e.g. certifying good long-term service.

An especially interesting kind of proof is a *testament*, namely a certification of a node about the suitability of its children as an heir to its position. In contrast to a grandparent, needing to make a fast decision during the repair process, such a testament is built over a long time of cooperation and may include many factors. Thus, it enforces exemplary behaviour to nodes willing to ascent in the topology. A simple way to use testaments, is by regularly submitting such a rating of the own children to the predecessor, providing it with far more consolidated information to choose its new child.

Note, that the chosen promoted node has no prior knowledge about its new children, which are its former siblings. To prevent a whitewashing, it is therefore important to initialize its own testament with the ratings made by the failed node. To do this, the grandparent has to forward the testament to the heir.

Another point to consider when designing the decision process, is its predictability. Clearly, a completely deterministic behaviour will be open to manipulation by well-informed attackers. Therefore, it is advised to add a random component, e.g. by equally choosing the node from some best portion of the candidates. A different modification would be to frequently choose the second-best candidate, thereby inhibiting lies about performance parameters, as long as attackers do not cooperate.

3.5 Reliability Estimation Via Long-Term Service

From the factors estimating the reliability of nodes, the participation time is one of the simplest. Furthermore, when statistically evaluating the distribution of participation times in live streaming systems [SM04], there is a high probability that old nodes will further continue to take part in the streaming system.

So, there is a concentration of long-living nodes on the high levels of the tree, the time between position changes grows. This effect automatically results from node churn under the precondition, that joining nodes are positioned as a leaf at lowest level (see later), but can also be actively encouraged by the design of the node promotion processes.

The ideal goal of such a mechanism must be to force the attacker to contribute so much exemplary effort to the streaming system, in order to reach an important position, that the resulting damage of its attack cannot compensate its costs. More specifically, the system has to be designed, such that the *efficiency* of an attack is as low as possible.

Additionally, information provided by a peer itself must always be mistrusted. A solution consists in measuring only the time spent in the current depth layer of the tree. This can be easily done by the peer's predecessor. Clearly, in case of a predecessor change, the new predecessor should initialize the time values based on the testament of the old predecessor. Due to its promotion, its own time value will be reset to zero.

3.6 Bootstrapping Joining Nodes

A last important design decision concerns the way joining nodes are attached to the existing topology. This decision affects both, the availability of topology information and the balance of the tree topology. A very simple method is a node insertion at the source of the stream. This way, the new node can be dropped down to a position optimal for the tree balance. However, during this process it gains information about the source and nodes from all tree layers.

A more common approach is the use of bootstrapping servers returning random nodes as entry points. Since the great majority of nodes has only low positions and no information about their rank is provided, the information leakage is bounded. The similar variant, returning only random leaf nodes would require a significantly increased management effort and a single instance with global knowledge. Furthermore, it would not avoid necessary balancing and optimization operations, since without them the generated topologies grow very deep.

4 A Brief Discussion of Existing Systems

In some systems (e.g. HGM [RES01]) there exists a central coordinator, which has global knowledge and assigns participating nodes to specific positions. But by construction, such a coordinator is a single point of failure, which may be easily attacked, if not concealed. Furthermore, usually the existence of such a central authority limits the size of the system, preventing a good scaling behavior.

The well-known SplitStream protocol [CDK+03] requires that each node knows its path to the source in every stripe, in order to avoid cycles. Hence, every node knows the source. In addition the delegation of nodes is based on their ID and allows joining nodes with a suitable ID to take over relevant positions immediately. Since these IDs contain a randomized component, a new node might be assigned to important positions purely by random, supporting an attacker with a large number of agents. Similar like SplitStream, some approaches like DagStream [LN06], rely on information flowing from nodes in higher levels of the tree to nodes residing in lower levels.

In approaches like Chunkyspread [VF06] or mTreebone [WXL07] the decision for node delegation and promotion is made by children nodes instead of their parents, which enables agents to lie.

The system proposed in [SWS07], operates with local topology knowledge and local repair mechanisms. The decision process for the promotion or degradation of a node is performed by its parent. However, this approach still has drawbacks. A child node does not only know its father, in addition it also obtains information about its grandfather, which is contacted by the child during a repair action.

5 A Push-Based Streaming System Utilizing a Manipulation Resistant Topology Repair Mechanism

Our approach is built at the basis of [SWS07], as described in section 4, and extends it by utilizing the building blocks presented in section 3. Only local topology information is used and the information flow is strictly directed from leaf nodes upwards the tree, so that the view of participating nodes is restricted to their parents in each stripe, instead of their grandparents as in [SWS07]. So in our approach, a node communicates with its one-hop predecessor only, while it has broader knowledge about its children and the total number of nodes below, since this is required to enable a balancing of the underlying subtrees.

The main difference to [SWS07] is the use of testaments for node promotion during repair actions. In the process, a proper candidate for a promotion is chosen by the grandfather according to the node's residence time, measured locally at the father node. Therewith, the grandfather has the repair initiative and not the children of the failed node, as in [SWS07]. This combination of mechanisms now offers the evaluation of peers based on their long-term behaviour and avoids making decisions based on untrusted, snapshot-like information.

Bootstrapping of joining nodes is done by inserting them at random nodes that already take part in the streaming. A bootstrapping server provides a joining node with a list of parent candidates, which will either accept it as a new child or pass it on to one of their children.

6 Experiments

In order to evaluate our system with regard to the effectiveness of the integrated building blocks discussed in section 3, a simulation study was conducted. The system was simulated in the presence of local sleeper attackers with different capabilities. We measured the ratio between potential damage, represented by the overall number of successors of all attacking nodes, and the bandwidth spent until this time.

Within the simulation, the stream is divided into 4 stripes distributed via 4 spanning trees. Summed up over all trees, every client has enough upload capacity to supply at most 8 children. The source is capable of forwarding every stripe 3 times and therefore has a capacity of 12. A total number of 250 nodes was simulated, with 95% of them being ordinary streaming clients and the remaining 5% being sleeper attackers with different capabilities. Ordinary nodes join uniformly at the beginning of the simulation between the first 10 and 50 seconds and leave the stream following a shifted pareto distribution with $k = 1.3$ and $x_{min} = 1$. To keep the node number at a constant level, leaving nodes rejoin again uniformly distributed between 5 and 10 seconds after their leave. The overall simulation time comprises 300 seconds. Obviously, this user behavior may not reflect the reality, but it allows to observe the system at a high load and enables us to draw conclusions on the systems operation at a more realistic user behavior with less node churn and longer streams. Attacker nodes join slightly later to an almost complete but not fully established streaming topology, since we assume attacks on already running and stabilized streaming systems. It is clear, that during the unnatural massive node join at the beginning of the experiments, there is no way to prevent agents from being positioned at high levels. So, the attacker nodes join uniformly distributed between the first 30 and 60 seconds and remain in streaming until the end of simulation. 32 simulation runs were conducted per parameter set and for every graph 97.5% confidence intervals were computed.

Figure 1(a) shows the average residence time per level for all spanning trees, i.e. the average time that nodes in a certain distance from the source remained at this position. As discussed in section 3, a reliability estimation based on the participation time of nodes in the system, should allow to move more reliable nodes to higher levels of the tree. As can be seen in the figure, this is the case for our system, since nodes closer to the source have growing residence times.

In addition, we simulated sleeper attackers with different additional capabilities to test our topology construction mechanisms and to observe if an attacker can exploit them to ascent in the topology. In our experiments, the agents were able to kill their fathers once per a certain time interval. These varied between 0 (a passive sleeper) and 50 seconds. It is assumed that all agents were controlled by one authority, therefore their damage and invested bandwidths combine.

Figure 1(b) shows the results for the ratio of maximum potential damage per run to the invested bandwidth until that point in time. As expected, this value is increased by a high attack frequency. However, the attack efficiency is very low for all intervals, such that the attackers had to forward multiple times more packets than are now not able to reach their destination. Furthermore, the efficiency increase of the active attackers is low, demonstrating that the topology repair mechanisms successfully reduce the impact of such strategies.

Figure 1(c) shows the ratio of achievable damage to invested bandwidth (attack "efficiency", see also section 2) of the passive and the most effective active attacker over time. Once more, the active attack is more successful, but at a very low level. The efficiency of both follows a characteristic development. The

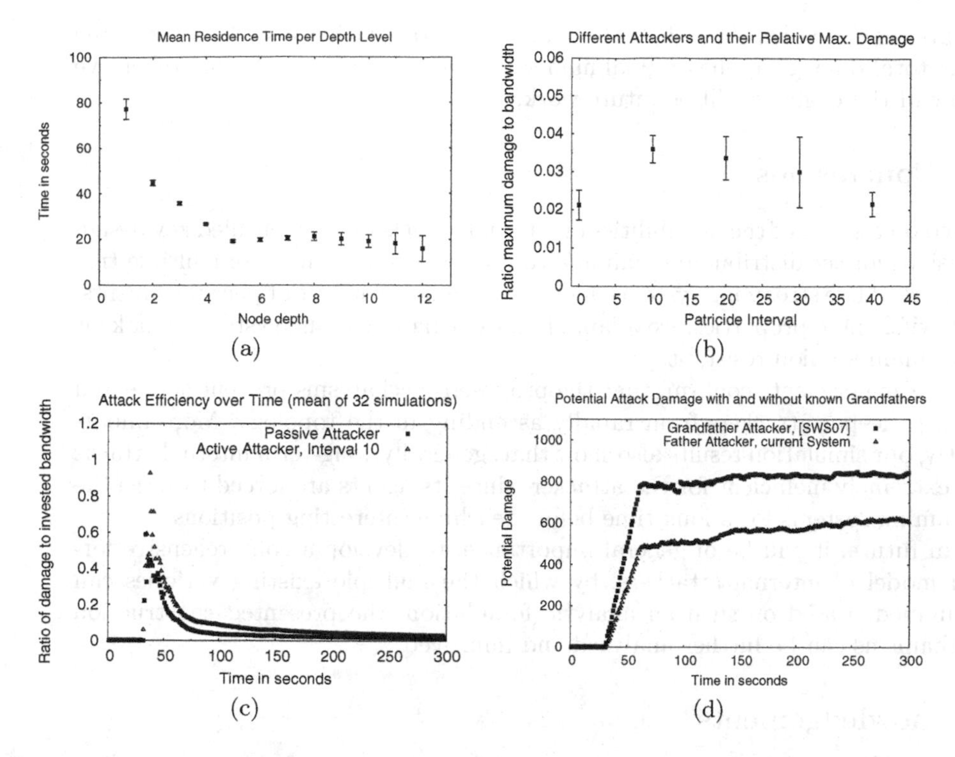

Fig. 1. (a) Mean residence time per level, (b)(c) attack efficiency (total number of successors in all stripes / invested bandwidth), (d) absolute potential damage of our improved streaming system in comparison to [SWS07]

highest benefit for an attacker lies between 40 and 50 seconds, shortly after joining the stream and after obtaining one or several children for its agents, since it has spent nearly no effort in terms of invested bandwidth. The attack efficiency quickly decreases when the attacking nodes stay longer in the system, in order to reach more important positions in the streaming topology. This observation gives further indication of the effectiveness of our topology building principles.

In order to compare our system to the approach mentioned in [SWS07], we simulated both systems in the presence of sleeper attackers. The topology knowledge of nodes in our system is restricted to the respective fathers in all stripes, whereas in [SWS07] peers also know their grandfathers.

Exploiting this knowledge, instead of disrupting the service by switching off itself, an agent in [SWS07] could kill all its grandfathers and in our improved system an agent could only kill all of its father nodes. Figure 1(c) shows the potential damage in our system in comparison to the potential damage caused by the attacker in [SWS07]. As can be seen, the appliance of the building blocks described in section 3 lowers the potential attack damage between 20% and 30% in comparison to [SWS07]. One might expect that the improvement is higher, but it has to be taken into account that many attackers have common grandfathers.

As first experiments show, half the number of grandfather attackers reach the same total damage as the original number of father attackers. A comprehensive study of these effects will be future work.

7 Conclusions

Based on a study of the possibilities of internal attackers, we identified key design decisions for the distributed repair and construction mechanisms of multiple-tree based P2P live streaming systems, including the new concept of peer testaments. Following these properties, we adapted an existing streaming system to make it more manipulation resistant.

Our experiments confirm, that the proposed mechanisms prevent active and passive sleeper attackers from rapidly ascending in the topology. More importantly, our simulation results also show that, generally, long-term internal attacks are extremely inefficient for the attacker, since its agents are forced to serve the streaming systems for a long time before reaching interesting positions.

In future, it will be of general importance, to develop a comprehensive formal model of internal attackers, by which the multiple existing varieties can be unified. Based on such an analytic foundation, the presented construction mechanisms can be further analyzed and improved.

Acknowledgements

We would like to thank Stephan Beyer and Michael Braun for their valuable help in implementing the simulation study.

References

[CDK+03] M. Castro, P. Druschel, A. Kermarrec, A. Nandi, A. Rowstron, and A. Singh. Splitstream: high-bandwidth multicast in cooperative environments. In *SOSP '03*, New York, NY, USA, 2003. ACM.

[Dou02] John R. Douceur. The sybil attack. In *IPTPS '01*, London, UK, 2002.

[LN06] J. Liang and K. Nahrstedt. Dagstream: locality aware and failure resilient peer-to-peer streaming. volume 6071. SPIE, 2006.

[RES01] V. Roca and A. El-Sayed. A host-based multicast (hbm) solution for group communications. In *ICN '01*. Springer-Verlag, 2001.

[RSS07] M. Rossberg, G. Schaefer, and T. Strufe. Using recurring costs for reputation management in peer-to-peer streaming systems. *SecureComm*, 2007.

[SM04] K. Sripanidkulchai and B. Maggs. An analysis of live streaming workloads on the internet. In *in Proc. of ACM IMC*, pages 41–54. ACM Press, 2004.

[SWS07] T. Strufe, J. Wildhagen, and G. Schäfer. Network-Efficient and Stable Overlay-Streaming Topologies (German: Netzwerkeffizienz und Stabilität von Overlay-Streaming-Topologien). In *KIVS*, 2007.

[VF06] J. Venkataraman and P. Francis. Chunkyspread: Multi-tree unstructured peer-to-peer multicast, 2006.

[WXL07] Feng Wang, Yongqiang Xiong, and Jiangchuan Liu. mtreebone: A hybrid tree/mesh overlay for application-layer live video multicast. *ICDCS*, 2007.

Turning the Tables: Using Wireless Communication Against an Attacker

Ivan Martinovic, Jens B. Schmitt

Distributed Computer Systems Lab (DISCO), University of Kaiserslautern, Germany

Abstract. In this paper, we propose a system leveraging the peculiarities of the wireless medium, such as the broadcast nature of wireless communication and the unpredictability of indoor signal propagation to achieve effective protection against attacks based on the injection of fake data in wireless sensor networks (WSNs). Using a real-world WSN deployment and a realistic implementation of an attacker, we analyze this protection scheme and demonstrate that neither position change, transmission power manipulation, nor complete knowledge of wireless parameters can help an attacker to successfully attack the network. As a result, this work demonstrates how the chaotic nature of radio communication, which is often considered a disadvantage in regard to security objectives, can be exploited to enhance protection and support implementation of lightweight security mechanisms.

1 Introduction

Using secrets in the protection design of wireless networks is an expensive and complex task. Most cryptographic techniques are trivially breakable if a secret is not adequately chosen, confidentially exchanged, and securely stored and protected. Hence, there are a number of methods which assist to fulfill these requirements, such as cryptographic hash functions, asymmetric key exchanges, tamper-resistant hardware, etc. Since these requirements increase the costs of the security design, especially in terms of protocol complexity and resource requirements, an additional advantage of using secrets is the previously mentioned "all-in-one" property. Once the secret is securely exchanged and stored, different objectives can be fulfilled at the same time and at no significantly higher costs. While this kind of a tradeoff is suitable for performance-capable devices common to wired computer networks, it faces wireless networks with an "all-or-nothing" choice. The problem is that if any of the requirements is not fulfilled, none of the security objectives can be guaranteed. This inflexibility and lack of a more modular design is in contrast to the heterogeneous nature of wireless networks and their applications. Security design of wireless networks requires a more fine-grained access to different tradeoffs between application goals and security objectives. For example, in a wireless sensor network (WSN) which is deployed within an environmental monitoring scenario, the main security objective is to capture authentic physical conditions of the environment, such as temperature or air humidity. While the confidentiality of these physical conditions is not crucial for the network security, it is highly important to guarantee that the decisions derived from aggregated data reflect the actual environmental conditions. An adversary should not be able to inject fake data and force the system to, e.g., rise a fire alarm. Hence, in this particular application the security design should focus on data authenticity. Moreover, the protection does not even need to guarantee the authenticity of every sampled data, as long as the overall state of the network cannot be manipulated and fooled, which implies that protection of the network can also be statistical in nature.

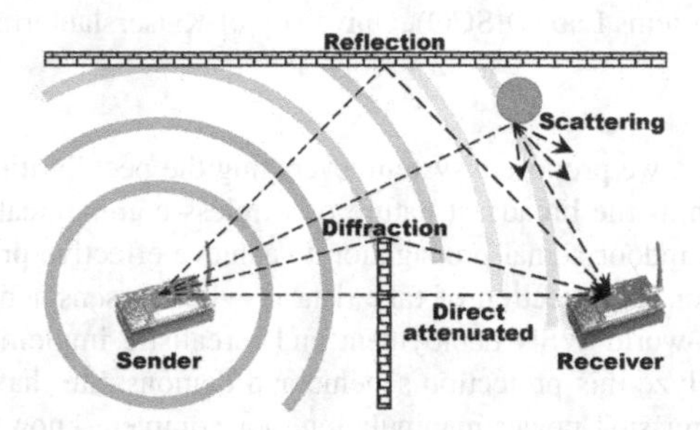

Fig. 1. Indoor radio propagation and different propagation phenomena: reflection, diffraction and scattering result in unpredictability of signal propagation within real-world environments.

2 Unpredictability of Signal Propagation

Operating within an indoor environment, a WSN may take advantage of access control offered by the "physical world", where walls, locked doors or other barriers for preventing physical intrusion establish the border between an outdoor attacker and the legitimate sensors. Although radio signals are able to trespass such barriers, the radio signal received from outside is strongly biased by various propagation effects such as reflection, absorption, diffusion, and scattering and therefore tainted with a significant amount of randomness (see Figure 1) [11]. Other than the attacker, legitimate senders and receivers within the WSN are positioned in an indoor area and their radio transmission has to penetrate fewer obstructions. By a planned placement, it is even possible to achieve Line-Of-Sight (LOS) between legitimate WSN nodes.

In this section, we deploy a real-world indoor WSN network in order to empirically evaluate the diversity of signal propagation. Our testbed is a network installed in our university lab using 8 wireless sensor sensors and an attacker placed outside the room, as shown in Figure 2. The wireless sensors are based on a MicaZ platform with CC2420 radios, allowing for 32 different transmission power settings and 8-bit resolution of received signal strength. The power measurements are reported in RSSI (Received Signal Strength Indicator), yet the conversion to dBm is easily computed by $P_{dBm} = RSSI_{VAL} + RSSI_{OFFSET}$, where $RSSI_{OFFSET} \approx -45$.

Considering the topology of the testbed depicted in Figure 2, an idealistic free-space model would provide the strongest RSS for the sensor which is in the attacker's closest proximity (M_1), while the most distant sensor (M_5) would measure the weakest RSS from the attacker's transmission. However, when looking at real-world measurements,

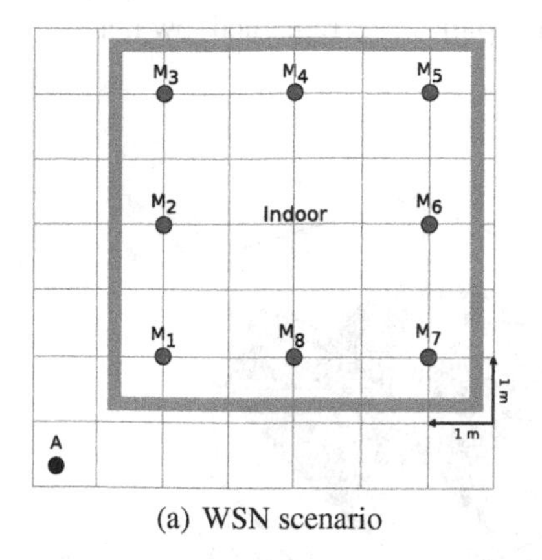

(a) WSN scenario

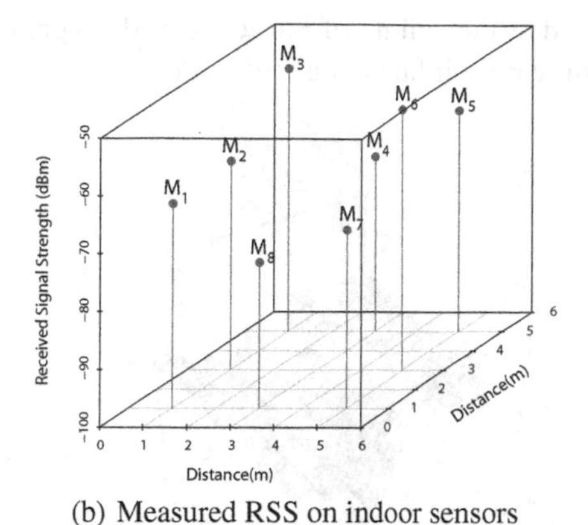

(b) Measured RSS on indoor sensors

Fig. 2. Residential monitoring scenario (a): a WSN with 8 sensors is deployed within a residence (indoor), while an attacker A attempts to inject fake data from outside. RSS unpredictability (b): signal strengths measured from an outdoor transmission on indoor sensors (refer to topology shown in (a)). The order of measured RSS is dominated by physical characteristics of environment and signal propagation effects.

the results are significantly different. The outdoor transmission which passes through different obstacles and is altered by various signal effects arrives highly randomized in an indoor environment. Hence, the order of RSS received at indoor sensors is completely shuffled. Figure 2 (b) shows measured RSS on every sensor using the topology from Figure 2 (a) averaged over 100 transmission. The sensor with the strongest RSS is M_3 ($\approx -55\,dBm$) and the one with the weakest RSS is M_8 ($\approx -75\,dBm$). In a free-space model, M_8 would have measured the second strongest RSS; moreover, this RSS relationship between sensors and attacker is changed with *any* alteration of sender's configuration of antenna orientation, physical position, or even a transmission frequency. To demonstrate the impact of frequency changes on RSS together with signal variability, we sampled long-term transmissions on every wireless channel without changing the positions of the sensors. The results measured at two different receivers are depicted in Figure 3(a) and (b). So for example, if the transmission is changed from channel 5 to channel 11 (i.e, 2430 MHz to 2460 MHz corresponding to channels 16 and 21 in IEEE 802.15.4, respectively), one receiver experiences an RSS decrease of $\approx 15\,dBm$, while another of merely $\approx 2\,dBm$. Yet, if the transmission is changed from channel 7 to channel 11, the second receiver measures an RSS increase of $\approx 12\,dBm$, while the RSS at the first receiver still decreases for $\approx 10\,dBm$. Consequently, a single frequency change may cause RSS to increase or decrease on different indoor receivers at the same time and the same position of the sender. This finding has important implication in a security context, it allows us to shuffle the order of sensors' RSS merely by switching between different transmission frequencies without changing the placement of the sensors. For example, if both indoor sensors transmit on channel 4, the order of their RSS is approximately equal, i.e., $M_1 \approx M_2$. Changing the transmission frequency, e.g., using channel 8, results in $M_1 > M_2$, and at channel 11 in $M_1 < M_2$. Moreover, since the sensors were placed at the ceiling of our test lab, the signal strength variation has remained low not significantly influencing their order.

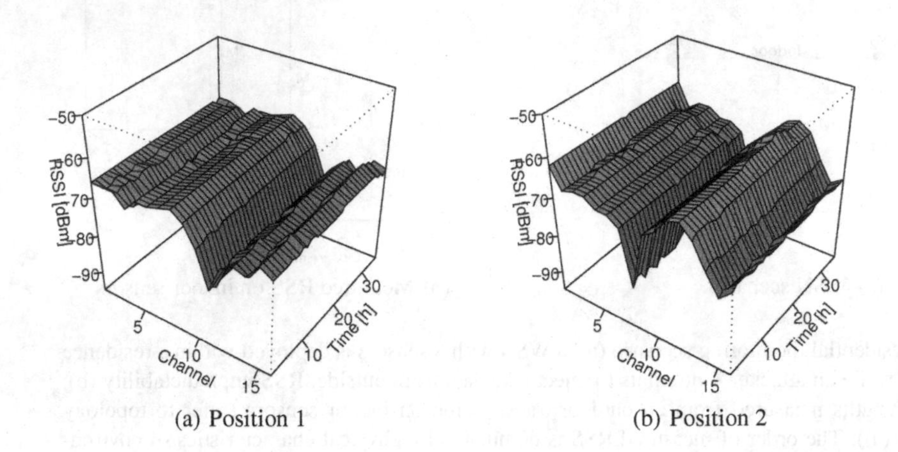

(a) Position 1

(b) Position 2

Fig. 3. Results of long-term sampling of RSS on all available wireless channels and two different physical positions (both receivers are $< 3m$ from the sender). .

3 Authentication Primitives

Leveraging the unpredictable and chaotic nature of signal propagation, our protection method is based on a single assumption – *two wireless transmissions from different physical positions cannot produce exactly the same signal propagation properties*. To facilitate this wireless peculiarity, we propose and implement two mechanisms for crypto-free authentication of frames exchanged within an indoor WSN: (i) *acceptance intervals*, and (ii) *dynamic configuration*. The acceptance intervals are used to detect frames whose transmission properties are significantly different from those of legitimate sensors, while the dynamic configuration of transmission properties within a WSN increases the unpredictability of signal propagation. They are defined as $[\mu - k\sigma, \mu + k\sigma]$ and based on empirical data measured during the deployment phase, where μ is the sample median, σ the standard deviation of a sample, and $k > 1$ is an environment-dependent constant defining the width of the interval, i.e., it describes within how many standard deviations the RSS is still considered to be legitimate. During the deployment phase, each sensor uses initial transmissions to create acceptance intervals on every other sensor (i.e., similar to *signalprints* used in [5] and more advanced approaches discussed in [3,5]). To successfully inject fake frames into the network, an attacker must find an appropriate *configuration* of wireless parameters, such as physical position, transmission frequency (the wireless channel), and a transmission power level to produce the received signal strength which satisfies the acceptance interval on all sensors. If any of legitimate sensors detects the impersonation (i.e., it measures an RSS of

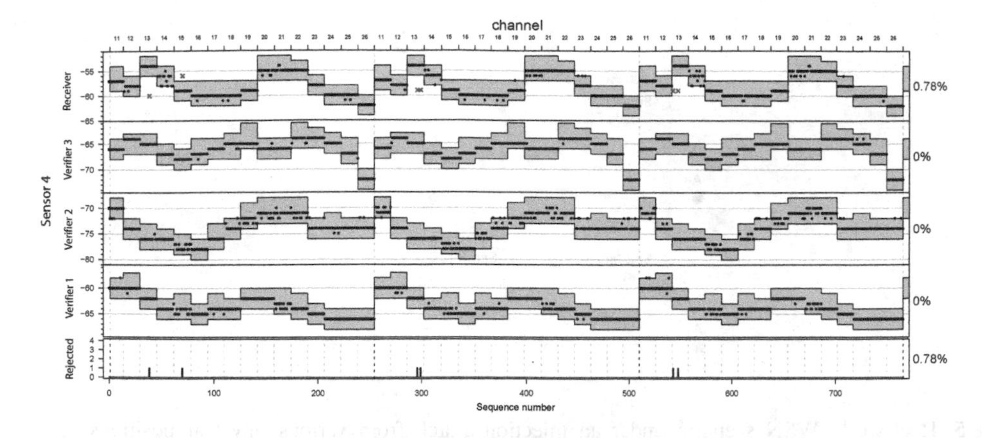

Fig. 4. Time-line of legitimate transmissions verified by 3 sensors and 1 receiver. The figure shows acceptance intervals at each node (gray area) and received frames (black dots as accepted frames, crosses as rejected). Using the same PRNG seed each sensor periodically changes the transmission frequency and thus it dynamically changes its acceptance intervals. The amount of false positives, i.e., legitimate frames discarded due to signal variation is low at 0.78%.

a frame not included in acceptance interval), the receiver is notified by a warning frame disclosing a sequence number of the injected frame.

Dynamic configuration is used to hinder an attacker in its brute-force search for a successful configuration. All WSN sensors are instantiated with the same PRNG seed which allows them to permute different transmission parameters defined during the deployment phase. So for example, one configuration would be to transmit on channel 15 with a transmission level 10, another to transmit on channel 22 with a transmission level 15. As a result, different configurations are assigned with different acceptance intervals. Even if an attacker is able to inject frames with a certain configuration, the attack is only successful during the same acceptance intervals.

To allow periodic change of acceptance intervals the WSN uses a simple synchronization method where a bases station periodically broadcasts a beacon to signal the change of the transmission parameters (e.g., every 2 minutes). An example can be seen in Figure 4 which shows a time-line of monitoring phase without the presence of an attacker. The sender's transmissions are verified on four sensors (three sensors and a base station). Although the acceptance intervals dynamically change (gray areas), the legitimate sender has no problem of correctly changing its transmission properties to fulfill acceptance intervals on other four sensors. This, as we investigate in the next section, presents a major channel for an attacker placed on other physical positions.

4 WSN Under Attack – A Real-World Analysis

We consider a static WSN network as depicted in Figure 5. It consists of three senders and one base station (receiver), hence for a successful injection, a frame must be received within the acceptance intervals of the receiver *and* the two other sensors ($sensor_{2,3}$).

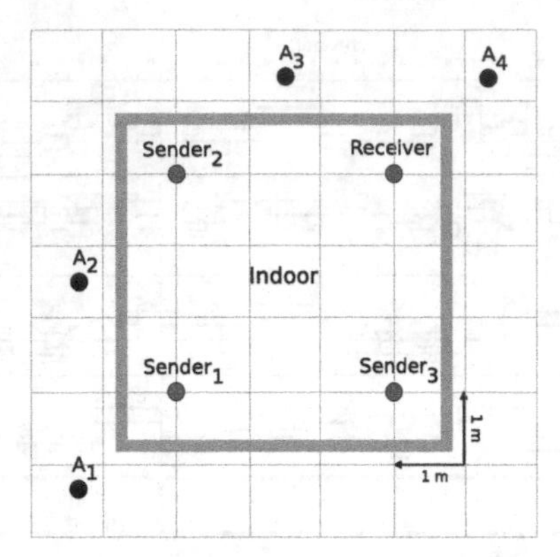

Fig. 5. Real-world WSN scenario under an injection attack from various physical positions (A_1, A_2, A_3, A_4).

Equal to previous measurements, the legitimate sensors were deployed on the ceiling of our university lab and the experiment was divided in two phases:

1. *Deployment phase:* Installation of sensors and configuration of transmission parameters, including initial measurements using different power levels and frequencies for defining the width of acceptance intervals, as well as a dynamic configuration change.
2. *Monitoring phase:* The network is in regular operation while being subject to an injection attack executed from various physical positions outside the deployment area.

4.1 Attacker Model and Countermeasures

The attacker is modeled with complete knowledge of the network, allowing it to observe the progress of its attack and it also knows the PRNG seeds installed on all sensors. Before attacking the network, the attacker sends probe frames to discover how many acceptance intervals have been defined and what power levels resulted in successful injection for each interval. The notification of an interval change is broadcast in clear and the attacker is able to promptly adapt its transmission power, obviating brute-force searching during the attack to keep the rate of frame injection as high as possible. It also attempts to take advantage of frame loss and different physical positions to sneak away from the verifying sensors in order to avoid detection.

As a result of this attacker model, there is *no secret information* among legitimate sensors. The security of this scheme only depends on its wireless characteristics, i.e., assumption that the attacker cannot physically access locations of the sensors.

Before we continue with the attack scenario, an appropriate reaction mechanism needs to be defined as a reaction to identified fake frames. There are various techniques to fulfill that task; some may be based on cryptography and applied only during the duration of an attack, while other, more lightweight reactions can be based on exposing the injected frames to the WSN, making it possible to exclude those frames from data aggregation. So for example, sensors which detect injection can notify the WSN segment and the base station by broadcasting the identifier of the fake frame.

While designing a sophisticated reaction mechanism is out of the scope of this work, we implemented a method similar to the aforementioned notification-based reaction to offer a comprehensive analysis of WSN protection. If any of the verifying sensors detects a frame outside its acceptance interval, it broadcasts a warning frame with the sequence number of the injected frame, which is then discarded from further in-network processing. Using this response method, the following section provides an overall analysis of the implemented WSN scenario under the real-world injection attack.

4.2 Impact of an Injection Attack

As shown in Figure 5, the attacker attempts to inject fake frames from different physical position (A_1, A_2, A_3, A_4). During the first $\approx 250s$ the attacker iterates over all power levels and selects those for which a frame was successfully injected at the receiver, since missing the receiver's intervals would result in frame rejection. To demonstrate the challenge with which the attacker is faced, Figure 6 provides a trace of attacking from the position A_2. Both upper sub-figures show the time-line of the attack at the two sensors and their dynamic interval selection, while lower two sub-figures provide relative frequencies of all accepted and rejected frames, as well as their RSS deviation from the mean of the acceptance intervals. As can be seen, the attacker promptly reacts to dynamic changes by adapting its transmission. While some intervals are easier to "break into" than others, the attacker's overall rate of success at the receiver is $\approx 50.8\%$ of all transmitted fake frames that are sent from position A_2. However, by transmitting with a power suitable for the receiver, the attacker cannot keep its frames within the intervals of the other sensors.

As previously mentioned, for each frame that misses any of the acceptance intervals of at least one sensor, the receiver is notified with a warning frame disclosing the sequence number of the injected frame. The attack results in 84.3% rejections at $verifier_2$. Actually, the median of attacker's RSS at $verifier_2$ exceeds the expected value by $\approx 10dBm$, which means that the transmission power (in mW) should be decreased by at least *10 times*. Such a decrease would consequently result in completely missing the acceptance intervals at the receiver. Hence, the only possibility for the attacker to continue its attack is to retry the complete procedure from another position, without any possibility of predicting the outcome. Importantly, these were only results for one receiver and a single verifier. Overall attack results from other positions using two verifiers are given in Table 1, which provides statistics of the attacker's success but also the reasons for its failure – frequency of injections detected by the verifying sensors, and missed intervals at the receiver. It also shows frame losses encountered at both sensors during an attempt of low-power injections – sending with a low power to produce frame loss at $verifier_{2,3}$ and thus avoid verification at those sensors. The low-power attack is less successful because the sensors are in close proximity to each other, thus it is unlikely that the RSS measured at the receiver is strong enough to match the acceptance intervals (e.g.,$-75dBm \leq RSS \leq -70dBm$), while at the same time being

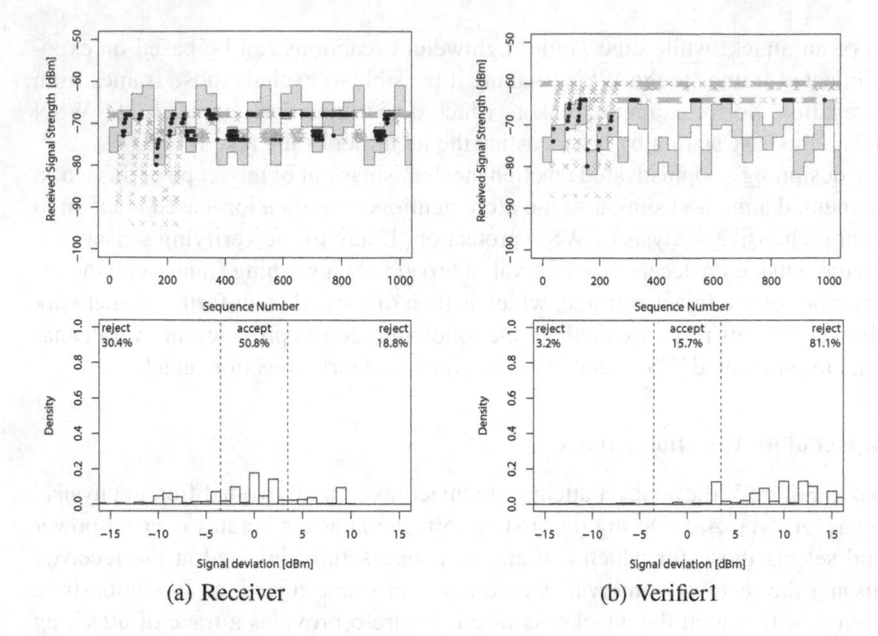

(a) Receiver (b) Verifier1

Fig. 6. Attacking an indoor WSN. Upper figures show a first few minutes of the attack, while lower figures provide statistics over the complete measurement. For a successful attack a frame must be received within acceptance intervals of all verifying sensors (due to space limitations the presented results are only of the receiver and only one verifying sensor.

below the sensitivity threshold of the other sensors (e.g., $RSS \leq -95\,dBm$). Even the highest frame loss rate of 7.25% at both sensors did not result in any successful injection.

To analyze the impact of dynamic frequency change during the injection attack, we proceeded with a slightly modified methodology. This time, the sensors were configured to use only one acceptance interval per wireless channel, but dynamically changed the transmission frequency using the same mechanism as described previously. Also, to illustrate the impact of the acceptance interval's width and its relation to injection success, we manually selected various widths (max. $10\,dBm$) and varied the number of sensors within the network.

The attacker model was also modified to increase the efficiency of injections. Before attacking, we manually searched for an appropriate configuration of physical position, antenna orientation, and power level to be able to use at least one frequency for successful injection at the receiver. The question we were interested in was if an attacker could find a configuration allowing it to successfully inject frames at the receiver using one wireless channel, and how many additional channels would be affected when using the same configuration (i.e., without changing the physical position).

The results of measurements using three different, randomly selected placements of indoor sensors are presented in Table 2 as the number of *secure wireless channels*, i.e., the frequencies which did not results in acceptance of any fake frame. So for example, a WSN with only two verifying sensors, and an interval width of $4\,dBm$, enables an

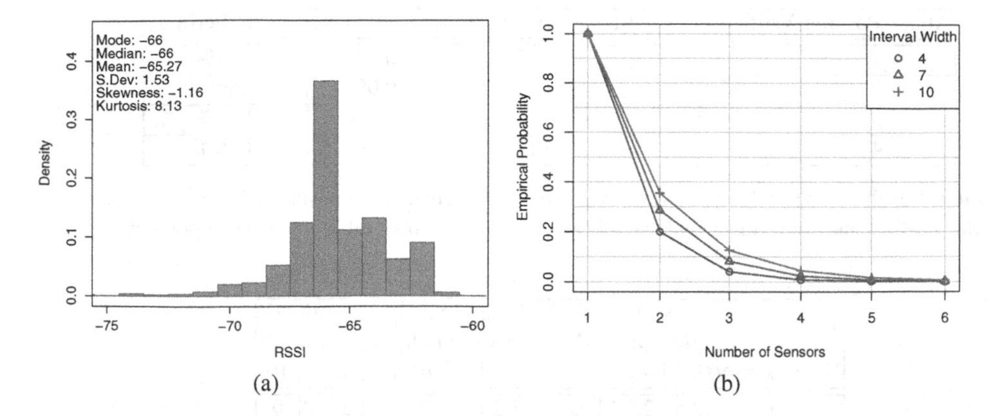

Fig. 7. Experimental analysis of attacking a real-world WSN network within a highly dynamic environment (resulting from frequent human movements as depicted in (a)). Due to a high signal variation, acceptance intervals increase their width to minimize the number of false positives. This presents a tradeoff to security, since it also increase the probability to inject fake data (i.e., increasing a number of false negatives). Yet, by adding additional sensor nodes into the network, probability for a successfull injection is decreasing (b).

injection of fake frames on eight channels, while the other eight are not possible to attack using the same configuration of transmission properties.

Similarly, using three sensors to verify the transmission, and the width of acceptance intervals set to $2dBm$ (i.e., very quiet environment), the attacker could use only three wireless channels (we select the worst result from three different scenarios) while the other 13 wireless channels did not allow for successful injection of any frame.

Obviously, if the environment where the WSN is operating is highly dynamic (e.g., due to frequent human movements and LOS disruptions), the network will experience a high number of false positives. Yet, this can be circumvent by additionally increasing the width of acceptance intervals. For example, Figure 7(a) depicts results conducted in a room with a large number of people moving. As expected this increased the signal strength variation and resulted in an interval width of ≈10 dBm which allowed for 8 % of successful injections. However, by installing more sensors, we could compensate for this disadvantage. Hence, there is a simple tradeoff provided by this scheme; by increasing the number of sensors we can increase the number of secure channels even in environments with a high variance of RSS. This tradeoff can be seen in Figure 7(b), which provides results of thorough empirical sampling of various physical positions used to attack the WSN network with different numbers of verifying sensors. After installing six verifying sensors we could not find any position that resulted in a single successful injection even if acceptance intervals were set to $10dBm$. Clearly, if the position of sensors changes or if significant long-term alteration of physical environment takes place, the initial measurements from the deployment phase should be initiated to recompute the acceptance intervals.

Attack Position	Verifiers Detected	Receiver Detected	Attack Succ.	Loss at Verifiers
1	50.4%	53.15%	0.0%	7.25%
2	82.5%	79,64%	0.0%	2.86%
3	66.1%	63.15%	0.0%	2.95%
4	75.0%	70.12%	0.0%	4.88%

Table 1. Results from attacking an indoor WSN from different outdoor positions. Frames detected by the verifiers and the receiver, and overall injection success over different physical positions.

	Scenario 1 Interval width				Scenario 2 Interval width				Scenario 3 interval width			
No. of sensors	2	4	6	10	2	4	6	10	2	4	6	10
1	5	2	2	0	7	2	1	0	5	2	0	0
2	12	8	6	2	14	6	1	0	9	4	2	0
3	15	14	10	8	16	13	13	5	13	8	7	6
4	15	15	15	12	16	15	15	14	16	14	12	11

Table 2. Number of *secure channels*, i.e., channels immune to injection attacks (of max. 16 available).

5 Related Work

Impersonation attacks constitute a fundamental security problem inherent to the broadcast nature of every wireless communication. A variety of research contributions is based on designing cryptographic solutions to offer both, authentication and confidentiality for WSN communication. Such designs commonly use symmetric ciphers. For example, IEEE 802.15.4 [1] uses AES in CBC-MAC mode of operation and supports 128-bit message authentication codes (MACs). There are also security frameworks using public-key cryptography such as TinyECC [7] which is based on Elliptic Curve Digital Signature Algorithm (ECDSA) enabling even 160-bit for both, secret key and a MAC computation, although with high computational costs on the magnitude of seconds.

However, such cryptography-based solutions simply transfer the concept of protection used in wired networks to significantly different wireless networks. To authenticate a frame, a device must first compute the MAC, and then decide whether to accept or to reject it. Since a wireless network can not provide physical control over the traffic, and wireless devices depend on battery power, arbitrary initiation of frame authentication or the key exchange often results in new resource-depletion vulnerabilities.

For this reason, the peculiarities of wireless communication have been the focus of many wireless security research papers which attempt to include them in the security design. In [3], Chen et al., design protection against spoofing attacks is based solely on physical properties of wireless communication. Using statistics based on cluster analysis, the authors demonstrate that both spoofing and attack location can be identified. Recently, in [10] Mathur et al., show that unpredictability of the signal propagation can be used to derive secret keys, hence avoiding the exchange of cryptographic material.

Various other research papers are concerned with physical properties of the radio propagation to augment the wireless security design, e.g., [14,2,6,13,12]. However, the contribution of this work significantly differs from the aforementioned research. Our solution neither requires specialized hardware, nor introduces complex message exchange, nor utilizes cryptographic primitives for authentication. Moreover, in contrast to often applied simulation-based analysis, this work practically demonstrates the feasibility of using radio signal properties for a security design. The closest research to our work is probably given by Demirbas et al. in [4]. The authors also take advantage of signal strengths to detect injections attacks and demonstrate their solution using Mica2 wireless sensors. While in their work, the authors attempt to minimize the randomness of signal strength by comparing the ratios of RSS values using redundant measurements, in this work we turn the tables and show that protection can be based on the wireless channel randomness directed against an attacker. Furthermore, our protection concept incurs no additional cost to the legitimate propagation, while [4] requires sending additional traffic even when the network is not being attacked.

The initial idea of this work is introduced in [9]. However, in this contribution we significantly extended our work by analyzing the feasibility of a long-term transmission frequency change and the security impact of varying both, the transmission power and frequency. The underlying paradigm of *security by wireless* is also demonstrated in [8], which tackles the problem of cryptographic (client) puzzles and using peculiarities of realistic signal propagation adapts it to comply with properties of wireless networks, especially the IEEE 802.11 technology.

6 Conclusion

The main purpose of this paper was to demonstrate how the chaotic nature of wireless communication can be used as an advantage and how it can assist in increasing security of WSNs. Rather than implementing additional protocols necessary for traditional security mechanisms, we designed practical and lightweight protection without requiring more features than the communication itself provides. By including such physical properties of wireless communication there is a number of advantages which supports construction of novel protection methods. In this paper, we showed how to extended authentication objective to protect not the content of transmission but the transmission itself, i.e., a wireless receiver is able to verify if transmission properties are authentic without verifying the data. This further implies that wireless devices may detect and reject fake transmissions without previously investing resource to correctly receive, then verify and finally reject a fake frame which is currently the case with cryptography methods. Finally, while using cryptographic authentication requires permanent data verification, the method introduced in this work requires additional resources only during an attack.

References

1. IEEE 802.15.4-2006. Part 15.4: Wireless Medium Access Control (MAC) and Physical Layer (PHY) Specifications for Low-Rate Wireless Personal Area Networks (WPANs). IEEE Standard, June 2006.

2. C. Castelluccia and P. Mutaf. Shake them up!: A Movement-based Pairing Protocol for CPU-constrained Devices. In *MobiSys '05: Proceedings of the 3rd International Conference on Mobile systems, Applications, and Services*, pages 51–64, June 2005.
3. Y. Chen, W. Trappe, and R. Martin. Detecting and localizing wireless spoofing attacks. In *Proceedings of the Fourth Annual IEEE Communications Society Conference on Sensor, Mesh, and Ad Hoc Communications and Networks*, pages 193–202, 2007.
4. M. Demirbas and Y. Song. An RSSI-based Scheme for Sybil Attack Detection in Wireless Sensor Networks. In *WOWMOM '06: Proceedings of the 2006 International Symposium on World of Wireless, Mobile and Multimedia Networks*, pages 564–570, June 2006.
5. D. B. Faria and D. R. Cheriton. Detecting Identity-based Attacks in Wireless Networks using Signalprints. In *WiSe '06: Proceedings of the 5th ACM workshop on Wireless Security*, pages 43–52, September 2006.
6. L. E. Holmquist, F. Mattern, B. Schiele, P. Alahuhta, M. Beigl, and H.-W. Gellersen. Smart-Its Friends: A Technique for Users to Easily Establish Connections between Smart Artefacts. In *UbiComp '01: Proceedings of the 3rd international conference on Ubiquitous Computing*, pages 116–122, September 2001.
7. A. Liu and P. Ning. TinyECC: A Configurable Library for Elliptic Curve Cryptography in Wireless Sensor Networks. In *Proceedings of the 7th International Conference on Information Processing in Sensor Networks, IPSN 2008*, pages 245–256, April 2008.
8. I. Martinovic, F. Zdarsky, M. Wilhelm, C. Wegmann, and J. Schmitt. Wireless Client Puzzles in IEEE 802.11 Networks: Security by Wireless. In *Proc. ACM Conference on Wireless Network Security (WiSec 2008)*, pages 43–52, Alexandria, VA, USA, March 2008.
9. Ivan Martinovic, Nicos Gollan, and Jens B. Schmitt. Firewalling Wireless Sensor Networks: Security by Wireless. In *Proceedings of the 33rd IEEE Conference on Local Computer Networks (LCN): Workshop on Practical Issues in Building Sensor Network Applications (SenseApp 2008)*, Montreal, Canada, October 2008. Accepted for publication.
10. S. Mathur, W. Trappe, N. Mandayam, C. Ye, and A. Reznik. Radio-Telepathy: Extracting a Secret Key from an Unauthenticated Wireless Channel. In *The 14th Annual International Conference on Mobile Computing and Networking (MobiCom)*. ACM Press, September 2008.
11. T. Rappaport. *Wireless Communications: Principles and Practice*. Prentice Hall PTR, Upper Saddle River, NJ, USA, 2001.
12. A. Varshavsky, A. LaMarca, and E. de Lar. Enabling Secure and Spontaneous Communication between Mobile Devices using Common Radio Environment. In *Proceedings of the Eighth IEEE Workshop on Mobile Computing Systems and Applications*, February 2007.
13. M. Čagalj, S. Čapkun, R. Rengaswamy, I. Tsigkogiannis, M. Srivastava, and J.-P. Hubaux. Integrity (I) Codes: Message Integrity Protection and Authentication Over Insecure Channels. In *SP '06: Proceedings of the 2006 IEEE Symposium on Security and Privacy (S&P'06)*, pages 280–294, May 2006.
14. S. Čapkun, R. Rengaswamy, I. Tsigkogiannis, and M. Srivastava. Implications of Radio Fingerprinting on the Security of Sensor Networks. In *Proceedings of the 3rd International Conference on Security and Privacy in Communication Networks*, September 2007.

Evaluation of Attack Countermeasures to Improve the DoS Robustness of RSerPool Systems by Simulations and Measurements

Xing Zhou[1], Thomas Dreibholz[2], Wencai Du[1], Erwin P. Rathgeb[2]

[1] Hainan University, College of Information Science and Technology
Renmin Avenue 58, 570228 Haikou, Hainan, China
{zhouxing,wencai}@hainu.edu.cn

[2] University of Duisburg-Essen, Institute for Experimental Mathematics
Ellernstrasse 29, 45326 Essen, Germany
{dreibh,rathgeb}@iem.uni-due.de

Abstract. The Reliable Server Pooling (RSerPool) architecture is the IETF's new standard for a lightweight server redundancy and session failover framework to support availability-critical applications. RSerPool combines the ideas from different research areas into a single, resource-efficient and unified architecture. While there have already been a number of research papers on its performance in general, the robustness against intentional attacks has not been intensively addressed yet. In particular, there have not been any analyses for real setups. Therefore, the goal of this paper is to provide a robustness analysis in order to outline the attack bandwidth which is necessary for a significant impact on RSerPool-based services. This analysis is based on lab measurements – using a real RSerPool system setup – as well as on measurements for comparison and validation. Furthermore, we present and evaluate countermeasure approaches to significantly reduce the impact of attacks.[1]

Keywords: Reliable Server Pooling, Security, Attacks, Denial of Service, Robustness, Performance Analysis

1 Introduction and Scope

Reliable Server Pooling (RSerPool, see [15]) denotes the IETF's new standard for a generic, application-independent server pool [7] and session management [3] framework. While there have already been a number of publications on the performance of RSerPool for load balancing [3, 4, 11, 22–24] and server failure handling [8], there has been very little research on its security and attack robustness. Until now, only basic concepts to avoid flooding the pool management with misinformation have been analysed by simulations in [9, 16]. The underlying transport protocol SCTP[2] already provides protection against blind flooding attacks [20] and the RFC [19] of RSerPool mandatorily requires applying mechanisms like TLS [14] or IPSEC [1] in order to ensure authenticity, integrity and confidentiality. Nevertheless, these techniques are still insufficient: in

[1] Funded by the State Administration of Foreign Experts Affairs, P. R. China (funding number 20084600036) and the German Research Foundation (Deutsche Forschungsgemeinschaft).

[2] Stream Control Transmission Protocol, see [17].

a distributed system, there is always a chance that an attacker compromises a legitimate component (e.g. by exploiting a software bug) and obtains the private key. It is therefore important to analyse the behaviour of the RSerPool protocols under attack situations.

The goal of this paper is to analyse the attack robustness of the RSerPool architecture by simulations using our RSerPool simulation model RSPSIM [6] as well as measurements in a lab setup based on our RSerPool implementation RSPLIB [3] – which is also the IETF's reference implementation, see [15, chapter 5] – by first showing the impact of different attack scenarios on the application performance. Using these analyses as a baseline performance level, we will present techniques to efficiently reduce the impact of such attacks.

2 The RSerPool Architecture

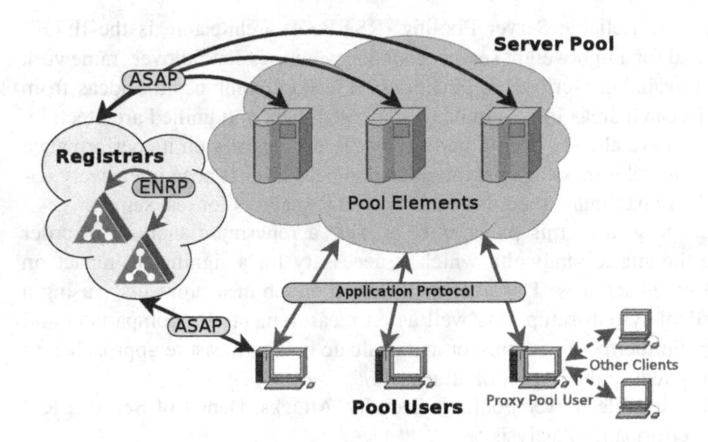

Fig. 1. The RSerPool Architecture

Figure 1 illustrates the RSerPool architecture [3, 15] which consists of three types of components: servers of a pool are called *pool elements* (PE), a client is denoted as *pool user* (PU). The *handlespace* – which is the set of all pools – is managed by redundant *pool registrars* (PR). Within the handlespace, each pool is identified by a unique *pool handle* (PH).

PRs of an *operation scope* synchronize their view of the handlespace by using the Endpoint haNdlespace Redundancy Protocol (ENRP) [21], transported via SCTP [13] and secured e.g. by TLS [14] or IPSEC [1]. Unlike Grid Computing [12], an operation scope is restricted to a single administrative domain. That is, all of its components are under the control of the same authority (e.g. a company or an organization). This property results in a small management overhead [7], which also allows for RSerPool usage on devices providing only limited memory and CPU resources (e.g. embedded systems like routers). Nevertheless, PEs may be distributed globally to continue their service even in case of localized disasters [5].

PEs choose an arbitrary PR of the operation scope to register into a pool by using the Aggregate Server Access Protocol (ASAP) [18], again transported via SCTP and using TLS or IPSEC. Within its pool, a PE is characterized by its PE ID, which is a randomly chosen 32-bit number. Upon registration at a PR, the chosen PR becomes the Home-PR (PR-H) of the newly registered PE. A PR-H is responsible for monitoring its PEs' availability by keep-alive messages (to be acknowledged by the PE within a given timeout) and propagates the information about its PEs to the other PRs of the operation scope via ENRP updates. PEs re-register regularly (in an interval denoted as *registration lifetime*) and for information updates.

In order to access the service of a pool given by its PH, a PU requests a PE selection from an arbitrary PR of the operation scope, again using ASAP. The PR selects the requested list of PE identities by applying a pool-specific selection rule, called *pool policy*. RSerPool supports two classes of load distribution policies: non-adaptive and adaptive algorithms [4]. While adaptive strategies base their assignment decisions on the current status of the processing elements (which of course requires up-to-date states), non-adaptive algorithms do not need such data. A basic set of adaptive and non-adaptive pool policies is defined in [10]. Relevant for this paper are the non-adaptive policies Round Robin (RR) and Random (RAND) as well as the adaptive policies Least Used (LU) and Least Used with Degradation (LUD). LU selects the least-used PE, according to up-to-date application-specific load information. Round robin selection is applied among multiple least-loaded PEs. LUD [24] furthermore introduces a *load decrement* constant which is added to the actual load each time a PE is selected. This mechanism compensates inaccurate load states due to delayed updates. An update resets the load to the actual load value again.

PUs may report unreachable PEs to a PR by using an ASAP Endpoint Unreachable message. A PR locally counts these reports for each PE and when reaching the threshold MaxBadPEReports [8] (default is 3 [18]), the PR may decide to remove the PE from the handlespace. The counter of a PE is reset upon its re-registration.

3 Quantifying an RSerPool System

For our quantitative performance analysis, we use the application model from [3]: the service provider side of an RSerPool system consists of a pool of PEs. Each PE has a request handling *capacity*, which we define in the abstract unit of calculations per second[3]. Each request consumes a certain number of calculations; we call this number *request size*. A PE can handle multiple requests simultaneously – in a processor sharing mode as provided by multitasking operating systems.

On the service user side, there is a set of PUs. The number of PUs can be given by the ratio between PUs and PEs (*PU:PE ratio*), which defines the parallelism of the request handling. Each PU generates a new request in an interval denoted as *request interval*. The requests are queued and sequentially assigned to PEs.

[3] An application-specific view of capacity may be mapped to this definition, e.g. CPU cycles, harddisk space, bandwidth share or memory usage.

The total delay for handling a request d_{Handling} is defined as the sum of queuing delay d_{Queuing}, startup delay d_{Startup} (dequeuing until reception of acceptance acknowledgement) and processing time $d_{\text{Processing}}$ (acceptance until finish):

$$d_{\text{Handling}} = d_{\text{Queuing}} + d_{\text{Startup}} + d_{\text{Processing}}. \quad (1)$$

That is, d_{Handling} not only incorporates the time required for processing the request, but also the latencies of queuing, server selection and message transport. The user-side performance metric is the *handling speed*, which is defined as:

$$\text{HandlingSpeed} = \frac{\text{RequestSize}}{d_{\text{Handling}}}.$$

For convenience reasons, the handling speed (in calculations/s) is represented in % of the average PE capacity.

Using the definitions above, it is possible to delineate the average system utilization (for a pool of NumPEs servers and a total pool capacity of PoolCapacity) as:

$$\text{SystemUtilization} = \text{NumPEs} * \text{puToPERatio} * \frac{\frac{\text{RequestSize}}{\text{RequestInterval}}}{\text{PoolCapacity}}. \quad (2)$$

Obviously, the provider-side performance metric is the system utilization, since only utilized servers gain revenue. In practise, a well-designed client/server system is dimensioned for a certain *target system utilization* of e.g. 50%. That is, by setting any two of the parameters (PU:PE ratio, request interval and request size), the value of the third one can be calculated using equation 2 (see [3] for detailed examples).

4 System Setup

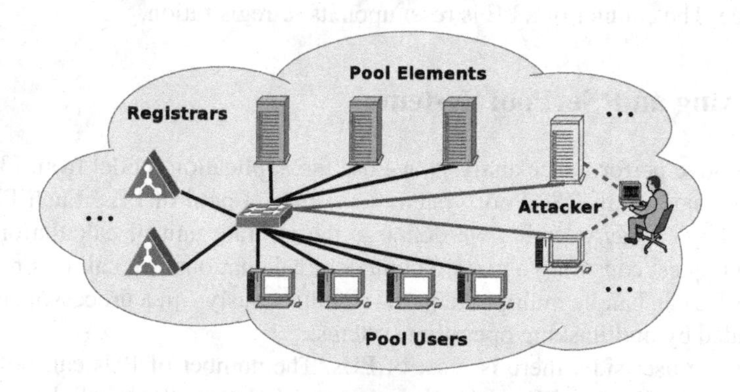

Fig. 2. The System Setup

For our performance analysis, we have used the OMNET++-based RSerPool simulation model RSPSIM [4, 6] as well as the implementation RSPLIB [3, 5] for measurements in a lab setup. Both – simulation model and implementation – contain the protocols ASAP [18] and ENRP [21], a PR module, an attacker module and PE as well as PU modules for the request handling scenario defined in section 3.

Unless otherwise specified, the basic simulation and measurement setup – which is also presented in figure 2 – uses the following parameter settings:

- The target system utilization is 50%. Request size and request interval are randomized using a negative exponential distribution (in order to provide a generic and application-independent analysis [3, 4]). There are 10 PEs; each one provides a capacity of 10^6 calculations/s.
- A PU:PE ratio of 3 is used (i.e. a non-critical setting as explained in [4]).
- We use request size:PE capacity setting of 10; i.e. being processed exclusively, the average processing takes 10s – see also [4].
- There is a single PR only, since we do not examine PR failure scenarios here (see [4] for the impact of multiple PRs). PEs re-register every 30s (registration lifetime) and on every load change of the adaptive LU and LUD policies.
- MaxBadPEReports is set to 3 (default value defined in [18]). A PU sends an Endpoint Unreachable if a contacted PE fails to respond within 10s (see also [8]).
- The system is attacked by a single attacker node.
- For the simulation, the simulated real-time is 120min; each simulation run is repeated at least 24 times with a different seed in order to achieve statistical accuracy.
- Each measurement run takes 15min; each run is repeated at least 3 times.

GNU R [6] is used for the statistical post-processing of the results. Each resulting plot shows the average values and their 95% confidence intervals.

5 The Impact of an Attacker

Attack targets of RSerPool systems are the PRs, PEs and PUs. Due to the restriction of RSerPool to a single administrative domain, a protection of the small number of PRs is assumed to be feasible [9, 16]. Instead, the most likely attack targets are the PEs and PUs. These components are significantly more numerous [3] and may be distributed over a larger, less controllable area [5]. For that reason, ASAP-based attacks are in the focus of our study. Initially, we will show that – without any protection mechanisms – even a *single* compromised PE or PU can already cause a Denial of Service (DoS).

5.1 An Attacker Masquerading as Pool Element

The goal of an attacker being able to perform PE registrations is clearly to perform as many fake registrations as possible. That is, each registration request simply has to contain a new (random) PE ID. The policy parameters may be set appropriately, i.e. a load of 0% (LU, LUD) and a load increment of 0% (LUD), to get the fake PE selected as frequently as possible. The underlying SCTP protocol [17,20] itself already prevents simple address spoofing: each network-layer address under which a PE is registered must be part of the SCTP association between PE and PR. The ASAP protocol [18] requires the addresses to be validated by SCTP. However, maintaining a registration

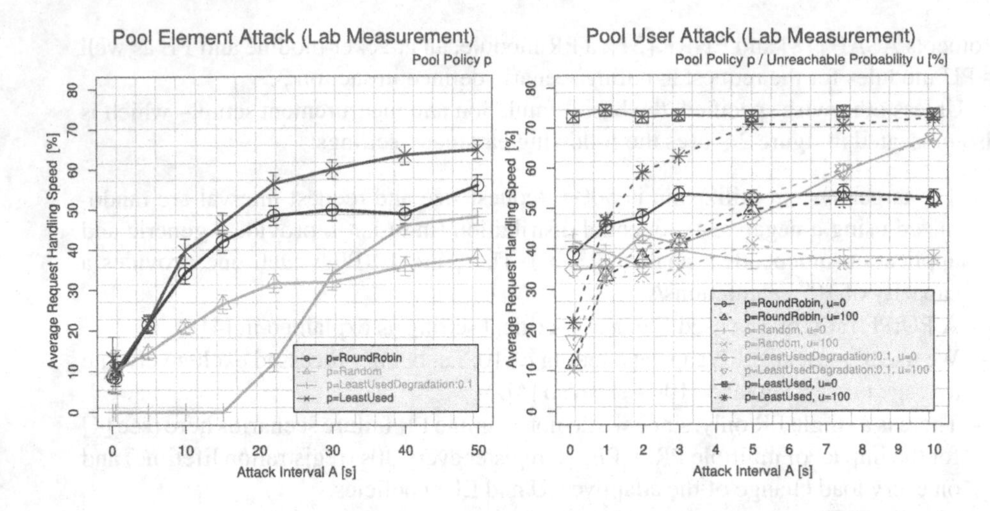

Fig. 3. The Impact of a PE/PU-Based Attacks without Countermeasures

association with the PE and silently dropping all incoming PU requests is already sufficient for an attacker.

The left-hand side of figure 3 shows the impact of varying the attack interval A (i.e. the time between two fake registrations) on the handling speed in the lab setup. Clearly, even an interval of 10s (i.e. one registration packet per 10s) is already sufficient to significantly decrease the performance. For the LUD policy [24], this already leads to a full DoS: an unloaded PE whose load does not increase when accepting a new request seems to be the most useful choice for each PU. That is, it leads to exclusively choosing fake PEs. Using smaller settings of A (e.g. here: 0.1s) a DoS is also reached for the other policies.

The corresponding simulation results show an analogous behaviour. Since we have presented such results already in [9,16], they have been omitted here.

5.2 An Attacker Masquerading as Pool User

PUs are the other means of ASAP-based attacks, especially their handle resolution requests and unreachability reports. Obviously, an attack scenario would be to flood the PR with handle resolution requests. However, the server selection as part of the handlespace management is very efficiently realizable [7] – but it is a fallacy to assume that simply performing some handle resolutions (without actually contacting any selected PE) cannot affect the service quality: on the right-hand side of figure 3, the impact of a handle resolution attack on the performance is presented for varying the attack interval A (i.e. the delay between two handle resolution requests) in the lab setup. For selected PE entries, an unreachability report (see section 2) is sent with probability u.

Even for u=0%, there is an impact on the performance of RR, due to the "stateful" [4] operation of RR: the round robin pointer is advanced by the selection procedure itself (i.e. without actually using a PE), causing the selection of less appropriate

PEs. Similarly, the load value is increased on each selection for LUD. In contrast, LU and RAND are "stateless" and therefore not affected by this attack. The impact of also reporting all PEs as being unreachable (here: u=100%) is disastrous: PEs are kicked out of the handlespace, and the handling speed quickly sinks and leads – here at about A=0.1s (i.e. only 10 reports/s) to a DoS. Since analogous simulation results have been discussed by us in [9, 16], we omit them here.

6 Applying Attack Countermeasures

Clearly, even a single attacker with a small attack bandwidth (i.e. a few messages/s) can achieve a complete DoS. Therefore, we discuss and analyse possible countermeasures for the PE and PU-based threats in the following section.

6.1 Countermeasures Against Pool Element Attacks

The key problem of the PE-based threat shown in subsection 5.1 is the attacker's ability to create a new fake PE with each of its registration messages. Only a few messages per second (i.e. even a modem connection) are sufficient to degrade the service. Therefore, an effective countermeasure is to restrict the number of PE registrations that a single PE identity is allowed to create. However, in order to retain the "lightweight" [7] property of RSerPool and to avoid synchronizing such numbers among PRs, we have put forward a new approach and introduce the concept of a *registration authorization ticket* [9] consisting of:

1. the pools's PH and a fixed PE ID,
2. minimum/maximum policy information settings (e.g. a lower limit for the load decrement of LUD) and
3. a signature by a trusted authority (to be explained below).

This ticket, provided by a PE to its PR-H as part of the ASAP registration, can be easily verified by checking its signature. Then, if it is valid, it is only necessary to ensure that the PE's policy settings are within the valid range specified in the ticket. An attacker stealing the identity of a real PE would only be able to masquerade as *this* specific PE. A PR only has to verify the authorization ticket. No protocol change or synchronization among the PRs is necessary. The additional runtime required is in $O(1)$. Clearly, the need for a trusted authority (e.g. a Kerberos service) adds an infrastructure requirement. However, since an operation scope is restricted to a single administrative domain (see section 2), this is feasible at reasonable costs.

To demonstrate the effectiveness of our countermeasure approach, figure 4 presents the handling speed results for an attack interval of A=0.1s per attacker for varying the number of attackers α. As shown in subsection 5.1, A=0.1s has already lead to a full DoS with only a *single* attacker.

Obviously, our countermeasure is quite effective: even for α=10, the handling speed only halves at most – but the service still stays operational and the attack impact is not even close to a DoS. Note, that α=10 here means that the attacker had successfully compromised as many nodes for obtaining registration authorization tickets as there are

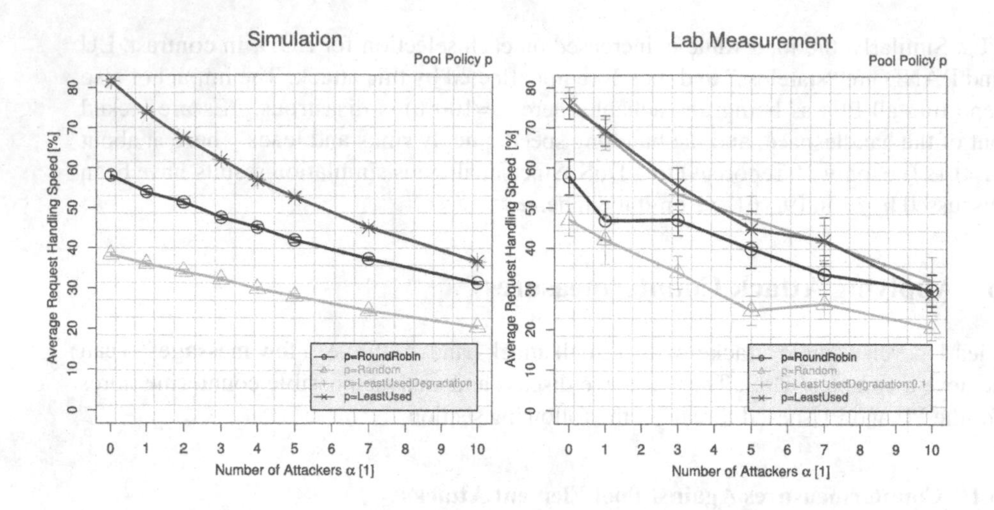

Fig. 4. Applying Countermeasures Against Pool-Element-Based Attacks

"real" PEs in the pool – which is assumed to be quite difficult in a controlled RSerPool operation scope (i.e. a single administrative domain, see section 2). The lab measurement results correspond to the simulation results, i.e. the mechanism also works effectively in a real setup. Note, that the slightly different handling speed levels of the lab measurements are caused by node and SCTP association setup latencies, which are – due to their complexity – not incorporated into the simulation model. Nevertheless, the obtained tendency of the results is clearly observable.

6.2 Countermeasures Against Pool User Attacks

The key threat of the handle resolution/failure report attack shown in subsection 5.2 is a PU's ability to impeach PEs – even for MaxBadPEReport>1. Our basic countermeasure idea is therefore to avoid counting multiple reports from the same PU. As for the PEs, it is necessary to introduce a PU identification which is certified by a trusted authority and can be verified by a PR (see subsection 6.1). Then, a PR simply has to memorize (described later) the PH for which a certain PU has reported unreachable PEs and to ignore multiple reports for the same pool. Since the unreachability count for each PE is a PR-local variable, no synchronization among PRs is necessary. That is, an attacker cannot cause harm by just sending its reports for the same PE to different PRs.

Instead of storing each reported PE (which could be exploited by sending a large amount of random IDs), we use a hash-based approach for a per-PU message blackboard: the function Ψ maps a PE's PH into a bucket:

$$\Psi(\mathrm{PH}) = h(\mathrm{PH}) \text{ MOD Buckets}.$$

h denotes an appropriate hash function: an attacker may not easily guess its behaviour. This property is provided by so called universal hash functions [2], which are – unlike cryptographic hash functions (e.g. MD5, SHA-256) also efficiently computable.

Each bucket contains the time stamps of the latest up to MaxEntries Endpoint Unreachables for the corresponding bucket. Then, the report rate can be calculated as:

$$\text{Rate} = \frac{\text{NumberOfTimeStamps}}{\text{TimeStamp}_{\text{Last}} - \text{TimeStamp}_{\text{First}}}. \quad (3)$$

Upon reception of an Endpoint Unreachable, it simply updates the reported PE's corresponding bucket entry. If the rate in equation 3 exceeds the configured threshold MaxEURate (Maximum Endpoint Unreachable Rate), the report is silently ignored. The effort for this operation is in $O(1)$, as well as the required per-PU storage space.

In a similar way, the same hash-based approach can be applied for handle resolutions with the corresponding threshold MaxHRRate (Maximum Handle Resolution Rate). However, unlike simply ignoring the request, the PR replies with an empty list – which means for the PU that the pool is currently empty.

Instead of specifying a fixed threshold, an alternative approach is presented in [16] by applying statistical anomaly detection: the behaviour of the majority of nodes is assumed to be "normal". Differing behaviour – which is necessary for an attack to be effective – is denoted as anomaly. However, this approach can – by definition – only detect attackers if their number is less than the number of legitimate components. Furthermore, obtaining the "normal" behaviour is more resource-intensive than simple thresholds.

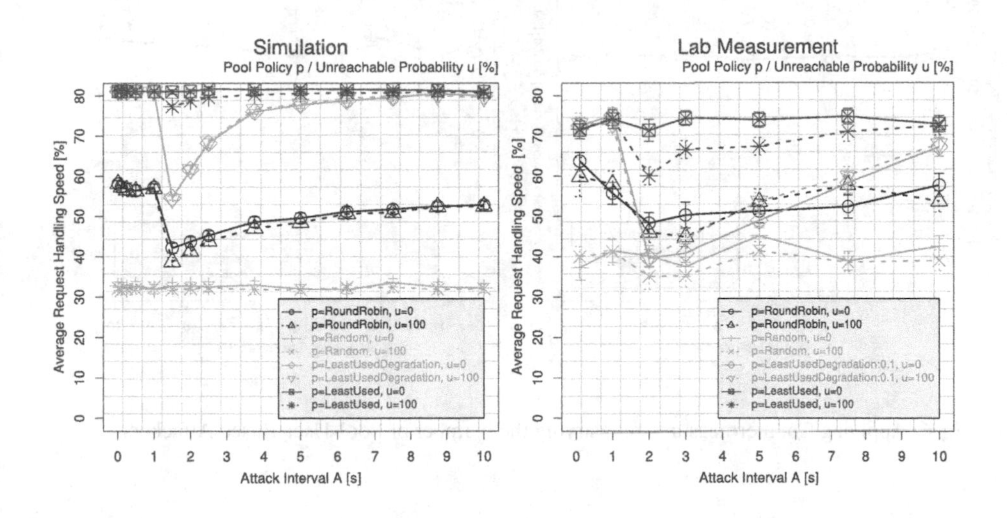

Fig. 5. Applying Countermeasures Against a Pool-User-Based Attack

The effectiveness of our approach for MaxHRRate=1 (which is 60 times more than the application's actual handle resolution rate) and MaxEURate=1 (which is by orders of magnitude higher than a real pool's PE failure rate) is shown by figure 5 for varying the attack interval of a single attacker in simulation (left-hand plot) and lab measurement (right-hand plot). The results are shown for two probabilities of sending Endpoint Unreachables for each selected entry: u=0% and u=100% (i.e. worst case).

Due to the "stateful" behaviour of the RAND and LUD policies, the attacker is able to reduce the handling speed until triggering the countermeasure mechanism. Then, the attacker is ignored and the performance remains as for attack-free scenarios. For the LU and RAND policies, even very small attack intervals (e.g. A=0.001 s) have no significant impact in the simulation. Only for LU and u=100%, a performance degradation can be observed in the measurement scenario: this effect is caused by the latency of the PE load state updates in the real network (which can vary depending on the SCTP protocol's flow control – which is not covered by the simulation model): since the load value of a PE only changes on reregistration, a least-loaded PE entry may be selected multiple times in sequence. That is, the attacker will send multiple unreachability reports for the same PE. As long as the threshold of MaxEURate is not yet reached, the PE entry may be removed. However, when the countermeasure threshold is reached, the attacker is ignored and the performance goes back to the level of attacker-free scenarios.

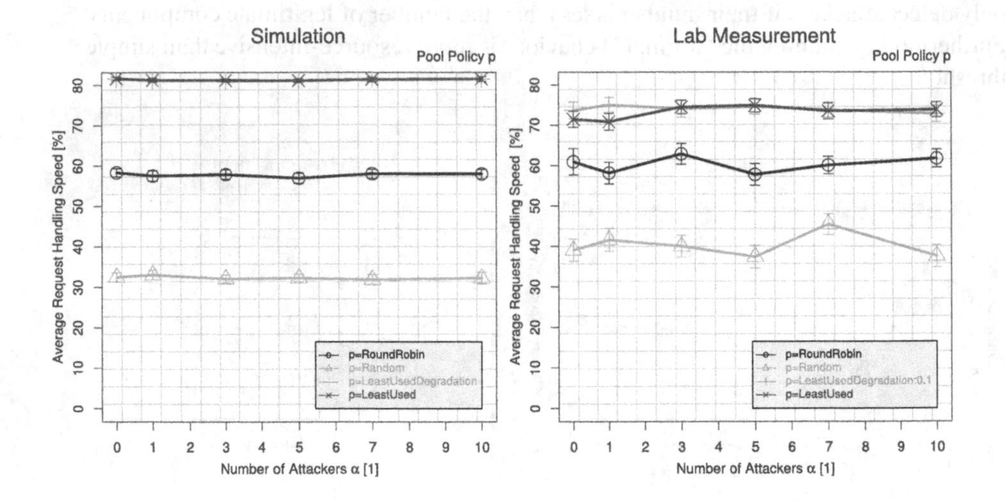

Fig. 6. Applying Countermeasures for Varying the Number of Pool-User-Based Attackers

Figure 6 presents the results for varying the number of attackers α with an attack interval of A=0.1 (for which a *single* attacker was able to cause a complete DoS without countermeasures, as shown in subsection 5.2). The attacker sends Endpoint Unreachables at a probability of u=100% for the selected PE entries (worst case). Clearly, the presented results show that even α=10 attackers have no significant impact on the performance – neither in simulation nor in reality – any more, due to the applied countermeasures.

7 Conclusions

In this paper, we have examined the two critical attack threats on RSerPool systems by both, simulations and corresponding lab measurements:

- PE-based attacks (registration) and
- PU-based attacks (handle resolution/failure report).

Without any protection, even a single attacker is easily able to achieve a complete DoS. For both types of attacks, we have introduced countermeasure approaches which are efficiently realizable with small memory and CPU requirements – as it is necessary for the "lightweight" RSerPool architecture. By simulations and lab measurements we have shown that these mechanisms work as expected and provide a significant performance gain – in comparison to an unprotected setup – in case of DoS attacks.

The ideas of our RSerPool research have been contributed into IETF's RSerPool standardization process, which has just reached a major milestone by publication of its basic protocol documents as RFCs. As part of our future work, it is also necessary to analyse the robustness of the ENRP protocol. Although the threat on the small number of PRs of an operation scope is significantly smaller, it is useful to obtain knowledge of possible attack scenarios. Furthermore, we intend to perform real-world security experiments in the PLANETLAB – again by using our RSerPool implementation RSPLIB. Our goal is to provide security and configuration guidelines for application developers and users of the IETF's new RSerPool standard.

References

1. S. Bellovin, J. Ioannidi, A. Keromytis, and R. Stewart. On the Use of Stream Control Transmission Protocol (SCTP) with IPsec. Standards Track RFC 3554, IETF, July 2003.
2. S. A. Crosby and D. S. Wallach. Denial of service via Algorithmic Complexity Attacks. In *Proceedings of the 12th USENIX Security Symposium*, pages 29–44, Washington, DC/U.S.A., Aug. 2003.
3. T. Dreibholz. *Reliable Server Pooling – Evaluation, Optimization and Extension of a Novel IETF Architecture*. PhD thesis, University of Duisburg-Essen, Faculty of Economics, Institute for Computer Science and Business Information Systems, Mar. 2007.
4. T. Dreibholz and E. P. Rathgeb. On the Performance of Reliable Server Pooling Systems. In *Proceedings of the IEEE Conference on Local Computer Networks (LCN) 30th Anniversary*, pages 200–208, Sydney/Australia, Nov. 2005. ISBN 0-7695-2421-4.
5. T. Dreibholz and E. P. Rathgeb. On Improving the Performance of Reliable Server Pooling Systems for Distance-Sensitive Distributed Applications. In *Proceedings of the 15. ITG/GI Fachtagung Kommunikation in Verteilten Systemen (KiVS)*, pages 39–50, Bern/Switzerland, Feb. 2007. ISBN 978-3-540-69962-0.
6. T. Dreibholz and E. P. Rathgeb. A Powerful Tool-Chain for Setup, Distributed Processing, Analysis and Debugging of OMNeT++ Simulations. In *Proceedings of the 1st ACM/ICST OMNeT++ Workshop*, Marseille/France, Mar. 2008. ISBN 978-963-9799-20-2.
7. T. Dreibholz and E. P. Rathgeb. An Evaluation of the Pool Maintenance Overhead in Reliable Server Pooling Systems. *SERSC International Journal on Hybrid Information Technology (IJHIT)*, 1(2):17–32, Apr. 2008.

8. T. Dreibholz and E. P. Rathgeb. Reliable Server Pooling – A Novel IETF Architecture for Availability-Sensitive Services. In *Proceedings of the 2nd IEEE International Conference on Digital Society (ICDS)*, pages 150–156, Sainte Luce/Martinique, Feb. 2008. ISBN 978-0-7695-3087-1.
9. T. Dreibholz, E. P. Rathgeb, and X. Zhou. On Robustness and Countermeasures of Reliable Server Pooling Systems against Denial of Service Attacks. In *Proceedings of the IFIP Networking*, pages 586–598, Singapore, May 2008. ISBN 978-3-540-79548-3.
10. T. Dreibholz and M. Tüxen. Reliable Server Pooling Policies. RFC 5356, IETF, Sept. 2008.
11. T. Dreibholz, X. Zhou, and E. P. Rathgeb. A Performance Evaluation of RSerPool Server Selection Policies in Varying Heterogeneous Capacity Scenarios. In *Proceedings of the 33rd IEEE EuroMirco Conference on Software Engineering and Advanced Applications*, pages 157–164, Lübeck/Germany, Aug. 2007. ISBN 0-7695-2977-1.
12. I. Foster. What is the Grid? A Three Point Checklist. *GRID Today*, July 2002.
13. C. Hohendorf, E. P. Rathgeb, E. Unurkhaan, and M. Tüxen. Secure End-to-End Transport Over SCTP. *Journal of Computers*, 2(4):31–40, June 2007.
14. A. Jungmaier, E. Rescorla, and M. Tüxen. Transport Layer Security over Stream Control Transmission Protocol. Standards Track RFC 3436, IETF, Dec. 2002.
15. P. Lei, L. Ong, M. Tüxen, and T. Dreibholz. An Overview of Reliable Server Pooling Protocols. Informational RFC 5351, IETF, Sept. 2008.
16. P. Schöttle, T. Dreibholz, and E. P. Rathgeb. On the Application of Anomaly Detection in Reliable Server Pooling Systems for Improved Robustness against Denial of Service Attacks. In *Proceedings of the 33rd IEEE Conference on Local Computer Networks (LCN)*, pages 207–214, Montreal/Canada, Oct. 2008. ISBN 978-1-4244-2413-9.
17. R. Stewart. Stream Control Transmission Protocol. Standards Track RFC 4960, IETF, Sept. 2007.
18. R. Stewart, Q. Xie, M. Stillman, and M. Tüxen. Aggregate Server Access Protcol (ASAP). RFC 5352, IETF, Sept. 2008.
19. M. Stillman, R. Gopal, E. Guttman, M. Holdrege, and S. Sengodan. Threats Introduced by RSerPool and Requirements for Security. RFC 5355, IETF, Sept. 2008.
20. E. Unurkhaan. *Secure End-to-End Transport - A new security extension for SCTP*. PhD thesis, University of Duisburg-Essen, Institute for Experimental Mathematics, July 2005.
21. Q. Xie, R. Stewart, M. Stillman, M. Tüxen, and A. Silverton. Endpoint Handlespace Redundancy Protocol (ENRP). RFC 5353, IETF, Sept. 2008.
22. X. Zhou, T. Dreibholz, and E. P. Rathgeb. A New Approach of Performance Improvement for Server Selection in Reliable Server Pooling Systems. In *Proceedings of the 15th IEEE International Conference on Advanced Computing and Communication (ADCOM)*, pages 117–121, Guwahati/India, Dec. 2007. ISBN 0-7695-3059-1.
23. X. Zhou, T. Dreibholz, and E. P. Rathgeb. Improving the Load Balancing Performance of Reliable Server Pooling in Heterogeneous Capacity Environments. In *Proceedings of the 3rd Asian Internet Engineering Conference (AINTEC)*, volume 4866 of *Lecture Notes in Computer Science*, pages 125–140. Springer, Nov. 2007. ISBN 978-3-540-76808-1.
24. X. Zhou, T. Dreibholz, and E. P. Rathgeb. A New Server Selection Strategy for Reliable Server Pooling in Widely Distributed Environments. In *Proceedings of the 2nd IEEE International Conference on Digital Society (ICDS)*, pages 171–177, Sainte Luce/Martinique, Feb. 2008. ISBN 978-0-7695-3087-1.

Towards a Generic Backup and Recovery Infrastructure for the German D-Grid Initiative

Markus Mathes, Steffen Heinzl, Bernd Freisleben

Department of Mathematics and Computer Science, University of Marburg
Hans-Meerwein-Str. 3, D-35032 Marburg, Germany
{mathes,heinzl,freisleb}@informatik.uni-marburg.de

Abstract. Grid computing is often used for conducting time-consuming experiments that produce large amounts of data. Since existing backup and recovery solutions based on GridFTP or RFT require in-depth knowledge, they are not suited for scientists who are not Grid computing experts. Most scientists prefer an easy to use solution to back up and recover their experimental results. The F&L-Grid project (a Grid providing services for research and education) is part of the German Grid Initiative (D-Grid) and is aimed at the design and development of the first generic backup and recovery infrastructure suitable for arbitrary Grid environments. This paper presents the current status of the ongoing F&L-Grid project and outlines the generic backup and recovery infrastructure in detail.

1 Introduction

Grid computing environments are heterogeneous collections of networked hard- and software components located at different sites and hosted by different organizations. Resource sharing and problem solving across boundaries of individual institutions are the main goals of Grid computing [1]. To enable users to access these resources in a convenient manner using standardized interfaces, service-oriented Grid middleware providing a Grid service stack that implements the Web Services Resource Framework (WSRF) [2] has been developed. Examples for such a service-oriented Grid middleware are the Globus Toolkit 4.x [3] and Unicore/GS [4]. Typically, they provide functionality for runtime components, execution and information management, security, and data handling. Using a service-oriented Grid middleware, applications are composed of several Grid services. A Grid service can be regarded as a small entity of functionality to implement parts of the entire application. Large applications are broken down into several Grid services which can be flexibly composed to form new applications. This allows recombining Grid services to different applications and thereby reduces redundancy and increases flexibility.

Due to their computational power, Grid computing environments are often used to conduct complex experiments, e.g. within high energy physics. Such experiments normally produce large amounts of data. For backup and recovery purposes, most service-oriented Grid middleware systems offer simple—often Grid service based—tools. For example, the Globus Toolkit offers *GridFTP* [5]—a command-line FTP solution for Grid environments—and *Reliable File Transfer (RFT)* [6]—a service-wrapper for GridFTP. These built-in backup and recovery solutions are often very complex and overburden scientists who simply want to back up or recover their data.

This paper presents a generic backup and recovery infrastructure developed within the F&L-Grid project. F&L-Grid is part of the German Grid Initiative (D-Grid) [7] and includes the following project partners: T-Systems Solutions for Research (SfR) and Karlsruhe Institute of Technology (KIT) as service providers, the German Research Network (DFN) as the network infrastructure provider, and the University of Marburg as the service developer.

The main contributions of the F&L-Grid project presented in this paper are:

- The general requirements of backup and recovery solutions in the context of Grid computing are investigated by the project partners.
- Based on the identified requirements, F&L-Grid proposes an easy to use backup and recovery infrastructure applicable within arbitrary Grid environments. Scientists are empowered to easily back up and recover their experimental results without intervention of an administrator.
- The proposed backup and recovery infrastructure uses an arbitrary commercial backup and recovery solution as its backend to ensure reliability. The details of the backend used are hidden from the scientist.

The rest of this paper is organized as follows. Section 2 gives an overview of the D-Grid Initiative, discusses requirements of the backup and recovery solution and presents its architectural blueprint. Section 3 presents implementation details. Further backup and recovery solutions for Grid environments are discussed in Section 4. Section 5 concludes the paper and outlines areas for future work.

2 Design of a Backup and Recovery Infrastructure for Grid Environments

The German Grid Initiative (D-Grid) [7] founded in 2003 is part of the e-Science framework of the German Federal Ministry of Education and Research (BMBF) [8]. The main objective of the D-Grid initiative is to build a sustainable Grid infrastructure in Germany to enable e-science. D-Grid consists of several community projects and the D-Grid Integration Project (DGI).

The F&L-Grid project presented in this paper aims at establishing a generic service-oriented Grid for research and education. The offered services are based on the infrastructure of the DFN [9] that interconnects the universities and research institutions all over Germany. In the current project phase, a service for backup and recovery is developed. In the context of this service, some of the research institutions act as service providers, others as service users and the DFN acts as a mediator between the service providers and the service users.

In the following subsections, the requirements of service users and service providers are discussed, pull-based vs. push-based and node-based vs. user-based backup/recovery are compared, different backup strategies are discussed, and an outline of the F&L-Grid architecture is presented.

2.1 Requirements Analysis

The key requirements identified by F&L-Grid users and providers are:

- **minimal invasiveness:** The backup and recovery service should not influence already existing operational procedures at the sites of the service providers.
- **usability:** Scientists should be empowered to easily back up and recover their experimental results without intervention of an administrator or calling a help desk, which is often necessary if a commcercial backup and recovery solution is used.
- **simple software rollout:** The software required at the sites of the users and providers should be easy to install. More precisely, a new version of the backup and recovery client at the user's site should be automatically retrieved without user intervention.
- **sustainability:** The developed backup and recovery service should be usable in the long term, i.e. beyond the project duration, and will be offered by the DFN and the service providers.
- **replaceable backup and recovery backend:** The dependence on a specific commercial backup and recovery backend should be avoided, so that in the future the underlying backup software can be changed.
- **independence of the operating system:** It must be possible to use the backup and recovery service from different operating systems. Otherwise, client for many different operating systems have to be maintained.
- **support of multiple interfaces:** The backup and recovery service should be available from inside of the Grid as well as from outside of the Grid.

2.2 Pull- vs. Push-Based Backup and Recovery

From the perspective of the user, backup and recovery can be realized in a pull- or push-based manner. A *pull-based* backup and recovery approach uses a predefined schedule to decide when to start a backup/recovery. For example, a backup can be run daily at 01:00 AM since utilization is normally low at night. A *push-based* backup and recovery is initiated by the user on-demand. For example, a scientist can back up the results of an experiment after the experiment has finished.

Since a push-based approach can be realized without further installation of software on the client machines and without bothering an administrator for installation and updates of the software, the push-based approach was favoured by the project partners.

2.3 User- vs. Node-Based Backup and Recovery

Many commercial backup solutions only support *node-based* backup and recovery due to the fact that the file system may differ significantly from node to node. The node-based backup and recovery strategy has a main disadvantage: a user who moves between several nodes can only recover data from the current node and not his/her entire data. To solve this problem, backup and recovery have to be organized in a *user-based* manner, which enables cross-node recovery of the entire user data.

In Figure 1(a), a node-base backup and recovery strategy is shown. User 1 and user 2 cannot recover their data after moving from node 1 to node 2 and from node 2 to node 3, respectively. Supporting a user-based backup and recovery strategy enables recovery after moving from one node to another, as shown in Figure 1(b).

Within F&L-Grid, a user-based backup and recovery strategy is realized.

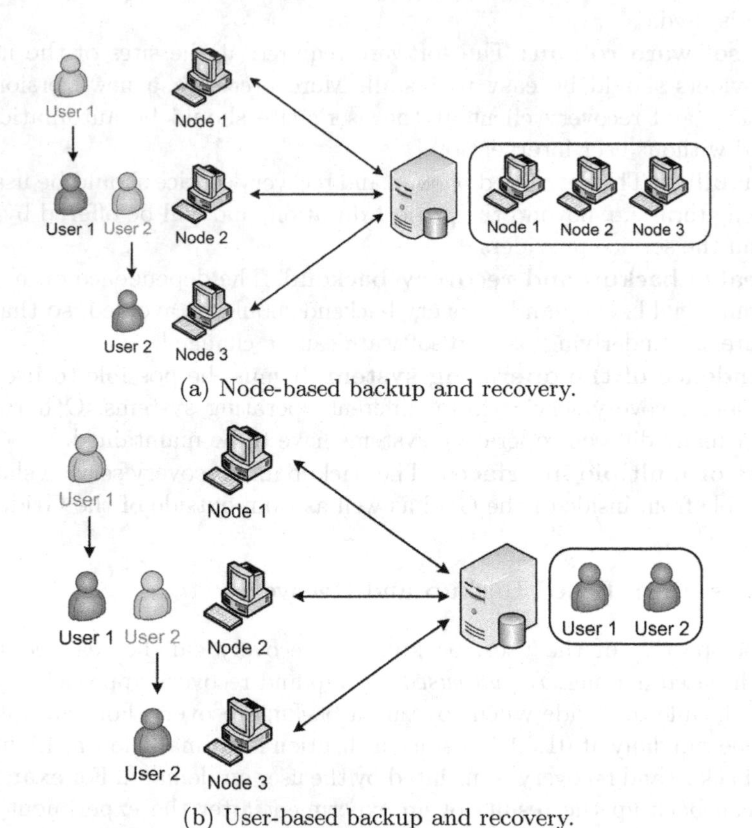

(a) Node-based backup and recovery.

(b) User-based backup and recovery.

Fig. 1. Example of a node- and user-based backup and recovery strategy.

2.4 Incremental, Differential, and Full Backup

Several backup strategies can be distinguished: incremental backup, differential backup, and full backup. A *full backup* contains all selected files. A *differential backup* contains all modified files since the last full backup. An *incremental backup* only includes files that have been modified since the last full or incremental backup.

In Figures 2(a), (b), and (c), examples for full, differential, and incremental backup of four files are shown. The dotted squares are files modified since the last backup, whereas the solid squares are not modified since the last backup. The (yellow) filled squares are backed up files in the current backup iteration, whereas the unfilled squares are not backed up in the current backup iteration.

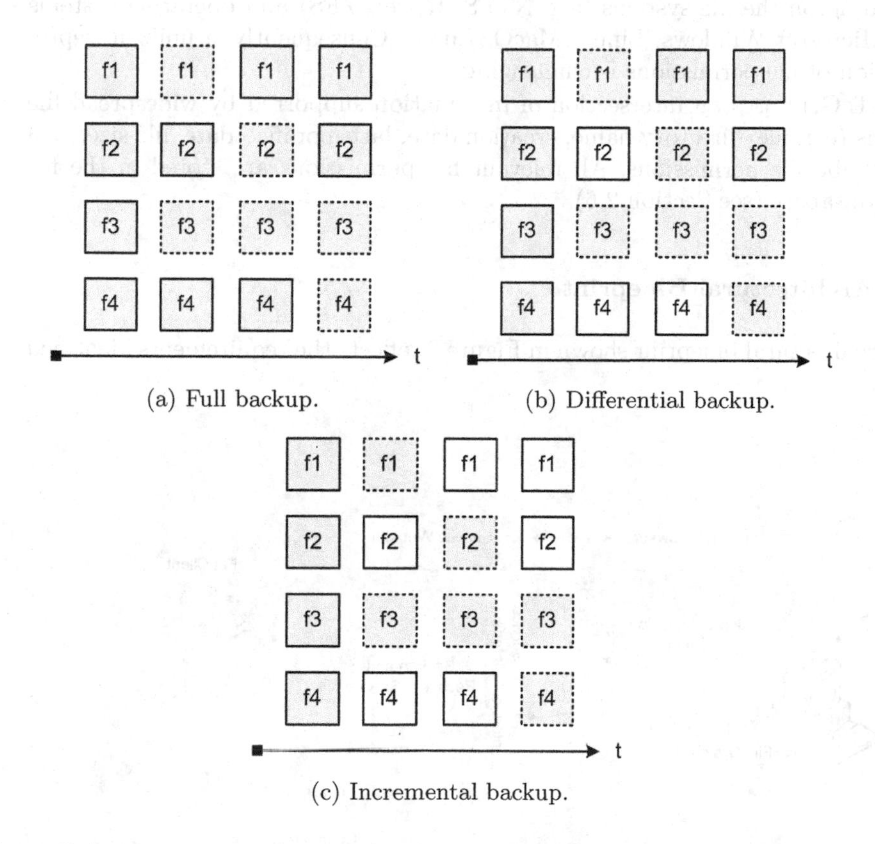

(a) Full backup. (b) Differential backup.

(c) Incremental backup.

Fig. 2. Example for different backup strategies (dotted squares are files modified since the last backup, colored squares are backed up files in the current backup iteration).

The main advantage of an incremental backup is a shorter backup time and low memory consumption because only modified files are backed up. To recover all files, the latest full backup and all incremental backups have to be recovered, resulting in a long recovery time. Using a differential backup strategy, recovery is much faster, since only the last full and differential backup have to be restored. This efficiency is paid with higher memory consumption.

Within F&L-Grid, the project partners have agreed on a full backup per backup iteration from the perspective of the fat client (see Section 2.6). This is necessary since the fat client cache holds the user data only temporarily, making a differential or incremental backup impossible for several backup and recovery solutions.

2.5 File Permissions

File permisssions for single users or complete user groups are handled differently depending on the file systems (e.g. NTFS, Reiser, ZFS) and operating systems (e.g. Microsoft Windows, Linux, MacOS) used. Consequently, a uniform representation of file permissions is challenging.

F&L-Grid uses an intersection of information supported by widespread file systems (e.g. file/directory name, creation date, last-modified date, file size, ...) to describe file permissions. All relevant file permissions are stored in the fat client database (see Section 2.6).

2.6 Architectural Blueprint

The architectural blueprint shown in Figure 3 reflects the requirements identified above.

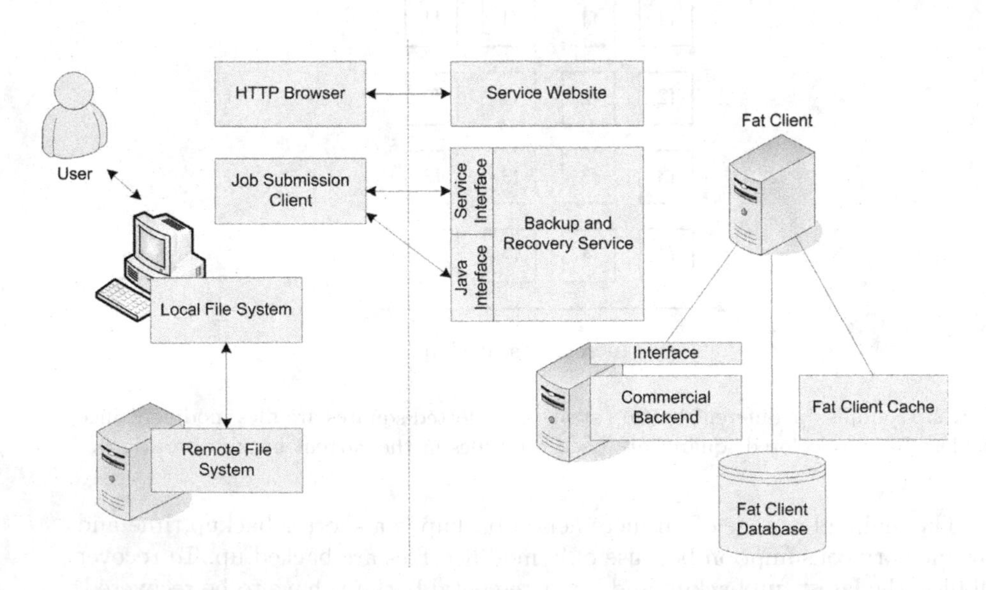

Fig. 3. Architecture of the F&L-Grid backup and recovery service.

At the client site, the user requires the so-called *job submission client* to access the backup and recovery infrastructure. This software is offered at a website and can be obtained using a simple web browser. Subsequently, the user may backup/recover a local file system or a remotely mounted file system.

The key component on the provider's site is the so-called *fat client*. The fat client permits access to the backup and recovery infrastructure and hides all painful details from the user. More precisely, the fat client controls the commercial backup and recovery backend, updates the fat client database, and manages the fat client cache. As the backup and recovery backend, an arbitrary commercial solution may be chosen, since the fat client uses a replaceable interface to access the backend. The fat client database logs all information relevant for accounting and billing purposes, e.g. how many backups a specific user has initiated. The *fat client cache* is a local store for all backup and recovery data. The commercial backend reads and writes data to the fat client cache, respectively. All these steps are coordinated by the backup and recovery service.

2.7 Backup

A backup job consists of six consecutive steps, as shown in Figure 4.

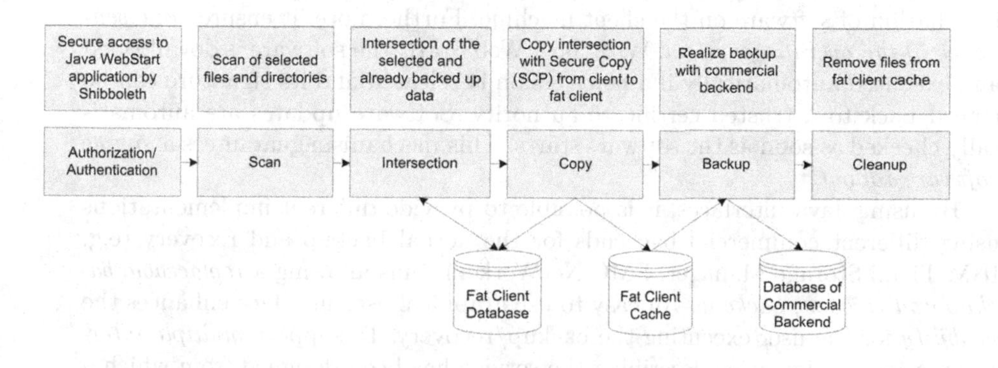

Fig. 4. Processing of a backup job.

1. **authentication/authorization:** The user who wants to initiate a backup process is identified and user rights are granted.
2. **scan:** The metadata (filename, last-modified timestamp, filesize, etc.) of all files/directories marked for backup are read and merged within a list.
3. **intersection:** To avoid unnecessary data movement between the user and the fat client, the intersection step removes all files/directories from the list that have not changed since the last backup or have been backed up before. For this purpose, already backed up files/directories for the current user are queried from the fat client database.
4. **copy:** All remaining files/directories are copied from the user node to the fat client cache using a secured communications channel.

5. **backup:** The commercial backup and recovery solution is triggered to back up the files/directories stored at the fat client cache. After a successful backup, the fat client database is updated to log the completed backup job.
6. **cleanup:** After completion of the backup job and logging, the fat client cache is cleaned, i.e. the corresponding files/directories are removed and the fat client database is updated.

3 Implementation Issues

This section gives an overview of the technologies selected for the implementation of the backup and recovery service, explains how the backup and recovery service can be accessed, and describes the processing of a backup job in detail.

3.1 Selection of Appropriate Technologies

Based on the identified requirements, the following technologies were chosen to implement the backup and recovery service.

To fulfill *minimal invasiveness*, we have chosen Java Web Start for the realization of the job submission client. A Java Runtime Environment (JRE) is installed on most computers nowadays, so that using Java does not induce the installation of software on the client machine. Furthermore, it ensures *independence of the operating system*. With Java Web Start, the software is downloaded and executed automatically if a new version is released and its signature can be traced back to a trusted certificate authority. Software updates are automatically checked as soon as the software starts. This mechanism guarantees a *simple software rollout.*

By using Java interfaces, it is possible to provide different implementations using different commercial backends for the actual backup and recovery (e.g. IBM Tivoli Storage Manager, EMC NetWorker), thus allowing a *replaceable backup and recovery backend.* An easy to use graphical user interface enhances the *usability* for the user executing the backup/recovery. To support *multiple interfaces*, a generic interface describing the service has been designed from which a Web Service Description Language (WSDL) [10] interface description or arbitrary other descriptions can be derived. To ensure *sustainability* of the service, the DFN has developed a business model settling the terms of use for the institutions using and the institutions providing the service.

According to a poll conducted by the ZKI Arbeitskreis Netzwerkdienste [14], 41 institutions in Germany were asked which backup software they use. Since 66% of these institutions are already using IBM Tivoli Storage Manager (TSM) as their backup and recovery solution, our prototypical implementation of the F&L-Grid backup and recovery service is also based on IBM TSM as backend. Since IBM TSM only supports a node-based backup/recovery, our implementation provides additional functionality to permit a user-based backup/recovery. Information required to permit a user-based backup/recovery, accouting, and billing are stored in the fat client database. Therefore, the fat client database provides a global view on the entire backup and recovery processes.

3.2 Accessing the Backup and Recovery Service

A user of the backup and recovery service requires the job submission client to access the service, i.e. to submit a backup or recovery job. For this purpose, the user browses a website that hosts the job submission client as a Java Web Start application. Consequently, the user only needs to retrieve the job submission client manually once. Subsequently, new versions of the job submission client are retrieved automatically by the Java Web Start technology.

To retrieve the software, the user must authenticate himself/herself against his/her home organization using Shibboleth [11] *(authentication phase)*, i.e. the user provides, for example, username and password to authenticate against the Shibboleth Identity Provider of his/her home organization. Shibboleth is used since it integrates well into the existing service portfolio of the DFN, which is also based on Shibboleth.

3.3 Submission of a Backup Job

A backup job is defined by selecting all relevant files/directories using the job submission client *(scan phase)*. The backup job indicates the selected directories and files by specifying their filenames, the node name, the user name, the last-modified timestamp, and the file permissions. This job object can then be sent to the backup and recovery service inside a Grid service invocation or, for example, as a serialized Java object, depending on the service interface. The service removes all files from the list of filenames that have not been changed since the last backup *(intersection phase)*. This can be done by querying the fat client database using JDBC. The modified list is returned to the job submission client that transfers the files to the fat client via the secure copy protocol (SCP) after initiating a secure shell (SSH) session *(copy phase)*. In our prototype, we use the Java Secure Channel (JSch) [12] library (that is also used by the very popular Eclipse IDE) for SSH and SCP implementation. When the data has been completely transferred, we start a TSM command-line client located on the fat client to back up the data to a TSM server *(backup phase)*. If the backup has been successfully completed, the job information is logged in the fat client database and the data is removed from the fat client cache *(cleanup phase)*. The file permissions are logged for each file as a plain string. Currently, UNIX file permissions are supported as well as Windows' basic NTFS permissions using the cacls (change access control lists) tool of Windows.

The type hierarchy of backup and recovery jobs is shown in Figure 5. The common characteristics of a `BackupJob` and a `RecoveryJob` are encapsulated in an interface `Job`. Both specialized jobs use a `FileDescription` to define the relevant files and directories. The `JobSerializer` is used to generate a Grid service invocation or a serialized Java object out of the backup and recovery jobs.

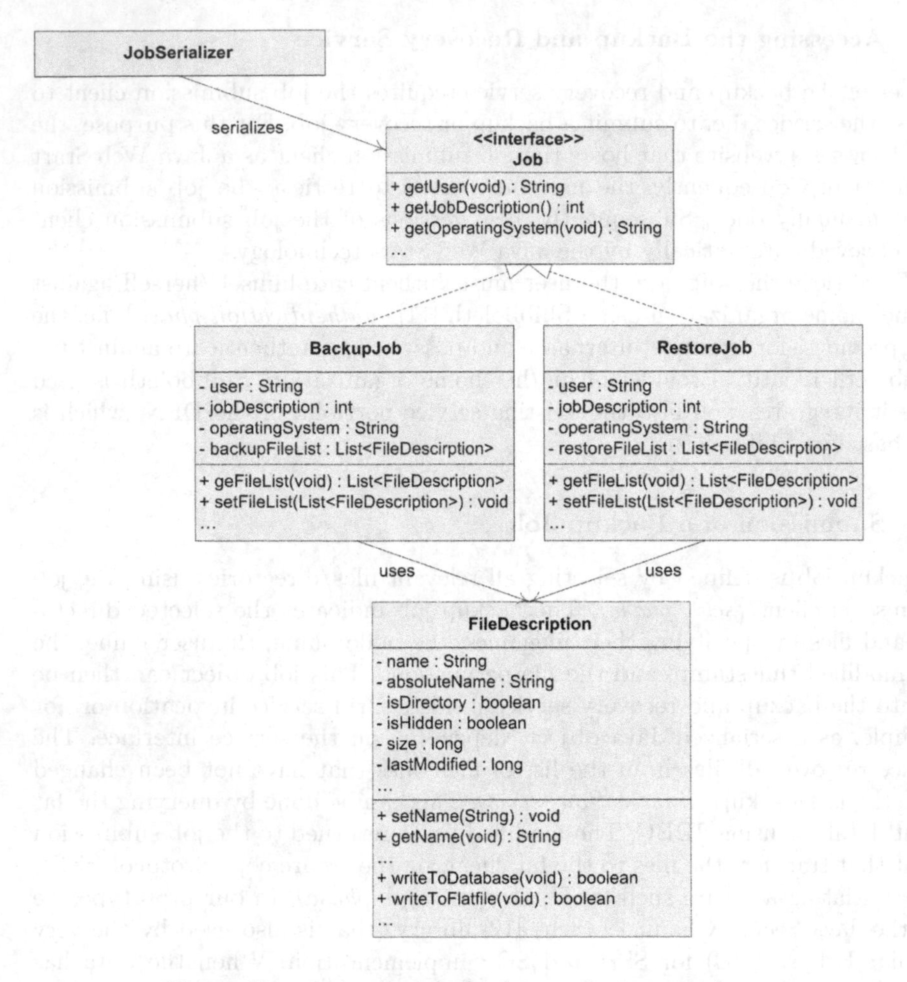

Fig. 5. Type hierarchy of a backup and recovery job.

4 Related Work

To the best of our knowledge, there are no generic backup and recovery solutions focusing on usability for Grid environments up to now. Consequently, work related to F&L-Grid reduces to standard technologies for data movement within Grid environments: GridFTP, RFT, RLS, and OGSA-DAI.

Current service-oriented Grid middleware innately offers data handling functionality. Based on this data handling components, research projects often build proprietary backup and recovery solutions. Consider, for example, the Globus Toolkit 4.x [3] that contains components for data movement (GridFTP and Reliable File Transfer (RFT)) and data replication (Replica Location Service (RLS)). GridFTP stems from the widely-used File Transfer Protocol (FTP) and supports the efficient, secure, and robust transfer of bulk data within Grid environments. The Globus Toolkit contains a GridFTP server (`globus-gridftp-server`) and a GridFTP command-line client (`globus-url-copy`) to host and retrieve data. RFT is a web service based interface to GridFTP which additionally permits scheduling of entire data movement jobs. The replication of data within Grid environments promises increased efficiency. To manage all replicas, the Globus Toolkit offers RLS, which is a simple registry for available replicas on different sites. Using middleware-specific data handling functionality results in two main problems:

1. the backup and recovery solutions can only hardly be reused,
2. in-depth knowledge of the middleware is required to use the backup and recovery solution which often overburdens simple users.

OGSA-DAI [13] provides services to access data from different sources like databases or flat files within the Grid. It also supports methods to query, transform, and deliver data in different ways. OGSA-DAI can be used as a simple backup service mostly for data replication but not for real backups leveraging reliable backup and recovery software.

5 Conclusions

In this paper, we have presented a generic infrastructure for backup and recovery in Grid environments. As part of the German Grid Initiative (D-Grid), the F&L-Grid project determined the requirements for a backup and recovery service from which an architecture for backup and recovery was derived. The infrastructure is easy to use and applicable within arbitrary service-oriented Grid environments and even for users outside the Grid. Scientists are empowered to easily back up and recover their experimental data without intervention of an administrator. As its backend, an arbitrary commercial backup and recovery solution can be used, which ensures reliability of the backups. The details of the particular backend used are hidden from the scientist.

In future work, we will support further file permissions including different inheritance schemes. Furthermore, an accounting and billing component will be developed that uses information from the fat client database to automatically bill submitted backup and recovery jobs.

Acknowledgements

This work is financially supported by the German Federal Ministry of Education and Research (BMBF) (D-Grid Initiative, F&L-Grid Project).

References

[1] I. Foster, C. Kesselman, and S. Tuecke. *The Anatomy of the Grid: Enabling Scalable Virtual Organizations.* In International Journal of High Performance Computing Applications, volume 15, pp. 200–222, 2001.

[2] OASIS: Web Services Resource Framework (WSRF).
http://www.oasis-open.org/committees/tc_home.php?wg_abbrev=wsrf.
[3] D. Petcu. *A Comprehensive Development Guide for the Globus Toolkit.* In Distributed Systems Online, volume 9, pp. 4–6, 2008.
[4] M. Romberg. *The UNICORE Architecture: Seamless Access to Distributed Resources.* In Proceedings of the 8th IEEE International Symposium on High Performance Distributed Computing (HPDC), IEEE Computer Society Press, pp. 287-293 1999.
[5] R. Kettimuthu. *GridFTP moves your Data and your News.* In International Science Grid This Week. July 2008,
http://www.isgtw.org/?pid=1001209.
[6] R.K. Madduri, C.S. Hood, and W.E. Allcock. Reliable File Transfer in Grid Environments. In Proceedings of the 27th Annual IEEE Conference on Local Computer Networks (LCN), IEEE Computer Society Press, pp. 737–738, 2002
[7] H. Neuroth, M. Kerzel, W. Gentzsch. *German Grid Initiative (D-Grid).* Niedersächsische Staats- und Universitätsbibliothek, ISBN 3938616997, 2007.
[8] German Federal Ministry of Education and Research (BMBF).
http://www.bmbf.de/.
[9] German Research Network (DFN). http://www.dfn.de/.
[10] W3C: Web Services Description Language (WSDL) 2.0, June 2006.
http://www.w3.org/TR/wsdl20/.
[11] R.O. Sinnott, J. Jiang, J. Watt, and O. Ajayi. *Shibboleth-based Access to and Usage of Grid Resources.* In Proceedings of the 7th IEEE/ACM International Conference on Grid Computing, IEEE Computer Society Press, 2006, pp. 136–143
[12] JSch – Java Secure Channel. http://www.jcraft.com/jsch/.
[13] M. Antonioletti, N.P. Chue Hong, A.C. Hume, M. Jackson, K. Karasavvas, A. Krause, J.M. Schopf, M.P. Atkinson, B. Dobrzelecki, M. Illingworth, N. McDonnell, M. Parsons, and E. Theocharopoulos. *OGSA-DAI 3.0 The Whats and the Whys.* In Proceedings of the UK e-Science All Hands Meeting 2007.
[14] Zentren für Kommunikation und Informationsverarbeitung in Lehre und Forschung e.V. (ZKI), Arbeitskreis Netzdienste.
http://www.zki.de/ak_nd/.

From Modelling to Execution of Enterprise Integration Scenarios: The GENIUS Tool

Thorsten Scheibler and Frank Leymann

Institute of Architecture of Application Systems (IAAS), Universität Stuttgart
Universitätsstr. 38, 70569 Stuttgart, Germany
{scheibler, leymann}@iaas.uni-stuttgart.de

Abstract. One of the predominant problems IT companies are facing today is Enterprise Application Integration (EAI). Most of the infrastructures built to tackle integration issues are proprietary because no standards exist for how to model, develop, and actually execute integration scenarios. EAI patterns gain importance for non-technical business users to ease and harmonize the development of EAI scenarios. These patterns describe recurring EAI challenges and propose possible solutions in an abstract way. Therefore, one can use those patterns to describe enterprise architectures in a technology neutral manner. However, patterns are documentation only used by developers and systems architects to decide how to implement an integration scenario manually. Thus, patterns are not theoretical thought to stand for artefacts that will immediately be executed. This paper presents a tool supporting a method how EAI patterns can be used to generate executable artefacts for various target platforms automatically using a model-driven development approach, hence turning patterns into something executable. Therefore, we introduce a continuous tool chain beginning at the design phase and ending in executing an integration solution in a completely automatically manner. For evaluation purposes we introduce a scenario demonstrating how the tool is utilized for modelling and actually executing an integration scenario.

1 Introduction

Nowadays, *Enterprise Application Integration (EAI)* is a major issue for most companies. Huge application landscapes exist comprising different kinds of IT artefacts (e.g. applications, services, data), in heterogeneous environments. Those independent artefacts need to be integrated and coordinated by an EAI solution in a loosely coupled manner. EAI therefore does not mean to create a single application distributed across several systems, but to build a system that uses such existing artefacts, adding new components, and coordinate their usage in the overall enterprise infrastructure. Typically, integration solutions are based on technologies, like *Enterprise Service Bus (ESB)* [3], *Message Queuing (MQ)* [15], or *Workflow Management Systems (WFMS)* [13].

During creation of such EAI solutions, recurring problems are solved multiple times using comparable approaches. These recurring problems and there solutions are generally described in terms of *Patterns* [1]. Apart from the well-established patterns in the field of object-oriented software design [11], there is an emerging area for creating patterns for software and enterprise architecture [2, 10]. [12] defines a set of patterns, covering prominent examples of situations encountered in message-based EAI scenarios. With those patterns EAI scenarios can be modelled easily. Even non technical persons (e.g. domain experts in designing system architectures) are able to develop integration architectures. Those patterns gain more and more importance in the field of enterprise application integration. Since they are public available and well documented, they serve as a base for system architects to specify integration solutions. However, this is only the first step in developing such a system. Basically, the development comprises three layers to be realised [16]: (i) the modelling layer where the overall scenario is modelled in an abstract way, (ii) the integration layer which glues different services together, and (iii) the application layer where the enterprise applications (legacy systems, databases,…) reside (see Figure 1).

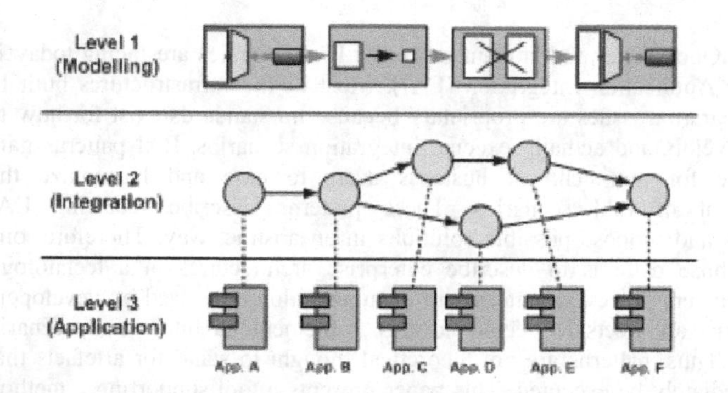

Fig. 1. Three levels of developing enterprise application integration scenarios

With the implementation of services at the lowest layer and the architecture of the desired system landscape at the top layer, no integrated solution exists describing how to connect both layers. This highlights a problem called the *Architecture-and-IT-gap*: a gap between people familiar with the overall architecture, business goals, and processes, and the people with in-depth knowledge of technical issues often decoupled from the former business goals and architectures. As worked out in [16], this gap can be filled by introducing a *Model-driven development (MDD)* [17] approach wherein the architecture described by means of EAI patterns can be transformed automatically into executable business processes by appropriate configuration parameters for those patterns. Integrating these architectural patterns for information systems into a tool chain that allows using them as user-centric models close the gap described. Based on our best knowledge, this is the first approach towards executable EAI patterns in a coherent manner.

Besides this method, no tool exists supporting the procedure. Nowadays, integration solutions on an architectural level are typically designed by IT architects using notations which are approved within their group but probably not by others. Several companies offer tools supporting system architects in developing integration solution (e.g. Aris IT Architect[1]). Hence, those tools do not use a standardized way of drawing integration architectures. [7] introduces a graphical editor in which some EAI patterns can be used to configure a flow in a certain ESB and automatically generate

[1] http://www.ids-scheer.com/en/Software/ARIS_Software/ARIS_IT_Architect/3741.html

executable code out of it. Though, this tool only supports a subset of patterns which can be reflected in the underlying middleware, and, furthermore, is only specialized on a proprietary middleware. It does not support any other technology and, therefore, lacks the ability of utilizing middleware technology of other vendors. [19] offers a domain-specific language allowing to execute EAI patterns on a .NET platform using Microsoft MQ. Yet, this approach is tightly coupled to an execution runtime and does not offer a method how other execution technologies can be included into the framework. Beside the academic research in this specific area, only one commercial tool is known: E2E Bridge[2]. It offers a model-driven integration approach by using UML as modelling technology and therefore uses a standardized notation. E2E Bridge uses UML interaction diagrams for describing integration scenarios, and thus models the behaviour of a system on a more technical level. This is in contrast to our work where an integration architecture is described leaving out interaction and technical details. Other publications dealing with application integration via an MDD approach, does not work with a common established Notation (e.g. [21] uses GME (Generic Modelling Environment) to design a domain specific modelling language). Thus, our work presented distinguished from related work that, on the one hand, it uses a common accepted and well established notation, and on the other hand does not make any assumptions about the execution environment.

The presented tool will close the gap between the architecture and the implementation in introducing the possibility of supporting various target platforms. Thus, our tool is not bound to a single execution environment. We provide a coherent tool chain (parameterized EAI patterns, modelling tool, generation algorithms, and deployment of executable artefacts) while being technology independent at the same time. In this paper we introduce the fundamentals for modelling executable EAI scenarios. Thereby, a multi-stage procedure is defined to model and execute integration scenarios. Following GENIUS is presented- a tool supporting this procedure. For evaluation purposes we introduce a scenario including modelling, generation and execution of an integration architecture. The paper concludes with a summary and an outlook of future work.

2 Modelling of EAI Scenarios

In this section we present the general procedure for modelling integrations scenarios with the help of parameterized EAI patterns. For the purpose of completeness we make an overview of parameterized EAI patterns, which form the basis of the method.

2.1 Parameterized EAI Patterns

EAI patterns provide a consistent vocabulary and visual notation framework to describe and model large-scale integration architectures across many technologies on a (technical) abstract level. E.g. a *Message Translator* points out that incoming massages have to be transformed into a new format which is needed at the filter after the translator (see Section 4). As worked out in [16] EAI patterns have to be described in a more formal way than existing descriptions. Thus, the so called *parameterized EAI patterns* are introduced. The parameters ease to specify EAI patterns concretely

[2] E2E Bridge: www.e3ebridge.com

and more precise. Evaluating EAI patterns four categories of properties which form the parameters and describe the patterns more specifically were identified [16]: (i) Input: the amount of incoming messages, (ii) Output: the amount of outgoing messages, (iii) Characteristics: the detailed behaviour of each pattern, which influences the generation of platform specific code, and (iv) Control: the formats of control messages and connections to management facilities of the infrastructure which dynamically lead to a new behaviour of a pattern at runtime.

In the proposed method, the parameterized EAI patterns act as a *platform independent model (PIM)* in terms of a *model-driven development* approach. This PIM serves as a basis for transformation algorithms that generate different executable artefacts. Those artefacts are called a *platform specific model (PSM)*, e.g. integration and application layers in Figure 1. According to MDD, the transformation of a PIM into a PSM is performed using a transformation engine based on a *platform model (PM)* and *marks*. These marks act as rules that steer the generation of appropriate artefacts in the transformation algorithms. In our case, marks are parameters of individual EAI patterns that are ingredients of an overall EAI solution. With such parameterized EAI patterns, a new way to develop a common basis for various transformation algorithms generating artefacts for various target platforms is introduced (see Figure 2).

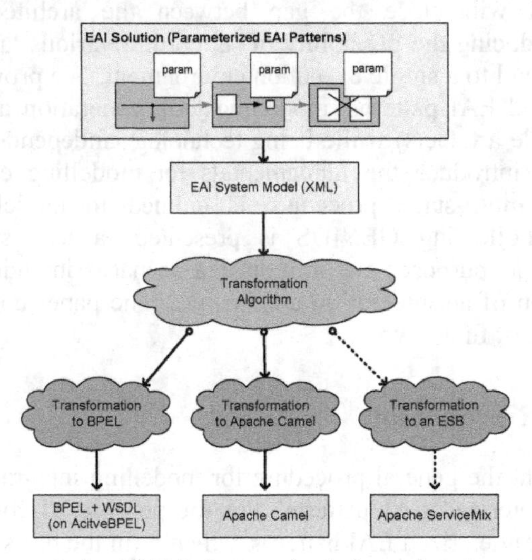

Fig. 2. Parameterized EAI Patterns as basis for various target platforms.

2.2 Model-Driven Development of Executable EAI Scenarios

The proposed method for developing executable EAI scenarios consists of three different steps. To be able to model integration scenarios within a tool, the EAI patterns together with the parameters have to be specified initially in a computer readable format (see Section 3.1). Another requirement is that existing or new applications have to be adapted that they all have a uniform interface description. This description will be used within the tool. As Web services (WS) [18] are nowadays the de facto standard for integrating heterogeneous applications, the interfaces have to be specified using *WSDL (Web Service Description Language)* [4]. This is the only requirement to the application landscape. In most of the cases these descriptions exist because the applications offer these descriptions or provide WS connectors already.

The first step in developing integration scenarios is modelling the architecture. In this step system architects develop a solution with the help of parameterized EAI patterns. These solutions describe architectures in general representing business use cases of a company (e.g. calculating loan allocations for customers, see Section 4). An independent tool was developed which supports the system architect in modelling integration solutions by letting him parameterize the needed EAI patterns according to the requirements of the use case. The architect models a system without specifying technical details only needed at runtime. Thus, when finishing this step the integration architecture is modelled in a platform independent manner readable by software, and can serve as a basis for transformation algorithms.

After finishing the modelling, the scenario has to be transformed into executable artefacts. These artefacts have to be installed on the appropriate infrastructure. To be able to install the integration solution it has to be enriched with technical information about the execution environment (e.g. addresses of servers, path to configuration data, etc.) during the transformation phase. This step is typically done by persons familiar with technical details of the infrastructure.

During the transformation into a platform specific model various steps are taking place. For instance, an archive is generated including all files needed at runtime (binary code, configuration data), or various applications are created, which have to be installed at different locations. When the model is transformed into executable artefacts and enriched with technical information needed at runtime, the system can be rolled out onto the executing infrastructure. This step can be done automatically since all information is available. After finishing the last step, the integration architecture can be executed. That is, the abstract model is automatically converted into executable integration logic.

3 GENIUS – A Tool for Modelling Executable EAI Scenarios

As business users are the target audience, the algorithm for transforming integration architectures into executable code is not enough. They require a graphical user interface supporting modelling of EAI architectures with parameterized EAI patterns and generating executable code out of it. The following sections describe the concepts including requirements of *GENIUS (Generating Enterprise Integration Executable Scenarios)* and present the architecture of the tool. Furthermore, we explain the concepts to achieve flexibility for implementing changed or new requirements. We conclude the chapter by introducing the core concepts of the generation algorithms.

3.1 Features of GENIUS

GENIUS provides a graphical user interface wherein a user can drag and drop various EAI patterns out of a toolbar into a visual editor pane and connect those patterns to build a messaging system representing the integration solution. The tool is built as a plug-in for Eclipse and therefore is based on standards like *Eclipse Modelling Framework (EMF)* [8] and *Graphical Editing Framework (GEF)* [9]. The user is aided during importing and linking the different patterns: the tool prohibits the combination of improper patterns, and examines continuously the system if information is missing. Errors are reported in the according error view.

Each EAI pattern can be parameterized through a configurations dialog. These parameters are used by the generation algorithm to steer the algorithm to produce according code. This generation takes place without the need for the user to write code on its own. Moreover, technical details are hidden from the user, e.g. the user has not to deal with interface names or binding information but rather with "high-level" information such as message names.

3.2 Architecture and Extension Mechanism

The underlying model, i.e. the representation of parameterized EAI patterns, is implemented using EMF. This library provides functionality of representing an object model, and the generation of a class hierarchy out of it (i.e. a MDD approach for modelling and implementation of object models). All EAI patterns are represented in the *EAI patterns model*. In Figure 3 a subset of this model is presented. The main class is denoted as *MessageSystem*. It contains all elements (i.e. patterns) which can be added to an integration solution. All patterns of the category *Channel* are represented by the class *Pipe* and its subclasses (e.g. *DataTypeChannel*). Filters are represented by the class *Filter* and all classes inheriting from that class (e.g. *ContentEnricher*, *Aggregator*). Using EMF as basis for the specification of parameterized EAI patterns eases the adaption of the model because of new requirements: new EAI patterns or new parameters are included by adding new sub-classes, or adding new attributes to an existing class. Since the EMF library automatically generates the implementation of a model to be used these changes are represented in the implementation as soon as the new code is generated. Therefore, it is not necessary at all to implement adoptions of the parameterized EAI patterns model by hand and enhancement of the EAI patterns model is realizable easily.

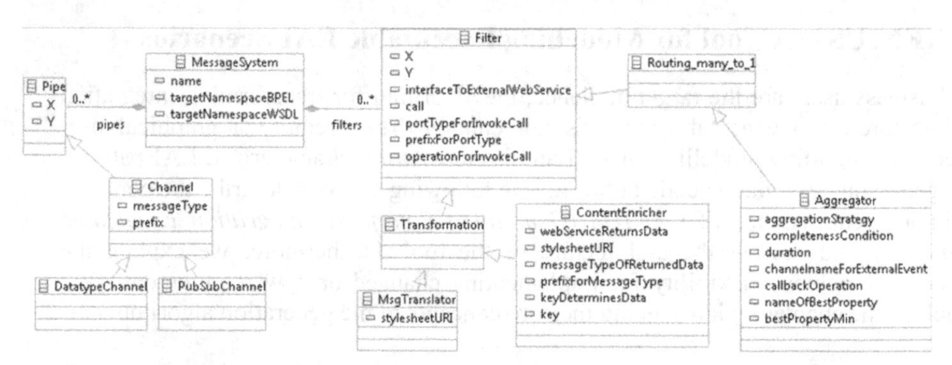

Fig. 3. EMF model of the system

Beside the model of EAI patterns and the graphical editing, the architecture supports the integration of different generation algorithms by a plug-in mechanism. Thus, the generation algorithm is not tightly coupled to the implementation of the editor. An algorithm plugs into the editor by adding a new action calling the new generation engine. The algorithm takes the modelled integration solution, and iterates through this model. The common behaviour of an algorithm is to generate single executable units for each pattern. Thus, each pattern is reflected as a "stand-alone" unit in the algorithm which generates appropriate executable code independent from other parts of the algorithm. Hence, modifications at a pattern can be done at exactly one place in the algorithm because no dependencies exist between single EAI patterns. Due to this modular approach new patterns can easily be integrated into the algorithm as well. The connection of single executable artefacts generated by single units has to be accomplished by the global part of the algorithm. This part cannot be modularized, since, the algorithm needs global knowledge about the integration solution (e.g. which pattern follows after which other pattern). Besides the extensibility of the EMF model reflecting the parameterized EAI patterns and the modular approach of the algorithms, some other parts of the tool has to be modified in case of changing requirements of parameterized EAI patterns, as well. New patterns possibly lead to a modification of the logic checking the proper configuration of EAI patterns as well as the logic checking the right connection of patterns.

3.3 Guarantee of Proper Configuration of Parameterized EAI Patterns

GENIUS focuses on people that are not familiar with the underlying technology which will actually run the integration scenario but are familiar with parameterized EAI patterns. However, as the complexity of an integration architecture increases, the retrieval of error increases, too. Thus, the tool supports the user during modelling an architecture reducing the creation of errors to a minimum.

Two different properties of the integration solution need to be continuously checked to avoid the modelling of an erroneous system: (i) are all included patterns configured properly, and, (ii) are all patterns connected properly. The logic verifying the configuration simply checks if the parameters of each pattern are set. The EMF model declares which parameters are mandatory and which are not. Thus, the logic checks the local setting without taking other information (like connected patterns) into account. For that, the second part of the logic comes into play. This part checks if the various patterns are properly connected. For instance, the logic inspects if the output message type of one pattern is similar to the input message type of the following filter connected via a channel. If not, the user is informed by the tool. Moreover, the logic prohibits connecting patterns, which do not fit. Thus, a user cannot even connect patterns that must not be connected (e.g. two filters with each other). The continuous verification of the modelled integration scenario during development leads to a correct solution which can be transformed into executable code.

3.4 Generation Algorithm

As mentioned above, the common behaviour of an algorithm is iterating through an EAI solution modelled by means of parameterized EAI patterns. The algorithm generates individual artefacts out of single filters (e.g. a message translator). These artefacts are glued together as specified by the channels. Thus, the algorithm generates an integrated application which can be installed on an appropriate environment where the integration architecture is executed. Depending on the targeting runtime, it is possible that more than one single application is generated. However, these applications need to be integrated as well (e.g. in terms of a routing description). As pointed out in Section 2.2, additional information need to be included (by the user) so that the algorithm can generate the required code, and can actually install the integration architecture on the target infrastructure.

4 Scenario: Developing an Integration Solution

In this section we present a scenario to demonstrate how to compose routing and transformation EAI patterns into an overall integration architecture. For this purpose, the GENIUS editor is used wherein patterns are parameterized so that executable code can be generated. In the second part the generated BPEL code is explained.

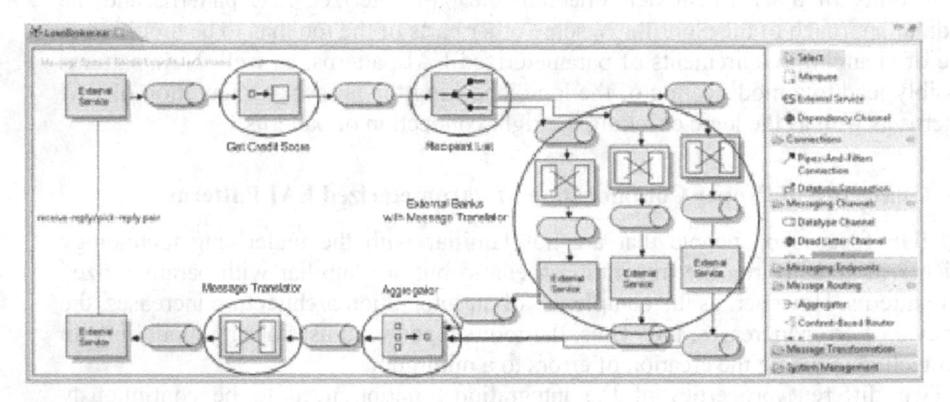

Fig. 4. Loan broker scenario modelled with Genius

4.1 Loan Broker Scenario with Parameterized EAI Pattern

The chosen scenario models the process of a customer obtaining quotes for a loan from various banks and selects the best offer. We simplified the process to demonstrate the important parts of the GENIUS tool and show how certain patterns can be parameterized. The scenario is based on the request for loan offers of a customer. Normally, the customer has to contact several banks, collect the offers, and chose the best one. The contacted banks investigate the customer's credit background to offer special credit rates. This procedure can be done by a broker collecting a loan request, enriches this request with all the information needed by a bank (credit score information), and sends the request to the responsible banks. At the end the broker chooses the best offer for the customer. Thus, the loan broker integrates various systems (credit agency, banks), and offers a service to the customer. The according integration solution modelled with EAI patterns in GENIUS can be seen in Figure 4. In this paper we do not go into detail of every parameterized EAI pattern. We present exemplarily the parameterization and according BPEL Code of three patterns.

In Figure 5.a the configuration dialog of the recipient list is shown. The user has selected that the recipient list is determined by an external service (via operation *getRecipients*) and is stored in the according message element (*recipientListtT*). The recipient list checks the content of this element and sends messages to banks when the bank is listed in the recipient list. The aggregator's parameters are shown in Figure 5.a. First, the completeness condition is set to *wait-for-all*. The aggregation strategy is described by comparing the value at the element *\\creditoffer\creditrate* the element with the lowest value is selected and the according message is transmitted without changes. The last step is translating the message coming from the aggregator to a message which is readable by the customer. Therefore, the message translator is parameterized by utilizing a XSL stylesheet to perform the transformation. The patterns external service, content enricher (get credit score), and all bank related patterns are not considered in this paper.

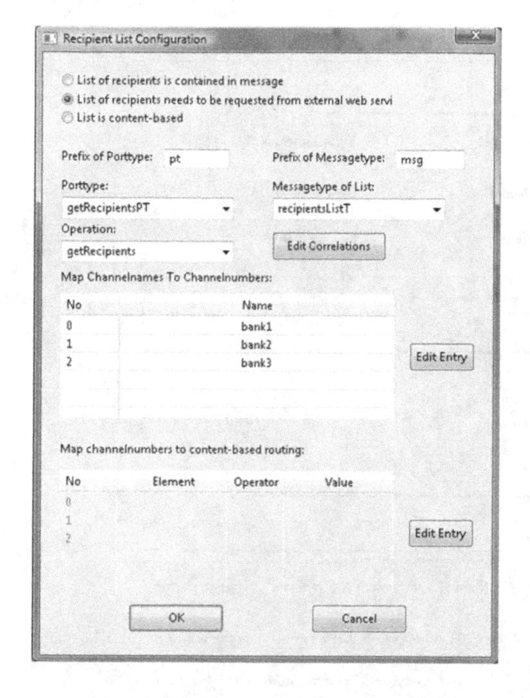

Fig. 5.a. Recipient list parameters

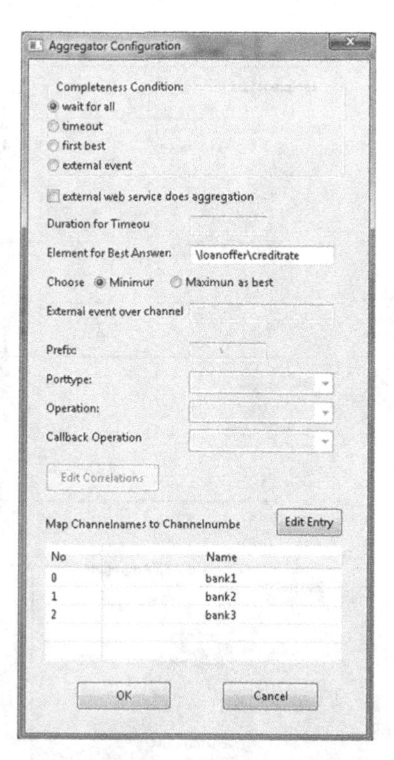

Fig. 5.b. Aggregator parameters

The overall EAI system model is configured as well. Beside the name of the system all needed WSDL and XSD files (definition of the external services, e.g. banks, and definition of the message files) are imported into the message system. These files are required for generating the appropriate executable code out of the EAI system model.

4.2 Generated BPEL Code

Based on the loan broker scenario shown above the generation algorithms can produce executable code. Currently, GENIUS supports two different target execution environments: (i) BPEL including needed WSDL, and (ii) Apache Camel [5] (an integration framework based on Apache Active MQ). In this paper we present the generation of BPEL.

The recipient list is transformed into BPEL as presented in Figure 6. The pattern starts with an invocation of the Web service representing the calculator of the recipient list. Afterwards, three if activities, one for each bank, check if the according bank name (e.g. bank1) is included within the recipient list. If this is true, a variable is set for the according bank. The links between recipient list pattern and each bank has a transition condition checking if the according variable for the bank is set. If this check is true the according bank is called.

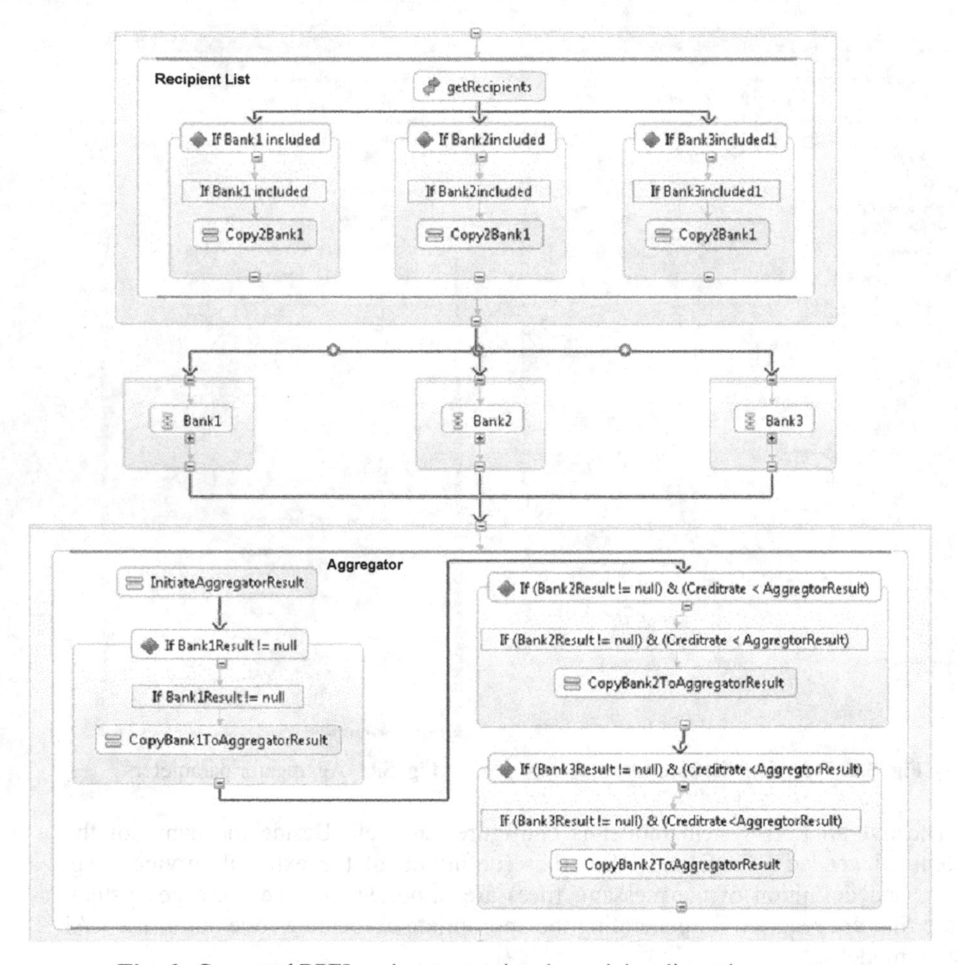

Fig. 6. Generated BPEL code representing the recipient list and aggregator

The aggregator is implemented using BPEL means only. At first the variable of the aggregator result variable is initiated (i.e. all values are set to default). If bank 1 was requested, the BPEL process receives an answer and thus the variable *bank1Result* is set. Next comparison is similar to the first one: if bank2result is set and the credit rate offer of this bank is smaller than the current rate in the aggregator result, the variable values are copied into the aggregator result variable. Same procedure holds for the last bank. At the end the aggregator variable is set with the offer of the bank including the smallest credit rate.

The *Message Translator* is implemented using an *Assign* activity utilizing a XSL stylesheet (BPEL method *doXslTransform*) describing how to transform the message to the according format. Note: this BPEL code is not represented in the figure.

5 Conclusion and Future Work

In this paper we introduced GENIUS, a tool supporting a method for modelling integration scenarios with the help of parameterized EAI patterns and the generation of executable code out of this model automatically. Therefore, we presented the parameterization of patterns which guides a generation algorithm to transform a platform independent model into a platform specific model according to the MDD paradigm. The methodology has been proven to be general enough to generate different artefacts for different execution environments (i.e. BPEL and Apache Camel). However, we will be integrating more target platforms to be supported by the tool. For example, [14] investigated how the parameterized EAI patterns can be mapped onto ESBs in theory and *Apache Service Mix* [6] in practice. Moreover, we introduced a scenario to evaluate the tool in a real world example. As the tool supports the modelling of this scenario and the generated code could be executed as well, the tool seems to be practical even for non technical persons. The last step-installing the application on the execution environment (i.e. deployment)- is done manually. This step has to be included into the tool as well to fully support the three levels of EAI: beginning at the modelling, generating of executable code afterwards, and finally, deploying and executing the code onto the execution environment.

In summary, we introduced a coherent method with a continuous tool chain (i.e. beginning at the modelling phase and ending at the execution of an integration solution) that can even be used by persons familiar with the overall architecture, business goals, and processes having not much knowledge about the actual technical environment.

Based on best practices we identified while modelling integration scenarios with EAI patterns, the tool should aid a user during modelling in special situations. In these situations a user chooses to add complex and composed patterns which are available as artefacts. As the name suggests those patterns are built up of basic patterns connected by channels to form coarse-grained units. When the user selects such a composed pattern the tool should prompt the user to select the precise basic patterns ("auto-completion"). For example, the *Scatter-Gather* pattern ends up with a *Splitter* at the beginning, an *Aggregator* at the end, and some patterns in between them. Hence, the user can decide whether he selects the offered possibilities or models his own solution when he wants to add a composed pattern to his model.

6 References[3]

[1] C Alexander. *The Timeless Way of Building*. Oxford University Press, August 1979.

[2] F. Buschmann, R. Meunier, H. Rohnert, P. Sommerlad, and M. Stal. *Pattern-Oriented Software Architecture*. Wiley, 1996.

[3] D. A Chappell. *Enterprise Service Bus. Theory in Practice*. O'Reilly Media, 2004.

[4] E. Christensen, F. Curbera, G. Meredith, and S. Weerawarana. Web Services Description Language (WSDL) 1.1, March 2001.

[5] Apache Software Foundation. *Apache Camel: a Spring based Integration Framework*. http://activemq.apache.org/camel/.

[6] Apache Software Foundation. *Apache ServiceMix: an Open Source ESB (Enterprise Service Bus)*. http://servicemix.apache.org.

[7] Apache Software Foundation. Cimero: a graphical eclipse tool for ServiceMix. http://servicemix.apache.org/cimero-editor.html.

[8] Eclipse Foundation. *Eclipse Modeling Framework (EMF)*. http://www.eclipse.org/emf.

[9] Eclipse Foundation. *Graphical Editor Framework (GEF)*. http://www.eclipse.org/gef.

[10] M. Fowler, D. Rice, and M. Foemmel. *Patterns of Enterprise Application Architecture*. Addison-Wesley Longman, Amsterdam, November 2002.

[11] E. Gamma, R. Helm, and R. E. Johnson. *Design Patterns. Elements of Reusable Object-Oriented Software*. Addison-Wesley Longman, Amsterdam, 1st edition, March 1995.

[12] G. Hohpe and B. Woolf. *Enterprise Integration Patterns: Designing, Building, and Deploying Messaging Solutions*. Addison-Wesley Professional, 2003.

[13] F. Leymann and D. Roller. *Production Workflow: Concepts and Techniques*. Prentice Hall International, September 1999.

[14] C. Mierzwa. *Architektur eines ESBs zur Unterstützung von EAI Patterns*. Diploma thesis (in German), Universität Stuttgart, March 2008.

[15] R. Monson-Haefel and D. Chappell. *Java Message Service*. O'Reilly, 2000.

[16] T. Scheibler and F. Leymann. A framework for executable enterprise application integration patterns. In *I-ESA 2008*, Germany, March 2008.

[17] M. Völter and T. Stahl. *Model-Driven Software Development*. Wiley & Sons, 1 edition, May 2006.

[18] S. Weerawarana, F. Curbera, F. Leymann, T. Storey, and D. F Ferguson. *Web Services Platform Architecture*. Prentice Hall, 2005.

[19] G. Hohpe. *Are "Pattern" and "Component" Antonyms?*. www.eaipatterns.com/ramblings.html, 2004.

[20] K. Balasubramanian, D.C. Schmidt, Z. Molnár, and Á. Lédeczi. *System Integration Using Model-Driven Engineering*. Designing Software-Intensive Systems: Methods and Principles, Information Science Reference, Idea Group Publishing, 2008

[3] Links' validity checked on 12/02/2008.

Pluggable Authorization and Distributed Enforcement with pam_xacml

Andreas Klenk[1,2], Tobias Heide[2],
Benoit Radier[3], Mikael Salaun[3], Georg Carle[1,2]

[1]TU München, Boltzmannstraße 3, 85748 München, Germany
[2]Wilhelm-Schickard-Institut, Sand 13, 72076 Tübingen, Germany
[3]France Télécom R&D, avenue Pierre Marzin 2, 22307 Lannion, France

Abstract. Access control is a critical functionality in distributed systems. Services and resources must be protected from unauthorized access. The prevalent practice is that service specific policies reside at the services and govern the access control. It is hard to keep distributed authorization policies consistent with the global security policy of an organization. A recent trend is to unify the different policies in one coherent authorization policy. XACML is a prominent XML standard for formulating authorization rules and for implementing different authorization models. Unifying authorization policies requires an integration of the authorization method with a large application base. The XACML standard does not provide a strategy for the integration of XACML with existing applications. We present pam_xacml, an authorization extension for the Pluggable Authentication Modules (PAM). We argue how existing applications can leverage XACML without modification and state the benefits of using our extended version of the authorization API for PAM. Our experimental results quantify the impact of security and connection establishment of using remote Policy Decision Points (PDP). Our approach provides a method for introducing XACML authorization into existing applications and is an important step towards unified authorization policies.

1 Introduction

Since the early days of the computers, the decision about permissible actions on a resource was critical. For a long time application specific configuration languages defined if and how the applications should act upon a request by specific subjects. These policies are sometimes hard to separate from the application configuration and are present at each instance of the application. The fact that the policies reside at the applications, distributed across the network, makes it difficult to to gain a coherent view of the access control decisions and to change these policies.
In recent years general purpose policy description languages emerged. These languages provide a method for formulating application independent policies that can be evaluated by general purpose Policy Decision Points (PDP). Policy languages [1][4][12][13] enable unified and centralized security policies that allow for

a better insight into the authorization decisions and facilitate timely changes to the security policy. As an important benefit, unified policies can be tested for compliance with a high level security policy. Model checkers can automatically test policies for redundancy, constraints, and safety properties, and can perform a change-impact analysis [7]. The eXtensible Access Control Markup Language (XACML) [19] standard enjoys growing popularity for specifying authorization policies. However, the use of policy languages is limited if they lack integration with applications.
The Pluggable Authentication Module (PAM) [22] is well established for providing unified authentication to applications. As a consequence, these applications become independent of the underlying authentication method (e.g. Kerberos, LDAP, Radius, and Smart Cards). Unfortunately such a solution is missing for authorization. This paper introduces the novel `pam_xacml` module for authorization with XACML. `pam_xacml` can be used for most existing applications that support PAM without the need for code modifications. An extension to the PAM conversation function enables even richer authorization decisions for applications that implement the new interface, and allows to return obligations for permissible actions. Introducing unified policies comes at the cost of additional communication with the PDP. The different deployment options of XACML PDPs have a significant impact on the performance of authorization. Authorization is a function that may happen multiple times at different applications during a single service request. Our experiments provide performance figures on the effect of multi-point authorization in distributed systems. This paper presents the following contributions, thereby motivating wide-spread use of XACML in distributed heterogeneous environments:

1. A PAM module for authorization decisions with XACML, usable for existing applications without modifications.
2. An extension of the PAM conversation function to provide more input for the authorization decisions and to return obligations to the application.
3. A study on the communication cost of distributed authorization and advice on different deployment options.

The remainder of this paper is structured as follows. Sec. 2 reviews related work on authorization in distributed systems. Sec. 3 describes our approach for use by many PAM enabled applications. Sec. 4 presents results from our measurement study with the prototype implementation.

2 Related Work

Authorization languages were subject to research and standardization during the last years. The Authorisation Specification Language was introduced in [12], Ponder [4] is a declarative language for security and management policies, X-RBAC [1] uses XML to express Role Based Access Control (RBAC) policies. We focus on the eXtensible Access Control Markup Language (XACML) [19] OASIS standard for authorization policies. XACML can take authorization rules

in XML and is able to implement different authorization models, such as Discretionary Access Control, Mandatory Access Control (MAC) and Role Based Access Control (RBAC). Positive experiences of using of XACML for access control in heterogeneous distributed systems have been reported in [18].
The IETF laid down the nomenclature and architecture commonly found in modern authorization systems [23], but did not specify concrete interfaces or messages. The Generic AAA (GAAA) [9] is one implementation that follows the ideas of the IETF framework. Follow up work on GAAA is done by [5]. Gheorghiu et al. introduced the General Authorization and Access API (GAAPI) [8]. Two IETF-Drafts have been written for this API, both of which are now expired. The Common Open Policy Service (COPS) [6] has a binary encoded policy interface that allows to contact a PDP, mainly for decisions on media level access control and QoS specifications. The Open Group published the Authorization (AZN) API standard in [21]. It describes a C interface for authorization based on the ISO-standard 10181-3. Applications can use the AZN-API for authorization requests. PERMIS is discussed in [3]. It uses a simplified version of the AZN-API introduced before. The authors in [11] propose an extension of the Java Authentication and Authorization Service for class-instance level access control with XACML, which is only available for Java programs.
The Security Assertion Markup Language (SAML) [2] defines an authorization decision query protocol. The CARDEA system [17] supports a PDP with SAML interface that can use XACML for its decisions. In case SAML serves as an interface to PDPs, it requires that the requesters of an authorization decision support the corresponding protocol binding, usually SOAP over HTTP. The public key cryptography for the verification of SAML documents also introduces complexity at the client. Our approach with `pam_xacml` shields the application from the communication interface with the PDP, by separating the PDP communication from the interface with the application.

3 Pluggable Authorization with XACML

This Section introduces `pam_xacml`, an authorization module based on the Linux Pluggable Authentication Modules (PAM) [22] for XACML [19] PDPs. Pluggable Authentication Modules were proposed by Sun Microsystems and were standardized by the Open Software Foundation in RFC 86.0 [22]. PAM allows for the development of authentication modules that can easily be plugged into the PAM library and hide the specifics of the authentication process from the applications. There also exist PAM modules that allow for basic authorization decisions. `pam_time` makes access dependent on the local time. `pam_ldap` retrieves user specific data (e.g. access levels) from the LDAP database, possibly using host name or time as selection criteria. All these methods are isolated and lack support for unified authorization policies.

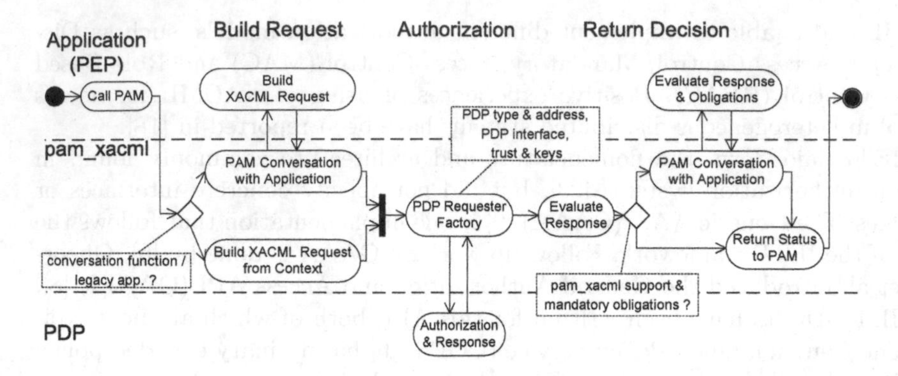

Fig. 1. Request Creation, Authorization at PDP and Response Evaluation

3.1 pam_xacml for Unmodified Applications That Support PAM

We introduce a PAM module to enable XACML authorization policies for arbitrary PAM enabled applications. pam_xacml[1] is an intermediary between application and XACML PDP (see Figure 1). The communication with the PDP works completely isolated from the application. The application is mainly concerned about the result of the authorization, hence it is sufficient for a PAM authorization module to fail upon negative decisions or succeed if all required modules returned positive results.
The authorization request can incorporate information from different sources. Existing PAM applications provide usually the user name and additional attributes which might not always be present, for instance, the address of the requester. Context information is accessible through the execution environment, for example, host name, system load, and local time. Services and databases can provide user related attributes, such as, account expiration date or account balance.
Any application that uses PAMs pam_acct_mgmt for account management or pam_sm_authenticate for authentication can simply add the pam_xacml module to the list of required PAM modules. PAM modules are stackable, that allows for rules that require all modules or a subset of the modules to succeed, for declaring a user to be authorized and be authenticated. We can take advantage of the existing authentication modules and demand a PAM configuration that enforces the user identities to be authenticated, before authorization is invoked. Using pam_xacml for authorization introduces a central instance in the system that allows to establish trust with PDPs, instead of configuring each application to authenticate and trust a given PDP. The keying material can be stored in one location of the OS, and thereby reduce the risk of the keys to become compromised. The module can monitor authorization requests and decisions and provide detailed log traces for the tracking of access requests and for the identification

[1] available at http://pamxacml.sourceforge.net

of possible attacks. The stacking of modules allows for the invocation of multiple PDPs for one authorization request by the application. An example of the stacking of pam_xacml is a scenario where the host has its own PDP for access control for local resources (e.g. files, applications), the PDP of the department decides upon access to the resources in the infrastructure (e.g. database, printer), whereas the corporate PDP decides if the organization wide business rules permit the request.
Another important aspect is the variety of communication methods that exist for querying remote XACML PDPs. SAML [2] allows for authorization requests and the transport of authorization decisions. SOAP [10] is a popular Web Service protocol that can be used to transport native XACML authorization requests. Data origin authentication, confidentiality, message integrity and replay protection introduce even more complexity for the communication. Viable options for secure authorization are HTTPS, port tunneling over SSH, or the use of WS-Security [15]. pam_xacml hides all these details from the application and provides great flexibility to introduce new access methods and additional PDPs to the infrastructure, with only minimal impact on the system configuration.

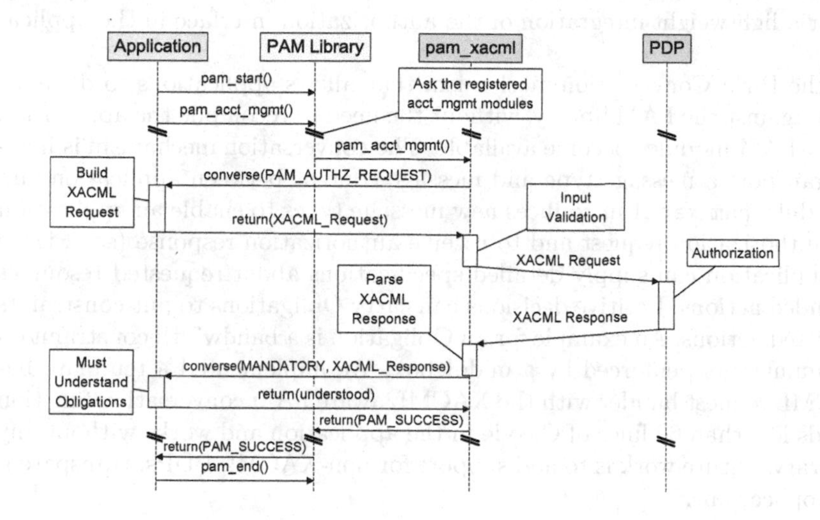

Fig. 2. Authorization with the PAM Conversation Mechanism

3.2 Applications with Authorization Interface

The prior Section assumed applications without any special support for pam_xacml. This limits the available information for the authorization. The application itself knows best about the parameters of the service request. The use of pam_xacml for existing applications can only regulate if access to an application as a whole should be possible. It has no means to limit access to certain actions on the application.

The basic idea is to give the application full control over the authorization by building the authorization request within the application. Authorization interfaces of applications are long lived, because they are linked to control flows deep within the programs. They must provide exhaustive information about the current situation and ensure effective enforcement of the access control decisions.We decided to go for the XACML policy language [19] for the interface with the application, because it has a set of common data types, well-defined semantic and has a straightforward XML language for authorization request and authorization response. The advantage of the XACML interface is, that it provides an migration path for applications that evolve towards using unified policies. These applications can start with `pam_xacml` to integrate support for XACML request and response XML documents and can be extended for native support of SAML XACML authorization later on. Alternative authorization interfaces with the application, such as AZN API [21] or GAAPI [8] can be added in the future.
The applications builds the raw XACML request and lets `pam_xacml` handle the communication and security. The application does not necessarily need to understand the XACML response, because `pam_xacml` parses the response and signals an authorization failure to PAM if the PDP denied access. This approach allows for a lightweight integration of the authorization interface in the application.
We use the PAM Conversation mechanism that allows applications to dynamically link against the PAM library, without the need to recompile the application when new PAM modules become available. The conversation mechanism is invoked to transport a message type and message content between application and PAM module. `pam_xacml` introduces new message types to enable an application to pass authorization request and to receive authorization response (see Figure 2). An application can supply detailed specifications about requested resources and intended actions. Positive decisions can carry Obligations to put constraints on permitted actions. An example for an Obligation is a bandwidth constraint on the communication, enforced by a middlebox. We implemented a template based XACML request builder with the XACML aware PAM conversation function that needs less than 60 lines of C code in the application and works without any XML library. Future work is to add support for non-XACML PDPs, transparent for the applications.

4 Experiments on Distributed Authorization

Policy enforcement is usually pessimistic as that it continues only with processing of a request, after a positive authorization decision was taken, hence it has a significant impact on session establishment. None of the publications we surveyed in Section 2 presented a detailed analysis on the performance of distributed authorization. We will focus on the impact of communication and cryptography, because no matter how fast a PDP policy engine implementation will become, the communication cost for making the request and receiving the decision will always be present.

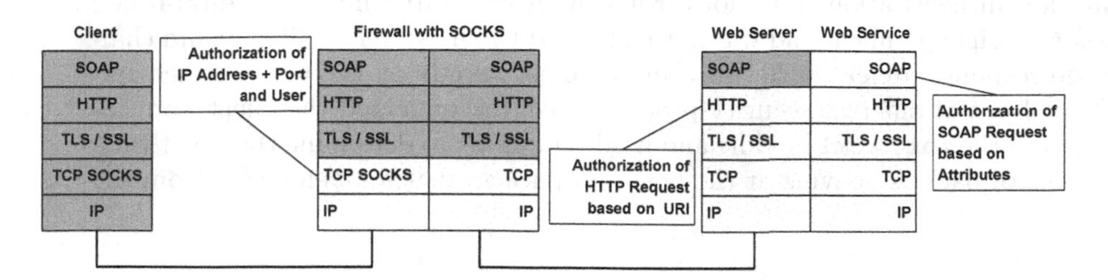

Fig. 3. Consequtive Authorization Decisions

4.1 Reference Scenario with Consecutive Authorization Decisions

Access control is guided by the principle of minimal exposure to adversaries. Services, applications and infrastructure have their own policy enforcement code in place. One service access usually involves multiple components, each of which must authorize the access. This architecture leads to multiple lines of defense that an intruder must circumvent. Service interfaces, for instance, are usually complex, and subject to change, making it hard to guarantee correct enforcement of access control decisions and assure the absence of exploits. As opposed to firewalls that are verifiable reference monitors and can filter most malicious requests, but lack insight into the application logic.
The Figure 3 introduces the reference scenario with consecutive authorizations of a SOAP request, using `pam_xacml` at each step. The firewall has an integrated SOCKS[16] server that relays communication to the web server after successful authentication and authorization of the requester. We used the SS5[2] SOCKS server and extended it to support bandwidth restrictions specified by XACML Obligations. SOCKS knows about user identities and requested service addresses. Hence, it can only authorize that a user is allowed to access the web sever at all. The web server in turn receives a HTTP request specifying an URI which can now be checked. The Web Service can authorize at the finest granularity, by using parameters like, intended action on the resource, resource specification, current state, and context for its authorization request. The Web Service and the PDP were accessible via SOAP interfaces through a stack of Apache Axis, the Tomcat servlet container and the Apache web server[3]. All machines were installed with a standard configuration of Fedora Core 4 and had an Intel Xeon 2.80GHz CPU with 1GB of memory, except the client which had an Intel Pentium 4 2.26GHz CPU with 512MB memory. The computers were connected by a 100MBit/s LAN with Round Trip Times (RTT) smaller than 0.1 milliseconds. We used different methods for issuing authorization requests to the PDP: plain SOAP, SOAP over TLS with the OpenSSL library and SOAP over an SSH tunnel. We used 1024bit RSA certificates for TLS server and client to assure

[2] http://ss5.sourceforge.net
[3] Apache, Tomcat, Axis available at http://www.apache.org

mutual authentication. Port forwarding with the SSH tunnel was established before each experiment and was authenticated by the server certificate and challenge response. Refer to [20] for a measurement study on the performance and throughput of different security protocols. We instrumented the client application and the `pam_xacml` module and used tcpdump[4] to determine the exact time stamps of packets arriving at the host and packets that are being sent from the host.

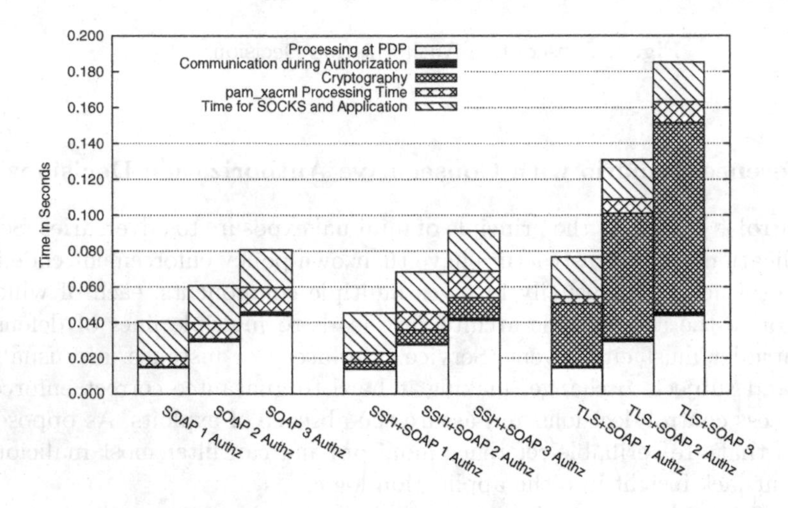

Fig. 4. Breakdown of Service Access Time for 1/2/3 Authorization Requests

4.2 Measurements

We were interested in the delay of single requests, for this reason, we made 100 requests with a time of 3 seconds between each request. We performed measurements for one, two or three consecutive authorizations, for each protocol binding (see Figure 4). The processing time for obtaining a decision at the PDP was virtually the same for all experiments. The interpretation of the performance numbers of the PDP is limited, because we use Sun's XACML[5] implementation with a simple policy, not comparable with real world policies. We determined the cost for a PDP decision without communication and SOAP overhead as 9 ms. The PDP decision inclusive the handling by the Operating System, the server and the SOAP processing took 15ms for one authorization. The `pam_xacml` module introduced a delay of at most 5ms for the PAM execution, the communication with the application and the XML processing. The delay for the whole communication was below 2ms. The signaling from the application with SOCKS

[4] http://www.tcpdump.org

[5] http://sunxacml.sourceforge.net

and the service request/response took 22ms in total. TLS cryptography introduced a significant overhead of 35ms for the connection handshake and derivation of the session key. The already established secure link with ssh took 4ms for the cryptography, only little more than the unencrypted messages.
In case of consecutive authorizations, the delay of all components involved in the authorization grows linearly with the number of authorization decisions. The whole process with 3 authorization requests takes a client between 90ms and 180ms over a secure link.

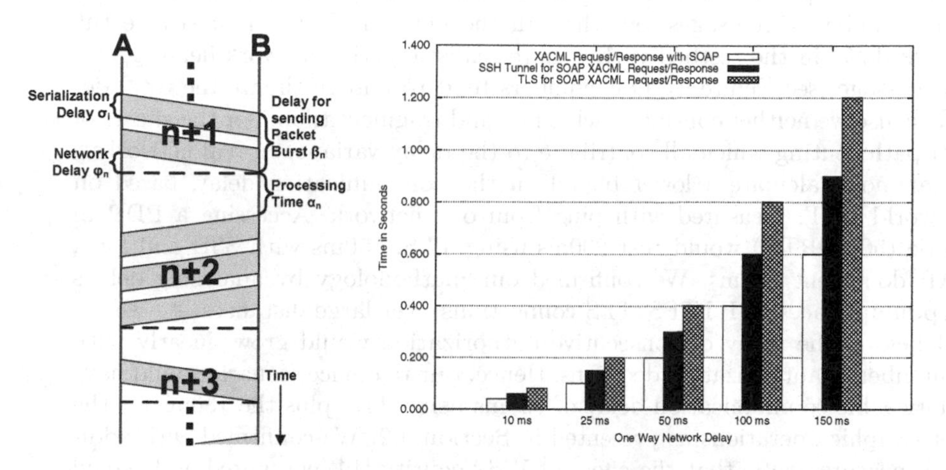

Fig. 5. Delay Contributions to Time for Authorization

Fig. 6. Impact of Propagation Delay on Authorization for different Communication Protocols

4.3 Impact of Propagation Delay

The impact of the communication on the authorization was negligible in the testbed. As many organizations have global scope, we want to estimate the impact of the propagation delay on the authorization.
Many factors contribute to the end-to-end delay of authorization (see Figure 5): The processing time α_n in the Operating System and within the client and service programs. The delay β_n for sending the packets that belong to one message waiting in the queue of the Operating System. The β_n delay consists mainly of the serialization delay σ_i of the individual packets. The σ_i can be calculated from the bandwidth of the link and size of the data to be sent. The bandwidth is usually constrained by the access network of client and server. The network delay φ_n is influenced by factors such as queuing and forwarding at routers, packet loss, effects of multi-path routing and most important, the distance of the link. The distance of the link determines the propagation delay at roughly $5\mu s$ per km. The time for a queued message to arrive at its destination is therefore $\beta_n + \varphi_n$. We observed always the same sequence of messages in our setup, for instance, only

after a request has been fully received a response was sent. We know the exact times α_n of each message after it has been completely received at a host and the first packet of the reply is going to be sent. We can approximate the T_{authz} for a complete authorization exchange as $T_{authz} \approx \sum \beta_n + \varphi_n + \alpha_n$, where n is one message during the authorization. We can estimate how larger propagation delays impact the authorization performance, because the processing time α_n is independent of the network delay and longer routes in the network have small impact on β_n. The effects of longer routes through the network is mostly independent of the packet size and is therefor dominated by φ_n which is dependent on the number of messages sent through the network. We can substitute the network delay in the testbed with a more realistic fictive network delay φ'_n for each message (see Figure 6). Our numbers tend to underestimate the total delay, because we neither consider packet loss and fragmentation, nor the effects of multi path routing which all contribute to the delay variance in real networks. We can now calculate a lower bound on the communication delay, based on real world RTT, measured with ping from our network. Accessing a PDP in Europe (50ms RTT) would cost 200ms using TLS, 150ms with SSH and for a SOAP document 100ms. We confirmed our methodology by analyzing delays of tcpdump traces of HTTPS/TLS connections over large distances. As we argued before, the delay of consecutive authorization would grow linearly with the number of authorization decisions. Hence, our reference scenario would have an noticeable communication delay of 600ms using TLS plus the 180ms for the cryptographic operations as presented in Section 4.2. We confirmed with additional measurements, that the effect of WS-Security [14] encrypted and signed SOAP documents experiences comparable network delay contributions as with our SOAP only scenario.
The conclusion from these results is to locate the PDP close to the applications that need authorization and to use a persistent secure channel. One optimization could be, albeit not always applicable, to use optimistic authorization to start processing a request before the decision is taken and to discard and roll back changes to system upon a negative outcome.

5 Conclusion

XACML is a policy language for authorization that is gaining momentum in research and standardization. It can greatly simplify administration if it allows to regulate access to resources in distributed systems with one policy set. The success of XACML as enabler for unified policies depends on the extent existing applications are able to issue authorization requests and act upon authorization decisions. We harvest the power of XACML for applications by providing an authorization module for the PAM system. It is pluggable into existing applications and is stackable to authorize with a sequence of PDPs for one request. Applications that use PAM for authentication or account verification can directly benefit from the `pam_xacml` module without any changes to the code. XACML support can simply be enabled in the PAM configuration of the application. As this mechanism is restricted in the information that it can obtain from the application, and as the enforcement decision boils down to permitting or denying access to an application in total, an application interface for authorization is desirable. We introduce new message types for the PAM conversation function, to allow an application to express all parameters relevant for authorization, such as the requesting subject, accessed resources or intended actions. The authorization response can contain obligations to restrict permissible actions. The proposed `pam_xacml` messaging interface allows for more powerful authorization compared to legacy applications and can open a migration path for application developers towards full XACML support, by first supporting the new PAM message types for authorization and adding communication interfaces for direct communication with the PDPs later on. A measurement study on the impact of consecutive authorization decisions showed the cost of using unified policies in distributed systems. We expect `pam_xacml` to have great potential for bringing XACML support to existing systems and for realizing unified policies.

References

1. Rafae Bhatti, James Joshi, Elisa Bertino, and Arif Ghafoor. Access Control in Dynamic XML-Based Web-Services with X-RBAC. In Liang-Jie Zhang, editor, *Proceedings of the International Conference on Web Services, ICWS '03, June 23 - 26, 2003, Las Vegas, Nevada, USA*, pages 243–249. CSREA Press, 2003.
2. Scott Cantor, John Kemp, Rob Philpott, and Eve Maler. Assertions and Protocols for the OASIS Security Assertion Markup Language (SAML) V2.0. Standard, OASIS, March 2005.
3. David W Chadwick and Alexander Otenko. The PERMIS X.509 Role Based Privilege Management Infrastructure. In *SACMAT'02*. ACM, June 3-4 2002.
4. N. Damianou, N. Dulay, E. C. Lupu, and M. Sloman. Ponder: a language for specifying security and management policies for distributed systems. *Imperial College Research Report DoC 2000/1*, 2000.
5. Yuri Demchenko, Leon Gommans, and Cees de Laat. Using SAML and XACML for Complex Authorisation Scenarios in Dynamic Resource Provisioning. In *ARES '07: Proceedings of the The Second International Conference on Availability, Reliability and Security*, pages 254–262, Washington, DC, USA, 2007. IEEE Computer Society.
6. David Durham, Jim Boyle, Ron Cohen, Shai Herzog, Raju Rajan, and Arun Sastry. *RFC 2748: The COPS (Common Open Policy Service) Protocol*. The Internet Society, January 2000.
7. Kathi Fisler, Shriram Krishnamurthi, Leo A. Meyerovich, and Michael Carl Tschantz. Verification and Change-Impact Analysis of Access-Control Policies. In *ICSE '05: Proceedings of the 27th international conference on Software engineering*, pages 196–205, New York, NY, USA, 2005. ACM.
8. Grig Gheorghiu, Tatyana Ryutov, and Clifford Neuman. Authorization for Metacomputing applications. In *Proceedings of the 7th IEEE International Symposium on High Performance Distributed Computing*, July 28-31 1998.
9. Leon Gommans, Cees de Laat, Bas van Oudenaarde, and Arie Taal. Authorization of a QoS path based on generic AAA. *Future Gener. Comput. Syst.*, 19(6):1009–1016, 2003.

10. Martin Gudgin, Marc Hadley, Noah Mendelsohn, Jean-Jacques Moreau, Henrik Frystyk Nielsen, Anish Karmarkar, and Yves Lafon. SOAP Version 1.2 Part 1: Messaging Framework (Second Edition). W3C Recommendation, April 2007.
11. Rajeev Gupta and Manish Bhide. A Generic XACML Based Declarative Authorization Scheme for Java. In Sabrina De Capitani di Vimercati, Paul F. Syverson, and Dieter Gollmann, editors, *ESORICS*, volume 3679 of *Lecture Notes in Computer Science*, pages 44–63. Springer, 2005.
12. Sushil Jajodia, Pierangela Samarati, and V. S. Subrahmanian. A Logical Language for Expressing Authorizations. In *SP '97: Proceedings of the 1997 IEEE Symposium on Security and Privacy*, page 31, Washington, DC, USA, 1997. IEEE Computer Society.
13. L. Kagal, T. Finin, and A. Joshi. A policy language for a pervasive computing environment, 2003.
14. Christiaan Lamprecht and Aad van Moorsel. Performance Measurement of Web Services Security Software. In *21st UK Performance Engineering Workshop*, 2005.
15. Kelvin Lawrence, Chris Kaler, Anthony Nadalin, Chris Kaler, Ronald Monzillo, and Phillip Hallam-Baker. Web Services Security: SOAP Message Security 1.1 (WS-Security 2004). W3C Recommendation, February 2006.
16. M. Leech, M. Ganis, Y. Lee, R. Kuris, D. Koblas, and L. Jones. RFC 1928, SOCKS Protocol Version 5, June 1996.
17. R. Lepro. Cardea: Dynamic access control in distributed systems. Technical Report NAS Technical Report NAS-03-020, NASA Advanced Supercomputing (NAS) Division, Moffett Field, CA 94035, November 2003.
18. Markus Lorch, Seth Proctor, Rebekah Lepro, Dennis Kafura, and Sumit Shah. First experiences using XACML for access control in distributed systems. In *XMLSEC '03: Proceedings of the 2003 ACM workshop on XML security*, pages 25–37, New York, NY, USA, 2003. ACM.
19. Tim Moses. eXtensible Access Control Markup Language (XACML) Version 2.0. OASIS Standard, February 2005.
20. Heiko Niedermayer, Andreas Klenk, and Georg Carle. The Networking Perspective of Security Performance - a Measurement Study. In *MMB 2006, Nürnberg, Germany*, March 2006.
21. The Open Group. *Authorization (AZN) API*. Jan. 2000. ISBN: 1-85912-266-3.
22. Vipin Samar and Roland J. Schemers. Unified Login with Pluggable Authentication Modules (PAM). Open Software Foundation: Request For Comments RFC 86.0, October 1995.
23. John R. Vollbrecht, Pat R. Calhoun, Stephen Farrell, Leon Gommans, George M. Gross, Betty de Bruijn, Cees T.A.M. de Laat, Matt Holdrege, and David W. Spence. *RFC 2904: AAA Authorization Framework*. The Internet Society, Aug. 2000.

Teil VII

Kurzbeiträge

Enhancing Application Layer Multicast Solutions by Wireless Underlay Support

Christian Hübsch and Oliver P. Waldhorst

Institute for Telematics, University of Karlsruhe (TH), Germany

Abstract. Application Layer Multicast (ALM) is an attractive solution to overcome the deployment problems of IP-Multicast. We show how to cope with the challenges of incorporating wireless devices into ALM protocols. As a first approach we extend the NICE protocol, significantly increasing its performance in scenarios with many devices connected through wireless LAN.

1 Introduction

Novel Internet applications such as radio and TV broadcasting, live video streaming, video conferencing and multiplayer games increase the demand for multicast communication. Unfortunately, IP Multicast is far from global deployment due to administrative, technical and bussiness issues. Application Layer Multicast (ALM) is an attractive solution to cope with these issues, since it implements multicast functionality on end systems, where it can easily be installed as a piece of software. Several approaches for ALM have been proposed in recent years [5], including popular approaches like *Narada* [6] and *NICE* [1]. The latter is described shortly in Section 2. Recent work focuses on building resilience and efficiency in the ALM topologies by considering heterogeneous and short-lived devices [7] or building inner-node disjoint multicast trees [8]. Other recent work has shown how to transparently employ ALM for applications based on IP Multicast [9].

ALM protocols face new problems due to an increasing number of devices that connect to the Internet using wireless technology like wireless LAN or cellular connections. Typically, such devices decrease ALM performance since they have lower connection bandwidth or may be located in a shared medium with limited capacity. While some existing approaches like [2] address ALM in wireless ad-hoc domains, most protocols only refer to member node capacities, not considering heterogeneous underlay properties. In this paper, we propose to incorporate awareness for wireless devices into ALM protocols. We present an extension of NICE denoted as *NICE with WireLess Integration* (*NICE-WLI*) (Section 3). As major features, in NICE-WLI (1) all device within the same wireless LAN are represented by a single gateway node within the NICE ALM-topology and (2) gateway nodes are not assigned demanding tasks like cluster leadership. We present initial performance results showing that NICE-WLI significantly reduces the traffic load in the wireless network (Section 4). The work presented in this paper is part of the Spontaneous Virtual Network (SpoVNet) project

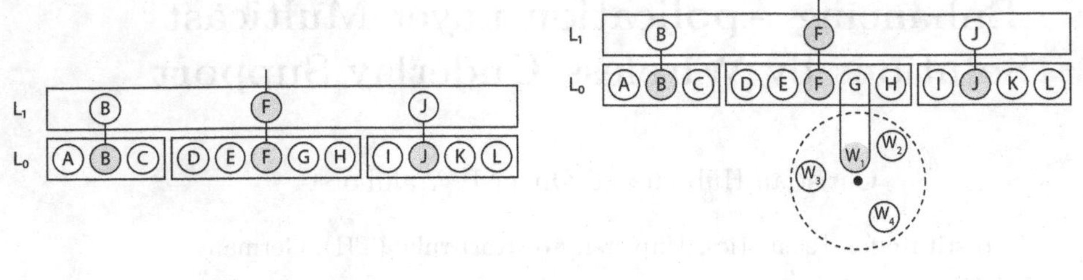

(a)The original NICE cluster hierarchy (b)Logical protocol parts in NICE-WLI

Fig. 1. The NICE cluster hierarchy and the NICE-WLI extension

(http://www.spovnet.de) and constitutes a step towards providing a SpoVNet group communication service.

2 Nice

The NICE protocol [1] is an overlay-based ALM protocol that has been developed in the context of the correspondent NICE project. NICE arranges its members in a hierarchical structure of clusters, aiming to provide communication in large scale groups. Members only exchange protocol maintenance messages inside the clusters they reside in, thus providing good scalability properties. Clustering is accomplished based on a distance metric between nodes (network latency in the original proposal). Each cluster in layer L_i elects a leader (starting with L_0 as the lowest layer), located in its graph-theoretic center. Cluster leaders form new logical clusters in a higher layer L_{i+1} which again elect leaders, resulting in a hierarchical structure of layered clusters. For data dissemination, cluster members send their data to all cluster neighbors, including the specific cluster leaders. The latter send the data to all nodes located in clusters they are leader of. Fig. 1(a) shows an exemplary hierarchy. We choose NICE for our considerations because of its popularity and good scalability properties. A detailed description can be found in [1].

3 NICE-WLI Protocol Design

This chapter describes the design of *NICE-WLI (NICE with WireLess Integration)* and its modifications to the original NICE protocol.

For employing NICE-WLI, we assume the existence of an out-of-band mechanism for discovering a node's local network context. This means every node is capable of knowing its connectivity properties, in case of NICE-WLI either the underlay connection via fixed network or its attendance in a particular wireless (WiFi) domain. In the latter case, also parameters like signal-to-noise ratio (SNR) to the access point as well as the used SSID is known.

The protocol enhancement is based on partitioning the overlay instance into two logical parts, the core part (which is identical with the conventional NICE) and the WiFi part. The WiFi part may split into multiple WiFi domains, each uniquely identified by the specific SSID and the access points' MAC address. In NICE-WLI, WiFi domains are handled as logical entities that are represented by exactly one L_0 cluster member in the overlay hierarchy (Fig. 1(b)). This member encapsulates the whole domain, both if it is the only WiFi node and if there are other nodes residing in the WiFi domain. This allows for minimizing wireless network traffic while keeping the wireless underlay drawbacks and properties out of the fixed network structure. The transition between the two protocol parts is accomplished by Gateway Nodes.

3.1 Gateway Nodes

A Gateway Node in NICE-WLI operates hybridly by communicating with the fixed network structure and also with the nodes in the connected WiFi domain. Being member of the WiFi domain itself, it is the only node in the WiFi domain that is also embedded in the NICE cluster hierarchy: Every Gateway Node is also a non-cluster-leader member in a L_0 cluster. A Gateway Node therefore represents all NICE members that are part of this WiFi domain and manages most protocol mechanisms and data forwarding. In Fig. 1(b), the Gateway Node is marked as W1. NICE-WLI always keeps Gateway Nodes out of the cluster leader disposition process. This is crucial, as one of the main design targets in NICE-WLI is communication efficiency and a cluster leadership may increase communication overhead in the Gateway Node up to $O(k \ log \ N)$ (k being the cluster size parameter in NICE) in the worst case, which is not desireable in shared mediums like WiFi domains. Also, cluster leaders occupy higher responsibility in terms of protocol stability, while WiFi domain members rather tend to be prone to errors. When more than one node resides in the same wireless domain, NICE-WLI aims at assigning the Gateway role to the one that is next to this domain's access point (in terms of SNR). Gateway Nodes define a new role a member can take in the overlay and are a key aspect in NICE-WLI.

3.2 Protocol Operation

This section describes the NICE-WLI protocol operation and how it handles to connect WiFi domains to an overlay instance efficiently. As long as members only join the overlay through fixed line connections, the overlay protocol operates as NICE does in its original proposal. As soon as a WiFi node wishes to join the overlay, it first checks the existence of a Gateway Node in the wireless domain. This is accomplished by broadcasting a *Gateway Discovery* message. Should no *Gateway Response* be received in a certain period of time, the node assumes to be the first overlay member in the specific WiFi domain and takes the role of the Gateway Node. Thereby it connects to the overlay and joins the L_0 cluster it belongs to in terms of network latency. If a Gateway Node responds to the *Discovery* in time, the joining node remains loosely coupled to the Gateway Node instead of joining the fixed network structure (W2, W3, W4 in Fig. 1(b)). Just like in the original NICE, nodes in NICE-WLI's core part exchange protocol information by sending periodic state messages (Heartbeats) to their cluster neighbors. This enables the current Gateway Node in a WiFi domain to inform the L_0 cluster members (especially the L_0 cluster leader) of its special role. By this, the cluster leader is capable of excluding the Gateway Node from the cluster leader determination process. Due to the central role of the Gateway Node, it should be chosen to have the best connectivity to the wireless network's access point. Because wireless nodes may be subject to mobility and varying conditions, NICE-WLI refines its roles periodically. Every node broadcasts its SNR per Heartbeat, enabling the Gateway Node to compare all participating members' quality of connection. Should one SNR exceed a specific difference to the current Gateway's (based on a Weighted Moving Average estimation), the Gateway role is transferred to this node, causing him to join the L_0 cluster. In case a node leaves the wireless domain, it has to be distinguished between Gateway Nodes and non-Gateway Nodes. In the latter case, the node may simply leave without any further protocol signaling, for no logical relationship had been established that should be released. If a Gateway Node leaves, it first has to sign off its L_0 cluster (like in NICE); additionally, it has to elect a new Gateway Node based on the current SNRs. If a Gateway Node leaves 'ungraceful', meaning the Gateway Node leaves unpredictably, both the NICE overlay and the wireless NICE-WLI part detect this by not receiving any further Heartbeats. The NICE overlay reacts like described in [1], while the wirless nodes begin to elect a new Gateway Node based on the SNRs they know from each others Heartbeats.

Finally, it may in some cases appear that two nodes take the role of the Gateway Node in a WiFi domain coincidentally. This may happen e.g. due to lost responses to *Gateway Discoveries*. In such cases, the Gateway Nodes recognize this situation by means of their mutual Heartbeat messaging and dissolve it. In phases of such duplicate Gateway Nodes, loops may occur in data forwarding (because both Gateway Nodes forward data they receive in the wireless domain to the fixed connection NICE part). To solve this, data packets hold a flag that marks them as being sent by a Gateway Node. If another Gateway Node receives such a packet, it does not forward the data, instead intiating the process of Gateway election to resolve the duplicate Gateway Nodes. In case data from wireless protocol parts reaches the core part anyhow, the specific L_0 cluster leader is able to detect duplicate packets based on their origin from Gateway Nodes from the same wireless domain.

3.3 Data Dissemination

While 3.2 described how NICE-WLI arranges nodes, this section discusses how data is disseminated in the overlay. Inside the core part, data is forwarded like desribed in [1], where cluster leaders send packets to all nodes located in clusters they are leader of. As soon as a data packet reaches a Gateway Node in a L_0 cluster, this Gateway Node has to disseminate the data in its WiFi domain, for there is no knowledge about the wireless part in the core parts. Additionally, the Gateway Node has to minimize wireless network traffic s.t. the medium is not occupied more than necessarily required. Therefore, upon reception in the

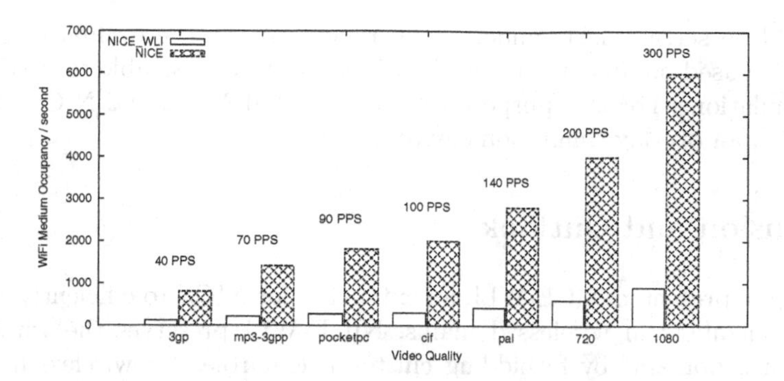

Fig. 2. Wireless Medium Occupancy in NICE-WLI

L_0 cluster, the Gateway Node broadcasts the data packet in its WiFi domain, reaching all protocol members with a single transmission.

Nodes in the wireless network wishing to send group-related data also broadcast their packets, reaching other wireless members including the Gateway Node. The Gateway Node then forwards the data to its L_0 cluster. While in the original NICE, cluster members unicast their data to all other cluster members and the cluster leader, this is different in NICE-WLI. To minimize the use of the shared medium, Gateway Nodes send data from the wireless network only to their L_0 cluster leader, allocating the medium only once. Knowing that the data's origin is a Gateway Node, the L_0 cluster leader disseminates the data to the remaining L_0 cluster members and all other nodes in clusters it is leader of.

4 Evaluation

In this section we analyze how much transmission overhead can be saved in WiFi domains by using NICE-WLI compared to NICE. In our estimation we assume an overlay of 1000 nodes of which are 5% connected through one wireless domain.

To appraise the savings in data dissemination, we have to presume an application that uses the overlay to send its data. In our case we look at video streaming in different quality levels, ranging from low-quality (3gp) to high-quality (HDTV) video. Fig. 2 shows the theoretic number of wireless media allocations, meaning how often the medium has to be allocated to transmit a packet to a wireless node, distinguished between the original NICE and NICE-WLI. Analysis with VLC [3] has shown that those qualities are connected to characteristic packet rates in data transfer (packets per second, approximated by PPS). We assume the video source to be a fixed overlay member node. In NICE, whenever a data packet has to be disseminated in the overlay (especially in the wireless domain), the packet has to be unicasted to every member node, allocating the shared medium. In NICE-WLI, the allocation is limited by broadcasting every data packet, reaching all wireless nodes with one transmission. We abstract from potential collisions and retransmissions in MAC layer. Clearly visible, the number of medium allocations in the WiFi domain is only a fractional amount of what it would be setting aside underlay awareness. While the evaluative estimation here is based on analytical considerations, we were also able to verify it based on simulations. For this purpose we implemented NICE and NICE-WLI in OverSim [4], an overlay simulation environment.

5 Conclusion and Outlook

In this paper we presented NICE-WLI, an extension for NICE to efficiently support overlay members in wireless domains. NICE-WLI preserves the wireless medium in such domains by forbidding cluster leader roles for wireless nodes while limiting protocol messaging and data dissemination overhead. This is promising, as more and more wireless domains arise, allowing connection to the Internet and its services, including application-layer solutions at a global scale. In the future we plan to evaluate the benefits in more detail, including exact MAC layer considerations and media allocation savings in cluster leadership prescription. Also, we look at how to minimize the drawbacks that come up with broadcasting (e.g. higher loss ratios in wireless environments).

This work is supported by the Landesstiftung Baden-Württemberg within the SpoVNet Project and by the "Concept for the Future" of the Karlsruhe Institute of Technology within the framework of the German Excellence Initiative. Additionally, we would like to thank Daniel Schmidt for his ideas and collaboration.

References

[1] Banerjee, S., Bhattacharjee, B., Kommareddy, G.: Scalable Application Layer Multicast. *Proc. SIGCOMM 2002*, Pittsburgh, PA, USA, 205–217, 2002.

[2] Bloedt, S.: Efficient End System Multicast for Mobile Ad Hoc Networks. *Proc. 2nd IEEE Annual Conf. on Pervasive Computing and Communications Workshops*, Orlando, FL, 75, 2004.

[3] VLC media player - The Cross-Platform Media Player and Streaming server. http://www.videolan.org/vlc/. September 2008.

[4] OverSim: The Overlay Simulation Framework. http://www.oversim.org/. September 2008.

[5] Hosseini, M., Ahmed, D.T., Shirmohammadi, S., Georganas, N.D.: A Survey of Application-Layer Multicast Protocols. *IEEE Communications Surveys & Tutorials* 9(3),58–74, 2007.

[6] Chu, Y., Rao, S., Seshan, S., and Zhang, H.: A case for end system multicast. *IEEE Journal on Selected Areas in Communications* 20(8), 1456–1471, 2002.

[7] Fu, X., Hogrefe, D., and Lei, J,: DMMP: A New Dynamic Mesh-based Overlay Multicast Protocol Framework. *Proc. 4th IEEE Consumer Communications and Networking Conf. (CCNC 2007)*, Las Vegas, NV, 1001–1006, 2007.

[8] Strufe, T., Wildhagen, J., and Schäfer, G.: Towards the construction of Attack Resistant and Efficient Overlay Streaming Topologies. *Electronic Notes in Theoretical Computer Science* 179, 111–121, 2007.

[9] Brogle, M., Milic, D., Braun, T.: Supporting IP Multicast Streaming Using Overlay Networks. *Proc. Int. Conf. on Heterogeneous Networking for Quality, Reliability, Security and Robustness (QShine 2007)*, Vancouver, Canada, 2007.

Strombasierte Struktur-Validierung von simple content in XML-Dokumenten

Jesper Zedlitz und Norbert Luttenberger

Christian-Albrechts-Universität zu Kiel
Institut für Informatik
AG Kommunikationssysteme

Zusammenfassung. XML-Dokumente mit einer großen Menge von *simple content* lassen sich bisher nur eingeschränkt überprüfen, da bei der Validierung hauptsächlich die Struktur des Dokumentenbaums, nicht jedoch des *simple content* selbst untersucht wird. In diesem Artikel wird am Beispiel des XML-basierten Datenformats *Observation and Measurements* (O&M)[1] vom Open Geospatial Consortium ein Verfahren vorgestellt, wie man solche XML-Dokumente speichereffizient validieren kann.

1 Einleitung

In verschiedenen Anwendungsumgebungen ist es erforderlich, große Mengen von schwach strukturierten[1] Daten als kompakte Textblöcke in XML-Dokumente einzubetten. Diese Vorgehensweise findet sich häufig z. B. bei der Übertragung und Archivierung von Sensordaten, die bei computergestützten Messungen anfallen.

Je nach Dauer und Umfang einer Messung möchte man diesen Strom nicht in seine einzelnen Komponenten (z. B. die einzelnen Messwerte) aufspalten und jede Komponente in ein Paar von XML *tags* "verpacken", da sich dadurch das Datenvolumen unangemessen vergrößern würde. Möchte man aber nun solche Messdaten mit anderen Forschern austauschen oder für eine spätere Auswertung abspeichern, dann empfiehlt es sich, Kontextinformation (z. B. Ort und Zeit der Messung, Kalibrierdaten usw.) gemeinsam mit den Sensordaten abzuspeichern. Die Kontextinformation bettet man in geeignete XML *tags* ein, wie sie z. B. vom Open Geospatial Consortium in den XML-basierten Sprachen O&M [1] und SensorML [2] definiert sind, und fügt dann dem Austauschdokument die "eigentlichen" Messdaten hinzu, indem man sie in ein XML-Element einbettet, dessen *content* gemäß XML Schema [3] als *simple content* spezifiziert ist, d. h. als Inhalt ohne tiefere XML-basierte Struktur.

XML-Dokumente, bei denen die Daten nicht mit der dazugehörigen Strukturbeschreibung übereinstimmen, deuten auf Fehler bei manueller Bearbeitung, fehlerhafte Hard- oder Software oder gar einen Manipulationsversuch hin. Je

[1] Unter schwach strukturierten Daten verstehen wir Daten mit positionsbasierter statt mit expliziter Typisierung, d. h. der Typ eines Datenelements ergibt sich aus der Position des Elements in einem Dokument bzw. in einem Datenstrom und der dazugehörigen, aber nicht enthaltene Strukturbeschreibung.

früher solche fehlerhaften Dokumente identifiziert werden, desto leichter fällt es, Maßnahmen zur Behebung der Fehlerquelle durchzuführen. Bei der Verarbeitung der Daten kann viel Aufwand gespart werden, wenn bereits im Vorfeld sichergestellt wurde, dass die Daten der erwarteten Struktur entsprechen. Dies triff nicht nur auf XML-Strukturen zu, sondern auch auf die Struktur von *simple content*, der in XML *tags* eingeschlossen. ist.

2 Validierung

Während für die Überprüfung der XML-Dokumentenstruktur Standardtechniken eingesetzt werden können, ergeben sich bei der Überprüfung der eigentlichen Nutzdaten eines O&M-Dokuments, die als *simple content* in einem XML-Element abgelegt sind, neue Probleme. Möglich wird eine Überprüfung der Nutzdaten erst dadurch, dass ihre Struktur im O&M-Dokument selbst definiert ist. Diese Struktur kann komplex sein und z. B. Listen variabler Länge enthalten, deren Größe erst innerhalb der Daten selbst festgelegt wird. Ein Beispiel für eine solche Definition in einem O&M-Dokument ist in Abb. 1 zu sehen. Es handelt sich um eine Messung, bei der zu einem Zeitwert und einer zweidimensionalen Ortskoordinate eine variable Anzahl von Meßwertpaaren (Druck und Temperatur) aufgezeichnet werden.

```
<elementType name="measurement">
  <DataRecord>
    <field name="time"><Time /></field>
    <field name="lat"><Quantity /></field>
    <field name="lon"><Quantity /></field>
    <field name="number-of-pairs"><Count gml:id="PAIR_COUNT" /></field>
    <field name="values">
      <DataArray>
        <elementCount ref="PAIR_COUNT" />
        <elementType name="value-pair">
          <DataRecord>
            <field name="pressure"><Quantity /></field>
            <field name="temperature"><Quantity /></field> ...
```

Abb. 1. Strukturdefinition für Meßwerte aus einem O&M-Dokument

Um eine speichereffiziente Validierung – gerade bei den hier typischerweise sehr großen XML-Dokumenten – zu ermöglichen, scheidet eine DOM-basierte XML-Verarbeitung, bei der das gesamte Dokument in den Speicher geladen wird, aus. Stattdessen wird eine strombasierte XML-Verarbeitung angewendet, bei der nur ein sehr kleiner Teil des Dokuments im Speicher gehalten werden muss.

Soll diese Technik bei Datenströmen (im Gegensatz zu Dateien, auf die Zugriff an beliebiger Stelle möglich ist) eingesetzt werden, ist es notwendig, dass die Struktur des *simple content*

1. unabhängig vom zu prüfenden Dokument im Voraus bekannt oder,
2. wenn sie im Dokument eingebettet ist, in Dokumentenreihenfolge vor dem *simple content* definiert wird.

Andernfalls müsste der gesamte Inhalt zwischengespeichert werden, bevor er gegen die später eingelesenen Strukturinformationen validiert werden kann – der Vorteil des geringen Speicherbedarfs bei der Validierung wäre dahin. Bei O&M ist diese Bedingung mit Fall 2 erfüllt, da das XML-Schema für O&M vorschreibt, dass die Elemente `elementType` und `encoding`, in denen Struktur und Serialisierung des *simple content* beschrieben sind, stets vor dem Element `values`, das die eigentlichen Messdaten enthält, stehen müssen (vgl. Abb. 2).

```
<DataArray>
  <elementCount>753</elementCount>
  <elementType name="measurement"><!-- siehe Abb. 1 --></elementType>
  <encoding>
    <BinaryBlock byteEncoding="base64" byteOrder="bigEndian">
  </encoding>
  <values>wEQAAAAAAABAdIZmZmZmZsBBgAAAAAAAQG22ZmZmZmbAPgAAAAAA
    AEBlvMzMzMzNwDkAAAAAAABAYBAAAAAAAMAOAAAAAAAAQFf49cKPXCnAL
  ...</values>
</DataArray>
```

Abb. 2. stark verkürzter Ausschnitt aus einem O&M-Dokument mit binärer Kodierung

Anders als bei der Validierung der Dokumentenstruktur üblich, wird hier kein Automat verwendet. Statt zu überprüfen, ob der nächste Wert passend ist (*push*), wird versucht, einen passenden Wert aus dem Datenstrom zu lesen (*pull*). Dies ist notwendig, da man bei binärem Inhalt mit variabler Länge (der möglicherweise noch über Datenelementgrenzen hinweg Base64-kodiert ist) nicht erkennen kann, wann ein Wert vollständig eingelesen ist und zur Überprüfung weitergereicht werden kann.

Bei Entscheidungsmöglichkeiten für gültige nächste Werte, wie es z. B. bei einer `union` in XML-Schema der Fall ist, kann es unter Umständen notwendig sein, mehrfach Daten auszulesen, und auf Gültigkeit zu überprüfen. Tauchen diese Entscheidungen selten – oder wie bei O&M gar nicht – auf, ist dies kein großer Nachteil für die Performance.

3 Validierung im Detail

Da es kein allgemeines Format zur Definition der Struktur von *simple content* gibt, müssen für die XML-basierte Sprache, in der die Grammatik des zu validierenden *simple content* beschrieben ist (im folgenden als SC-Schema bezeichnet), drei Komponenten erstellt werden:

1. Repräsentation der Strukturdefinition
2. passende Kontrollelemente
3. pull-Operationen für das schrittweise Einlesen des *simple content*

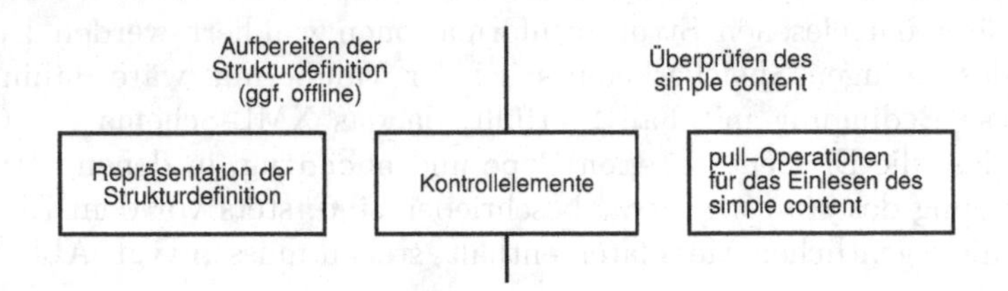

Abb. 3. Übersicht über die drei Komponenten und deren Einsatz während der Validierung

Mit diesen drei Komponenten und einem Programm, das das Zusammenspiel der Komponenten steuert, läuft die Validierung folgendermaßen ab: Vom XML-Parser werden Parser-Ereignisse entgegengenommen. Bei Auftreten der Strukturdefinition (bei O&M: `elementType`) wird im Speicher die *Repräsentation der Strukturdefinition* erzeugt und passende *Kontrollelemente* generiert. Sobald das XML-Element auftritt, das die Kodierung beschreibt (bei O&M: `encoding`), wird ein Objekt mit den zugehörigen *pull-Operationen für simple content* instantiiert. Sobald der XML-Parser den zu prüfenden *simple content* erreicht, wird der Datenstrom an die *Kontrollelemente* übergeben. Diese lesen mit Hilfe der *pull-Operationen für simple content* solange Zeichen aus dem Datenstrom, bis der Datenstrom vollständig abgearbeitet ist oder ein Fehler auftritt.

Im Folgenden werden diese drei Komponenten genauer beschrieben, wobei jeweils zunächst erläutert wird, was allgemein für jede Komponente zu beachten ist. Anschließend wird auf spezielle Aspekte bei der Verarbeitung von O&M-Dokumenten hingewiesen.

3.1 Repräsentation der Strukturdefinition

Damit der in einem XML-Dokument eingebettete *simple content* validiert werden kann, muss dessen Struktur bekannt sein. Diese Strukturinformation muss bei der strombasierten Verarbeitung extrahiert und in einer für die Validierung geeigneten Form zur Verfügung gestellt werden. Diese Aufgabe wird von der ersten Komponente übernommen. Beim Einlesen der Definition aus dem XML-Dokument muss beachtet werden, dass nur der Teilbaum in den Speicher geladen wird, der die Definition enthält und nicht unnötige Teile des Dokuments, die für großen Speicherverbrauch sorgen würden.

Wie in Abb. 2 zu sehen, ist bei O&M zu beachten, dass Teile der Strukturdefinition (`elementCount`, `elementType`) zusammen mit den Nutzdaten (`values`) Kindelemente eines gemeinsamen Elternelements (hier: `DataArray`) sind. Es darf daher nicht der gesamte Elternelement verarbeitet werden, sondern zunächst nur die Strukturdefinition.

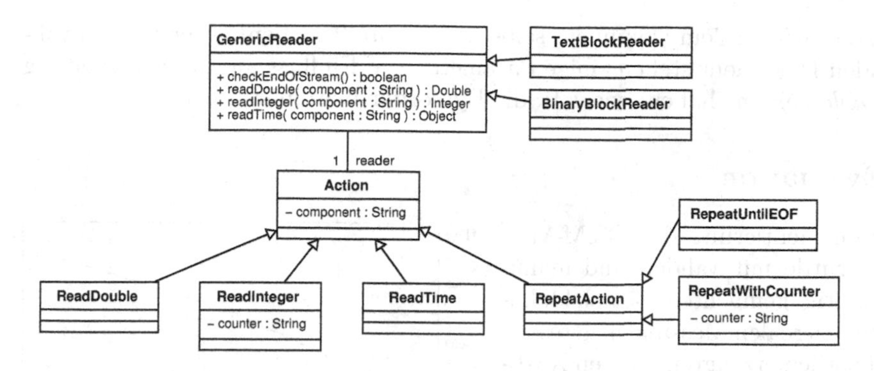

Abb. 4. Klassen der Kontrollelemente (Mitte) und Klassen mit pull-Operationen für simple content (oben) zum Validieren von O&M-Dokumenten

3.2 Kontrollelemente

Aus der mit Hilfe der ersten Komponente ausgelesenen Definition der Struktur werden speziell an das jeweilige SC-Schema angepasste Kontrollelemente erzeugt, die den Ablauf des Einlesens, d. h. der pull-Operationen, steuern. Dies sind typischerweise Aktionen zum Einlesen und Überprüfen eines Wertes und Konstrukte für Schleifen. Ein Kontrollelement liefert `false` zurück, wenn seine Aufgabe nicht erfüllt werden konnte, also der *simple content* an dieser Stelle nicht der vorgegebenen Struktur entspricht. Die Kontrollelemente arbeiten dabei unabhängig von der konkreten Serialisierung der Daten. Dazu greifen sie auf ein (jedoch vom jeweiligen SC-Schema abhängiges) Interface zu, das von den pull-Operationen (s. nächstes Kapitel), implementiert wird.

Bei O&M ist die Menge der Kontrollelemente recht übersichtlich:

- Lesen eines Wertes (double, integer, boolean, string, token, time)
- Wiederholen einer Menge von Aktionen bis zum Ende des Datenstroms
- n-faches Wiederholen einer Menge von Aktionen

3.3 pull-Operationen für simple content

Je nachdem, welche Arten von Serialisierung im SC-Schema vorgesehen sind, werden eine oder mehrere Klassen mit passenden pull-Operationen zum Verarbeiten des *simple content* Datenstroms erstellt. Da sie durch ein Interface von den übrigen Komponenten getrennt sind, muss hier über die Struktur der Daten nichts bekannt sein. Jede pull-Operation hat die Aufgabe, zu einem angeforderten Datentyp einen passenden Wert aus dem Datenstrom zu lesen. Enthält der Datenstrom an der aktuelle Position keinen Wert des Datentyps liefert die Operation einen Nullwert zurück.

Da für O&M zwei Arten von Serialisierung unterstützt werden sollen, benötigt man zwei Mengen von Operationen: pull-Operationen für `TextBlock` und pull-Operationen für `BinaryBlock`. Welche Opertion für ein Dokument eingesetzt wird, steht erst in dem Dokument selbst (vgl. Abb. 2). Ebenfalls erst im zu validierenden Dokument stehen einige Parameter, die Einfluss auf die Verarbeitung des *simple content* haben, wie z. B. die Byteorder bei binären Daten.

4 Evaluation

Die Implementierung des O&M-Validators wurde mit validen und manuell ungültig gemachten Beispieldokumenten aus realen Messungen getestet. Mit künstlich erzeugten, großen XML-Dokumente wurde untersucht, ob die Laufzeit linear von der Größe des Eingabedokuments abhängt. Abb. 5 zeigt, dass dies der Fall ist.

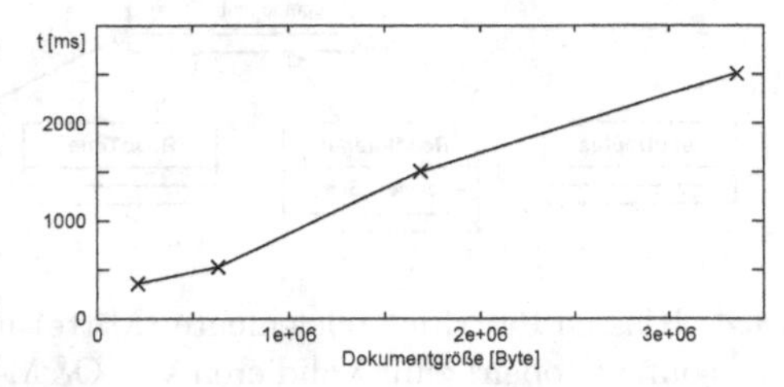

Abb. 5. Laufzeit der Validierung des *simple content*

Der Speicherverbrauch ist unabhängig von der Größe des zu verarbeitenden Dokuments und wird im Wesentlichen von der Länge einiger programminterner Puffer bestimmt, wie z. B. der vom XML-Parser am Stück gelesenen Zeichen aus dem *simple content* und der vorkonfigurierten maximalen Anzahl von Zeichen, die während der Verarbeitung eines `TextBlock` bei der Suche nach einem Trennzeichen eingelesen werden.

5 Ausblick

Es wurde gezeigt, wie man für SC-Schemas speicher- und zeiteffizient überprüfen kann, ob der in einem Dokument enthaltene *simple content* dieser Definition entspricht. Dieses Verfahren funktioniert auch dann, wenn das SC-Schema verschiedene Serialisierungen für die Daten verwendet, die zu unterschiedlichem Aussehen des *simple content* führen.

Manche XML-basierte Sprachen wie Scalable Vector Graphics (SVG) enthalten große Mengen *simple content* nicht nur in XML-Elemente sondern auch in XML-Attributen. Das vorgestellte Verfahren kann auch hierfür genutzt werden, jedoch müsste man dazu einen noch besser auf strombasierte Verarbeitung angepassten XML-Parser entwickeln, der alle Attribute eines Element nicht wie der SAX-Parser gemeinsam übergibt, sondern als einzelne Parser-Ereignisse.

Literaturverzeichnis

1. Cox, S. et al.: Observations and Measurements OpenGIS® Implementation Specification (2007)
2. Botts, M. et al.: Sensor Model Language (SensorML) OpenGIS® Implementation Specification (2007)
3. H. Thompson, D. Beech, M. Maloney, N. Mendelsohn et al.: XML Schema Part 1: Structures Second Edition W3C Recommendation (2004)

CLIO – A Cross-Layer Information Service for Overlay Network Optimization

Dirk Haage, Ralph Holz, Heiko Niedermayer, and Pavel Laskov

Wilhelm-Schickard-Institut für Informatik - Universität Tübingen, Germany

Abstract. New overlay-based services aim to provide properties like resilience, availability or QoS. To achieve this, automatic organization and optimization is required, which again demands accurate information on the network. Collecting and exchanging this data has a significant impact on the network, especially if several overlays are used on the same host. In this paper, we provide a survey of the current state of the art and identify challenges which must be addressed in order for new overlay-based services to be successful. We present our own solution CLIO, a cross-layer information service for overlays. CLIO provides information for the automatic creation and optimization of overlays. The service supports multiple overlays on the same node, the provided information is overlay-independent, and collected information is reused.

1 Introduction

The Internet's underlying infrastructure connects heterogeneous networks ranging from classic Ethernet to WiFi, or 3G mobile communication networks. However, the functionality of IP is often considered insufficient, as it lacks desired features such as group communication, path diversity, or quick adaptation to changes. Hence new services often deploy their own overlays on top of the Internet. A typical example is peer-to-peer based Voice-over-IP telephony, e.g. P2PSIP [1] and Skype [2].

Several proposals for the 'Future Internet' are based on self-organizing overlays. The Autonomic Network Architecture (ANA) [3], Ambient Networks [4] or our own work, SpoVNet [5], use overlays to streamline complex networks. SpoVNet provides e.g. an underlay abstraction and generic services for applications to simplify the utilization of overlays.

An essential problem to be addressed by all self-organizing overlay network architectures is overlay optimization under massive usage. In this paper, we identify the requirements and challenges of overlay optimization and present our concept of a cross-layer information service (CLIO) that is aimed at efficient overlay management.

2 Challenges and State of the Art

Overlays have various advantages: Thanks to independent routing and redundancy mechanisms, they can provide higher resilience and availability [6,7]. More complex services, e. g. end system multicast/anycast or distributed storage, are also possible. Overlays hide the details of the underlying network layers, leveraging simpler APIs for applications. Furthermore, it is possible to find alternative paths in the Internet providing better properties such as QoS, low latency, and resource availability[8].

However, these properties are hard to achieve without interaction between an overlay and the underlying layers. The following challenges faced by modern overlay-based applications can be identified:

Challenge 1: Application-Specific Overlay Optimization. Overlays must be optimized with regard to the requirements of the application that uses them. These requirements can differ widely. Video streaming in a multicast tree, e. g. requires participating nodes to offer certain bandwidths with respect to their upstream and downstream links. Massively multiplayer online games, on the other hand, require certain latencies between nodes. The requirements of applications that run on the same overlay can thus be in conflict, making it difficult to 'hardcode' an overlay that would satisfy all of them.

Challenge 2: Collecting Information About the Underlay. Knowledge about underlying layers allows better optimization of overlays. The challenge is to obtain accurate and reliable information about a dynamically changing underlay infrastructure. Some recent overlay implementations realize a limited measurement functionality, e. g. round-trip time measurements [9]. However, there are more possibilities to use network measurement results in overlays. Besides accuracy, a key requirement to such a measurement system is scalability with respect to the number of nodes in an overlay and the number of overlays on a host.

Challenge 3: Low Impact on the Network. Currently, the impact of overlay measurements on the network is relatively low, as most overlay networks make only little use of it, if at all. Measurement data intensively collected in many overlays can be quite voluminous. Hence, the applied mechanisms should minimize the measurement impact on the network by enabling the reuse and optimization of measurements across several overlays.

These challenges suggest a *consolidation* of the overlay measurement functionality in a dedicated component, denoted here as a 'cross-layer information service'. This component must clearly be distributed, as a centralized service contradicts all paradigms of self-organizing overlays. It should deliver measurements to applications via a well-defined and overlay-independent interface while minimizing the measurement effort by capitalizing on the 'economy of scale'. The following requirements are imposed on such a service.

Accuracy: The service must provide the most accurate information possible to multiple overlays running in parallel.

Efficiency: Resources must be used efficiently. The service must be scalable with respect to the number of overlays on a host, the number of nodes in each overlay and the number of overlays in a network. The measurement overhead (e. g. active measurements and inter-node communication) must be minimized.

Anonymity and Privacy: Privacy issues become important when data is shared between different entities. It is essential that the data acquired does not leak overlay-specific information between overlays (e. g. identity of nodes, etc.).

Simplicity: The complexity of information gathering must be hidden inside the service. Simple interfaces are essential for sharing information across hetergeneous overlays.

Conventional network management techniques do not meet these requirements. Most network management systems gather data at a central point of operation. The Management Information Base (MIB) concept of the Simple Network Management Protocol (SNMP) offers a good representation of data, but neither does SNMP provide a measurement infrastructure with a generic interface nor does it address overlays. Ganglia [10] is a tool for managing large distributed systems. However, it focuses on node properties rather than link properties, which are crucial for overlay optimization.

Most techniques for overlay optimization have been developed for one particular overlay, and often with respect to only one metric [11,9]. A more comprehensive approach is presented in [12]. The described routing underlay allows optimization of the overlay via primitives. The functions return the best metric-dependent next hop or a path between two hosts without revealing information to the requestor. Applications, however, can only use available metrics. Multi-dimensional metrics are not addressed.

Furthermore, several approaches are currently discussed to provide ISP-specific network information to overlay applications [13,14,15]. These concepts introduce a central point in a network sharing insight about the networks internal structure. In contrast to CLIO, these solutions do not involve end hosts but run entirely on a provider's infrastructure. Thus, CLIO can be seen as a concept that is complementary to these approaches.

3 CLIO – A Cross-Layer Information Service for Overlays

The design of CLIO is intended to address all the requiements specified in Section 2. As part of the SpoVNet architecture [5], CLIO is to be deployed in overlays in which applications can request connectivity with special requirements (e.g. security, latency, QoS) in an abstract way, and free from any network-specific concerns. Each application instantiates its own overlay with its own identifier space. An overlay can be optimized according to an application-defined metric. The goal of CLIO is to provide measurement information for optimization of application-specific overlays. Additional SpoVNet services, such as multicast or event notification, may instantiate their own overlays, therefore CLIO has to deal with multiple overlays, each with different optimization metrics. CLIO gathers a multitude of information and can remote-query other hosts for status information. A generic interface makes this data available to overlays on the host.

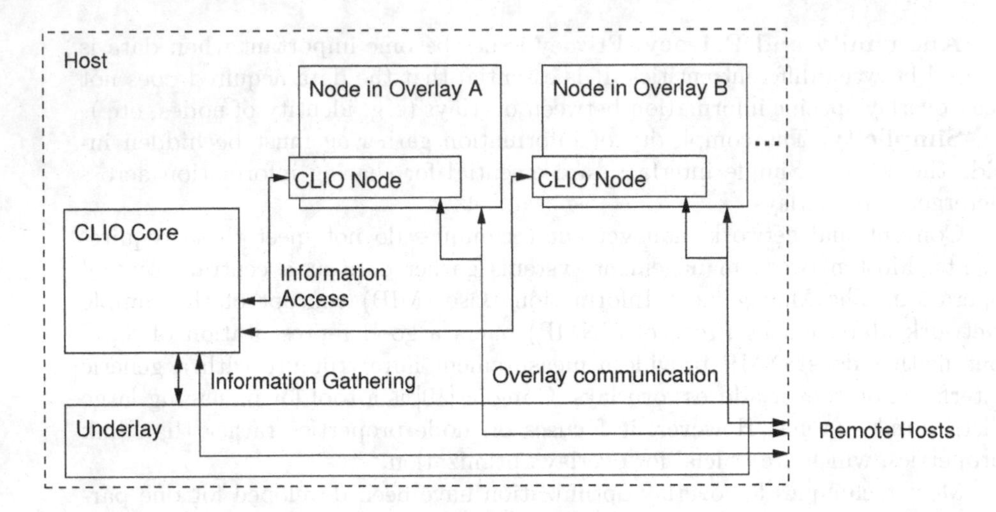

Fig. 1. The CLIO architecture and information flow.

3.1 Inner Workings

CLIO consists of two parts. This reflects the need for a component that operates on the semantics of the underlying networks and for a further component that can interact with the overlays on the host. The *Core Component* is responsible for most of the functionality: taking measurements and monitoring, pre-processing of data and data storage, and finally request management and aggregation. The *Node Component* is the link to an overlay node that uses CLIO. It provides the Interface for the applications to request data items. Furthermore, it gives the core access to selected overlays function, e. g. it resolves the overlay identifiers to underlay identifiers (i.e. IP addresses). The architecture and interaction of the components are shown in Figure 1. While the core component works in underlay notation (e. g. IP in the current Internet), the node component for each overlay uses the overlay-specific identifiers to deliver measurement results.

3.2 Data Representation and Generic Interface

Irrespective of its internal data structure, CLIO presents its information via key:value pairs. Data items can only be queried in overlay-specific notation. Each overlay sees the information based on its own namespace. Available data items have unique keys, e.g. RTT, or RTTDeviation. Data items can be node-specific information (e. g. network type, load) and link-specific (e. g. bandwidth, MTU, RTT), while a link is an underlay connection between to nodes.

Overlays access the data through the generic interface. This interface can remain stable even if the methods for the information gathering change. This enables later optimization or exchange of the measurement and prediction algorithms.

Queries can be made as a one-time request, a periodic update or a triggered notification when a value has changed. This allows flexible and asynchronous data access for the applications on the one hand, and efficient measurement scheduling for the CLIO service on the other. If two requests are made for the same data, CLIO attempts to execute the measurements only once. This also helps to reduce the number of measurements and the traffic for information exchange between nodes.

4 Discussion and Conclusion

The proposed cross-layer information service offers several features for automatic creation and maintenance of multiple overlay networks. These features can be classified into the following three categories.

Access to Information: CLIO offers a generic interface for gathering up-to-date network information. It enables overlay-based applications to optimize their communication without collecting this information themselves. This eases application development and allows efficient usage of resources. For security reasons, data is collected in the underlay notation and is translated for each overlay into its own overlay notation. Hence, it is not possible for an application to gain knowledge about other overlays running on the same host.

Efficient Data Maintenance: CLIO implements several mechanisms aimed at minimizing the impact on a network. Measurements are only initiated by request, consequently, unless CLIO is used by any overlay, resource usage is near zero. If a host is involved in several overlays with little or no overlap, CLIO has the same impact on a network as each overlay would have without using CLIO. For overlapping overlays, resource usage is reduced considerably by CLIO through measurement order aggregation and result caching. Furthermore, CLIO offers an important advantage for bootstrapping of overlays: Previously collected information is available immediately. This can speed up the creation and initial optimization of overlays.

Enhancing Services: The data collected by CLIO can be used for additional services. Even though the overlays work on top of a best-effort network, more complex requirements like 'probabilistic' QoS support can be addressed by the means of network measurements. Furthermore, applications can adapt to varying QoS levels by utilizing the up-do-date measurements. For example, if the desired quality of service cannot be met anymore, an application may try to obtain a different link from the base overlay software. A further attractive feature offered by our approach is the possibility of 'forward diagnostics'. Dynamically changing underlay infrastructures bear the risk of performance degradation as well as security incidents. The information provided by our service can be used to identify anomalous conditions *before* they affect the functionality. Thus, countermeasures can be initiated early enough, to maintain efficiency and resilience of both the overlay and CLIO.

We have implemented a first version of CLIO for use in a demonstrator including a number of measurement modules. We are currently continuing the development with the goal of carrying out performance measurements and evaluating its utility in the SpoVNet architecture.

References

1. P2PSIP Status Pages. http://tools.ietf.org/wg/p2psip/ (April 2008)
2. Baset, S.A., Schulzrinne, H.: An analysis of the Skype Peer-to-Peer Internet telephony protocol. arXiv:cs/0412017v1, http://arxiv.org/abs/cs/0412017v1 (2004)
3. ANA: Autonomic Network Architecture. http://www.ana-project.org/ (Feb 2008)
4. L. Cheng et al.: Service-aware overlay adaptation in Ambient Networks. In: Proc. of the International Multi-Conference on Computing in the Global Information Technology (ICCGI '06). (2006)
5. The SpoVNet Consortium: SpoVNet: An Architecture for Supporting Future Internet Applications. In: Proc. 7th Würzburg Workshop on IP: Joint EuroFGI and ITG Workshop on "Visions of Future Generation Networks". (2007)
6. D. Andersen et al.: Resilient overlay networks. In: Proc. of the 18th ACM symposium on Operating systems principles (SOSP 2001). (2001)
7. Gummadi, K., Gummadi, R., Gribble, S., Ratnasamy, S., Stoica, I.: The impact of dht routing geometry on resilience and proximity. In: Proc. 2003 Conference on Applications, Technologies, Architectures, and Protocols for Computer Communications. (2003) 381–394
8. Stefan Savage et al.: The end-to-end effects of internet path selection. SIGCOMM Comput. Commun. Rev. (1999)
9. A. Rowstron, P. Druschel: Pastry: Scalable, distributed object location and routing for large-scale Peer-to-Peer systems. In: Proc. of the IFIP/ACM International Conference on Distributed Systems Platforms, Heidelberg, Germany (Middleware 2001). (2001)
10. Ganglia Monitoring System. http://ganglia.info (April 2008)
11. J. Han et al.: Topology aware overlay networks. In: Proc. 24th Annual Joint Conference of the IEEE Computer and Communications Societies (INFOCOM 2005). (2005)
12. A. Nakao et al.: A routing underlay for overlay networks. In: Proc. of the 2003 conference on Applications, Technologies, Architectures, and Protocols for Computer Communications (SIGCOMM '03). (2003)
13. Aggarwal, V., Feldmann, A.: Locality-aware p2p query search with isp collaboration. Networks and Heterogeneous Media **3**(2) (2008)
14. Xie, H., Yang, Y.R., Krishnamurthy, A., Liu, Y.G., Silberschatz, A.: P4p: provider portal for applications. SIGCOMM Comput. Commun. Rev. **38**(4) (2008) 351–362
15. Hilt, V., Rimac, I., Tomsu, M., Gurbani, V., Marocco, E.: A Survey on Research on the Application-Layer Traffic Optimization (ALTO) Problem. Internet-Draft draft-hilt-alto-survey-00, Internet Engineering Task Force (July 2008) Work in progress.

Improving TCP's Robustness to Packet Reordering

Arnd Hannemann Alexander Zimmermann Lennart Schulte

Department of Computer Science, Informatik 4
RWTH Aachen University, Ahornstr. 55, 52074 Aachen, Germany
{hannemann,zimmermann,schulte}@nets.rwth-aachen.de

Abstract. TCP was designed for fixed, wired networks. As a result TCP performs suboptimal in networks with a high degree of parallelism and frequent topology changes, e.g., in wireless mesh networks. One reason for this is standard TCP's behavior in presence of packet reordering.
In this paper we introduce a novel backwards compatible method how TCP's performance can be improved in face of packet reordering. Our scheme is a receiver only modification that enables detection of packet reordering and appropriately changes TCP's behavior. It also employs already established TCP extensions. This paper presents preliminary evaluation results of the implementation in our testbed.

1 Motivation

The most widespread transport protocol within the Internet today is the Transmission Control Protocol (TCP). Ideally, TCP should work efficiently under any network condition. But the standard TCP was optimized for wired networks and shows shortcomings in newly emerging networks like wireless mesh networks (WMNs). One reason is that most algorithms around TCP were designed with the premise that all packets arrive in the same order as they were send. While even in the Internet this assumption is not always true (see [1]), it is certainly false for networks with a high degree of parallelism (e.g., link aggregation or multipath routing in WMNs).

The main cause of performance degradation of TCP flows experiencing packet reordering is TCP's coupling between error and congestion control mechanisms. It is based on the assumption that packet loss is an indication of network congestion. Upon detection of a packet loss TCP retransmits the presumably lost packet and backs off its transmission rate by decreasing its congestion window (CWND). Thereby, TCP uses two strategies to detect packet loss.

The first one is the absence of acknowledgements for a certain time, also referred to as the retransmission timeout (RTO). When such a timeout occurs, the TCP sender will enter the *slow-start* phase and reset its congestion window to one segment.

The second strategy relies on feedback from the receiver that packets other than the next expected one arrived. By means of the sequence number contained in each packet the receiver generates a duplicate acknowledgment (DUPACK) for every *out-of-order* packet. If the sender receives a certain number (called duplicate acknowledgment threshold (DUPTHRESH)) of such DUPACKs it will consider the segment referred to by the DUPACKs to be lost and perform a *fast retransmit* accompanied with a reduction of the CWND. In standard TCP implementations DUPTHRESH is equal to 3. It is important to note that modern TCP implementations use variations like SACK-TCP [3] or forward acknowledgment (FACK) [5] of the above scheme, if the TCP selective acknowledgment (SACK) option was negotiated for a given TCP flow.

In case of real packet loss the fast retransmit scheme can severely speed up TCP's loss recovery and increase overall performance. But it becomes also clear that the assumption that out-of-order packets indicate packet loss and therefore congestion is no longer true when a TCP flow is experience packet reordering. If segments arrive out-of-order at the receiver due to reordering, they will cause spurious retransmits and unnecessary CWND reductions.

2 Related Work

In literature there are several methods which try to improve TCP performance in the presence of packet reordering. For example approaches like RR-TCP [2] and TCP-NCR [8] attempt to improve the robustness against reordering by raising DUPTHRESH at the TCP sender, to avoid spurious retransmissions and unnecessary CWND reductions.

While TCP-NCR sets DUPTHRESH unconditionally to CWND, regardless whether packet reordering is happening in the network or not, the authors of RR-TCP point out that increasing DUPTHRESH is not without cost. Greater DUPTHRESH values make the TCP sender react more slowly on real packet drops thus increases latency for upper layers and receivers will need more buffer space to buffer all out-of-order segments until missing segments finally arrive.

RR-TCP addresses these problems by aggregating reordering events into a histogram and uses this histogram to adjust the DUPTHRESH in a way such that it corresponds to a certain percentage of avoided spurious fast retransmits. The authors showed increased throughput performance compared to SACK-TCP. However, their approach has some serious drawbacks. The additional state which is needed at the TCP sender is not marginal and because a significant number of reordering events is needed to construct a meaningful histogram this method is only suitable for long lived flows.

The authors of the sender-only modification TCP-PR [4] propose to entirely ignore DUPACKs and duplicate selective acknowledgments (DSACKs) for loss recovery purposes and suggest to utilize timers instead. Such timers similar to the RTO timer should indicate whether a segment got lost or not. However, for this method to work especially in networks like WMNs, where delay spikes are very common, a large minimum timeout value must be chosen to avoid spurious retransmission. Thereby the TCP connection may stale for long times in case of real packet losses.

The authors of [7] take an entirely different approach. Their receiver side modification aims specifically at recovering from reordering induced by a link-layer retransmission scheme, which does not attempt to deliver packets in-order. With the delayed duplicate acknowledgement scheme the TCP receiver delays DUPACKs, which would trigger fast-retransmit at the sender, for a certain amount of time. That is the TCP receiver responds to the first two subsequent out-of-order segments with immediate DUPACKs but refrains from sending further DUPACKs in response to out-of-order segments. Instead upon arrival of the third out-of-order segment a timer is started. If this timer expires before the next expected segment arrives all deferred DUPACKs are released. Otherwise they are just discarded. Their scheme is applied regardless whether reordering is perceived or not with a fixed value for the delay.

In our proposal we pick up the idea of deferring information, which would needlessly trigger retransmission at the receiver side and extend the scheme to dynamically adjust itself to the actual network conditions.

3 Algorithm

The basic idea is a receiver only modification where the requirement of sending acknowledgments (ACKs) directly in response to out-of-order segments is relaxed when reordering in the network is detected. However, standard TCP behaviour should not be altered in case no reordering is present. Furthermore, DUPACKs should be delayed exactly long enough, to resolve the expected reordering and short enough to recover as fast as possible from real packet loss.

The proposed modification consists of two parts. The first part is a mechanism to detect and determine the degree of segment reordering at the receiver side. The second part is an appropriate reaction on detected reordering. To detect reordered packets the proposed solution utilizes the TCP timestamps option. To measure the degree of reordering the *reordering late time offset* [6], which indicates the lateness in terms of buffer time that is needed to resolve the reordering, is computed for each reordered packet.

To calculate the reordering late time offset for an incoming segment, the out-of-order queue is searched for segments which must have been sent after the incoming segment, by comparing the sequence number and timestamp value of the incoming segment with every entry in the out-of-order queue. If the incoming segment is a retransmitted segment, only entries with a timestamp value which is genuinely greater than the segment's timestamp value are considered to be sent afterwards by the TCP sender. If the incoming segment is an original transmission, entries, which have an equal timestamp value but a larger sequence number, are considered to be sent afterwards as well. The late time offset can then be calculated by subtracting the earliest reception time of the mentioned out-of-order entries from the segment's receive time.

To decide, whether the incoming segment is a retransmission or not, the out-of-order queue is searched for an entry, that has a larger sequence number and at the same time a smaller timestamp value than the incoming segment. Such an entry indicates that the incoming segment was sent after a segment with higher sequence number was already transmitted.

To keep the additionally needed state minimal a weighted average of the late time offset over the detected reordering events is computed, similar to what is done to calculate the TCP retransmission timer. The proposed method updates the exponentially weighted moving averages (EWMAs) for every k-th reordering event (an incoming segment which is classified as beeing reordered) with a reordering late time offset of $\mathtt{OFF}_k$ as follows:

$$\begin{aligned} \mathtt{SOFF}_k &= (1-\alpha)\cdot \mathtt{SOFF}_{k-1} + \alpha \cdot \mathtt{OFF}_k \\ \mathtt{SOFFVAR}_k &= (1-\beta)\cdot \mathtt{SOFFVAR}_{k-1} + \beta \cdot \ \mathtt{SOFF}_{k-1} - \mathtt{OFF}_k \end{aligned}$$

$\mathtt{SOFF}_1$ and $\mathtt{SOFFVAR}_1$ are initialized upon detection of the first reordering event with $\mathtt{OFF}_1$ and $0.5\cdot\mathtt{OFF}_1$ respectively. α and β are configurable smoothing factors between 0 and 1.

The reaction on detected reordering consists of delaying DUPACKs, beginning with the third DUPACK caused by subsequent out-of-order segments. If the next expected in-sequence segment arrives in time, all scheduled DUPACKs are discarded. Otherwise, outstanding DUPACKs are released. The time for which DUPACKs are delayed is computed with help of the average measured reordering late time offset. This implies that DUPACKs are never delayed, if the affected connection never experienced any reordering. Moreover, DUPACKs are never delayed for more than 100ms to avoid spurious RTOs.

The deferral time is given by $\mathtt{DEFTIME} = \min\ \mathtt{SOFF} + m\cdot\mathtt{SOFFVAR}, 100\mathrm{ms}$. The factor m is used to weight the variance estimator.

4 Implementation

We implemented our proposed scheme in our testbed UMIC-Mesh.net [9]. UMIC-Mesh.net is a hybrid wireless mesh network testbed, setup in the complex of the Computer Science buildings at the RWTH Aachen University. Currently, 51 mesh routers are deployed in two four-story buildings. All mesh routers are located in different offices at different floors. Unlike wireless-friendly cubicle environments, our buildings have rooms with floor-to-ceiling walls and solid wooden doors. Thus, three routers were distributed across every floor. For a more complete description of the testbed, we refer to [9].

The algorithm proposed in this paper is based on the vanilla Linux kernel in version 2.6.24.3. The evaluation scenario consists of a TCP sender connected to a wired backbone, within the Internet and a TCP receiver, which is located in our testbed. The receiver communicates wirelessly with a mesh gateway over two wireless links which are operated on different frequency bands (2.4GHz and 5.8GHz) establishing two separate paths from the mesh gateway to the TCP receiver.

For evaluation four different TCP variants were used, namely NewReno, SACK-TCP, FACK and NewReno with the modifications described in this paper. For each variant three different test-runs were performed, where the server performs bulk TCP transfers to the client while the aggregated throughput is measured. In test-run A only one flow is used to transfer data from the server to the client in a way that only one wireless link is utilized. This test-run is performed to determine the throughput of one single flow of the tested TCP variant without packet reordering present. In Test-run B the server transfers data to the client with enabled link aggregation, employing both wireless links. Thereby the TCP connection will likely experience serious reordering. The last test-run C runs without link aggregation, but with two wireless links employed. This is achieved by utilizing two parallel TCP connections with different destination addresses. To compute the throughput of this run the throughput of both flows is combined. Because no reordering is induced the combined value should indicate the maximum achievable throughput with link aggregation, if TCP were absolutely immune to packet reordering.

Every combination of test-run and TCP variant was repeated for 250 times. This lead to a total of 3000 measurements. The averages computed from these values are shown in Figure 1. As one can see run A and C show the same results regardless of the TCP variant. This was expected since no reordering takes place in any of those runs. The fact that the modified NewReno variant has equal performance with the other TCP variants in test-run A and test-run C shows that the adaptive reordering detection indeed works, i.e. no performance degradation, if no packet reordering is present. The results of test-run B show that standard TCP implementation experience severe performance degradation in face of packet reordering. Test-run C shows an average throughput of approximately 36.6 Mb/s. In test-run B NewReno achieved in average 22.75 Mb/s. If 36 Mb/s is considered the maximum possible, it uses only 63.2% of the available bandwidth, SACK-TCP and FACK perform even slightly worse. The gain achieved by our modified NewReno is 4.74% compared to standard NewReno.

5 Conclusion and Future Work

As discussed in section 1 and verified by measurements presented in section 4, existing TCP implementations experience problems when used in networks that induce packet reordering. We presented and evaluated a novel method how a TCP receiver can be modified to improve TCP's robustness to packet reordering.

The paper presents preliminary results only. Although, the proposed modification showed a decent performance boost, roughly one third of the theoretically possible bandwidth remained unused. Further research is needed to explore possibilities to use this idle bandwidth.

In the used implementation reasonable but arbitrary values for the weighting factors within the late time offset mean and variance estimator were used. Hence, future work should evaluate how to tune these variables, for instance by investigation of measured reordering late time offsets in real-world scenarios.

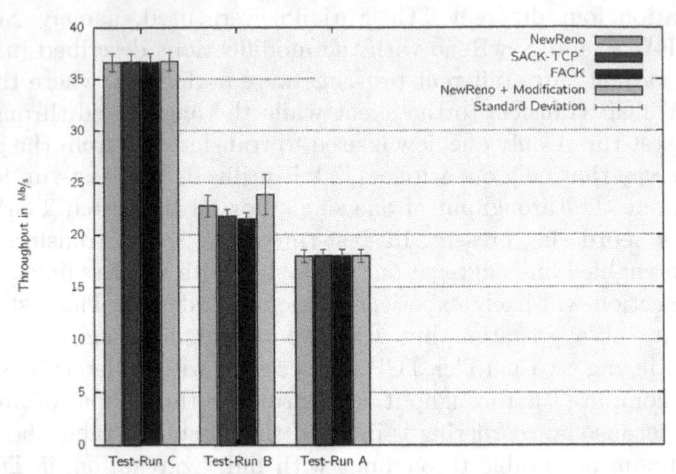

Fig. 1. Average throughput per run and TCP variant

References

1. J. C. R. Bennett, C. Partridge, and N. Shectman. Packet reordering is not pathological network behavior. *IEEE/ACM Transactions on Networking*, 7(6):789–798, 1999.
2. Bhandarkar, A. L. N. Reddy, M. Allman, and E. Blanton. Improving the robustness of TCP to non-congestion events. RFC 4653, August 2006.
3. E. Blanton, M. Allman, K. Fall, and L. Wang. A conservative selective acknowledgment (SACK)-based loss recovery algorithm for TCP. RFC 3517, April 2003.
4. S. Bohacek, J. P. Hespanha, J. Lee, C. Lim, and K. Obraczka. TCP-PR: TCP for persistent packet reordering. In *Proc. of the 23rd Int. Conf. on Distributed Computing Systems (ICDCS '03)*, page 222, Washington, DC, USA, 2003. IEEE Computer Society.
5. Matthew Mathis and Jamshid Mahdavi. Forward acknowledgement: Refining TCP congestion control. In *Proc. of the Special Interest Group on Data Communication (SIGCOMM '96)*, pages 281–291, 8 1996.
6. A. Morton, L. Ciavattone, G. Ramachandran, S. Shalunov, and J. Perser. Packet reordering metrics. RFC 4737, November 2006.
7. Nitin H. Vaidya, Milten N. Mehta, Charles E. Perkins, and Gabriel Montenegro. Delayed duplicate acknowledgements: a TCP-unaware approach to improve performance of TCP over wireless. *Wireless Communications and Mobile Computing*,2(1):59–70, 12 2001.
8. M. Zhang, B. Karp, S. Floyd, and L. Peterson. RR-TCP: A reordering-robust TCP with DSACK. In *Proc. of the 11th IEEE Int. Conf. on Networking Protocols (ICNP '03)*, pages 95–106, 2003.
9. Alexander Zimmermann, Daniel Schaffrath, Martin Wenig, Arnd Hannemann, Mesut Güneş, and Sadeq Ali Makram. Performance evaluation of a hybrid testbed for wireless mesh networks. In *Proc. of the 4th IEEE Int. Conf. on Mobile Ad-hoc and Sensor Systems (MASS'07)*. IEEE Computer Society Press, 2007.

Banishing Patch-Cables from LAN Parties
Using Ad-hoc P2P Multicast as a Substitute?

Peter Baumung

Institute of Telematics, Universität Karlsruhe (TH)

Abstract. Although playing real-time multi-player games online over the Internet became more and more popular in the past few years, people still enjoy meeting for so-called *"LAN Parties"* because of higher social interaction. As the number of participants increases, the deployment of the required infrastructure (i.e. the LAN) however gets more and more bothersome. With the current availability of computers featuring WLAN support, substituting the LAN by an infrastructureless ad-hoc network seems a long awaited and time-saving step. This paper investigates how the wireless environment, its scarce bandwidth and the strong requirements of multi-player games regarding packet latencies constrain the number of a WLAN party's participants.

1 Introduction

With increasing bandwidth available in private Internet connections, online and real-time multi-player games (such as first person shooters) became more and more popular in the past years. A major and well-known drawback of these games however is the lack of social interaction, since players never get a true impression of their opponents. Although a regression is noticeable, the convenience of private Internet connections could not cause online games to fully supersede so-called *LAN Parties*. Here, people actually *meet* in one locality and run their favourite game over a locally deployed infrastructure, i.e. a *local area network* (LAN).

Although they get more and more cumbersome to deploy for an increasing number of participants, LANs have been the standard communication infrastructure of LAN parties for more than a decade. Interestingly, however, the devices interconnected within the LAN have evolved: Indeed, with the increasing performance of notebook computers, people have welcomed the relief of carried weight and required space. As they are commonly equipped with WLAN adapters, notebooks however can, with their WLAN adapters switched to *ad-hoc mode*, communicate without the need of any infrastructure. To provide an adequate support for games one must, on the one hand, bear in mind the traffic emitted by typical applications and, on the other hand, understand the differences when migrating from a fixed to a wireless network.

In current multi-player games, one dedicated node usually acts as a *server node* which in a first step gathers *position and velocity updates* as well as *event information* (use of weapons or "respawns") from all player nodes. In a second step, this data is sent equally to all player nodes. For achieving accurate movements in the game both steps are performed 25 times per second.

With a (semi-)broadcast medium becoming available in a wireless environment, the resulting number of medium accesses (possibly several hundreds per second) has a key impact on the success of data forwarding and thus affects the gaming experience. Indeed, with the information requiring to be delivered to other players within about $150ms$ [1], colliding medium accesses and resulting exponential back-off times used by WLAN adapters for resolving collisions can quickly lead to rising latencies and, thus, a worsening gaming experience.

In the following section we propose a strategy for keeping the number of medium accesses needed for data forwarding as low as possible. We then evaluate the strategy within standard LAN party scenarios by referring to network simulations: We thus study the wireless medium's impact on the feasibility of WLAN parties and investigate the effect of different MAC configurations. Eventually, we conclude the paper by giving a short summary.

2 Ad-hoc P2P Multicast as a Patch-Cable Substitute

For enabling communication within the wireless environment we rely on P2P multicast approaches, since these can easily be deployed and do not require operating system extensions as multicast routing protocols would. With P2P multicast protocols, an *overlay network* (such as [2,3]) is set up between all player nodes using standard transport links as e.g. provided by UDP. The overlay network is used for forwarding a player's periodic updates to all player nodes. As shown in Fig. 1.a), this "standard" overlay forwarding causes data dissemination to be highly inefficient: This results from the consecutive medium accesses that are required for forwarding a single update to all player nodes. Since in LAN party scenarios, however, player nodes usually find themselves very close to each other, the communication's efficiency can be improved by using the wireless medium's broadcast capability. To do so, we employ our technique of *Local Broadcast Clusters* (LBCs, [4]), which works as follows.

Whenever a player node joins the game, it attempts to detect a so-called *virtual server* by listening for the latter's periodic heartbeats. On a successful detection the player node becomes an *LBC player node* and uses the virtual server for data dissemination as detailed below. If, however, the server detection fails, the player node declares itself as a new virtual server. By periodically emitting heartbeats via broadcasts the new virtual server creates its LBC and, hereby, provides access for other joining player nodes. Note that, in contrary to LBC player nodes, virtual servers *do* join the overlay network. They, thus, become *overlay player nodes* that are interconnected via overlay links.

When an LBC player node emits a position and velocity update, the information is sent to the nearby virtual server. The latter, using a broadcast, forwards the update to other LBC player nodes in its vicinity. Additionally, the virtual server sends the information via potentially existing overlay links to distant virtual servers. These then take care of broadcasting the information to their respective LBC player nodes. As a consequence, this technique does not require all player nodes to be within each other's transmission range: Given the existence

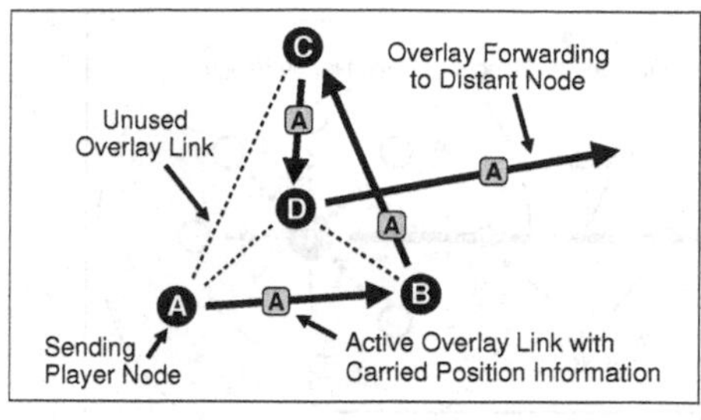

a) "Standard" Overlay Forwarding

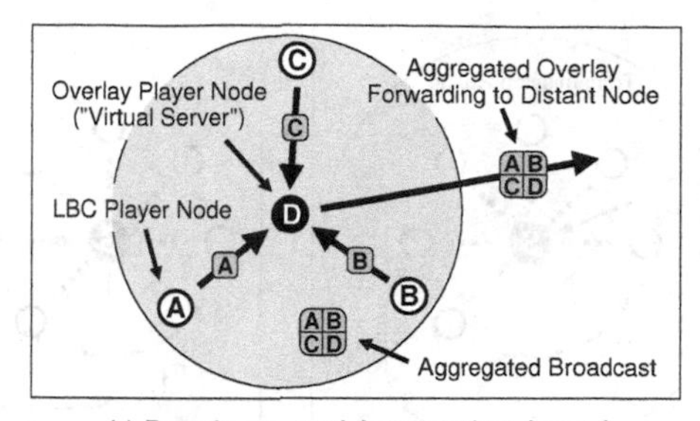

b) Broadcast- and Aggregation-based Overlay Forwarding

Fig. 1. Standard vs. broadcast and aggregation-based overlay forwarding.

of a multi-hop routing protocol, we also provide support for fully distributed, multi-hop WLAN parties.

To further reduce the number of required medium accesses we apply a special data aggregation strategy: A virtual server receiving an update from an LBC player node not immediately forwards the information. Instead, the information is buffered until the virtual server sends its next own update. Note that the delay implied by buffering is included in the forwarded updates: This enables player nodes to extrapolate the movement of other players according to the latter's position and velocity information. The entire mechanism of broadcast and aggregation based data forwarding is depicted in Fig. 1.b). Also note that the buffering delay of up to $40ms$ constrains the number of times updates can be buffered before reaching the critical latency of $150ms$.

3 Scenario Modelling

In this paper we study two different WLAN party scenarios. For the first scenario, visible in the left of Fig. 2, player nodes are placed, as in a typical LAN party scenario, within an area of 20x20m^2. The player node in the area's centre is the first to join the game. It, thus, becomes a virtual server and provides access to all other nodes which, hence, become LBC player nodes. As we increase the number of players, we expect the latencies of player updates to rise and, at some point, reach the critical threshold of $150ms$. Since we ascribe this to an increasing number of colliding medium access and ongoing MAC retransmissions, we in this paper investigate a second, distributed scenario.

As shown in the right of Fig. 2, the distributed scenario reduces the number of medium accesses around the server by splitting a large WLAN party into two smaller clusters. The resulting scenario, thus, consists of two virtual servers which gather player updates from their respective LBC player nodes. Using the (multi-hop) overlay link each virtual server then forwards the gathered and aggregated information to the distant virtual server which, then, broadcasts the information to its LBC player nodes with its own, next update.

We assume a constant size for position and velocity information and a variable size of additional event information. We thus model traffic by letting each player

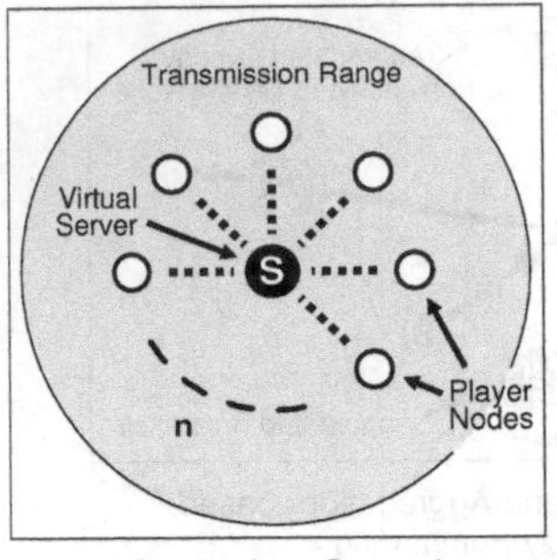

a) Single–hop Scenario

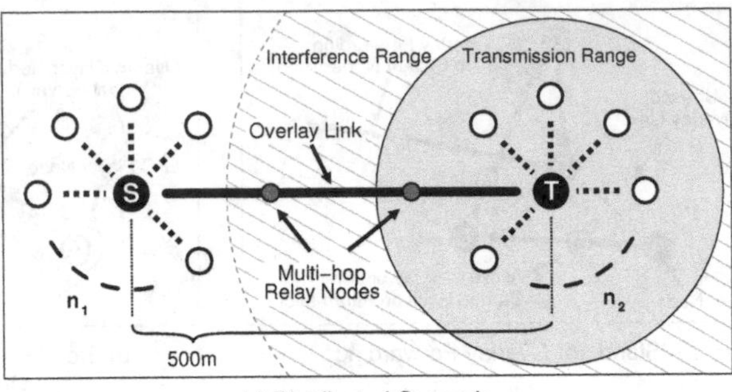

b) Distributed Scenario

Fig. 2. Single-hop and distributed scenario as modelled for the investigations.

node send a packet with a size randomly chosen between 32 and 48 bytes every 40*ms*. Depending on the actual number of participating players, the resulting size for aggregated player information reaches several hundred bytes and potentially more than 1 KByte.

The simulation experiments were conducted with GloMoSim [5] featuring IEEE 802.11b with 2 MBit/s as MAC and AODV for establishing routes in the distributed (multi-hop) scenario. Unless otherwise stated, transmission power is set to 3.9*dBm*, resulting in a transmission range of 175*m* and an interference range of 353*m* respectively. While the interference range shows to be uninteresting for the first scenario, it is of major importance in the distributed scenario. Indeed, when splitting the WLAN party, it must be guaranteed that the communication inside each cluster does not affect the distant cluster. Considering the transmission and interference range we, thus, place the virtual servers 500*m* from each other. We bridge the distance using 2 multi-hop relay nodes (resulting in a 3 hop overlay-link) which only forward traffic and do not join the game.

4 Simulation Results

The results of our simulation experiments are obtained using 40 random number generation seeds and shown in Fig. 3. While we plot the number of participating players on the x axis, we show the percentage of updates with a latency beyond 150*ms* (classified as “not delivered in time”) on the y axis including 95% confidence intervals.

As can be seen for the single-hop scenario, the amount of updates that are delivered with a latency above 150*ms* can be neglected for up to 21 players. With the 22nd player joining, however, about 5% of all updates are no longer delivered in time, perceivable through a worsening gaming experience. With more players joining delays drastically increase, resulting in an unacceptable game performance.

Despite the reduction of medium accesses around the virtual servers, the distributed scenario shows a performance far worse than the original single-hop

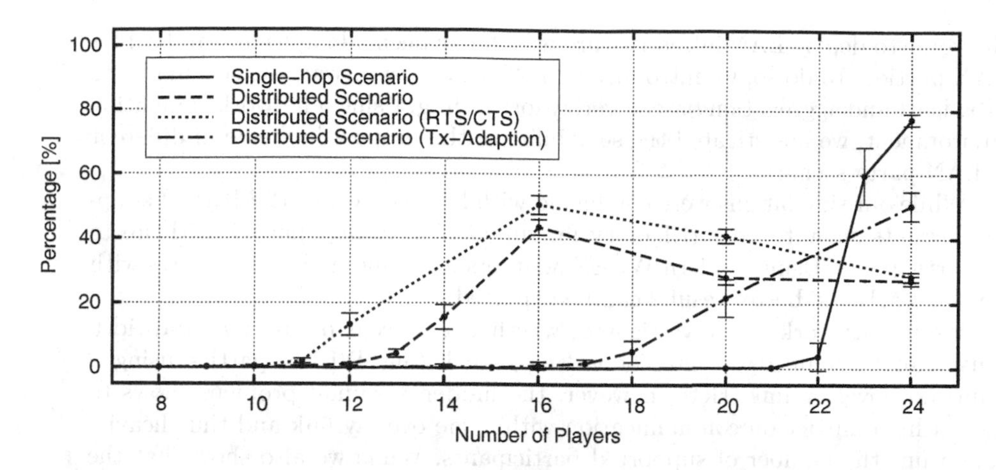

Fig. 3. Percentage of updates not delivered in time.

scenario. While this observation at first seems surprising, it can be ascribed to the wireless (semi-)broadcast medium and its well-known hidden terminal problem [6]. Indeed, although both clusters are clearly separated and do not influence their opposite's communication, the forwarding of aggregated data along the multi-hop overlay link suffers from heavy interference implied by the communication within the clusters. Because of resulting exponential back-off increases and ongoing MAC retransmissions, latencies quickly rise and thus lead to unacceptable performance for 13 (and more) players.

Activating the RTS/CTS extension introduced for the IEEE 802.11 standard does not lead to a performance increase, but results in a further decrease of supported players: Indeed, the sending of RTS and CTS packets implies additional medium accesses, resulting in heavier interferences and degrading performance. The percentage of updates not delivered in time, thus, already shows a slight increase for 10 players.

A possible option for reducing the extent of interferences and facilitate the communication along the overlay link is to lower the transmission power of LBC player nodes. Indeed, the latter are located within a few meters from their virtual server and, hence, do not require a full transmission range of $175m$. As a consequence, we for the final evaluations set the transmission power of LBC player nodes to -13dBm, which results in a transmission range of $25m$ and an interference range of $79m$ respectively. As can be seen from the diagram, this leads to a drastic performance increase in the distributed scenario: The percentage of updates not delivered in time only starts rising slowly with 16 players. However, the results achieved in the single-hop scenario can still not be matched.

5 Summary and Conclusion

We in this work investigated, whether 802.11b WLAN adapters operated in ad-hoc mode in combination with P2P multicast protocols can substitute a bothersome to deploy LAN infrastructure, which has been a long time standard for LAN parties. To do so, we introduced an efficient data forwarding scheme using broadcast and aggregation based overlay forwarding. Using a network simulation environment, we investigated the scalability of the proposed scheme in different WLAN party scenarios.

While our simulations were conducted with low bandwidth (2 MBit/s) adapters, results show to be satisfactory for supporting WLAN parties with up to 21 participants. Using modern WLAN adapters featuring higher data-rates with up to 54 MBit/s, better results can be expected.

We in this work also investigated, whether a concept of spacial bandwidth reuse can be applied by interconnecting two distant WLAN parties using a multi-hop overlay link. Here, however, the hidden terminal problem shows to have a high impact on communication within the overlay link and thus heavily constrains the number of supported participants. While we also show that the RTS/CTS extension worsens the results because of additional medium accesses, we observe an increase of performance by reducing the transmission power of LBC player nodes: We although provide evidence that results from single-hop scenarios cannot be matched.

Concluding, we can say that, for moderately sized LAN parties (i.e. *"meeting at a friends home"*), the approach investigated in this paper shows to be a proper alternative to a true and bothersome to deploy LAN. It is, however, inadequate for bigger parties which can feature several hundred participants and, therefore, rely on a professionally deployed and costly infrastructure.

References

1. Beigbeder T., Coughlan R., Lusher C., et al: *"The Effects of Loss and Latency on User Performance in Unreal Tournament 2003"*, ACM Network and System Support for Games Workshop, Portland (USA), September 2004
2. Ge M., Krishnamurthy S., Faloutsos, M.: *"Overlay Multicasting for Ad Hoc Networks"*, The Third Medditteranean Ad Hoc Networking Workshop, Bordum (Turkey), June 2004
3. Baumung P.: *"TrAM: Cross-Layer Efficient Application-Layer Multicast in Mobile Ad-hoc Networks"*, The IEEE Wireless Communications and Networking Conference, Hong Kong (China), March 2007
4. Baumung P.: *"On the Modular Composition of Scalable Application-Layer Multicast Services for Mobile Ad-hoc Networks"*, The International Workshop on Wireless Ad-hoc and Sensor Networks, New York (USA), June 2006
5. Zeng X., Bagrodia R., Gerla M.: *"GloMoSim: a Library for Parallel Simulation of Large-scale Wireless Networks"*, The 12th Workshop on Parallel and Distributed Simulation, Banff (Canada), May 1999
6. Jayasuriya A., Perreau S., Dadej A., et al: *"Hidden vs. Exposed Terminal Problem in ad hoc Networks"*, The Australian Telecommunications, Networks and Architecture Conference, Sydney (AU), December 2004

A Middleware for the Controlled Information Exchange Between Online Games and Internet Applications

Sonja Bergsträßer[1], Tomas Hildebrandt[1], Christoph Rensing[1], Ralf Steinmetz[1]

[1]KOM – Multimedia Communications Lab, TU-Darmstadt {sonja.bergstraesser, tomas.hildebrandt, christoph.rensing, ralf.steinmetz}@KOM.tu-darmstadt.de

Abstract. Multiplayer Online Games (MOGs) are a thriving market leading to a multiplicity of game related internet applications. Enabling information exchange between games and these applications is essential, but still an unsolved challenge. Our Virtual Context Based Service (VCBS) middleware enables such an information exchange. The VCBS middleware is an interface between games and other internet applications, which also supports community activities. In this paper we describe the architecture of the VCBS middleware and its components, and introduce our concept for generic MOG interfaces.

1. Introduction

Today most internet applications are client-server applications (e.g. websites, networked virtual environments, voice-chat tools or shared calendars). Especially networked virtual environments like Multiplayer Online Games (MOGs) are isolated from other internet applications. Nevertheless various internet applications related to MOGs develop around these games, e.g. community portals, knowledge bases, communication and collaboration tools. We call these internet applications and related services the environment of MOGs. Normally there are no interconnections between the different servers and between different client applications and the data contained in one application can not be used in another one.

While there are first approaches for the utilization of game related information, yet no generic concept for information exchange between MOGs and other internet applications exists. We have developed such a concept which in addition supports community activities [1]. Based on this concept we introduce a middleware solution, the Virtual Context Based Service (VCBS) architecture, to enable data exchange between game clients and servers and other internet applications and to provide means for community participation. In addition our middleware includes a data flow control mechanism to avoid abuse of game related information. Cheat prevention is a serious issue in gaming research and discussed in various papers (e.g. [2, 3]).

We give an overview on different attempts to enable information access or user participation in the MOG area in section 2. Section 3 introduces virtual context based services and describes the VCBS middleware in detail. In section 4 we show how our architecture can be utilized. Finally we summarize this article in section 5.

2. Related Work

Hardly any general concept exists, about how information exchange between a game and its environment can be realized. Also the involvement of game communities is quite limited in most cases. For both scenarios only isolated applications and specialized approaches can be found. In the following we give a short overview of the current situation and introduce some of the existing approaches.

The users of MOGs form communities which actively participate in the evolution of games and shape them through the creation of large data collections, guidelines, and even custom tools and game add-ons. The commitment of the gamers to their games is generally very strong and the exchange and communication between gamers are essential elements. The request of game communities for creative participation is increasing and possibilities to adapt games and the gaming experience to the user will be a crucial factor for the success of a MOG in the future. Today we are already aware of the fact that fast growth of user count and binding a critical mass of users to a game is not only important for its development but decides on its success or failure [4]. The support of community development within the game [5] and in the game environment improves the binding of users to the game and thus is one success factor. Especially in the Massively Multiplayer Online Role-Playing Game (MMORPG) market, which is highly competitive, only MMORPGs with strong communities can be successful.

In some genres like First Person Shooters (FPS) the game industry has begun to open itself to the game community and some games already include editors to modify the game itself. But especially MMORPGs, which are based on player interaction and live through their communities, shield themselves from the outside world. One approach to provide selected ingame information is the developer driven game data presentation. Special internet portals where e.g. character information can be retrieved are operated by different game developers or publishers (e.g. WoW Amory [6] or ET:QW Stats [7]). A different approach is the usage of launch platforms coupled with community applications. This approach mainly focuses on awareness aspects and teaming and emphasizes communication applications (e.g. ESL Wire [8] or Steam Community [9]). Additionally third parties begin to utilize the opportunities given (e.g. World of Warcraft is providing an API which allows the retrieval of stored ingame information) and present available ingame information on web portals or community platforms (e.g. buffed [10] or xchar [11]).

The main drawbacks of current approaches beside the lack of a generic solution are coupling to one information source, specialization of applications, and no time synchronous or real-time data usage. The approaches are each strongly coupled to one kind of information source only, although only very few and limited information is available at all. The applications are very specialized: developer driven data representation portals only present data (no interaction is possible), launch platforms are mainly server browsers combined with buddy lists and web portals include community features enriched with limited game information. The time synchronous usage of data is not possible and thus no data exchange is feasible while a gamer is playing a game. In addition there are no concepts for the prevention of cheating while ingame information is exchanged with the game environment. In order to prevent cheating most of the games simply do not allow any outside connection to the outside or retrieval of ingame information from the outside at all.

3. Virtual Context Based Services

The goal of Virtual Context Based Services (VCBS) is to provide services to the user regarding his current situation in a virtual environment [1]. The VCBS enable information exchange between a virtual environment and other applications. In addition the VCBS include a control mechanism for the information flow and thus complies with the given requirements. In the following we subsume the VCBS concept, shortly introduce our generic game interfaces and describe the architecture of the VCBS middleware and its components.

3.1 Virtual Parameters and Virtual Context

The virtual situation of a gamer's character (or avatar) can be described using different parameters, e.g. location in the virtual world, current action or character properties. These virtual parameters specify the virtual context of a user and his character. We have defined an XML based virtual parameter description language which is valid for MOGs in general. Thus generic game interfaces can be described and extended for specific genres and if needed also for specific games. This allows us to define an abstract interface for MOGs and include special needs of different genres and games. The virtual parameters are the base for the definition of an interface between games and other internet applications. We have defined four parameter sets (general, location, character and status) specifying the different categories of virtual parameters. The general set provides information about the player (e.g. player name), the game time (e.g. session time) and the server (e.g. server name), the other three sets about the virtual character and his situation in the virtual world. The location set provides position and area information (e.g. area name), the character set includes general information about the virtual character (e.g. skills) and the status set is about the current state of the character (e.g. health) and includes grouping information.

3.2 VCBS Middleware Architecture

The VCBS middleware consists of a **VCBS Client** on the client system, a **VCBS Registry** and **VCBS Servers** (see Figure 1). It also defines an interface for external services. The different services (e.g. a web platform providing gamer statistics, a wiki including situation related guidelines or a voice tool for group communication) are not part of the VCBS architecture and can be provided independently. This gives anybody the opportunity to provide services (e.g. game developers, the game community or third parties). Services are coupled with the game through the VCBS middleware. Hence they can utilize ingame information, react on ingame events and provide data regarding the current situation of a gamer.

The **VCBS Registry** manages all parts of the VCBS architecture, the registered services and user accounts. Before a service can be used with the VCBS architecture it has to be registered with the VCBS Registry (*service registration* (1)). The registration data includes a service description which is stored in the Registry. The Registry checks during service registration, if a service is authorized to get the requested client information based on the rule set defined by the game (to check if the requested information is approved for the situations the service is designed for). It distributes the users to the VCBS Servers (to ensure the scalability of the system) and maintains the servers using *status updates* (2) (e.g. "new appointed gamer").

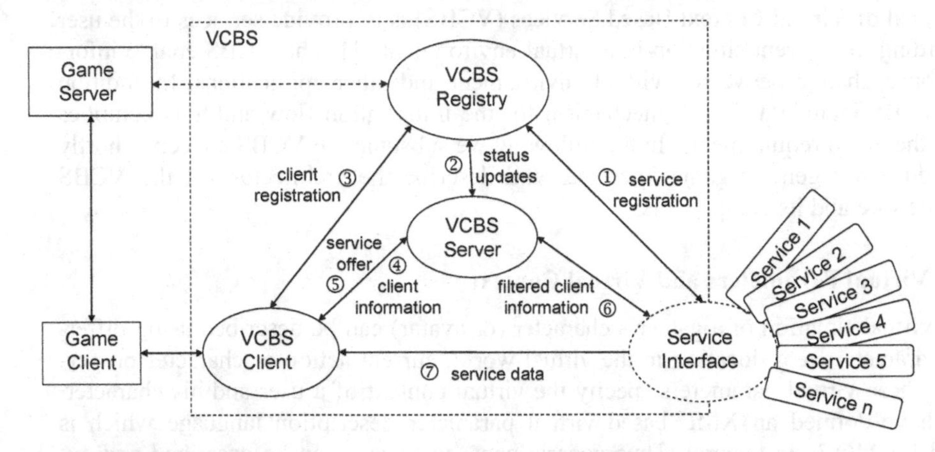

Figure 1. VCBS middleware: architecture overview and information flow

The **VCBS Client** is located at the gamer's system (client system). It handles the registration of the user (*client registration* (3)) and interacts with the user. The VCBS Client receives the virtual parameters from the game and integrates outgame service data into the game. The game interface of the VCBS Clients use plug-ins to handle different game APIs. When a user is online in a virtual world of a supported game, the VCBS Client regularly sends the game client information containing the virtual parameters (*client information* (4)) to the assigned VCBS Server.

The **VCBS Server** receives the game client information updates from the VCBS Client and offers available and suited services to the user (*service offer* (5)) through the VCBS Client. The Servers are responsible for the processing of the game client information. They decide which services are offered to the gamer and which information is forwarded to the external services. The matching is done based on the virtual situation of the user and two options for matching virtual situations to services are included in the VCBS middleware: parameter and event-based matching. Using parameter matching the VCBS Server compares the game client information with the service description. With event-based matching the VCBS Client reacts on events indicating changes of the user's context in the game. There is also the possibility to use other matching schemes. If a matching scheme triggers, the VCBS Server verifies the corresponding service, checks if the parameters are approved regarding the game based rule set and offers it to the gamer. Thus a control mechanism based on the virtual situation of a user is integrated into the information flow. If a gamer chooses to use a offered service, the VCBS Server forwards the relevant parameters to the corresponding service (*filtered client information* (6)). Then the service can process the client information, utilize the information or send his resulting data (*service data* (7)) to the VCBS Client. The data is then integrated into the game by the VCBS Client. If the situation of the user changes and the service is not matching the situation anymore the VCBS Server stops sending the *filtered client information.*

4. Usage Scenarios

There are multiple usage scenarios for the VCBS middleware which can be mainly divided into two categories. In the first category are internet applications using status information about the gamer outside of the game (e.g. at a web portal like gamerlist.net where a gamer wants to show information about himself to the community). The second category includes services which provide ingame user support.
We are currently developing "**gamerlist.net**" a community platform where gamers present themselves, their games, their relationships to other gamers and their community activities. It is used to increase the visibility of a gamer and his activities for the game community. This information can be used to support grouping, provide statistics, enable the comparison of gamers with others and so on. The platform utilizes the VCBS middleware in order to access ingame information, e.g. to show which game a user is currently playing, display his game statistics or (if possible and allowed by the game) his current ingame location. The ingame information is obtained by a service, which is part of gamerlist.net. This ensures that only information which is allowed to be shown is displayed on the platform and that the information access is standardized.
The **Service User Interface** (SUI) is an extension of the UI of a game. To include a service into a game an ingame representation of the service must be provided. With this ingame service representation, the user can interact and access the service data. An ingame representation of a service can be realized with the SUI. An example service we are using with the SUI is the "Fisherman's Friend" service. It supports a user when he goes fishing in a virtual environment. When the user's character is standing at a virtual lake or river and takes a fishing rod in his hands the "Fisherman's Friend" service is offered to him. The service offer is based on the virtual context parameters, the coordinates and the used equipment in this example. The service data can include the fishes that can be caught there, the probability of catching the different species, whether the difficulty of the waters is suited for the character skill or which other fishing sites might be interesting to go to. To obtain this information (which is normally not provided directly by the game itself) the client information is collected by an external service while a character is fishing in the virtual world. The information is processed, and with more people using the service the obtained information is improved. The data from the service is embedded into the game by the VCBS middleware.

5. Summary

The information exchange and service invocation between different virtual environments and internet applications is an important issue, especially concerning gaming and game worlds. The evolution of MOGs in that direction is currently just at the beginning. Isolated approaches exist but they do not satisfy the needs. All approaches presented in the related work section are only first and non-systematic steps to open games to other applications or community participation.

This creates needs for a generalization of interfaces and communication mechanisms, which satisfies the interests of the community for flexible influence opportunities and complies with the requirements of the game industry for a protection of the game against forbidden modifications and the ensuring of fairness. It is important to consider the unique features of the different games or genres. But it is also important to find similarities and include the wide variety of games and gamers.

With the Virtual Contact Based Services and the VCBS middleware we offer the first generic connection of MOGs with internet applications. By offering a loose coupling our solution can be used to support all networked gaming scenarios. In conclusion the VCBS satisfy the identified requirements by enabling information exchange between games and internet applications and opening games to community participation while preventing abuse of game related information. We have already tested our VCBS concept with games which provide an API where we can obtain virtual parameters or ingame events. With our solution we want to provide game developers a framework so that they can open their games for the participation of the game community and use the high creative potential and developing power.

6. References

1. Bergsträßer S., Hildebrandt T., Lehmann L., Rensing C., Steinmetz R. Virtual Context Based Services for Support of Interaction in Virtual Worlds. In: Grenville Armitage: Netgames 2007, 6th Annual Workshop on Network and Systems Support for Games, p. 111--116, Melbourne, Australia, September 2007
2. Chambers, C., Feng, W., Feng, W., and Saha, D. 2005. Mitigating information exposure to cheaters in real-time strategy games. In Proceedings of the international Workshop on Network and Operating Systems Support For Digital Audio and Video (NOSSDAV '05), Stevenson, Washington, USA, June 13 - 14, 2005
3. Li, K., Ding, S., McCreary, D., and Webb, S. 2004. Analysis of state exposure control to prevent cheating in online games. In Proceedings of the 14th international Workshop on Network and Operating Systems Support For Digital Audio and Video (NOSSDAV '04), Cork, Ireland, June 16 - 18, 2004
4. Strain, Jeff: How to create a successful MMO, Games Convention Developers Conference (GCDC), Leipzig, 2007, http://eu.guildwars.com/press/article/jeffgc2007/
5. Ducheneaut, N., Yee, N., Nickell, E., and Moore, R. J. 2007. The life and death of online gaming communities: a look at guilds in world of warcraft. In Proceedings of the SIGCHI Conference on Human Factors in Computing Systems, San Jose, California, USA, April 28 - May 03, 2007
6. The World of Warcraft Armory, http://eu.wowarmory.com/, last accessed 12.09.08
7. Enemy Territory: Quake Wars Stats, http://stats.enemyterritory.com/, last accessed 12.09.08
8. ESL: ESL Wire, http://www.esl.eu/de/wire, last accessed 10.09.08
9. Steam Community, https://steamcommunity.com/, last accessed 10.09.08
10. buffed.de: Das Portal für Onlinespiele, http://www.buffed.de/, last accessed 12.09.08
11. xchar: WoW meets real life, http://www.xchar.de/, last accessed 10.09.08

Re-sequencing Buffer Occupancy of a Concurrent Multipath Transmission Mechanism for Transport System Virtualization

K. Tutschku[1], T. Zinner[2], A. Nakao[3,4] and P. Tran-Gia[2]

[1]Universität Wien, Professur "Future Communication",
Universitätsstrasse 10, 1090 Wien, Austria.

[2]Universität Würzburg, Lehrstuhl für Informatik III,
Am Hubland, 97074 Würzburg, Germany.

[3]University of Tokyo, Graduate School of Interdisciplinary Information Studies,
7-3-1, Hongo, Bunkyo-ku, Tokyo 113-0033, Japan.

[4]also with the NICT (National Institute for Communication and Information Technology), 1-33-16, Hakusan, Bunkyo-ku, Tokyo, 113-0001, Japan.

Abstract. From the viewpoint of a methodology, the concept of *Network Virtualization (NV)* extends beyond pure operational issues. In this paper, we will first transfer the concept of location independence of resources, as known in operating systems, to the area of data transport in communication networks. This idea is denoted as *transport system virtualization (TSV)*. We will outline an example for TSV which uses *concurrent multipath (CMP)* transmission and discuss an important performance issue of CMP transmission, the *re-sequencing buffer occupancy probability distribution*. The investigation of this probability distribution gives insights in how to select the set of paths when using CMP transmission for transport system virtualization.

1 Introduction

For practitioners, the concept of *Network Virtualization (NV)* enables the consolidation of multiple networks or overlays into a single physical system. Thus, NV may lower the required amount of hardware (capital expenditures, CAPEX) and of operational expenditures (OPEX) of multiple network structures since less systems have to be configured. As a result, NV is considered mainly as an operational technique.

From the viewpoint of a methodology, the concept of NV extends beyond the above outlined asset and operational issues. One of the main benefit of virtualization techniques is the *abstraction of computer resources*. An operating system, for example, may provide virtual memory to an application program. This memory gives the program the feeling that it can use a contiguous working memory, while in fact it may be physically fragmented and may even overflow on to disk storage. The actual location of the data in the physically memory doesn't matter and is hidden. Thus, this virtualization technique makes the resource "memory" independent from its physical "location". In this paper, we transfer the concept of location independence of resources to the area of data transport in communication networks. This idea will be denoted here as *transport system virtualization (TSV)*.

The short paper is structured as follows. First, we will outline briefly the idea of TSV. Then, we detail an example for TSV using a *concurrent multipath (CMP)* transmission mechanism. Finally, we discuss an important performance issue in CMP transmission, which is the *re-sequencing buffer occupancy probability distribution*. The investigation of this probability distribution gives insights in how to select the set of paths used in a TSV mechanism using CMP transfer.

2 Transport System Virtualization

The idea of *tranport system virtualization* is motivated partly by the abstraction introduced in P2P content distribution networks (CDNs). Advanced P2P CDNs, such as eDeonkey or BitTorrent, apply the concept of *multi-source download*. Here, a peer downloads multiple parts of a file in parallel from different peers. As a result, the downloading peer doesn't rely any more on a single peer which provides the data, and the reliability is increased. The providing peers are typically selected such that the throughput is optimized. The actual physical location of the file doesn't matter. Thus, these P2P CDNs can be viewed as an abstract and almost infinite storage for the data files. Thus, an abstraction of a storage resource, similar to the example of virtual memory in the introduction, is achieved.

The above outlined abstraction of a storage resource is transferred to the area of data transport. *Transport System Virtualization (TSV)* can be viewed as an abstraction concept for data transport resources. Hereby, the physical location of the transport resource doesn't matter as long as this resource is accessible. In TSV an abstract data transport resource can be combined from one or more physical or overlay data transport resources. Such a resource can be, e.g., a leased line, a wave length path, an overlay link, or an IP forwarding capability to a certain destination. These resources can be used preclusive or concurrently and can be located in even different physical networks or administrative domains. Thus, an abstract transport resource exhibits again the feature of location independence.

3 Implementing TSV Using Concurrent Multipath Transfer in Advanced Routing Overlays

A scalable approach for routing overlays is the concept of *one-hop source routing*, [1,2]. Hereby, the user data is forwarded to a specific intermediate node, denoted as One-hop Source Router (OSR), which then relays the traffic to its destination using ordinary IP routing. The details of this architecture can be found in [2] and in accompanying paper to this short paper [3].

The TSV in the considered OSR architecture is achieved by a *Concurrent Multipath (CMP)* transfer mechanism. The mechanism combines multiple overlay paths (even from different overlays) into a single virtual high-capacity pipe. The combined paths are used in parallel by sending data packets concurrently

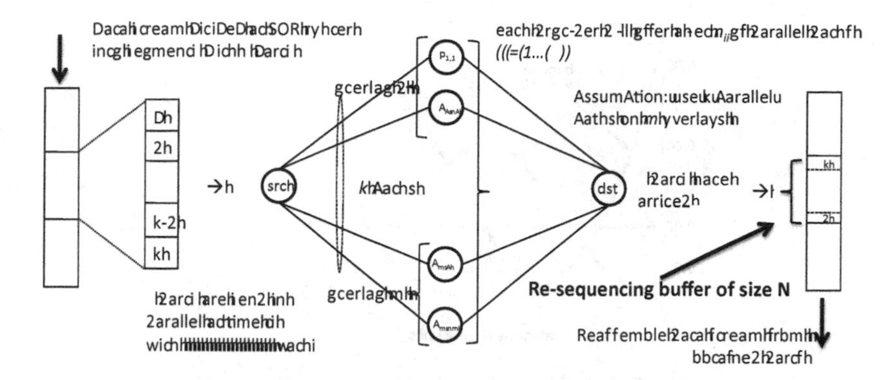

Fig. 1: Transmission Mechanism

on different overlay paths. This principle is also know as *stripping*. The paths which form the virtual pipe are chosen by the ingress router out of large number of potential paths, cf. [2] and [3]. The *path oracle* discovers the available paths, i.e. the components of the abstract data transport resource. Current discussions suggest that a path oracle can be provided by the network operator or by other institutions [4]. Altogether, the CMP mechanism combined with the path oracle facilitates an abstraction of a data transport resource. Instead using a single fixed data transport resource, the system relies now on location independent, multiple and varying resources.

Figure 1 shows a detailed model of the stripping mechanism. The data stream is divided into segments which are split into k smaller parts. The k parts are transmitted by the set of paths, i.e. in parallel on k different overlay links. The receiving router reassembles these parts. Unfortunately, the parts can arrive at the receiving router after different time intervals since they experience stochastically varying delay. Therefore, it is possible that parts arrive "out of order".[1]

Part or packet re-ordering may have a severe impact on the application performance. In order to level this behavior, the receiving router maintains a finite re-sequencing buffer. However, when the re-sequencing buffer is filled and the receiving router is still waiting for parts, part loss can still occur. This loss of parts is harmful for the application and should be minimized. Therefore, an important objective in operation of the system is to minimize the re-sequencing buffer occupancy. This can be achieved by a selection of paths with appropriate delay characteristics. The influence of path delay and its distribution on the buffer size is discussed next.

4 Re-sequencing Buffer Occupancy in Concurrent Multipath Transport

The performance of the CMP mechanisms is investigated by time discrete, event-based simulations. The simulation model assumes a continuous data stream. The

[1] Please note that part re-ordering can only happen between different paths. The order of parts on a path is maintained since packets typically can not overtake each other.

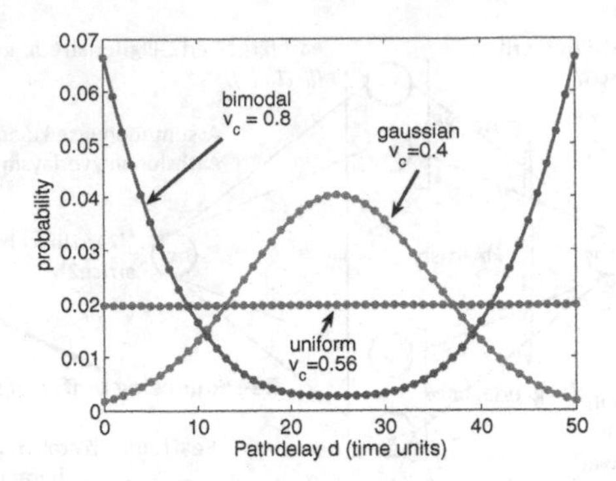

Fig. 2: Used distributions

stream is divided into parts which are send in parallel on either two or three paths. The delay on the paths is modeled by discrete delay distributions with a resolution of one time unit. A packet is transmitted every time unit on a path.

4.1 Impact of Type of Delay Distribution

In a first simulation study, the impact of the type of delay distribution on the buffer occupancy is investigated. Therefore, three different path delay distributions are considered for the paths: a truncated gaussian (label *gaus*), a uniform (*uni*) and a bimodal distribution (*bi*). The probability density functions (PDFs) of the distributions are depicted in Figure 2. The mean delay value for each the distributions is $E[d] = 25$, the minimum delay is $d_{min} = 0$ and the maximum delay $d_{max} = 50$. The coefficient of variation c_v varies between $v_c = 0.4$ for the gaussian distribution to $v_c = 0.8$ for the bimodal distribution. We decided to investigate these distributions in order to evaluate the system behavior under highly different condition, e.g. gaussian vs. bimodal delay.

We start with the investigation of two concurrent paths. The buffer occupancies for different delay combinations are depicted in Figure 3. The y-axis denotes the probability of the packets stored in the re-sequencing buffer, assigned on the x-axis. For the sake of clarity we plotted only the *bi,bi* buffer occupancy distribution with confidence intervals for a confidence level of 99%.[2]

For the case of two gaussian delay distributions, the buffer occupancy is left leaning and higher buffer occupancies are not very likely. However, for two bimodal delay distributions a large fraction of the probability mass covers a buffer occupancy bigger than 30 packets. It should be noted that the maximum buffer occupancy in the investigated scenario $o_{max} = 50$. As we see, the type and the variation of the path delay have a major influence on the buffer occupancy of the receiver. We can conclude that the buffer occupancy is not invariant to the delay distribution of the used paths.

In Figure 4 the buffer occupancies for three concurrent paths and different delay distributions are shown. It should be noticed, that the maximum buffer

[2] The size of the confidence intervals for the other curves is similar.

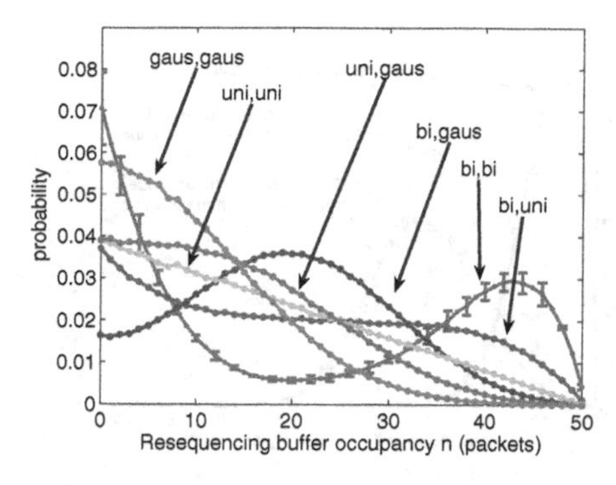

Fig. 3: Buffer occupancy for two paths

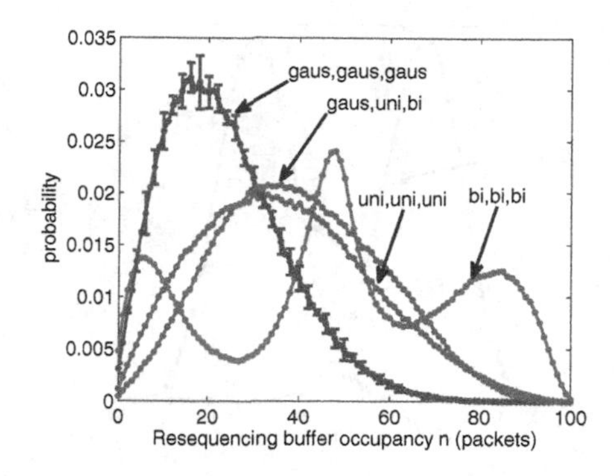

Fig. 4: Buffer occupancy for three paths

occupancy in this scenario $o_{max} = 100$. That denotes the worst case which can occur if a packet over one path has the maximum delay. In this case up to 100 packets might be transmitted over the other paths and have to be stored in the buffer until the next packet in sequence arrives.

Furthermore it can also be seen, that the buffer occupancy for three gaussian distributions is the smallest. For three times uniform and for one delay distribution of each type the occupancy is rather the same and higher than in the only-gaussian case. For three times bimodal the buffer occupation is the highest of the investigated scenarios, and a noticeable part of the of the probability mass covers an occupancy bigger than 60 packets.

4.2 Path Selection Criteria

In a second simulation study we investigates the criteria for path selection. Intuitively, a path selection algorithm should select those paths, which provide the shortest delay. This is of typical interest when the traffic comes from an interactive application which requires realtime responsiveness, but is leveled when non-interactive traffic is considered. For the investigation, we considered two truncated Poisson-like delay distributions with mean packet delay of $E[d] = 17$ and $E[d] = 34$ and with the same standard deviation of 4.1, cf. Fig.5.

Figure 6 shows actually four buffer occupancy distributions: a) all paths have the same low mean delay, b) all paths have the same high mean delay, c) two paths have low and one path a high mean delay, and d) two paths have high and one path a low mean delay. A close look at Figure 6 shows that the case a) and b) have the same buffer occupancy distribution. This indicates that the pure delay has no impact on the buffer occupancy. For the cases c) and d) it is outstanding that case d) with two high delay paths has a better performance in terms of occupancy than case c). This is very remarkable since intuitively more paths with lower delay should yield better performance. However, the coefficient of variation is lower for the high delay path and therefore the two high delay paths are more immune against delay variation. In turn, this yields a low buffer

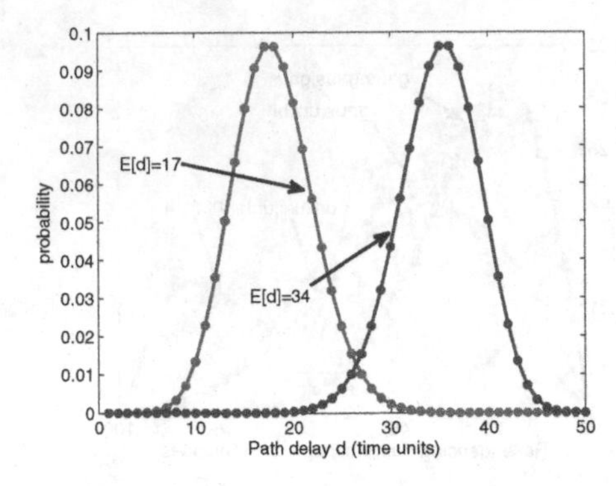

Fig. 5: Poisson-like Delay Distributions

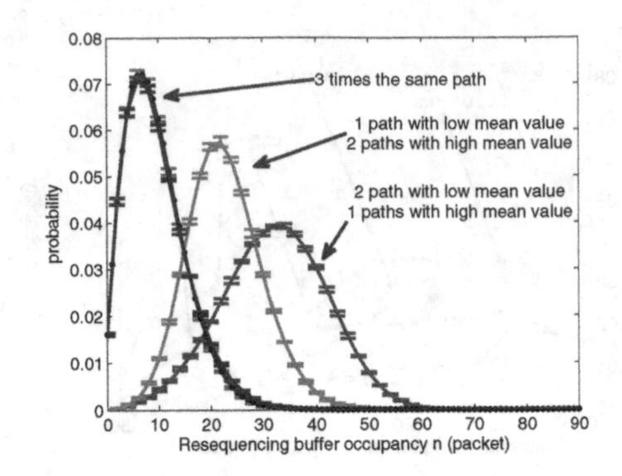

Fig. 6: Buffer occupancy considering Poisson-like Delay Distributions

occupany. These simple investigation shows that also the second moment of the path delay has to be considered in a real world path selection algorithms.

5 Conclusion

In this paper we have introduced the idea of *transport system virtualization (TSV)*, which provides a location independent abstraction for data transport resources. We have outlined the TSV concept by the example of *concurrent multipath (CMP)* transmission in one-hop source routing overlays and discussed an important performance issue of CMP transmission, the *re-sequencing buffer occupancy probability distribution* under the influence of the delay distribution on used the paths in the CMP mechanism. The performance evaluation shows that the delay and its distribution type has significant influence on the buffer occupancy. However, the intuitive approach of considering only mean delay is not sufficient. The second moment of the delay, which determines the coefficient of variation of the delay, influences strongly the buffer occupancy. More path selection criteria will be investigated in the future.

References

1. K. Gummadi, H. Madhyastha, S. Gribble, H. Levy, and D. Wetherall, "Improving the reliability of internet paths with one-hop source routing," in *Proc. OSDI'04*, San Francisco, Ca., USA, Dec. 2004.
2. S. Khor and A. Nakao, "AI-RON-E: Prophecy of One-hop Source Routers," in *Proc. of Globecom08*, New Orleans, LA., Nov./Dec. 2008.
3. K. Tutschku, T. Zinner, A. Nakao, and P. Tran-Gia, "Network Virtualization: Implementation Steps Towards the Future Internet," in *Proc. of the Workshop on Overlay and Network Virtualization at KiVS 2009*, Kasel, Germany, Mar. 2009.
4. V. Aggarwal, A. Feldmann, and C. Scheideler, "Can isps and p2p systems co-operate for improved performance?.," *ACM SIGCOMM CCR*, vol. 37, no. 3, Jul. 2007.

Designing a Decentralized Traffic Information System – AutoNomos

Axel Wegener[1], Horst Hellbrück[2], Stefan Fischer[1], Björn Hendriks[3], Christiane Schmidt[3] and Sándor P. Fekete[3]

[1] Institute of Telematics, University of Lübeck, Germany, {wegener,fischer}@itm.uni-luebeck.de

[2] Department of Electrical Engineering, University of Applied Sciences Lübeck, Germany, hellbrueck@fh-luebeck.de

[3] Institute of Operating Systems and Computer Networks, Braunschweig University of Technology, Germany, {b.hendriks,c.schmidt,s.fekete}@tu-bs.de

Abstract. We propose a decentralized traffic information system—AutoNomos—that is based on a thorough investigation of the properties of traffic and recommends a hierarchical data aggregation and forwarding for providing individualized information and support to road users. Our approach differs from work in the field by consequently applying local rules and local decentralized data processing, which turns out to be a key property of robust and scalable computing systems. We present a flexible VANET middleware that assists the application development by providing generic functionality for traffic applications. We discuss the architectural design of the overall system and provide solutions of important design concepts demonstrating the innovation of the approach.

1 Introduction

Existing Traffic Information Systems (TIS) with fixed infrastructure and centralized control are complex to install and expensive. Additionally, most of them provide outdated or incorrect predictions. The imprecise analysis and forecast results from the fact that only a fraction of the road system is monitored.

In the recent past a lot of effort has been spent on developing TISs that use a Vehicular Ad-Hoc Network (VANET) for communication. TISs monitor road conditions and allow single vehicles to optimize their individual driving route as well as they improve the overall traffic flow. These applications span hundreds of square kilometers and measure traffic density or detect and avoid traffic jams.

In future, all these applications will work simultaneously and will deal with unreliable ad-hoc communication, the limited view of single vehicles and the resulting inconsistent states, also the interpretation of data between the vehicles need to be defined consistently. Our AutoNomos approach assists the application development by acting as a flexible VANET middleware providing generic functionality for collaborative traffic applications.

The next section provides an overview of related work. We present our AutoNomos middleware approach with its key concepts and architecture in Section 3. The paper concludes with a summary and directions for future work.

2 Related Work

We discuss the related work in two steps: first, decentralized traffic information systems, since those represent the major field of applications for our approach; second, an overview of existing middleware approaches.

In the scope of the German research program *Fleetnet* (2000-2003) and *Network On Wheels* (2004-2008) techniques for lower layers like radio interface, medium access and routing have been developed. Some groups dealt with applications like internet integration as well as TIS (see [1]).

Based on these research programs, the Car-2-Car Consortium was founded to achieve a standardized frequency allocation and compatible lower layer protocols between manufacturers (see internet draft for VANET communication [2], moreover, an EU-wide frequency band is currently reserved for VANETs).

In SOTIS (Self-Organized Traffic Information System [3]), the road is partitioned virtually into fixed sized segments, depending on the type of the road. Measured traffic density and mean velocity is distributed within the network without further processing or aggregation. Thus, similar to centralized approaches the problem of data processing and applying of strategies remains unsolved.

Various middleware techniques have been developed in the related research area of Mobile Ad-Hoc Networks (MANETs) to assist application programmers in order to keep such a large system manageable. We follow the classification of [4] and for clarification, we add one representative approach.

Since MANETs often monitor their environment, **event based programming** presents an obvious strategy. Classification of and reactions to certain events define the behavior of network nodes (cf. [5]). Since communication costs grow with increasing distance between nodes, actions are triggered by **local rules** based on nearby data (cf. [6]). In MANETs measured data is more important than (error-prone) nodes. A **data centric** approach hides communication aspects from the application programmer (cf. [7]). **Virtual machines** offer two advantages. On the one hand, the heterogeneity of network nodes can be hidden by providing a virtual machine on nodes as shown in [8]. On the other hand, a program can be modeled as a mobile agent that copies itself from one node to the other in order to complete a desired task (cf. [9]). Most middleware approaches provide **communication abstraction** to relieve the application programmer from the network communication part as shown, e.g., in [10].

Currently, research addresses various fields within inter-vehicle communication like medium access and applications, but we still lack comfortable programming abstractions for VANETs. Abstractions in related work are also advantageous for VANETs; thus, we incorporate them into our proposed AutoNomos approach in the next section.

3 AutoNomos Architecture

In this section, we present our *AutoNomos* architecture and provide an easy and structured programming model. In order to achieve this, two key concepts are used. *Hovering Data Clouds* (HDCs) virtually store local data and are not bound to a specific vehicle. The higher level structure of *Organic Information Complexes* (OICs) handle large scale traffic structures. After introducing HDCs and OICs, we describe the used data dissemination scheme and introduce the software architecture inside the vehicles. A traffic jam scenario illustrates our approach in the following.

3.1 Hovering Data Clouds

In most cases data relates to some phenomenon that occurs on the road. If—as in road traffic—the network nodes move, it is no longer advantageous to bind data to individual nodes in an uncorrelated way. Instead, *Hovering Data Clouds* (HDCs) store data that is pinned to phenomena or specific locations and no longer bound to nodes; data moves independent of its carriers to follow its phenomenon. The set of nodes holding specific data can even change completely, passing the data on to oncoming nodes in the phenomenon's area. We have described this key concept in detail in [11] and have demonstrated the feasibility of the concept.

Fig. 1. A Hovering Data Cloud at traffic jam's back warns approaching vehicles.

Figure 1 shows an HDC at the back of a traffic jam. The first vehicles, that brake due to an obstruction, detect their deceleration below a certain threshold and send their positions to oncoming vehicles. Thus, with every braking vehicle, more data is gathered until a *Traffic Jam Back* HDC is established at the vehicles' positions. Due to slightly different local knowledge, vehicles may establish slightly different HDCs, that get correlated later on, approaching a common understanding. HDCs disseminate their data as *data units* for two reasons: first, vehicles in the phenomenon's area need to maintain the HDC (intra-HDC communication); second, vehicles outside the HDC's area get informed about the HDC's phenomenon (inter-HDC communication). We will deepen this thought in the software architecture part.

3.2 Organic Information Complexes

As described above, HDCs detect and follow traffic phenomena in a simple and efficient way. To obtain higher level information, data of several spatially distributed phenomena and their particular HDCs need to be aggregated. Figure 2 shows how an Organic Information Complex (OIC) achieves this objective by hierarchically aggregation.

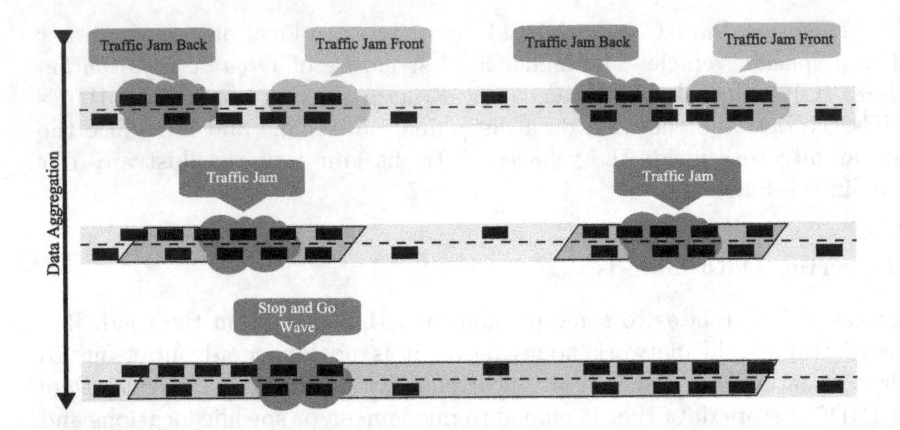

Fig. 2. Data aggregation to recognize a traffic jam by an Organic Information Complex

The topmost picture shows *Traffic Jam Back* HDCs and *Traffic Jam Front* HDCs as a result of local measurements of each vehicle. Those HDCs disseminate *data units*, that describe their observed phenomena. When data units of matching phenomena get together, *Traffic Jam* OICs are derived in this example as result of the first aggregation (cf. middle part of Figure 2). The aggregated data is the traffic jam's length and its movement over time, which could not be observed by one particular HDC.

To store the newly gathered information, again an HDC is used that arises just where the accordant data gets aggregated. Different views of the same phenomenon get correlated to approach a common understanding. Thus, instead of struggling with consistency of data, the AutoNomos system is able to turn the table and achieves a high robustness from redundant data processing—just by its design of evolving HDCs.

This aggregation process is repeated in a hierarchical manner. The lower part of Figure 2 shows a *Stop and Go Wave* as end result.

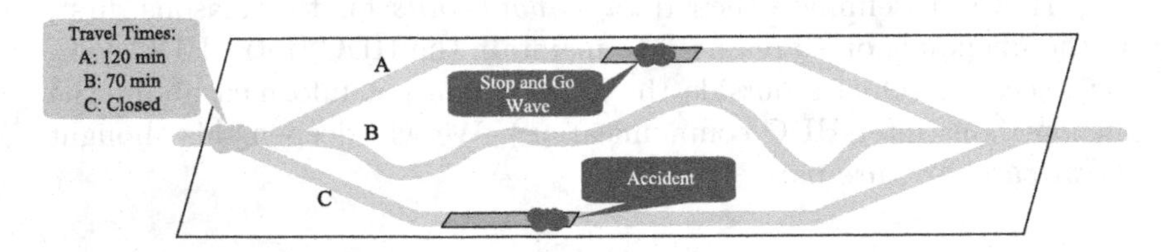

Fig. 3. Organic Information Complex on a road network aggregates travel suggestions

We continue with this example by looking from a higher perspective to a road network as depicted in Figure 3. Here, OICs discovered congestions on roads *A* and *C*. Those again send out data units towards incoming vehicles containing information about their monitored phenomena. When these data units reach intersections on the road network a journey time prediction for road sections arises as result of the aggregation process that helps to choose an appropriate route. Due to this in-network data aggregation, the overall system remains scalable.

HDCs and OICs are very flexible and form themselves self-organized wherever necessary. Also correlation and aggregation is not restricted to fixed location, but happens as a result of matching data. Thereby, data structures and algorithms are not limited by our middleware; instead, application developers define HDCs and OICs as well as correlation and aggregation mechanisms to build their own applications.

3.3 Data Dissemination Protocol AutoCast

For the efficient intra- as well as inter-HDC communication between vehicles, we developed the *AutoCast* data dissemination protocol. AutoCast is optimized for scalability and dynamics as well as density variations in networks. A sending node/vehicle encapsulates data into *data units*, that contains a dissemination region, time stamp, lifetime and the data itself. The AutoCast transport layer on every vehicle handles a local set of data units automatically and offers transport service to the upper layers.

AutoCast itself adapts to network density, by implementing probabilistic flooding when the network is very dense. On the other extreme, if the network is sparse and partitioned, periodic beacons enable storing and forwarding of data units in an efficient way. Thereby, vehicles do not switch between these operating modes, but rather adapt their behavior smoothly based only on local rules. For protocol details and evaluation of AutoCast we refer to [12].

3.4 Software Architecture

After introducing the key concepts of HDCs, OICs and AutoCast, Figure 4 provides the software architecture that is implemented in every vehicle. Our approach assumes the availability of wireless broadcast communication, e.g., DSRC/WAVE based on IEEE 802.11p [13]. Based on the broadcast communication, our first layer (*Transport Layer*) provides AutoCast for robust data dissemination as introduced in the last section.

The second layer (*HDC Layer*) stores and processes data units. Therefore, a data repository stores all locally known HDCs, representing the status of a node. The HDC repositories of nearby vehicles do not need to be fully consistent, but converge to a common understanding by ongoing correlation.

HDCs are created by *Data Mining* of local physical sensors; relevant data (e.g., black ice that provokes the ESP system) is filtered out and fed into data units for further processing.

The central processing component on the HDC layer is the *Correlation Handling*. Here, all incoming data units are processed—no matter if they result (1) from local sensors, (2) from the transport layer, which means from other vehicles

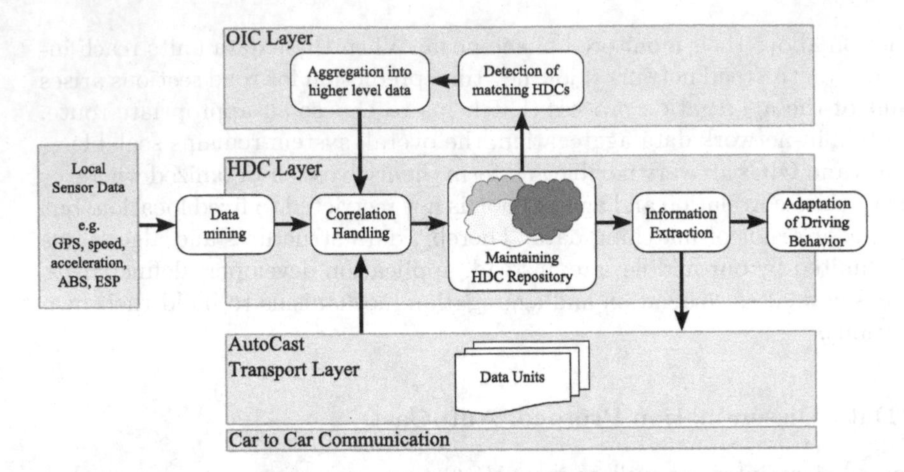

Fig. 4. Software Components available on a every Vehicle.

or (3) from the upper layer. The incoming data units are correlated to stored HDCs from the *HDC Repository* as exemplified in Section 3.1. If correlation functions identify one or more HDCs in the repository that correlate with the oncoming data unit, the particular HDCs get refreshed by applying update rules. Otherwise, a new HDC is formed based on the new data unit.

The HDC repository is maintained periodically to remove HDCs that are outdated or out of scope.

The *Information Extraction* component periodically generates data units from the stored HDCs that are disseminated by AutoCast. Such a data unit contains either a report, e.g., for approaching vehicles, with only a digest of the HDC's data (inter-HDC communication), or the complete data of an HDC to establish the same HDC in other vehicles. Doing so, an HDC can follow its phenomenon (intra-HDC communication).

Besides sending data units, extracted data can also be given to the *Adaptation of Driving Behavior* component. We foresee *Adaptable Distributed Strategies* (ADS), which are, e.g., able to dissolve traffic jams by local rules. Due to space limits, a detailed analysis of ADS is out of the scope of this paper.

The *OIC Layer* observes the HDC repository for matching HDCs that can be aggregated into a new, higher level HDC as demonstrated in Section 3.2. Once identified, the *Aggregation* component of the OIC layer semantically combines the particular HDCs into a higher level data unit, that is fed back into the correlation handling module of the HDC layer.

4 Conclusion and Future Work

In this article we propose a decentralized self-organizing traffic information system—namely AutoNomos—to match the challenges of road traffic as dynamic and unpredictable large scale system, where, e.g., the occurrence and behavior of traffic jams is unforeseeable. We presented our system design and introduced the concepts of *Hovering Data Clouds* and *Organic Information Complexes*, that allow for the required data correlation and aggregation as well as information extraction to improve traffic flow. Application developers can implement VANET applications based on our approach that run concurrently without interfering with each other.

In the next step of our system development we will complete the implementation of the AutoNomos system and specify the application programming interface for the proposed middleware. In addition, we will further improve the algorithm for traffic jam detection and implement *Adaptable Distributed Strategies* to improve the overall road traffic performance.

References

1. W. Franz, H. Hartenstein, and M. Mauve. *Inter-Vehicle-Communications Based on Ad Hoc Networking Principles.* Universitätsverlag Karlsruhe, 2005.
2. R. Baldessari, A. Festag, and M. Lenardi. C2C-C Consortium Requirements for Usage of NEMO in VANETs. Internet Draft, http://www.ietf.org/internet-drafts/draft-baldessari-c2ccc-nemo-req-00.txt, 2007.
3. L. Wischhof, A. Ebner, H. Rohling, et al. Sotis - a self-organizing traffic information system. *Proc. of the 57th IEEE Vehicular Technology Conference*, 2003.
4. K. Römer. Programming paradigms and middleware for sensor networks. *GI/ITG Fachgespräch Sensornetze*, 2004.
5. S. Li, S. H. Son, and J. A. Stankovic. Event detection services using data service middleware in distributed sensor networks. *Information Processing In Sensor Networks: 2nd International Workshop*, 2003.
6. K. Terfloth, G. Wittenburg, and J. Schiller. FACTS - a rule-based middleware architecture for wireless sensor networks. *Proc. of the First IEEE International Conference on Communication System Software and Middleware*, 2006.
7. S. R. Madden, M. J. Franklin, J. M. Hellerstein, et al. Tinydb: an acquisitional query processing system for sensor networks. *ACM Trans. Database Syst.*, 30(1):122–173, 2005.
8. D. Gorgen, H. Frey, and C. Hiedels. JANE – the java ad hoc network development environment. *Proc. of the 40th Annual Simulation Symposium*, 2007.
9. S. Dolev, S. Gilbert, E. Schiller, et al. Autonomous virtual mobile nodes. Technical report, 2005.
10. D. Pfisterer, C. Buschmann, H. Hellbrück, et al. Data-type centric middleware synthesis for wireless sensor network application development. *Proc. of the 5th Annual Mediterranean Ad Hoc Networking Workshop*, 2006.
11. A. Wegener, E. M. Schiller, H. Hellbrück, et al. Hovering data clouds: A decentralized and self-organizing information system. *Proc. of International Workshop on Self-Organizing Systems*, 2006.
12. A. Wegener, H. Hellbrück, S. Fischer, et al. Autocast: An adaptive data dissemination protocol for traffic information systems. *Proc. of the 66th IEEE Vehicular Technology Conference*, 2007.
13. D. Jiang, V. Taliwal, A. Meier, et al. Design of 5.9 ghz dsrc-based vehicular safety communication. *IEEE Wireless Communications*, 13(5):36–43, Oct. 2006.

Teil VIII

Preisträger

UMTS Radio Network Planning: Mastering Cell Coupling for Capacity Optimization
Zusammenfassung der Dissertation

Hans-Florian Geerdes

Zuse-Institut Berlin (ZIB), Takustr. 7, 14195 Berlin

Bei der Planung von UMTS-Funknetzen sollen zelluläre Mobilfunksysteme der dritten Generation so konfiguriert werden, dass sie bei geringen Kosten eine maximale Netzabdeckung und Kapazität bieten. UMTS kann dank einer neuen Funkschnittstelle mehr Nutzer bedienen als die Vorgängersysteme. Die genaue Kapazität einer Zelle ist allerdings schwierig zu bestimmen; sie hängt von der Position der Nutzer, den jeweiligen Verbindungsanforderungen und dem Zustand des Funkkanals ab. Die Zellen eines Netzes müssen außerdem gemeinsam betrachtet werden, weil sie durch Interferenz gekoppelt sind. Statische Systemmodelle berücksichtigen dies alles und liefern in der Praxis die Informationen für die Funknetzplanung. Sie werden allerdings schnell sehr groß, weil sie alle Verbindungen explizit abbilden. Um die erwartete Leistungsfähigkeit eines Netzes unter zufälligen Schwankungen der Eingangsgrößen genau zu berechnen, benötigt man zudem zeitaufwändige Simulationen. Die bekannten Optimierungsmethoden basieren daher entweder auf vereinfachten Kapazitätsmodellen, oder auf Modellen, die so komplex sind, dass sie theoretisch kaum analysiert werden können.

Die Arbeit entwickelt neue Modelle und Methoden für diese Problemstellung. Im ersten Schritt werden Interferenzkopplungs-Komplementaritätssystemen eingeführt, die über das neue Konzept der perfekten Lastkontrolle alle Nutzer implizit abbilden. Die Größe des Modells hängt damit nur noch von der Anzahl der Zellen ab. In diesem Rahmen lassen sich erwartete Zelllasten und Blockierungswahrscheinlichkeiten ohne Simulation in erster Näherung über die erwartete Interferenzkopplung approximieren. Rechenexperimente mit wirklichkeitsnahen Daten belegen, dass das neue Systemmodell zutreffend ist und bestätigen die Methoden zur Kapazitätsschätzung.

Der so gefundene deterministische Schätzer für die Netzkapazität geht schließlich in die Zielfunktion eines neuen Modells zur Kapazitätsoptimierung ein. Das Modell ist in geschlossener Form angegeben; damit ermöglicht es neue gemischt-ganzzahlige lineare Formulierungen und strukturelle Einsichten, zum Beispiel untere Schranken. In vier Fallstudien auf großen Planungsszenarien laufen in der Arbeit entwickelte heuristische Methoden schnell und erfolgreich und liefern hocheffiziente Netzkonfigurationen.

Diese Ergebnisse schaffen ein prägnantes Verständnis von UMTS-Funknetzen auf Zellebene. Damit wird ein neuer Zugang zur Kapazitätsplanung aufgezeigt, der in der Praxis eine effektive Behandlung von großen Planungsproblemen ermöglicht und sich auch auf andere moderne Mobilfunksysteme übertragen lässt.

Stochastic Packet Loss Model to Evaluate QoE Impairments

Oliver Hohlfeld

Deutsche Telekom Laboratories / TU Berlin, Ernst-Reuter-Platz 7, 10587 Berlin
oliver@net.t-labs.tu-berlin.de

Abstract. With provisioning of broadband access for mass market—even in wireless and mobile networks—multimedia content, especially real-time streaming of high-quality audio and video, is extensively viewed and exchanged over the Internet. Quality of Experience (QoE) aspects, describing the service quality perceived by the user, is a vital factor in ensuring customer satisfaction in today's communication networks. Frameworks for accessing quality degradations in streamed video currently are investigated as a complex multi-layered research topic, involving network traffic load, codec functions and measures of user perception of video quality.

Based on backbone traffic and DVB-H packet loss traces, stochastic models for the packet loss process are evaluated and discussed. Within this area, we provide a Markovian generator for packet loss pattern for studying the impact of impairments on the Quality of Experience. The main contribution is a new parameter estimation technique for Markovian point processes. Second-order statistics for the distribution of the number of lost packets over multiple time-scales are derived by moment generating functions. Moment matching is used to adapt a Markov process to error pattern observed in multiple time-scales. The second-order statistics in multiple time-scales is equivalent to the autocorrelation function of a process. An explicit analytical expression is derived for the Gilbert-Elliott model to compute the statistics on arbitrary scales based on four model parameters, which gives clear insight for the reverse process of parameter adaptation to observed statistics in relevant time-scales.

The experience in applying the results to to several scenarios in fixed and wireless communication networks suggest that the classical 2-state Gilbert-Elliott model already captures a wide range of observed loss pattern. The proposed approach leads to a closer match in multiple time-scales than classical methods with more flexibility to include information from different time-scales, enabling a simple and useful fit for long traces of traffic and packet loss processes.

The analytical study of loss pattern is supplemented with a qualitative investigation of their effects on QoE metrics for video transmission. In general, impairments of video sequences are sensitive to different assumptions on loss processes yielding different reaction in coding of slices and frames, which stresses the importance of refering to the most relevant pattern. A comparison of 2400 impaired video sequences led to strong evidence that uniform packet losses produce a larger distortion than busty packet losses at the same and sufficiently high loss-rate, since the former affect more frames on the video coding layers. Moreover, the results suggest that impairments at the video layer are affected by the applied parameter estimation technique.

References

1. Oliver Hohlfeld. Statistical error model to impair an H.264 decoder. Master's thesis, TU Darmstadt, March 2008. KOM-D-0310.

Unsynchronized Energy-Efficient Medium Access Control and Routing in Wireless Sensor Networks

Philipp Hurni

Institute of Computer Science and Applied Mathematics
University of Bern, Switzerland
hurni@iam.unibe.ch

This master thesis investigates optimizations on recently proposed fully unsynchronized power saving sensor MAC protocols. In contrast to many other sensor MAC protocols, unsynchronized sensor MAC protocols renounce on any kind of network- or cluster-wide synchronization for channel access coordination and maintenance of a common wake-sleep pattern, because in wireless sensor networks with low traffic requirements, the overhead for maintaining synchronization is likely to exceed the energy spent for the actual data traffic.
The implementation of the unsynchronized power saving protocol WiseMAC in a simulator and on real sensor hardware forms the entry point of the master thesis. The thesis discusses the choice of appropriate and realistic parameter values for the simulator environment and WiseMAC simulation model by comparing the protocol performance in simulation and on real hardware.
We suggest optimizations of the broadcast operation mode of WiseMAC to achieve a higher energy-efficiency. We exploit local knowledge of the neighboring nodes' wake-up schedules. Experiments in simulation and with the real-world prototype implementation approve the superior energy-efficiency of the scheme further called *best-instants broadcast* compared to existing techniques.
We propose an alternative allocation and arrangement scheme of the node's wake-up intervals is discussed to avert performance degrading systematic overhearing and fairness effects of WiseMAC's fixed static wake-up pattern, as problems may arise when two neighboring nodes share a similar wake pattern. We developed a scheme to let the nodes' wake-up window move in-between fixed intervals in respect to a linear movement-function, which leads to a more reliable overhearing avoidance and a lower risk of systematic overhearing, yet retaining the deterministic nature of the wake-ups.
We outline a mechanism to improve the adaptivity of the WiseMAC protocol in cases of traffic between multiple senders and one receiver basing on a so-called stay-awake promise. Cases with multiple nodes aiming to forward data over certain receivers are likely to occur in wireless sensor network topologies. Bottleneck nodes often have to forward data of large subtrees. Experiments on the simulator approve performance gains in respect to throughput and latency.
On the routing layer, the thesis integrates the on-demand routing protocol AODV and evaluates the performance of the combination with the energy saving MAC. Efforts are undertaken to integrate a multipath-protocol to balance load in a wireless sensor network and achieve a higher network lifetime.

Novel Network Architecture for Optical Burst Transport

Christoph M. Gauger

Institute of Communication Networks and Computer Engineering (IKR), University of Stuttgart, Germany**

Optical transport networks form the backbone of communication networks by cost-efficiently and reliably offering huge bandwidth [1]. However, flexibility, manageability, and multi-layer integration have remained as key challenges. While optical burst switching (OBS)—a highly dynamic network architecture with statistical multiplexing directly in the optical layer [2]—improved the flexibility it still lacked several practical network design requirements.

The thesis [3] develops, models, and evaluates the novel Optical Burst Transport Network architecture (OBTN). In a hybrid approach [4], OBTN combines an optically burst-switched layer with a dense wavelength-switched virtual topology layer. Together with an alternative, constrained routing scheme and a network dimensioning process it achieves flexibility, high service quality, and resource efficiency. Also, it opens up an evolution path from today's networks. Comprehensive evaluations by event-driven simulation demonstrate the performance of OBTN and exhibit the impact of its key building blocks.

The figure compares the required burst-switch ports and physical wavelength layer links for OBS, OBTN (several values of the dimensioning parameter, β), and a reference Burst-over-Circuit Switching (BoCS) architecture (normalized to a minimal, static traffic dimensioning at a burst loss probability of 10^{-5}. Compared to OBS and BoCS, OBTN reduces the number of high complexity burst-switched ports. Compared to OBS, OBTN trades them off by more economic wavelength layer links. This yields an overall more cost-efficient network design.

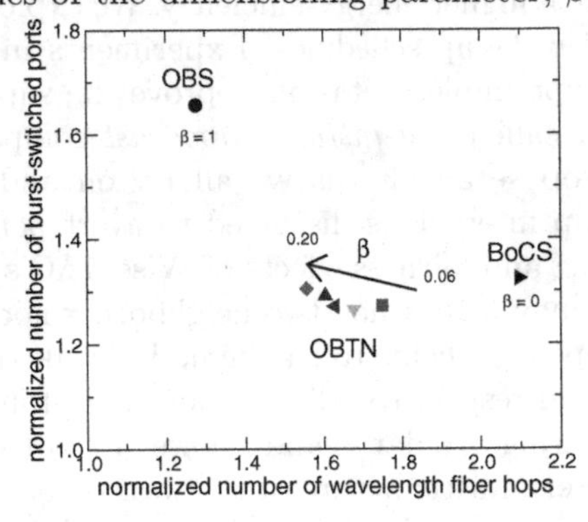

1. B. Mukherjee. *Optical WDM Networks*. Springer, 2006.
2. C. Qiao et al. Optical burst switching. *Journal of High Speed Networks*, 1999.
3. C. Gauger. Novel network architecture for optical burst transport. *Dissertation, University of Stuttgart*, 2006. Electronic Publication at elib.uni-stuttgart.de.
4. C. Gauger, P. Kühn et al. Hybrid optical network architectures: bringing packets and circuits together. *IEEE Communications Magazine*, 2006.

** All research while at IKR and at the University of California at Davis. The author thanks Prof. P. Kühn and Prof. B. Mukherjee for their invaluable support and guidance. He is now with The Boston Consulting Group, gauger.christoph@bcg.com

Abstract: Lightweight Authentication for HIP

Tobias Heer

RWTH Aachen University, Distributed Systems Group, Aachen, Germany

In recent years numerous solutions for overcoming the architectural constraints of the Internet have emerged. One of the most promising among them is the *Host Identity Protocol* (HIP) [2], which was recently approved as an experimental standard by the IETF. HIP adds an additional protocol layer between TCP and IP to implement the Identifier/Locator split. Apart from mobility and multihoming, HIP supports host authentication, payload encryption, and a cryptographic namespace without requiring changes to the network infrastructure or network applications. However, especially mobile devices with tightly limited CPU resources are slowed down by HIP. Its poor performance on these mobile devices is a result of the extensive use of public-key (PK) cryptography for securing the main protocol functions.

Lightweight HIP (LHIP) [1] is a HIP protocol extension that enables HIP to offer mobility and multihoming support without the use of PK cryptography. To achieve this, the LHIP authentication layer secures HIP mobility signaling messages with lightweight interactive hash-chain-based (IHC) signatures [3]. We have extended the IHC signature scheme in order to secure it against Man-In-The-Middle attacks and to improve its efficiency. The improved IHC signature scheme is easier to handle for middleboxes (e.g., HIP-aware firewalls) and improves the throughput of the IHC signature scheme. The performance measurements of the IHC signatures show that they are inexpensive in terms of CPU usage. However, they require more messages to be exchanged. LHIP also allows to transform an ongoing LHIP association into a full HIP association, enabling mobile devices to dynamically adapt to increased security requirements.

LHIP succeeds in providing decentralized end-host mobility to CPU-constrained devices. It reduces the computational cost of the relevant HIP protocol functionality to less than 2.5% compared to HIP using common key lengths of 1024 bit as Host Identities. We hope that LHIP will support the deployment of HIP on a broader scale by making HIP and LHIP an attractive and efficient combination for mobile devices.

References

1. T. Heer. Lightweight hip. In A. Gurtov, editor, *Host Identity Protocol (HIP): Towards the Secure Mobile Internet*, chapter 8. Wiley and Sons, 2008.
2. R. Moskowitz, P. Nikander, P. Jokela, and T. Henderson. Host Identity Protocol. RFC 5201 (Experimental), Apr. 2008.
3. V. Torvinen and J. Ylitalo. Weak Context Establishment Procedure for Mobility Management and Multi-Homing. *Communications And Multimedia Security: 8th IFIP TC-6 TC-11 Conference on Communications and Multimedia Security, Sept. 15-18, 2004, Windermere, The Lake District, United Kingdom*, 2005.

Author Index

Druck: Mercedes-Druck, Berlin
Bindung: Stein + Lehmann, Berlin

Printing: Mercedes-Druck, Berlin
Binding: Stein+Lehmann, Berlin